HOWELL HARRIS

A page from Howell Harris's Diary on the day that he and his followers decided to separate from the Methodist clergy, 7 June 1750. (by permission of the Historical Society of the Presbyterian Church of Wales.)

HOWELL HARRIS

From Conversion to Separation
1735–1750

GERAINT TUDUR

UNIVERSITY OF WALES PRESS
CARDIFF
2000

© Geraint Tudur, 2000

First published 2000
Reprinted 2002

British Library Cataloguing-in-Publication Data.
A catalogue record for this book is available from the British Library.

ISBN 0–7083–1618–2

*All rights reserved. No part of this book may be reproduced, stored in a retrieval system, or transmitted, in any form or by any means, electronic, mechanical, photocopying, recording or otherwise, without clearance from the University of Wales Press, 10 Columbus Walk, Brigantine Place, Cardiff, CF10 4UP.
Website: www.wales.ac.uk/press*

The right of Geraint Tudur to be identified as author of this work has been asserted by him in accordance with the Copyright, Designs and Patents Act 1988.

Typeset by Action Publishing Technology, Gloucester.
Printed in Great Britain by Dinefwr Press, Llandybïe

I'm teulu oll,
ac yn arbennig i'm Mam,
er cof am fy nhad,
Robert Tudur Jones

Contents

Frontispiece: a page from Howell Harris's Diary

Editor's Foreword	ix
Preface	x
Map of Wales	xii
List of Abbreviations	xiii
1 Howell Harris the Diarist	1
2 The Making of a Revivalist	13
3 A Mission from God	38
4 God's Little Parliaments	63
5 The Church of England	92
6 The Opposition to Methodism	119
7 Controversy and Division	151
8 The Prophetess	195
9 Postscript	229
Notes	235
Select Bibliography	298
Index	307

Editor's Foreword

The Centre for the Advanced Study of Religion in Wales was established in 1998 to encourage scholarly research and to contribute towards a wider understanding of the history of religion among the Welsh people. The publication of this book, the third under the auspices of the Centre, is welcomed as partial fulfilment of those aims.

Protestant Nonconformity became the dominant expression of Christian faith in Wales during the nineteenth century, inspired in part by the Evangelical Revival and the emergence of Methodism. This is the first critical and detailed study of Howell Harris's diaries, giving an insight into the aspirations and frustrations of this enigmatic man who was one of the most significant of the Revival's leaders. Geraint Tudur's book brings a fresh insight into Harris's character and the development of the Evangelical Revival in Wales up to the separation of 1750. In so doing, he corrects some of the more infamous misconceptions of the past.

The publication of this book is certain to help advance our knowledge of Welsh religious history and set it alongside comparative studies of the Revival as it advanced in other countries.

Robert Pope
on behalf of
The Centre for the Advanced Study of Religion in Wales,
University of Wales, Bangor

Preface

It is a measure of Howell Harris's greatness that despite all criticism, both contemporary and later, he remains one of the giants of eighteenth-century Wales, if not of Welsh history in general. Much has been written about him, but, despite many of the facts concerning his life being made known, in many ways the man himself has remained an enigma. While Dr Geoffrey Nuttall pointed the student of Welsh Methodism in the right direction through his revealing glimpse into Harris's mind and soul in *Howel Harris, The Last Enthusiast* (Cardiff, 1965), a broader analysis of Harris's life and work is needed in order that the events of the first fifteen years of the Revival in Wales can be better understood. Only with the emergence of a clearer picture of the founder of Welsh Methodism will the formative years of the movement come into focus.

It is hoped that this book will contribute to this process. Based on a D.Phil. thesis submitted to the Faculty of Theology at Oxford University in 1989, it is an attempt to understand the man who contributed so much to the development of religion in Wales, and to do so through his own writings, principally his Diaries. These were, for the most part, studied and partially transcribed during a period of eighteen months spent at the National Library of Wales at Aberystwyth, the first three months being devoted to mastering Harris's difficult handwriting. Further transcripts were made during numerous subsequent visits, but progress was much hindered by a constant need to magnify the text and the occasional use of artificial ultra-violet light. Previous published transcriptions of the Diaries, made by others, were checked alongside the original, and as some errors were discovered, corrections are made at the relevant points in this study.

Due to the draconian limits of the thesis, one chapter had to be removed before submission. This was a study of the opposition encountered by Harris as an early Methodist leader. This has now been restored, and, though curtailed, it emphasizes the hardships which the Methodists were forced to endure as they endeavoured to proclaim their message. Several other parts of the thesis were modified prior to publication, but references to source materials, especially the Diaries, were retained in the hope that they may facilitate further studies by others in the future.

Naturally, I am indebted to many people for helping me to research my thesis and prepare it for publication. I am grateful to the Historical Society of the Presbyterian Church of Wales for allowing me access to the Howell Harris manuscripts, and to my supervisor, Dr J. D. Walsh of Jesus College, not only for his guidance and sound advice during my Oxford days, but also for his seemingly endless patience after I was ordained at Cardiff. There, the members and deacons of Ebeneser Welsh Congregational Church allowed me time to pursue my studies even though I was employed as their full-time minister; for this I will always be thankful. During my initial long stay at Aberystwyth, and during countless visits afterwards, the staff of the National Library of Wales looked after me with kindness, efficiency and courtesy, and to them, and to the staff of numerous other libraries and archives, I now offer my most sincere thanks. Following my arrival at Bangor, my colleagues at the School of Theology and Religious Studies and in the Centre for the Advanced Study of Religion in Wales have encouraged and supported me; I thank them for their interest in my work. I am also grateful to Research Centre Wales for a grant towards publication costs. Special thanks are due to the staff of the University of Wales Press for their guidance in all things pertaining to this publication, and for the excellent quality of their work.

Carolyn, my wife, has always been a pillar of support throughout the years, while Dafydd, Llywelyn and Gruffudd, my three sons, have never complained despite being deprived of the occasional holiday. I thank them for their love and for bearing with me as I endeavoured to bring this work to a conclusion.

Though my father died while this book was being prepared for publication, I cannot but express my debt to him, and to my mother, for opening my eyes to the riches of my Welsh Christian heritage. It was at my father's feet during my undergraduate days at Bangor that I became interested in the history of the Evangelical Revival: for that reason, I dedicate this book to all my family, but especially to my mother, in loving memory of my father.

Geraint Tudur
Bangor

WALES

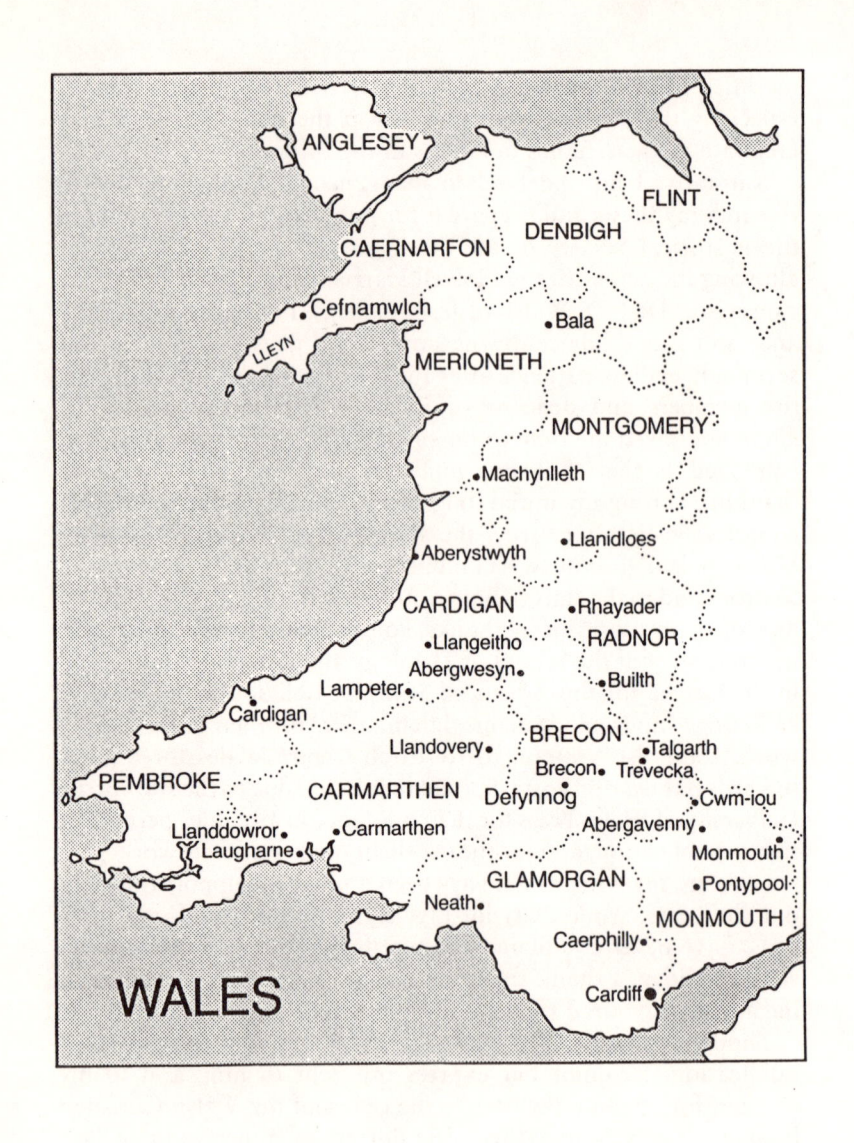

Abbreviations

BA	Howell Harris, *A Brief Account of the Life of Howell Harris, Esq.* (Trevecka, 1791).
DEB	Donald M. Lewis (ed.), *The Blackwell Dictionary of Evangelical Biography, 1730–1860*, 2 vols. (Oxford, 1995).
Diary	The manuscript Diaries of Howell Harris, Calvinistic Methodist Archives, National Library of Wales, Aberystwyth.
DNB	Leslie Stephen and Sidney Lee (eds.), *The Dictionary of National Biography*, 22 vols. (London, 1908–9).
DR	Eifion Evans, *Daniel Rowland* (Edinburgh, 1985).
DWB	J. E. Lloyd and R. T. Jenkins (eds.), *The Dictionary of Welsh Biography* (London, 1959).
HHDR	Richard Bennett, *Howell Harris and the Dawn of Revival*, translated by Gomer M. Roberts (Bridgend, 1987).
HHL	John Thickens, *Howel Harris yn Llundain* (Caernarfon, 1938).
HHLE	G. F. Nuttall, *Howel Harris: The Last Enthusiast* (Cardiff, 1965).
HHRS	Tom Beynon, *Howell Harris, Reformer and Soldier* (Caernarvon, 1958).
HHVL	Tom Beynon, *Howell Harris's Visits to London* (Aberystwyth, 1960).
HHVP	Tom Beynon, *Howell Harris's Visits to Pembrokeshire* (Aberystwyth, 1966).
HMGC	Gomer M. Roberts (ed.), *Hanes Methodistiaeth Galfinaidd Cymru*, vol. 1 (Caernarfon, 1973).
JHS	*The Journal of the Historical Society of the Presbyterian Church of Wales* (Caernarfon, 1916–)

ABBREVIATIONS

JWJ	N. Curnock (ed.), *The Journal of the Rev. John Wesley, A.M.,* 8 vols. (London, 1909–16).
LHH	Hugh J. Hughes, *Life of Howell Harris* (Newport, 1892).
MTU	Richard Bennett, *Methodistiaeth Trefaldwyn Uchaf* (Bala, 1929).
NLW	National Library of Wales, Aberystwyth.
POD	Gomer M. Roberts, *Portread o Ddiwygiwr* (Caernarfon, 1969).
STL I and II	Gomer M. Roberts (ed.), *Selected Trevecka Letters (1742–1747)* (Caernarfon, 1956) and *idem, Selected Trevecka Letters (1747–1794)* (Caernarfon, 1962).
TL	M. H. Jones, *The Trevecka Letters* (Caernarfon, 1932).
TM	John Morgan Jones and William Morgan, *Y Tadau Methodistaidd,* 2 vols. (Abertawe, 1895).

Chapter 1
Howell Harris the Diarist

Despite his invaluable contribution to the development of the Methodist movement in Wales during the eighteenth century, very little has appeared in print which has critically examined the life and work of Howell Harris. This has not been as a result of a shortage of source material; Harris left a vast amount of manuscripts for future generations to use in their assessment of his labours,[1] a collection so large that the task of reading, transcribing and extracting the relevant information has proved too daunting for many historians to undertake.

Among these manuscripts, the main source of information about Harris's life is the collection of his personal Diaries which span the period between 1735 and 1773, from the time of his conversion at the age of twenty-one to his death, aged fifty-nine. Although hitherto unpublished in their entirety, extracts have occasionally appeared in the *Journal of the Historical Society of the Presbyterian Church of Wales*, and a considerable contribution has been made to their study by Tom Beynon, a Calvinistic Methodist minister, in his three volumes, *Howell Harris, Reformer and Soldier* (Caernarfon, 1958), *Howell Harris's Visits to London* (Aberystwyth, 1960) and *Howell Harris's Visits to Pembrokeshire* (Aberystwyth, 1966). However, G. F. Nuttall's comment[2] that 'Beynon's editing of the Journals leaves the serious student with a good deal of work on his hands' must be borne in mind when using his transcriptions, for all three volumes are marred by the absence of any kind of annotation to indicate where and why the text has been edited. Even so, they are useful in that they serve as guides to the contents of the various Diaries transcribed by Beynon, and valuable as an introduction to the original manuscripts.

Views concerning the historical significance of the Diaries and the practicability of publishing them in their entirety have varied considerably over the years. J. H. Davies,[3] an eminent Welsh bibliographer, considered that such a project would be a complete waste of time and money,[4] while E. O. Davies,[5] a Calvinistic Methodist minister, held that 'full justice can never be done to the almost super-human labours of Howell Harris until these Diaries are examined, and their substance made known in some form or another'.[6] Dr D. Martyn Lloyd-Jones declared that 'as spiritual autobiography, [the collection] is practically unrivalled',[7] and at the close of a lecture to the Historical Society of the Presbyterian Church of Wales in 1964, the editor of its *Journal*, Gomer M. Roberts, appealed for the publication of the Diaries before the year 2000.[8] Sadly, this dream was not fulfilled; the mammoth task of systematic transcription has not yet begun.

Harris was a prolific writer, and 284 volumes of his Diaries are extant. In 1730, his brother Joseph, having received some correspondence from home, encouraged him to 'use his endeavours to mend his handwriting',[9] and it is regrettable that he did not heed his advice, as the Diaries are always difficult to read on account of Harris's barely legible handwriting and his constant use of abbreviations. Moreover, in certain parts of the collection, deterioration of the ink has further compounded the problems of the transcriber, and since Harris did not use a margin, words and sentences written near the edges of the pages often pose particular difficulty for the reader.

Entries were made in the Diaries at various times during the day, and the events of the evening often recorded on the following morning. Eighteen of the early manuscripts were written in Latin, possibly because Harris wished to improve his command of that language before matriculating at Oxford University,[10] but probably as an effective means of safeguarding the contents from prying eyes. By December 1736 he had given up this practice and from then on wrote in English. The fact that he did not choose to write in his native Welsh is not unusual, for English was regarded at that time as a hallmark of sophistication.

Several pages were used to record the events of a single day, which led to a certain amount of repetition when Harris wrote of his thoughts or feelings. Most entries were composed in great haste and appear at times disjointed. At certain times Harris also formed patterns while writing by dividing the pages into quarters and writing in different directions in each of the four sections; on other occasions he formed oblongs or diamonds with the words in the centre of the page. Although it may be put down to coincidence, this practice seems to have emerged soon after Harris visited Bristol and London for the first time. It may, therefore, have been intended to make the Diary appear difficult to read during a period when itinerants were regarded with suspicion because of the Jacobite threat, and the Crown agents were active in attempting to uncover all forms of subversive activities. However, it could be argued that such a practice would be likely to arouse more rather than less suspicion. Whatever the motive, Harris went to great lengths to form these patterns.

When he began keeping his Diaries, Harris did not intend that they should be published. Their initial purpose was to enable him to 'watch more close' his personal conduct[11] and act as a Protestant confessional wherein he would be able to record 'all the sins of the past Day, of omission and Commission, against God, myself or my Neighbour in Thought, Word or Deed'.[12] This was done 'by accurate Recollections, what I did, saw, heard or Read'. All quarrels, sinful thoughts and imaginations, together with the misapplication of any spare hour, any neglect of an opportunity to do good and anything else in which his conscience accused him of being guilty of a breach of God's Law, were to be included in order that he would be able fully to confess his sins before God 'in a proper form' and also 'pray against them'.

Oral confession to a priest had, to a large extent, been abandoned in England at the time of the Reformation, but written confession, usually in the form of a diary, soon became an alternative for many Protestants.[13] The Puritan diarists recorded their progress in both spiritual and material matters in order, on the one hand, to evaluate their own performance, and on the other, to remind themselves of the greatness of God's mercy towards them. Thus the diaries, in their contents if not in their appearance, often resembled account books; a catalogue of the individual's sins and failures counterbalanced by the wealth of God's grace and mercy.[14] This element of remembering God's particular goodness towards an individual received especial emphasis as it was believed that the diarist would thus be prevented from succumbing to ingratitude and unfaithfulness.[15] This called for extensive self-examination, a tradition which remained basically unchanged well into the eighteenth century.[16]

Harris unwittingly became part of it. His original objective of simply confessing his sin always remained a fundamental part of his discipline of keeping a Diary and although his view of the nature and purpose of the Diaries developed as the years went by, confession remained throughout an integral part of the entries. But, as in the Puritan tradition, he also included accounts of his thoughts and labours, to act as a record of his life by which it would be possible for him later to assess whether he grew or decreased in a spiritual sense.[17] Also in true Puritan fashion he came to see the hand of God in the most prosaic of daily occurrences,[18] a belief which made necessary the continued detailed recording of the events of each day. Failure to do so could easily result in the omission of some essential fact or event which would totally undermine the value of the discipline. In order to be able to draw valid conclusions from the entries, all the necessary information had to be included, but Harris was then faced with the difficulty of knowing what on any particular day was relevant to his spiritual progress. He therefore felt himself obliged to include as much detail as possible in each entry, though this did not prevent anxiety at the end of the day that he had omitted something of significance.[19]

This need for detail was further intensified by Harris's belief in divine guidance. Communications from God were not an unusual phenomenon in his experience.[20] Convinced that he had experienced the sovereign grace of God and that no one could restrict the work of the Holy Spirit, he believed that God worked among men and communicated with His chosen people in whatever way pleased Him. Thus, when Harris was uncertain whether he was to continue with his evangelistic mission in the spring of 1736, he says that he prayed 'for an infallible sign in order to know if God was commanding [him] to read [aloud, from devotional books, at his meetings]'. His prayer was answered as 'the Spirit descended with tears and unusual tenderness' upon him, 'an infallible assurance that [he] was to continue'.[21] As the years went by he carried his belief to its logical conclusion, that God took an active interest in even the most unimportant details of the individual's life. This resulted in prayers being offered on a wide range of subjects; for example, whether or not he was being faithful to God in his actions,[22] the possibility of buying a clock,[23] the outcome of the war with France,[24] the planting of fir trees around his home[25] and the purchase of underwear for his wife.[26]

Harris was without doubt an 'enthusiast', in the contemporary understanding of the word.[27] He believed that he was, in a sense, directly inspired by the Holy Spirit in ways which were not only discernible in their long-term fruits, but perceptible immediately and intuitively, or at least after their impact and significance had been registered, by self-scrutiny after the event. To record such 'impressions' of the Holy Ghost, and the spiritual 'frames' or sensations in the mind which reflected their presence, was a major purpose of the Diaries, as it was of other evangelical journals, notably that of George Whitefield.[28] Behind evangelical autobiography and diary-keeping lay the belief that close study of God's activity, both in the world and in the soul, could help the believer to build up a dossier of recorded instances of the Spirit's work. By constantly recording the influences of the Spirit, their patterns and configurations could be ascertained in such a way as to offer guidance to the believer as he moved along the difficult path of his spiritual pilgrimage.

Harris's belief in the active presence of God and the transforming nature of the Gospel, coupled with the personal sense of mission which was rooted in his conversion experience of 1735, led him to be critical of both the increasing rationalism and the quietism that were to be seen in the eighteenth century.[29] He refused the notion that God was to be understood as a distant ideal of perfection, and similarly refused to embrace the suggestion that He could be discovered in some mystical manner in the inner man.[30] God had not only given a general revelation of Himself in creation, but had also given a particular revelation in Jesus Christ, and continued to reveal His mind and will through His Word in the Scriptures and through the activity of the Spirit. It was His revelation to the individual soul that led to salvation; through grace, the love of God was shed abroad in the heart.[31] But, while the sinner was the object of this free grace, he was not to remain passive.[32] Faith may have been 'the fundamental grace in the spiritual work', but it was also 'the genuine spring of all obedience'.[33] Harris recognized the biblical emphasis on the need for man to work out his own salvation,[34] and the transforming power of the encounter with God was to be manifested by outward and visible change. Salvation was more than an inward experience;[35] he expected faith to beget action.

This was certainly true in his own case. He gained prominence among his contemporaries through the abundance of energy and depth of commitment that he displayed. Through the pages of the Diaries he can be seen praying, preaching and exhorting, often at great length but always with a seemingly untiring spirit, even in the face of the most violent opposition. His determination to submit to God's will – that he should proclaim the Gospel – and his conviction that God was actively engaged in that work through him, remained a fundamental part of his personal faith throughout his life and sustained him through all the difficulties which he encountered.

Preaching was one aspect of the work in which Harris excelled, though he often preferred to describe the activity as 'exhorting'.[36] He was undoubtedly an extremely powerful preacher and managed, even in the early days, to draw crowds of auditors.[37] During that period, it seems that he did not preach from specific scriptural texts as was his later custom, but rather in submission to whatever divine guidance he believed himself to be receiving at the time,[38] and though many of his sermons are quoted at length in the Diaries, it is obvious that they needed both the character of the man and the unction of the Spirit to bring them to life. They do, however, enable us to study the contents of the message which made such an impact upon so many.

Harris's approach was to make his sermons intensely personal so that each individual member of his congregation would feel the effect of his words. He often began with a direct challenge to the conscience. As the majority of his auditors were at least nominal members of the Church of England, Harris would remind them that God had a valid claim on their lives as they had been baptized within His Church and in His name during their infancy. Their unfaithfulness to Him and the sinfulness of their lives rendered them open to the horrors of divine judgement unless they repented and believed the Gospel. One who had heard him speak in Carmarthenshire said that he preached the Law in all its severity and declared that unless God could have the sinner's heart for Himself, He would see him torn, body and soul, by the devils at the hour of death and in the Day of Judgement.[39] It is not surprising that many were deeply moved by his words.[40] This threat of judgement would remain Harris's constant theme until his congregation had been convinced of their sin, and it was only when they were visibly suffering under the burden of their guilt that he would speak of the promise of salvation found in the Gospel. The sharp transition from the 'terrors' of the Law and the threat of damnation, to the 'balm and sweetness' of the Gospel, with its offer of grace to the guilty sinner, had immense force when used by a powerful preacher like Harris. The antinomies of the Gospel message, sin and grace, Law and Gospel, heaven and hell, had all the more dramatic force when they were related not only to their biblical foundation, but – as in Harris's case – to personal experience, past and present.

Harris described this process of bringing his auditors face to face with their sinful condition as 'cutting' and 'cruel',[41] but it was not confined to spiritual matters, as he had much to say about the social life of his period. While preaching he would set about opposing the evils of his day, the casual attitude shown by many towards smuggling,[42] the robbing of shipwrecks[43] and cockfighting.[44] He opposed any social activity which he believed to be undermining the morals of the people. Therefore, his campaign to win souls also involved striving for what contemporaries knew as a reformation of manners; 'all the gaiety, sports and dancing' were to be exposed in the hope that people would see the folly of their ways and turn to God.[45] He encouraged them to show honesty and integrity in all their activities, not in order to qualify for salvation but in order that they might glorify God.

Being unordained, Harris was forced to take to the open air to deliver his message. During his lifetime he often claimed that he was the first of the Methodist leaders, in both England and Wales, to begin field preaching;[46] he also claimed that he was the first to be converted and that the Revival had begun through him.[47] This was not purely the result of his ego. He believed himself to have been guided by God not only through the Scriptures but directly, by the Spirit.[48] He was convinced that he was a chosen vessel[49] and, although dogged for many years by doubts and fears that he was deceiving himself, he could not deny or forget the early experiences through which he believed he had been called. As a result, the early years of the Diary are full of prayers that God would prove to him that he had been called and sent out among his fellow countrymen to preach the Gospel. It was thus of continual use to Harris as a means to assure himself of his own credentials. All the feelings of insecurity and doubt were written in so that the Diaries became a record not only of God's particular dealings with him as an individual but also as a revivalist, and an essential tool in the task of preserving for the future details of the divine guidance which had been given to enable him to serve God and lead the Methodist movement. There is no doubt that even in the early years of the Revival he had become aware of his own importance as a public figure and that he realized the historical significance of the records that he kept.[50] He therefore began to write with an eye on posterity and in 1738 wrote, 'I think I write this Diary that I may see the secret working of Grace, sin, corruption and nature and if possibly it may be useful to others.'[51] The possibility of publishing extracts from the Diaries had by that time occurred to him, but on suggesting this to Griffith Jones of Llanddowror,[52] he was advised to pursue the idea no further. He therefore 'resolved again . . . not to publish',[53] but still hoped that they would be of benefit to future generations. In 1741 he wrote:

> I feel I must write all observations thus, and the Lord will rise some or other to read and understand it. O! that this should be blessed to be of use to His lambs while He has a Church, when I shall be in the dust, and to encourage poor seekers to come to Him and to bring glory to Him. That is what I aim at in writing it.[54]

This was still on his mind three years later when he wrote: 'I saw wisdom enough in God to gift some person, when I am in the grave, to draw out somewhat out of them that may be of use.'[55] In 1748 he set out what he considered to be the vital elements of his Diaries. These were: '1. an account of the visits I have from my dear Lord. 2. the teachings I have too. 3. the Places where I discourse and the substance of what I preach and 4. some general observations.'[56] Though he did not mention confession, it was still a prominent part of each entry, essential to the process of self-examination and the foundation upon which all else was built.

As with other religious diarists before him, Harris regarded reflection as an essential part of the spiritual process, and was convinced by 1738 that he possessed a particular gift of being able 'to note the workings of Grace' on his soul.[57] But, while other writers referred back to earlier entries in their diaries and journals,[58] Harris only referred to the actual experiences, as if he had never written about them before. It is true that he often referred to the Diary, thus displaying, as Dr Nuttall observed, 'marks of the true diarist',[59] but he did not cite the contents of earlier entries either for his own benefit or that of a future reader. The Diaries were confined to the events of the day and, if relevant, recollections from the past. Therefore, on reaching the anniversary of a particular event, such as the various stages of his conversion, Harris wrote an account of that day as he remembered it without reference to any previous observations or conclusions that he had included in his entries on similar anniversaries in the past.

Although Beynon expressed the view that Harris's Diaries were 'an unbiased story of his pilgrimage',[60] it is highly questionable whether he achieved a high degree of detachment in his view of himself. Beginning with the premise that he was a totally depraved sinner,[61] a notion which coloured his assessment of his motives and actions, he was always exceedingly self-critical, and many of his statements cannot be accepted at face value. His self-image needs to be considered in the light of his religious convictions, and the Diaries' impression of an overscrupulous introvert obsessed by a desire to fulfil his duty towards God and to see all around him submit to the same discipline must be balanced against our wider knowledge of the writer's character. Through his magnetic personality Harris was able not only to attract many thousands to hear him preach but also to join him in society meetings in various parts of the country. Moreover, he was able to draw a large number of his followers to make their home with him at Trevecka following his separation from Daniel Rowland in 1750. The Diaries thus give too negative a picture of Harris's personality and its interaction with others. If the impression is given that his character and demeanour lacked many of the finer qualities expected of a man of God, it is as well to remember, not only that they are the writings of a fallible individual facing the various temptations of a highly public life, who has through his own record of his activities exposed himself to the criticism of later generations enjoying the benefit of hindsight, but also that such Diaries can never give a full picture of the writer when the main theme of his composition is a critical self-examination.[62]

In reading the Diaries, Harris's integrity can never be doubted. In order to achieve his purpose in composing them, he realized that they would have to be a true record of his experiences. Mistakes were inevitable since most entries were made in haste, but there is never any suggestion that he set out to deceive a future reader or that he was – in his own conviction – less than honest with himself. No doubt in some respects he was self-deceiving, not sufficiently aware of his own motivation, especially of his ability to interpret his own opinions and desires as guidance from the Holy Spirit. But the ingenuous frankness of his narrative accounts and self-revelations makes them extremely valuable as a source. The fact that the Diaries composed after 1737 were written in the hope that they might be of use to posterity does not decrease their value as a truthful account of the period. The fact remains that Harris did not wish, or have the time, to arrange his material in a way that would colour the reader's view. As Dr Nuttall has pointed out, 'he wrote as he felt. Everything went pouring in, all the quick changes of mercurial temperament.'[63]

The Diary was the dissecting table upon which his experiences and feelings were examined. Therefore, though he travelled extensively around Wales, there are but few references to the geography of the country or the climate on the day that he undertook his journey. In most entries it was not the simple chronological account of what was happening around him that was of interest to him; it was what was happening *within* him that commanded his attention. The result is that several consecutive pages are often filled with meditations, prayers and spiritual observations, and in the case of themes which caused him particular worry or anxiety, such as impending legal hearings or concern about his own personal salvation, these are repeated at such length that the reading of the Diary becomes, in the words of M. H. Jones, 'a tedious and laborious business'.[64] It does, however, allow a view of the inner man, not a carefully concocted image of how Harris might have wanted us to see him. The large amount of material that he left and the haste in which he wrote have in some ways guaranteed the evidential probity of the sources which he has left us to consider, particularly in their revelation of the author's beliefs, attitudes and feelings.

In addition to the Diaries, a large collection of Harris's letters is also extant. These were catalogued by M. H. Jones in the 1920s, and his inventory was published in 1932 under the title *The Trevecka Letters*. Due to the fact that many of them are comparatively brief documents, more effort has been made to secure their publication than that of the Diaries, with the result that they are more widely available for study. A great deal of the transcribing of the letters was done by Gomer M. Roberts, and two volumes edited by him have been published under the title *Selected Trevecka Letters*.[65] Again, many letters have appeared over the years in the *Journal of the Historical Society of the Presbyterian Church of Wales*, and many have been published in the numerous volumes which have appeared in the past on Harris and the Methodist movement in Wales.

The earliest letters in the collection are those of Howell's brothers, Joseph and Thomas, to their parents during the period 1725–35, but following his conversion Howell also became a diligent letter-writer and safeguarded for posterity not only the letters that he received but also drafts or copies of the letters which he sent. The complete Trevecka letter collection, including the letters which belong to the period after Harris's death, comprises of nearly 3,000 manuscript documents dating between 1725 and 1797, and those which were composed during Harris's lifetime number in excess of 2,800.

The significance of the Trevecka manuscripts lies in the fact that they have safeguarded what is in effect a day-by-day account of the life, thoughts, aspirations and disappointments of one of the leaders of the Methodist movement in Wales. Although much of the content is of a personal nature, this should not be regarded as detracting from their value, but rather as the constituent which makes them valuable and poignantly evocative of the trials and temptations, challenges and joys which an eighteenth-century revivalist experienced.

In any study of Harris's life, the Diaries and the letters serve as a lens through which the man and his work can be examined. Due to the meticulous care which he took to include all information which he considered relevant, the Diaries allow us an unexpected amount of magnification of the period and of the man himself, while the letters serve as a useful means of substantiating some of the claims that he made. It is doubtful whether, in the voluminous annals of eighteenth-century evangelicalism, anything similar has survived on this scale, or carried intimate self-revelation to such an extent. Though a comparison with the journals of the other great leaders of the Revival will not be possible until Harris's

Diaries are finally published in their entirety, it is worth noting that they have a frankness and immediacy lacking in John Wesley's celebrated *Journal*, which was written for rapid publication and thus underwent stages of highly self-conscious editorial selection and revision before it emerged in its definitive form. Wesley was not only far more cautious about revealing his inner self than Harris, but was also very much concerned with his audience and with the effect that the account of his life, his teachings and judgements would have upon a reading public. His *Journal* was thus intended not only to record but to justify the actions and doctrines of the author. It was as much a tract as a journal. Whitefield's much shorter published *Journal* also had a similar purpose, though the ingenuousness of its self-revelation makes it more similar to Harris's Diaries in some respects. But Whitefield's frankness caused huge offence and gave such ammunition to his critics that his essay in journal writing, or at least journal publication, came to an abrupt and premature end. Later editions appeared, indeed, but with offending passages carefully excised.

The 284 volumes of Harris's Diaries are unique in providing an amazingly detailed, frank and unedited account of a revivalist's life during a period of extraordinary religious activity and ferment. This book is devoted to the picture of the Welsh Revival which emerges through the Diaries. It does not, therefore, claim to be an inclusive study of Welsh Calvinistic Methodism as a movement, but is directed to the more limited (but still exacting) task of charting the course of its greatest early leader as it is revealed in an autobiographical record of unique frankness, detail and length.

Chapter 2
The Making of a Revivalist

During a ceremony conducted at Talgarth parish church in Breconshire on 5 September 1702, Howell Powell,[1] a native of Llangadog in Carmarthenshire, was married to Susannah Powell who belonged to a long-established family in the county.[2] A joiner by trade, he had migrated to the area at the turn of the century[3] and was most probably employed on the Ashburnham estate which owned lands in both parishes. It is not known where they made their home during the early years of their married life, but in 1706 they were given a plot of land by Susannah's brother Thomas, who was the blacksmith at Trevecka, upon which they built a house.[4] It was there, at 'Trefeca Fach',[5] that Howell Harris was later born.

He was the youngest of three brothers; Joseph was born in 1704, Thomas in 1707 and Howell on 23 January 1714.[6] Though the family belonged to the lower middle class of society, the father being a joiner and a freeholder 'of the lesser sort',[7] the three sons managed to improve their social position, Joseph by being appointed assay master at the Royal Mint, and Thomas by amassing a considerable fortune as a tailor in London, then becoming a Breconshire landowner, and later the high sheriff of the county.[8] Howell, who had not learned any particular trade during his youth or been ordained as his family seemed to have wished,[9] succeeded through his itinerant ministry in assuming the role, if not the orders, of a clergyman. Then, by establishing a religious community known as the 'Trevecka Family' in the 1750s, he managed to raise himself even higher up the social ladder to the level of a landowner.[10] His social standing was further reinforced by the large number of labourers and craftsmen at his disposal within the 'Family'; this small army gave him a measure of respectability which allowed him to fraternize with local gentry and to become an honorary member of the Brecknockshire Agricultural Society established by them in 1755.[11]

13

Howell showed early signs of religiosity. During his upbringing, emphasis was put on traditional Christian values, and the impression given in his later testimony is that his parents were devout Anglicans, genuinely concerned about the education and spiritual welfare of their children.[12] Consequently, the three sons were taught the rudiments of the faith and brought up within the fold of the Church, and though Howell could later say that he was attending church services with an ulterior motive, namely to see the girls, the significant fact is that he was there.

The family came to the conclusion, as they began to think of his future, that a career in the Church would be desirable; as early as October 1730 it was suggested that he should consider becoming a clergyman.[13] Howell had by that time attended schools at Talgarth and Llanfihangel Tal-y-llyn, and in 1728 had entered the grammar school at Llwyn-llwyd,[14] where he was introduced to Latin and Greek. This, his eldest brother believed, was a good foundation upon which to proceed, but the death of their father in March 1731 threw the plans into confusion.

It is against this background of solid Anglican piety that Harris's account of his own life prior to his conversion must be understood. By putting pen to paper he unwittingly became part of a tradition of Christian 'experience writing' that dated back to the days of the early Church. With the post-Reformation increase in literacy and the Protestant emphasis on the individual's response to the Gospel, interest developed in written accounts of personal experiences, which was reflected by the publication of a treatise on the subject in 1656.[15] This emphasized the duty of keeping a record of God's mercies and encouraged the reader to include details not only of traumatic experiences such as conversion, but also of ordinary everyday events, as every detail was believed to be of interest to God.

This characteristic is also to be found in Harris's Diaries. In an attempt to assess the significance of his conversion experience, which took place over a period of several weeks during the spring of 1735, and in order to chronicle the change that had been wrought in him, he took a long view over the years of his youth from the higher moral and spiritual ground upon which he then stood. The process was a form of spiritual catharsis through which he unburdened himself of the guilt of his past sins by confessing them to God. But, from the vantage point of his conversion, it was difficult to see past events in perspective, with the result that his view of his childhood days was distorted and lacking in the common sense which allows that the pranks of young boys are a natural part of growing up. When he began writing, Harris was very much aware of the demands of God's Law and the severity of His judgement, and in keeping with the general genre of diary-keeping painted himself in darker colours than were necessary in order to magnify the glories of free grace.[16]

In keeping with the Puritan notion that conversion consisted of 'peace, disturbance, and then peace again',[17] Harris seemed eager to prove that his own 'disturbance', or conviction of sin, had begun much earlier than 1735. Having listed a long catalogue of childhood sins, he admits that in 1731 his conscience 'was not quite hardened nor altogether asleep'; it was not unusual for him to spend time in meditation, neither was he unaccustomed to praying. By 1733 he had begun 'to be anxious and to grieve somewhat for sin', and though he still continued in it, he became 'conscious of the wretchedness of such a life'. By 1734 he felt that he had no hope 'being such a prey of the devil', and confessed:

> My thoughts were evil in church and I had no religion but one of form. My chief object was to delude young women. I studied their dispositions and acted accordingly: to the religious, I became religious, pleasant to the pliant, weighty to the grave, and merry to the light headed. I, however, grew conscious that I was doing wrong, and prayed – Pity me, O God![18]

It appears, therefore, that long before the conversion experience of 1735 the Anglican spirituality which had been part of Harris's upbringing had made him aware of his own sinfulness and anxious about his condition, a pattern visible in many similar conversion accounts.[19]

It was on Palm Sunday 1735 that the conversion experience truly began. The parishioners at Talgarth had been neglectful of their duty of attending Holy Communion, and Pryce Davies, the vicar,[20] was 'using arguments to prove the necessity of receiving the Sacrament' in an attempt to persuade them to be present at the communion on the following Sunday, it being Easter.[21] As he spoke to the congregation,[22] he argued with them, saying, 'If you are not fit to come to the Lord's Table, you are not fit to come to Church, you are not fit to live, nor fit to die.'[23] These words made a deep impression upon Harris's mind;[24] they led him to resolve to be present at the communion on the following Sunday and also to carry through a radical change of his way of life.[25]

His attempts at personal reform began immediately. On his way home from church, he met a neighbour with whom he had quarrelled, and approached him to seek reconciliation.[26] A week later he attended the communion, but on hearing the words of the confession became aware that they were, in his case, meaningless; the remembrance of his sins was not grievous to him, neither was their burden intolerable. This absence of inward grief led him to conclude that as he was approaching the communion table with a lie in his mouth he should withdraw without partaking of the Sacrament. However, his conscience was quietened as he remembered the vow he had made to lead a new life. With that resolution in his mind he approached the table to receive 'the Pledge of God's dying Love'.[27] This was the first time he had partaken of the Sacrament.[28]

During the following week he began to be more serious and thoughtful;[29] he prayed often and strove to keep his thoughts fixed on God. On the Sunday after Easter he communicated 'by chance' at nearby Llan-gors[30] but as the days went by his determination weakened, so that by 20 April he had slipped back into his old ways.[31] On that Sunday, contrary to his usual custom of returning home to Trevecka and attending church at Talgarth, he remained at Trebinsiwn where he lodged while teaching at Llangasty,[32] and there came across a copy of *The Whole Duty of Man*,[33] a 'manual of godly living' which epitomized 'the pietistic, inward looking, non-controversial brand of Anglicanism which emerged during the 1650s'.[34] In the preface the author declared his intention of providing 'a Short and Plain Direction to the very meanest Readers, to behave themselves so in this World, that they may be happy for ever in the next', and in over 400 pages gave advice on such subjects as observing the Lord's day, honouring God's word, reverencing the sacraments, praying, fasting and performing duties to one's neighbour.[35] Harris admitted, 'As soon as I began reading it, I was convinced, that in every branch of my Duty to God, to myself and to my neighbours, I was guilty, and had fallen short.'[36] His conviction of sin was further intensified as he later read Bryan Duppa's *Holy Rules and Helps to Devotion* (London, 1675), another publication from the 'Holy

Living' school. He was particularly affected by 'The examination by way of articles upon the moral law', which posed questions based on God's commandments; the exercise led Harris to realize the extent of his spiritual shortcomings and to see that if he was judged by the standards of the Law, he would be 'undone forever'.[37]

He renewed his efforts to live a better life and attempted to subdue sin by prayer, fasting and denying himself the usual comforts of day-to-day life.[38] In his quest for moral strictness he became so confident that he could soon challenge his conscience to accuse him, if it could, of any sin.[39] He later admitted, however, that he had progressed no further than an outward, superficial change, and that his religion was rooted in mere conformity to a few rules seen in a book.[40] In retrospect he saw that he was, notwithstanding his confidence, 'in a damnable state and in danger of final destruction'.[41]

Having gone to the belfry of Llangasty church to pray during May, he felt a strong desire to give himself to God.[42] This was followed by doubt concerning the wisdom of such an action; he feared that submission would lead to a restriction upon his personal liberty and involve accepting the challenge of living a sinless life.[43] But, he claimed, 'this persuasion was different from all others I ever had, for tho' it did not force me as we would a Dog, it worked so irresistibly on me that I could not stand against it but was obliged to yield.'[44] 'I was made willing', he wrote later, 'to bid adieu to all things temporal and to choose the Lord for my portion.'[45] 'I believe', he added, 'I was then effectually called to be a follower of the Lamb.' In 1741 he analysed the experience thus:[46] 'tho' I had been called before, then did Christ come in.'[47]

The battle was not yet over and Harris now found himself facing numerous temptations.[48] Not only was he troubled by uncertainty concerning whether or not he had been accepted by God, he was even tempted at times to doubt God's existence.[49] As Sunday, 25 May, approached, he was torn by his suspicions and conscious that Satan was raging within him 'with a sore temptation to atheism'.[50] His only comfort was that he had read in Lewis Bayly's *The Practice of Piety* (1610), 'that if we go to the Sacrament, simply believing in the Lord Jesus Christ, we should receive forgiveness of all our sin.'[51] The passage which gave him such succour was, most probably: 'As thou eatest the Bread, imagine that thou seest Christ upon the Cross, and by his unspeakable torments fully satisfying God's Justice for thy sinnes [sic], and strive to be as verily partaker of the spiritual grace, as of the Elemental signs.'[52] In church, Harris was enabled to bring his burden of sin to Christ, whom he saw dying on the Cross.[53] It was then that the personal aspect of the Saviour's work was impressed upon his mind. 'I was convinced by the Holy Ghost', he said, 'that Christ died for me.' 'I went to the feast believing and expecting a Deliverance and it was given to me ... I went home fully satisfied that my sins were forgiven.'[54] But he was again to find himself beset by worries, fearing that he would lose his new-found peace and forgiveness. Believing that he had to be on his guard at all times, he continued fasting and praying, and refrained from conversing with old friends as that might have led him to sin. In all aspects of his life he enforced a rigorous discipline and remained hesitant and fearful until the next experience which took place during June.

On the 18th of that month, he was again at prayer at Llangasty church. 'I felt suddenly', he says, 'my heart melting within me like wax before the fire with love to God my Saviour.'[55]

> Then was a cry in my inmost soul, which I was totally unacquainted with before, Abba Father!, Abba Father! I could not help calling God my Father; I knew that I was his child and that He loved me and heard me. My soul being filled and satiated, crying, 'Tis enough, I am satisfied. Give me strength and I will follow Thee through fire and water.'[56]

In 1741, recalling the events of this day, Harris said that it was then that he received 'the Spirit of adoption'. He at last believed himself to be 'in God'; he could ask anything of Him; he was 'filled', and 'longing to be thus for ever'.[57] He knew, not only that he was a child of God, but that God had accepted him as one of His own.

His assurance of salvation did not last long. Throughout this period he had continued working as a teacher and kept school at Llangasty Tal-y-llyn.[58] During one of his classes, he became angry towards one of his pupils, and later recalled his thoughts on that day. 'Somewhat said in me, "Now thou art fallen from Grace" ... I felt then such hatred to myself for offending against all this love and losing this love that it was a great mercy I did not destroy myself.'[59] Fearing that he had fallen from grace and firm in the belief that he was in a worse condition than ever, he said that God pitied him, 'and soon sent that word home to my soul, I CHANGE NOT.'[60]

These words from Malachi 3:6 led Harris to realize that his salvation rested, not on his own faithfulness to God, but on God's faithfulness to him. 'Therefore', he reasoned, 'though I change, yet because he changeth not, I [am] secure.' Through this realization he was 'entirely freed from all fears and found uninterrupted rest in the love and faithfulness of God [his] Saviour'.[61]

During this series of experiences, many changes took place in Harris's life. On 22 May he began to keep a diary, a discipline which he kept up until his death in 1773. Three days later he adopted a rigid framework for his day-to-day life consisting of prayer, Bible study, restraint in social activity, meditation, confession, good works and the observance of the Sabbath. His understanding of the nature of the Christian life had been moulded by the books he had read and his solemn vow on 25 May was that he would follow the directions of *The Practice of Piety* and *The Whole Duty of Man*, as he believed that they would regulate his life 'according to the Scripture'.[62]

He soon discovered, however, that he could not be content without adapting this framework to suit his own personal needs. The 'Holy Living' literature did little to promote experiential religion; in its fear of 'enthusiasm', the Anglicanism of the Interregnum had relegated discussion of faith, grace, conversion, election and similar subjects to the sidelines,[63] and Harris found that while the books instructed him in the way to find God, they did not elaborate on the ways in which God would reveal Himself to him.[64] Central to his own experience thus far had been an awareness that God not only expected submission and obedience but also wished to be in communion with him.[65] Consequently, Harris could not rest until he had either found, or formed, a theology which could balance these two aspects satisfactorily in his mind, but his doctrinal ignorance[66] and the lack of mature Christian fellowship[67] greatly hindered his progress, and it was many years before he could feel completely at ease with regard to his relationship to God. His failure to work out a clear theological standpoint and his inability to identify himself totally with the traditional Arminian or Calvinistic camps led to agonizing bouts of insecurity, which in turn led to overwhelming loneliness.[68]

At the same time he was filled with a missionary zeal. Natural piety and teachings gleaned from books had already led to attempts to induce his family and friends to join him in his devotions,[69] and during June he began reading to neighbours various literary extracts concerning the Sacrament and church attendance.[70] Having learned that it was his duty to visit the sick, he called at Tredwstan to see an elderly man, and as he read to him the neighbours gathered to listen. Later, he felt that it was also his duty to speak to those who had formerly been his companions and this led to Sunday afternoon visits to three villages, most probably Trevecka, Talgarth and Llan-gors. Still employed at Llangasty, he walked back to Trevecka during the week to conduct small devotional meetings which emphasized the need for congruence of profession and practice. This was the beginning of his ministry.

Opposition was encountered from the outset. He was derided by some and pitied by others.[71] Attempts were made to frighten him in order to curb his zeal, but as the advice given him was so tainted by 'the wisdom of this world' he found it unacceptable.[72] Motivated by a desire to express his gratitude to God, he could not desist; his awareness of God's love spurred him on, not only to read to others but also to sell his possessions in order to give to the poor.[73] Such conduct, coupled as it was with a critical attitude towards others[74] would, sooner or later, lead to accusations of 'enthusiasm', as would the sight of Harris gathering together a clique of overzealous followers who argued that they were, through their lifestyle, preserving or restoring the discipline of the Church.[75] Most Anglicans viewed his actions with deep suspicion, particularly as the vicar was not involved. Without clerical leadership, his meetings, led as they were by an unauthorized layman, could easily be taken to be conventicles, and the sudden interest in religion as the reappearance of Puritan separatism.[76]

Undaunted by popular fears, Harris regarded the Established Church as a mission field. Not only did the view of rich and poor 'going as if it were hand in hand in the broad way to ruin' disturb him, he was also concerned about the ministers, and believed that they were not in earnest and that they were failing to display 'any feeling sense of the love of Christ'.[77] Their instructions were delivered in such an indifferent manner, and had such little effect upon their hearers, that Harris could say that he had never seen anyone awakened through their preaching.[78] Finding those from among the clergy with whom he was acquainted unwilling to listen to his criticism, he soon gave up his attempts to convince them of the need for reform, but his efforts among the lay members of the Church continued as they gathered at his home to hear him read. Death and judgement, he said, were the main themes of his conversation, together with the need for both frequent prayer and communion. Through his interest in the reformation of individuals, Harris was within weeks of his conversion aware of its significance to the Church as a whole. He knew that the renewal of the body began with the renewal of each individual member.[79]

His conviction of the benefit of receiving monthly communion motivated Harris to write an anonymous letter to the vicar of Talgarth during August 1735.[80] In it he informed him that some of his parishioners had joined together 'in a Strict Observance of [their] Duty', and while admitting their ignorance of the 'Heavenly Road' suggested the possibility of communicating once a month, hoping that together with his 'pious endeavours' as vicar and their 'observation and performance', it would prove to be an 'effectual Means to kindle [the] Heavenly Spark' which otherwise was in danger of dying out.

Following a brief stay at Oxford in November,[81] Harris returned home and resumed his activities, not only within his own parish but also in the neighbouring parishes of Llan-gors and Llangasty, by going from house to house to read and exhort. At the same time he attempted to educate himself through reading and during December derived great benefit from John Pearson's *Exposition of the Creed* (1659), a book which Harris claimed was instrumental in removing the last remnants of atheism from his mind. As he had relinquished his teaching post at Llangasty he also became more public in his activities and attended fairs at Talgarth where he openly denounced the gentry, the 'carnal' clergy and all evil-doers. His efforts met with dramatic success, and according to his own reports, family worship was set up in many houses while crowds attended church services in general and the communion in particular.[82] Consequently, it was difficult for Harris to understand the opposition of the local magistrates and clergy to his efforts.

The response of his own minister perplexed him greatly. In a letter sent to Harris on 27 February 1736,[83] Pryce Davies made a clear statement of the objections he held as a clergyman to his religious zeal. He had believed that Harris's initial efforts to instruct his neighbours on the nature of the Sacrament and on the fulfilment of their duty 'proceeded from a pious and charitable disposition', but as he had now begun to deliver public lectures from house to house and 'even within the limits of the Church',[84] Davies believed the time had come for him to be informed of his sin and error. The task of giving religious instruction to the people, Pryce Davies held, did not belong to the laity 'any further than privately in their own families', and through careful reference to the Bible Harris would be able to see 'the heavy judgements which God inflicted upon the sacrilege and impiety of those who audaciously presumed to invade the office ministerial'. Davies was here evidently aware of the substantial literary critique of 'enthusiasm' which had accumulated in previous decades and which the Evangelical Revival was about to kindle into new life. Harris's gatherings of awakened souls instantly aroused the fear of seditious conventicles which was by now ingrained into the clerical mind. For a professed Anglican to form private devotional groups was to some extent suspect in itself, but when the organizer was a layman, the offence was greatly compounded. Harris had undercut the pastoral authority of the priest over his flock; he had seduced 'ignorant and illiterate people and by cunning insinuations from house to house' had imbued them with views which were his own, not those of the Church. All this was dangerously reminiscent of the Civil War and the Commonwealth: if Harris would only study the history of the Church in those disorderly days, he would be able to see the 'dismal and lamentable effects of a factious zeal and a puritanical sanctity'. Like most Anglican priests of his day, Pryce Davies saw the practice of extempore prayer as a mark of religious individualism and lawlessness, depreciating the liturgical forms of the Book of Common Prayer. For Harris privately to expound the contents of *The Whole Duty of Man* and follow this 'with a long extempore prayer with repetitions, tautologies &c', was a 'heavy crime'. 'Pray consider', he asked, 'how odiously this savours of fanaticism and hypocrisy.' If he could not be persuaded to mend his ways, the vicar threatened to inform his brother Joseph of these developments in the hope that he would be able to exercise some influence over him. Should that fail, the bishop would then be acquainted with the facts, which would create an insurmountable obstacle to Harris's ever being ordained.

This letter, together with the threats of some magistrates to prosecute those who opened their houses to him,[85] and a deterioration in his own health,[86] led Harris briefly to suspend his activities.[87] The dilemma in which he now found himself weighed heavily on his mind; he could either obey the vicar, give up his exhorting and be ordained by the bishop, or refuse to obey, continue in his efforts and forfeit ordination. He was totally at a loss as to how he should proceed.

It was at this time that he came into contact with the Dissenters. William Herbert, who at one time had been a member of the Independent congregation at Tredwstan but had since joined the Baptists at Trosgoed, and Phillip Morgan, a Baptist preacher, attempted to persuade him to leave the Church, arguing that there was more life among the Baptists and that they would welcome him with open arms.[88] After the rebuke from his own minister, such an invitation seemed attractive, though Harris had to admit that not everyone in the Established Church opposed him.

On the anniversary of his first spiritual experience at Talgarth, Harris, in his predicament, requested that God would give him 'an infallible sign' to indicate whether he was to continue exhorting until Easter.[89] That sign should be a movement of the Spirit resulting in either 'Tears or Softness'. If it was not forthcoming, he promised he would then cease from all his activities and set about preparing himself for ordination in the usual way. But the Spirit descended 'with Tears and unusual softness and infallible Certainty', convincing him that he was to continue. He was now able to proceed with confidence, and wrote: 'I promised, in the midst of swords, fire and fury to read, not fearing to have my Guts torn in pieces, entirely relying on God for my Qualification.'[90] This began a dependency on direct indications of the divine will which set Harris apart as an 'enthusiast'. Believing in an 'immediate communion with God',[91] it became his custom to seek guidance in every aspect of his day-to-day life, a characteristic which led him to be viewed with suspicion in an age which emphasized moderation and discouraged all forms of fanaticism. Harris was undaunted by this response; he believed that he had already witnessed God's willingness to guide him during his conversion and held that his communion with God was a natural response to the divine initiative. This was, therefore, to become a prominent feature of his spiritual life, accentuated by the loneliness which he experienced following his conversion. But even when he came into contact with others of similar beliefs to his own he found that he was still in need of divine guidance. The Anglicans encouraged him to give up exhorting while the Dissenters encouraged him to give up the Church. Harris wanted to continue exhorting within the Church, and, finding himself unable to decide which party represented God's will, he believed that the only way to progress was to appeal directly to God Himself.

Revelations of the divine will came to Harris in many ways, but there was always a strong emphasis on the subjective element. In 1739 he spoke of 'a strong Inclination in [his] own Breast',[92] while in 1748 he 'felt' an answer was given him.[93] In 1744, while writing to Griffith Jones, he said: 'on asking about going back to see him I had att last an answer (O! the Privilege of having [an] answer from God by the Holy Spirit!) by his being laid in my soul in such a manner that I could not help going to see him.'[94] Again, while unsure where he was to lodge at New Inn, Monmouthshire, in 1745, Harris says that 'he had freedom to ask the Lord', and 'He shewed me where [to stay], by shining on me and letting me have a farther glympse than ever of the Glory set before me, where I shall soon be.'[95] As already mentioned, specific signs were sometimes requested either to confirm or deny a proposition. In 1741, while seeking guidance on whether or not he should go to London, Harris requested that God would incline others to give him money, both as a sign and to enable him to undertake the journey.[96] Other unsolicited signs were also regarded as significant. A cock crowing out of time was an omen of Harris's own death, while the chattering of magpies signified the coming of trials and battles.[97] This interest in portents and omens, displaying a blend of folkloristic beliefs and orthodox Christianity, was not unusual, as demonstrated in Edmund Jones's celebrated study, *A Relation of Apparitions of Spirits* (Newport, 1813).

G. F. Nuttall observed that 'religion ... often invaded Harris' dreamworld',[98] but although it is beyond doubt that he believed it possible for God to make his will known through dreams,[99] it is surprising how few examples exist of Harris interpreting dreams as divine messages. Most of those mentioned in his Diaries were fantasies concerning his work, or the effects of sin which served to remind him of his frailty. One attempt at interpreting a dream is to be found in 1744 when, in his sleep, Harris heard his father's voice calling his mother. This, he believed, was a sign of his mother's imminent death.[100]

The impression must not be given that Harris so emphasized direct guidance that he neglected to consult the authority of the Bible in his efforts to discern the will of God. Sometimes this took the form of *sortes Biblicae*: early in 1738 he wrote in his Diary, 'I took out the Bible hoping that God would shew me what he would have me do.' At random, the book opened in Revelations 3, 'whence [came] such assuring Love that I can't express it, such zeal that fear is entirely taken away.'[101] In a more general sense, but far more importantly, Harris saw God as revealing His will through the reading and preaching of the Word. In 1741 he declared that 'God speaks to none but thro' His Word now',[102] and though this may appear inconsistent with his views at other times it seems that he was attempting to give expression to the principle that God did not speak contrary to his revealed will in Scripture and that the Spirit corroborated the Word. Three years later while expressing gratitude for being shown in spirit that the Methodists were conforming to God's will, he wrote, 'O! the Glory of this Priviledge [sic], – to know not only in general [through Scripture] but in particular actions [through direct guidance], we are in His Will and Love.'[103]

It is perhaps at this point that Harris himself comes closest to 'enthusiasm'. His belief in the continuous presence of the Holy Spirit led him to expect divine guidance in the form of inward 'impressions' even in the minutiae of his personal life. Though always accepting the necessity of testing the validity of such immediate influences of the Spirit against the prescriptions of the written Word,[104] he anticipated more perceptible and direct assistance than many clerical leaders of the Revival allowed for. He came close to the young Whitefield, whose published *Journal* gave instances of direct guidance which were seized upon by his critics and used for decades in an attempt to discredit the movement.[105] After his painful experience of illuminist extravagance on the fringes of the Great Awakening in America, Whitefield had been forced to confess that he had overemphasized 'inward impressions' and published 'too soon and too explicitly' what should have remained private or been related after his death.[106]

Harris does not seem to have felt the need for any such retraction. Perhaps this can be explained by his comparative isolation in Wales, where highly supernaturalistic religious beliefs were current, and often synthesized with Protestant orthodoxy.[107] He would no doubt have distanced himself from those who carried spiritual revelation to extreme lengths, such as the despised French Prophets[108] who were still active in the 1730s and 1740s, but he nevertheless expected spiritual influences which were direct and not mediated through the Word or the constituted 'means of grace'.

Harris had a craving for divine validation of his actions, though he was aware of the dangers which this entailed. While praying that God would direct him so that he would 'infallibly know' His will, he wrote in 1737: 'how hard it is to distinguish whether our Thoughts, Words and actions grow from self Love, self Interest, self Pride or Love to Christ... Religion may be a cloak to hide my ends and Designs.'[109] Such subjective views of divine guidance and revelation were unacceptable to many, not least to Griffith Jones of Llanddowror, who, in a sermon preached in 1741 warned against 'the spirit of error' which was displayed 'when we lean on our own experiences before [the] Word'. His warning to his auditors that they should 'beware of giving way ... to a spirit of delusion' was taken by Harris as directed at him personally.[110] In 1748 Whitefield reinforced this message. By this time he had recanted his earlier dependence on 'inward impressions', admitting that by his actions he had 'given some wrong touches to God's ark, and hurt the blessed cause' he sought to defend.[111] While on a visit to Wales, he preached at Watford against 'revelations and following Impulses',[112] perhaps in response to Harris's increased dependency upon them during that period. Harris, on the other hand, continued throughout his life to insist on the validity of the divine guidance he received. Rather like Wesley, he saw his own career in the Revival as so extraordinary and so marked by success, that he regarded his role as quasi-prophetic or even quasi-apostolic, blessed by an unusual degree of divine guidance. In 1749 he claimed that there was always a 'Moses' among God's people, invested with the authority of the apostles.[113] Though, of course, he could not prove the existence of this high degree of inspiration by miracles as many critics of the Revival demanded, he nevertheless claimed that the success of his ministry evidenced the fact of divine guidance.[114]

Having received confirmation that he was to continue exhorting until Easter, Harris could claim that, rather than resisting ecclesiastical authority, he was now submitting to the higher authority of God. He declared himself willing to forfeit his life, reputation and career for the sake of the work and with renewed determination set out to conquer new territory, travelling under the cover of darkness in order to avoid persecution, as far as Talach-ddu, four miles to the west, and Cathedin, four and a half miles to the south.

The Dissenters' interest in his activities continued, notwithstanding his reluctance to be identified with them. Conscious that the majority of the populace gave their allegiance to the Church and were strongly opposed to Nonconformity, he resisted the temptation of drawing too close to the Dissenters for fear that they would interpret this as an indication that he was about to join them. By attending the services at Talgarth on Sundays, and showing himself loyal to the Church, he believed it would be safe for him to meet with the Dissenters during the week, but this failed to deflect criticism. Because of his association with the Independents of Tredwstan, he was soon regarded as having joined them, with the result that many of his hearers deserted him and joined the ranks of his persecutors.[115] Local opposition was further inflamed by the fact that some of his followers were at this time struck by a form of frenzy, probably resulting from their conviction of sin,[116] a phenomenon his enemies used to their advantage.

Harris was still buffeted by feelings of loneliness which were now heightened by opposition and the loss of support. Convinced that there were other Anglicans with similar beliefs to his own who would support him if he made their acquaintance, he decided that he would continue with what support he had until he met them.[117] In the meantime, if his work was regarded by the ecclesiastical authorities as sufficient reason for not allowing him to be ordained, he could comfort himself with the thought that ordination would confine him to a single parish. There were advantages in remaining unordained: he would be free from parochial responsibilities, answerable only to God and able to enlarge his sphere of activity without restriction. But he also wished to be accepted by the Church and this, together with the hope of his family that he would one day be admitted into Holy Orders, kept him from discarding the possibility. He realized that there were other problems that could prevent his ordination. In a letter to his brother Joseph, he wrote:

> Some say the Bishop comes to his Diocess [sic] about Midsummer but I am told he ordains none till upwards of 6 months above 22, which will be an Objection to me, if I could in other Respects come off, which I have not assurance enough to trust.[118]

It was during May that he heard, almost certainly through the Dissenters, of two clergymen who would probably give him a sympathetic ear and possibly assist him.[119] One was Thomas Jones of Cwm-iou in Monmouthshire,[120] the other, Griffith Jones of Llanddowror. Both were diligent workers, but more significantly Calvinists, a fact which was to influence Harris in due course. In another letter to Joseph, he wrote of Griffith Jones, that

> he devotes himself entirely to the Duties of his Function ... If I could be introduced to him, he could befriend me; he would draw my Character in its due light to the Bishop and easily answer the objection of Nonage and Imperfection in the learned Languages.[121]

Griffith Jones[122] was born at Penboyr, Carmarthenshire, in 1683 and educated at a local school. Having begun his career as a shepherd, he decided to enter the ministry and attended the grammar school at Carmarthen. Ordained deacon and priest during September 1708, he became rector of Llanddowror in 1716 under the patronage of Sir John Philipps,[123] and remained there until his death in 1761. Though primarily remembered for his immeasurable contribution to the development of education in Wales through the circulating schools founded by him in the 1730s, it must be remembered that he was also a powerful preacher and a gifted spiritual leader. His endeavours incurred the wrath of his bishop in 1714, when he was accused of 'going about preaching on week days in Churches, Churchyards, and sometimes on the mountains to hundreds of auditors'.[124] Large congregations flocked to Llanddowror to hear him; as a result he has been described as the morning star of the Methodist Revival.[125]

Encouraged by William Williams[126] of Tredwstan, Harris went to Llanddowror to meet Griffith Jones during the last week of May, and in a letter to Joseph gave an account of the visit and of the advice he had been given.[127] Griffith Jones believed that Harris's age would be reasonable grounds for dismissing his application for ordination, but assured him that if he was unable to find employment as a teacher in the Talgarth area he would help him in the meantime. This left Harris doubting the wisdom of making an application during the summer of 1736, it being regarded an affront to the bishop to offer for ordination while still under age. Griffith Jones also added that, had he not recently taken a nephew[128] to assist him, he would have been prepared to help Harris 'to one of the two churches he [had] himself'.

The visit to Llanddowror marked an important stage in Harris's career. It introduced him to a new range of personal contacts and to some of the voluntary religious movements which were already at work in the Church. The meeting also widened his view of the religious world and helped to break down the insularity which had thus far restricted his vision. One of Griffith Jones's patrons was Bridget Bevan, the wife of Arthur Bevan, the Member of Parliament for Carmarthen from 1727 to 1741.[129] Another was his brother-in-law, Sir John Philipps, and all three were deeply involved in the activities of the SPCK[130] and were in contact with a number of continental religious leaders, among whom were A. H. Francke and A. W. Boehm.[131] John Philipps was also familiar with the Wesleys and Whitefield during their days at Oxford. Griffith Jones would therefore have known of developments not only in London but in other parts of the country; he would also have been cognizant of events abroad. By visiting Llanddowror, Harris would have been made aware of this wider religious scene, and it is noteworthy that he was dreaming of emulating Francke by setting up an alms house at Trevecka as early as December 1736.[132]

Now he had found respectable and influential friends who were willing to give him the advice and support he had sought for so long. Griffith Jones, fulfilling as he did Harris's heartfelt need for companionship, was held in such high esteem by him that he could say:

> Pray let me not want the favour of your advice for I'll be directed by you, nor shall I take any new steps without consulting you ... for you are in

my eyes My Master's Steward and I am one of the Day Labourers, who having consulted our great Master and His Word I am in hopes of receiving His particular Commands through your Mouth.[133]

Following his visit, Griffith Jones decided that no harm would come from Harris's submitting an application for ordination during the bishop's visit to Wales during July.[134] He therefore advised him first to seek the support of some of the local clergy, as six signatures were required on his testimonial, and then, on obtaining the support of the signatories, to submit his application. It is significant that on approaching the clergy Harris found them to be 'exceeding kind',[135] either because they were unwilling to see him and his followers forced out of the Church or because they were pacified by the loss of support that he had experienced during the spring. Pleased that they and a Justice of the Peace were ready to pledge him their support, Harris's hopes were raised 'to a High Pitch'; God was clearing a path so that he could enter Holy Orders.

His appearance before Nicholas Claggett[136] resulted in a bitter disappointment; moreover, the bishop's response threw him into confusion. Since Harris believed that he 'had things so well drawn up and notwithstanding met such Treatment', it made him 'utterly despair of ever having publick Authority to serve Mankind from this Bishop'[137] and raised serious doubts in his mind concerning his work. Was he right in thinking himself wiser or better than his opponents? Was it possible that exhorting was indeed contrary to God's Law and sinful? Through anxiety he found that he had lost his zeal and 'could not speak to the People with greater effect than any other Person', but after visiting some friends and resuming his work yet again, he saw 'extraordinary success' which quickly restored his sinking spirits.

However great his disappointment, Harris now knew that there were some among the Anglican clergy and laity who supported him. Llanddowror had become a source of comfort and encouragement, and it was to Griffith Jones, and those around him, that he turned for advice. But this prop was soon to be removed. During August 1736 Harris spent a fortnight at Llanddowror and there met Edward Dalton,[138] a member of Griffith Jones's congregation. Though a man of firm religious principles, Dalton found difficulty in appreciating Harris's boundless energy and zeal, and attempted to persuade him of the benefits of moderation in both outlook and conduct. Hearing him remark 'that Satan could disguise himself as an angel of light', Harris began to suspect that he had been deceiving himself and that all the apparent success he had hitherto enjoyed had not been due to the power of God's Spirit. Dalton's advice led him to curb his spiritual spontaneity, but in so doing he found that he had 'lost much of the simplicity and sweet communion with God' which he experienced when despised and vilified by those around him. Religion, he found, became a burden, while fear began to trouble him.

> I lost my assurance by listening to Mr Dalton who called it fanaticism, the work of the devil. I lost my first love – when I could not let anybody alone without telling him of his wretchedness, and when there was such power among us, that I was often on my feet all night for three nights in succession, and unable to desist. He advised me not to be so zealous; that God never asks such a thing of us. I soon yielded, not knowing that it was flesh and blood that loved that doctrine until the Lord had left me . . . I lost my testimony by listening to those who called it spiritual pride, and in consequence I was in bondage for three years.[139]

Dalton's views were partly endorsed by Griffith Jones who, in an attempt to make Harris acceptable to the bishop, had advised him to give up his itinerant ministry and set up a school at Trevecka. This he did, but he was later to claim that 'submitting to Mr Griffith Jones cost [him] three years of uncertainty'.[140]

The significance of this incident has not been sufficiently emphasized in the past.[141] Having come through his conversion experience and found what he described as 'uninterrupted rest in the Love and faithfulness of God',[142] and having weathered the storms of opposition, persecution and vilification, Harris's self-confidence and conviction that he had acted in obedience to God's will in attempting to bring others to Christ was greatly undermined by Dalton and Griffith Jones. Furthermore, his anxiety was not confined to doubt about the nature of the work he had undertaken, but, as will be seen, included doubts about the validity of his own spiritual experiences during the spring of 1735. Harris could not deny that they had taken place but now questioned their significance. Bennett's statement[143] that 'from now on [Harris] spent much of his time in fighting his fears, and the corruption of his own heart' is literally true, for as Harris observed, it was a battle that was to rage within him for three years, until the summer of 1739. Though able to continue travelling, preaching and exhorting with astounding success, it was a desperately unhappy young man who wrote of his innermost feelings in his Diaries. It seems ironic that since his conversion Harris had longed for fellowship with mature, understanding Christians, and in meeting Griffith Jones had regarded him as an answer to his prayers. But within three months, directly as a result of Jones's intervention in his work, Harris was experiencing a serious spiritual crisis so deep as to convince him that he had never undergone the experience of regeneration.

Back at Trevecka, Harris opened a school, as suggested by Griffith Jones, but continued to exhort during the evenings. On 8 October he wrote to Llanddowror to report his progress and included in the letter an interesting reference to his activities. 'Private societies begin to be formed. I have not 6 Nights att home [sic] since I came down. I hope they take root.'[144] This is the first clear reference to the societies in Harris's writings; they had obviously been the subject of discussion between him and Griffith Jones at Llanddowror. It is surprising that he mentions them at all, for Jones had encouraged him to cease itinerating and devote himself to his studies in order to strengthen his candidacy for ordination.[145] While it is possible that he was being honest and admitting that he had not conformed with his mentor's wishes, another possibility is that Griffith Jones wanted Harris to be able to inform the bishop that he was a teacher by profession, thus making him a more acceptable candidate. At the same time, he may have told him that he was free to work locally during the evenings to establish private societies such as the ones seen in London from the latter part of the previous century, and which had been the subject of the famous tract written by Josiah Woodward entitled *An Account of the Religious Societies in the City of London* (1697). If Harris had insisted on being allowed to do at least something to nurture his converts, such activity may have been regarded as being possibly more acceptable to the bishop.

More new societies were formed towards the end of 1736[146] through Harris's association with John Games, the precentor at Talgarth church.[147] Games visited farms and villages to teach young people to sing psalms,[148] and Harris took advantage of the opportunity to go with him to exhort those who attended the classes. As this activity was regarded as being under the auspices of the Church there was no opposition to it, and Harris was thus able to visit other neighbouring parishes with Games during the winter.[149]

It was through these singing classes that he went, towards the end of 1736, to Y Wernos, a remote farm in the parish of Llandyfalle in Breconshire, and established what he later came to regard as the first 'permanent' society. In November 1738 he recalled that it was 'near this time 2 years, in '36' that God had brought him there 'through the means of singing Psalms with the Teacher',[150] and in 1745 he wrote that it was at Wernos that 'all this great work that has spread it self over Wales ... began, and the first society settled'.[151]

From the beginning of 1737 Harris's main concern was whether he was going to remain within the Church of England or join the Dissenters. Early in January he received a letter from William Herbert, the Baptist who had broached the subject with him a few months previously, in which he attempted to persuade Harris of the folly of keeping the new converts within the Church.[152] Having cured 'many scabby sheep', would it not be better for them to be put in 'some Enclosure by themselves', he asked, thus illustrating the difference between the Religious Societies and the Baptist congregations which were based on the 'gathered church' principle, according to which the regenerate sinners separated from the world into an association of 'visible saints'.[153] To allow the new converts to remain within the Church of England would, according to Herbert, lead to their corruption; 'one scabby sheep spoils the whole flock'.

The thought of joining the Dissenters certainly appeared attractive to Harris. While they had supported him in all his efforts, he had seen considerable opposition from within his own Church; the laity, the clergy and the bishop had all expressed their disapproval of his conduct. His allegiance to the Church had not only been questioned but also severely tested, and it seemed that life among the Dissenters could hardly be more difficult than what he had already experienced. Further opposition at this juncture served only to intensify his dilemma,[154] and while trying to decide whether or not he was going to remain in the Church, Harris agonized over the advantages and disadvantages for several weeks.

There was need for a balanced assessment of the situation. Any consideration of the possibility of joining the Baptists meant that Harris would have to examine their doctrine, and on the same day that he received William Herbert's letter we find him 'reading Controversies about Baptism'.[155] In February he remarked that both Dissenters and Churchmen liked in him only what pleased them,[156] and, seeing him taking an interest in the Dissenters, Pryce Davies softened his approach and warned him not to leave the Church.[157] Harris admitted to himself that he had no wish to do so as he never enjoyed 'as good Communion with God anywhere else',[158] and fully realized that he was in danger of being 'prejudiced against the Principles of the Established Church without examining them, by looking at the wicked lives of its Professors' and by pondering on the way they had persecuted him. Caught between the cross-currents of Anglican and Nonconformist Calvinism represented by Griffith Jones and William Herbert, he was determined to consider both sides of the argument, and became 'more humble and sincere in [his] prayers' and 'cooly examined both sides'.[159]

Others beside Pryce Davies realized the folly of forcing Harris out of the Church, and many clergymen who had previously shown themselves opposed to his work now mellowed considerably in their attitude towards him.[160] However, it is abundantly clear from the Diaries that these clergymen offered Harris their friendship at a price – his disapproval of the Dissenters. But while he was initially willing to respond to their wishes, he soon discovered that he could not continue on account of his conscience. While dining with David Lloyd, vicar of Llandyfalle, he found that he had been 'very negligent ... condemning the Dissenters' and was duly 'accused by conscience that [he] did not act with serenity enough'.[161] On meeting Pryce Davies at Talgarth and telling him of his opposition to the Dissenters,[162] he said that 'it left a guilt in me'. He suspected that his attempts to please his fellow men were not pleasing to God.

Owing to his fear of being accused of disloyalty to the Church, Harris also thought it prudent to praise her at every opportunity, though his motives were, in his own view, not entirely honourable. At Bolgoed, he says, he 'cried up the Church in order to escape persecution'[163] but then feared that by so doing, he had grieved the Spirit. The tension within him increased when he realized that he lacked unction at a house where he again 'cried up the Church', but enjoyed 'vast zeal' at another where he avoided the subject.[164] He confessed that he saw little that he would condemn in the Church. 'I never saw anything wanting in the Church of England but these', he wrote:

1. a Privilege of meeting together as a Society to consult about points of Salvation, [and] self examination.
2. More home preaching [on] the necessity of Regeneration in the Pulpit with familiar teaching, Catechising and instructing private[ly] in families and publick; an Inspection [of] the Life of every Communicant, the reason for their absenting [themselves] to be taken by some set apart for that Business, Deacons &c., with an Examination on the Saturday before, [in] publick, before they are admitted to Christ's Table, and to have the Sacrament monthly.
3. More familiarity between the Pastors and the Sheep.[165]

These were deficiencies which Harris believed needed to be reformed. His critique seems to have been founded upon the fact that apart from the sacraments, the Church provided matins, evensong, a recognized form of liturgy and little else. There was a failure to provide effectively for discipleship in small fraternal groups,[166] and it was Harris's conviction that people needed more to sustain them on their spiritual pilgrimage. However, he did not regard this as sufficient reason to secede from the Church, especially as the Dissenters were not without fault. In their eagerness to see their own churches grow, Harris cynically believed that they regarded attachment to their particular congregations as more important than an attachment to Christ,[167] and such sentiments, together with the fact that he was again consorting with the clergy, led the Dissenters to be as critical of him as he was of them. While he, on the one hand, 'spake something against the Dissenters' at a society meeting at Bolgoed,[168] they, on the other, accused him a week later of being opposed to extempore prayer.[169] Ten days later he heard that he was to be sent for to dispute with the Baptists,[170] and though at first inclined to accept the invitation, he decided that he would attend only to incite 'the Parties to love'. This did not prevent him from being 'zealous against the Baptists'[171] or 'talking against Dissenters'.[172] He declared, 'I am prodigious strict for securing all that are in our Church in it and resolve against the Dissenters.'[173] He found himself in the curious position of standing between the two parties, being to the Dissenters an Anglican, and to the Anglicans a Dissenter. The result was that during February he was able to claim that he was being attacked by both sides,[174] and his prayers for guidance reflect his deep anguish.

> O! God, what shall I do? ... I am tossed this way and that way by men of various opinions. I am at Thy feet to be directed aright. O! fix me where Thou wilt; show me from Thy Word, Thy Spirit, Thy Servants, Dreams or some means what is Thy will and I am ready by the assistance of Thy spirit to act so.[175]

Harris decided to stay within the Church. His bias had always been in her favour owing to his upbringing and the advice he received not only from Pryce Davies but also from Griffith Jones.[176] By April he was able to rejoice not only that 'open prophane [sic] sinners' were being converted but also that 'each was secured from dissenting'.[177] At the same time he was persuaded that his prayers had been answered and that God was saying, 'Be true to [the] Church of England.'[178] But, as was so often the case with Wesley, so also with Harris; it was pragmatism which finally settled the issue.[179] The Church was 'in Doctrine good',[180] and the spiritual home of the majority he hoped to convert. He wrote in the spring of 1737:

> As I was converted my self in this ruined Church, and was fed here ... and as its principles appear to me to be sound, O! pardon me if I did wrong in crying this up in order to have more liberty to teach other poor souls.[181]

His aim was not simply to secure a congregation for himself but to reach the people in vast numbers and bring them to Christ. In order to be able to do this he was prepared to remain within the Church, despite her weaknesses, if that made him more acceptable to the populace. He believed, as did Wesley, that as the work gathered momentum, he would then be able to press for the reformation of the deficiencies he saw.[182] Dissent was numerically far weaker than Anglicanism, much despised and ridiculed, and Harris, like Wesley, dreamed not of small minority sectarian groups, a form of spiritual 'remnant', but of a renewed majority, a spiritually blessed Church and nation.[183] He could never be content with the renewal of a local congregation; his prayers were for 'Mercy and Pity to the Church' in its entirety. The breadth of his concern encompassed a nation in which 'so many 10,000 souls starve' and led to claims that he was willing 'to be annihilated to profit all the Church' even though it was 'torn to pieces by its sin and ignorance'.[184] This view of the scale of the task to be accomplished set Harris apart from both the clergy and the Dissenters and it was also the reason why he remained faithful to the Church of England throughout his life.

Chapter 3
A Mission from God

Though having no conscious theological standpoint at the time of his conversion, Harris had naturally been influenced by the Arminianism which he had heard preached at the parish church. He was not, however, as Arminian in his views as some have suggested,[1] for even as early as July 1736 we find him denouncing contemporary 'Arminian' teaching in a letter to Griffith Jones.

> I have occasion to fear the Spirit that acted in the Apostles and Primitive Christians does not bear the rule now in our Church, for being strangers themselves to Regeneration, I never hear 'em [the clergy] preach that Doctrine and 'tis plain by their Arminian Tenets and their laying such great stress upon Externals, Modes and Ceremonies that they never felt the powerful Operation of the Blessed Spirit.[2]

Though Harris described himself as a 'strong Arminian' at this time and claimed that Arminianism was 'in [his] head',[3] it is very doubtful whether he possessed any clear or positive doctrinal system.[4] His theology was based largely on his personal experience.[5] Such 'Arminianism' as he possessed was largely negative, resting on the rejection of predestinarian ideas of free grace which was characteristic of most Anglicans of his time. His idea of salvation during this early period was simple: repentance, faith and the accomplishment of duty towards God and man. There was little mention of the significance of Christ's death.[6]

This was, however, the form of piety taught by *The Practice of Piety* and *The Whole Duty of Man*, and without further teaching it is difficult to see how it would have been possible for Harris to advance from that position. It was the same brand of teaching that he had heard from the clergy and condemned so bitterly in his letter to Griffith Jones, the only difference being that he believed that the fulfilment of duty was to be preceded by regeneration, an event which enabled man to endure the hardships of the discipline necessary to succeed. It was at the time of regeneration that the Spirit was given, which enabled the sinner to live in obedience to God. Salvation was not by faith alone but by faith and obedience.

This was totally unacceptable to the Dissenters who, because of their Calvinism, emphasized the free grace of God and election. In their disputes with Harris it was the latter of these two subjects that caused the most controversy as they opposed him at the society meetings.[7] But on 30 March 1737, during a church service, Harris saw that there was 'such a thing' as election through the reading of John 17, and the words of John 6.44 – 'No man can come to me, except the Father which hath sent me draw him' – raised further doubts in his mind concerning his opposition to the doctrine.

There were three major factors which contributed to Harris's final acceptance of the doctrines of election and free grace. The first was that the Dissenters argued with him on the basis of his own personal experience.[8] It was put to him that he was unable to fulfil any spiritual duty except through the grace of God. Grace preceded any action by him; repentance was the result of the work of grace, not grace the result of repentance. 'I was silenced', he wrote, 'my own experience condemned me.'[9] He recognized that it was in response to God's call that he had repented, but admitted that although he had become aware of both the experiential and biblical evidence, he was still reluctant to submit to it.

The second factor was William Herbert's words following a bout of illness which had brought him close to death. Herbert claimed that in his weakness, he had realized 'that all Duties were of no use to him' and that it was Christ alone who could answer for him. Harris was deeply moved and said that it was then that he 'began to mention much of Christ's Love and sufferings' while exhorting.[10] Before this, he said, 'I put all on the man to work – I knew nothing of free grace tho' I did inwardly feel I could do nothing.'[11] The third factor was the preaching of Thomas Lewis,[12] the curate of Merthyr Cynog in Breconshire, with whom Harris became acquainted during the summer of 1737. The son of an Evangelical clergyman, it was he who first enlightened him 'to see the Doctrine of Free Grace',[13] but after the initial enlightenment there followed a period during which Harris grappled with the significance of what he had learned.[14] He came to the conclusion that his defective understanding of the process of salvation clearly proved that he had never received Christ, and this confirmed the suspicions already in his mind since the previous autumn when, owing to the advice he had received from Edward Dalton at Llanddowror, his assurance of salvation had been undermined. This fear concerning his own condition did not, however, prevent him from acknowledging and accepting the objective truth of the doctrine of free grace.

While this development was taking place in Harris's mind, another change was occurring in his method of teaching within the societies. Until May 1737[15] his exhortations had been based on devotional books such as those which had contributed towards his own conversion. After reading extracts from them, he would proceed to explain the contents to his auditors, but this method was now abandoned. The books were put aside as Harris began to speak extemporarily, thus allowing himself the freedom to choose his own theme.[16] Although he used various terms to describe this activity,[17] his reading and exhorting had now developed into preaching.

During the summer Harris met two men who were to become prominent figures in Wales during the eighteenth century. The first was Howel Davies,[18] who, though he had come to Talgarth to teach at a school which had been set up in opposition to Harris's own, was later to became his assistant at Trevecka.[19] A native of Monmouthshire, he was ordained deacon in 1739, and priest in 1740. After serving briefly as curate to Griffith Jones at Llandeilo Abercywyn he moved to Llys-y-frân, Pembrokeshire, in 1741. He remained an active Methodist throughout his life but during his latter years confined himself to his own county, thus becoming known as the 'Apostle of Pembrokeshire'.

Davies was converted under Harris's ministry,[20] and thereafter their friendship developed into a close spiritual bond, again satisfying Harris's intense need for companionship. During September they joined together in a covenant with God, and 'Love boiled to Howel Davies' as they made 'the Dedication of Self to Christ'.[21] Similar personal covenants were made by the Puritans;[22] while conducting an active Christian witness in a hostile society, they found it helpful to make explicit in written form the covenant which was written on their hearts. Harris and Davies followed the same pattern. On 12 September 1737, they resolved to enter into a covenant on the following Wednesday, binding themselves not only to God but also to one another.

Here, for Harris, was a friendship similar to that of David and Jonathan in the Old Testament. He praised God for giving him 'a Companion so faithful and diligent', and rejoiced that all his 'former desires about a friend were answered in him'.[23] But Davies was soon to leave Trevecka, 'being asked to go',[24] most probably by Griffith Jones who was at that time in the process of developing his system of circulating schools.[25] This involved the setting up of classes in various localities to teach people to read, usually during the winter months when there was less to be done on the farms. Once the pupils had been taught, the teacher would proceed to another locality.

It is unlikely that Davies went to Llanddowror at Harris's instigation, as Richard Bennett suggests.[26] His departure came as a total surprise to Harris and it was news that he found difficult to accept.[27] They parted during December at the end of the school term, as Harris was setting out on another journey to Carmarthenshire. On his return home early in 1738, he was informed of a further development which had occurred during his absence; he had been dismissed from his post as a teacher because his constant itinerating had rendered him unable to perform his duties properly.[28] Though distressed at first, he soon found that the freedom accompanying unemployment could be used to his advantage to enlarge his sphere of activity.[29]

The second person whom Harris met during the summer was Daniel Rowland of Llangeitho.[30] Born at Nantcwnlle in Cardiganshire, the son of the vicar of Nantcwnlle and Llangeitho, he was educated, according to tradition, at the grammar school at Hereford and ordained deacon in 1734. Priested in 1735, he was appointed curate to his brother John at the parishes of Nantcwnlle and Llangeitho, and underwent a profound spiritual experience under the ministry of Griffith Jones. His own ministry was first dominated by the preaching of divine judgement, but following advice from Phillip Pugh, an Independent minister,[31] he began preaching the grace of God. Having met Harris during 1737, they became the leaders of the Methodist movement in Wales and co-operated to promote their cause until 1750, when, as a result of sharp differences, they separated. Following his brother's death in 1760, the parish of Llangeitho was given to

Rowland's son, and Rowland himself was dismissed from his curacy in 1763 because of his Methodist activities. He remained at Llangeitho but efforts to secure his reinstatement met with failure. He died on 20 October 1790, aged 77.

A spiritual awakening had occurred under Rowland's ministry independently from that at Trevecka when, in a similar way to Harris, he called the people to repentance through the proclamation of God's judgement.[32] The two men met unexpectedly at the parish church at Defynnog, Breconshire,[33] on 13 August 1737,[34] Rowland having gone there most probably as a result of his acquaintance with Griffith Jones.[35] Harris was impressed by what he heard and saw, and wrote: 'Upon hearing the sermon, and seeing the gifts given him and the amazing power and authority with which he spoke, and the effects it had upon the people, I was made indeed thankful, and my heart burned with love to God and him.'[36] Many years later he claimed that Rowland was 'surrounded by glory in the pulpit'.[37] A friendship was struck between them which 'to all eternity [would] never end'.[38]

Long before his dismissal from his school, Harris had begun to travel outside Breconshire. During the summer of 1737 he had accepted an invitation by John Williams,[39] who was later to become his father-in-law, to exhort in Radnorshire, and during the autumn had agreed to act as a supervisor over Griffith Jones's circulating schools.[40] This activity justified his travelling around the country and made up for the fact that the singing classes conducted by John Games had come to an end. Frequent journeys to Llanddowror[41] provided him with fresh pastures, and his knowledge of another, labouring in the same manner as himself at Llangeitho, gave him additional confidence.[42] The shift of emphasis in his doctrine also contributed to a more scriptural ministry, and his new practice of speaking without a book led to the need to draw texts from the Bible. All these factors contributed to a more public ministry characterized by field-preaching, and although Harris had served his apprenticeship as an open-air preacher at the Talgarth fairs during the winter of 1735–6, it was during the latter half of 1737 that his open-air ministry, and possibly the Revival itself, began in earnest. It was from that time that the congregations numbered in the hundreds, sometimes in the thousands,[43] and although some exaggeration would be expected in Harris's figures, the dramatic increase proves beyond doubt that an important milestone had been reached for both Revival and Revivalist. 'After this', he claimed, 'I readily complied with every invitation, and went wherever I was sent for, by day and night, discoursing generally three or four, and sometimes, five and six hours a day, to crowded auditories.'[44]

In the story of Harris's spiritual development the experience he enjoyed on 8 February 1738 has a unique place. Daniel Rowland was preaching at Gwenddwr in Breconshire, and while listening to his sermon on Proverbs 8.32 Harris was overwhelmed. He claimed that he had never before 'seen' that Christ was 'pleading' for him in heaven but now saw His love in such depth that his understanding was cleared; he saw in Christ a solid foundation upon which to build and was 'willing to go about and leave all'. 'Today', he wrote, 'was an extraordinary day to my Soul. I see myself more on Christ.'[45] He was later to claim that it was then that he 'was brought to the knowledge of the truth about Christ' and that Rowland had been the means of bringing it about.[46]

His appearance as a field-preacher excited the attention of Dissenters outside the immediate vicinity of Trevecka. As early as August 1737 he had received a letter from an Independent minister, Rees Davies of Abergavenny,[47] encouraging him to 'go on ... with [his] flaming zeal', but cautioning him against seeking ordination since his 'extensive usefulness [would] be much abridged and stinted within the limits of a parochial sphere'.[48] Davies was not alone in wishing him well. By the end of the fourth decade of the eighteenth century, many Dissenting ministers were longing for some form of spiritual awakening[49] and strove to prepare for the day that God would send it among them; Edmund Jones of Pontypool,[50] James Davies of Merthyr, Henry Davies of Blaen-gwrach and Phillip Pugh of Cardiganshire[51] among the Independents; Miles Harry, again of Pontypool, Enoch Francis of Newcastle Emlyn[52] and James Roberts of Ross[53] among the Baptists. These and others, many of them involved in itinerant ministries,[54] saw in Harris's success a means of furthering the cause of the gospel in Wales, and for that reason wrote to him when they heard of his work.

David Williams of Pwll-y-pant[55] hoped that he would visit Bedwellte in Monmouthshire, 'in the Power and Might of [God's] Spirit',[56] while Henry Davies said that many would have been 'very glad to see and hear [him]' as 'many thousands' were longing for him to visit Glamorgan.[57] Others similarly invited him to their areas;[58] Harris accepted and met with considerable success,[59] as shown by the letter sent to him by David Williams.

> The two days service with us has been attended with marvellous success. The churches and meetings are crowded, Sabbath-breaking goes down ... I cannot but forbear thinking (without any partiality) but that your coming here was from God, and that God himself, in the might and power of his Spirit, was pleased to come with you.[60]

Co-operation with the Dissenters lasted until the beginning of the 1740s and ended because of essential differences between the two movements. Disagreements concerning doctrine and church polity, together with various personality clashes and tensions, arising from the thorny issue of which congregations the new converts should join, all contributed to their inability to coexist within the same organization.[61] In a surprisingly short period, Methodism and Dissent drifted apart.

Through the extension of his activities and the constant neglect of his own physical welfare, Harris was soon to suffer another breakdown in his health. This confined him to his home for several weeks and it is during this period that we find him writing 'Directions to the Societies' in order to secure their continuance during his absence.[62] After his recovery he resumed his travels and spent the remainder of the year itinerating through most of south Wales.

Although immersed in his work, he was far from possessing the confidence, conviction and assurance he enjoyed at the time of his first campaign during the winter of 1735–6. Not only was he doubtful of the scriptural legality of the work he had undertaken, he was also still unable to escape the uncertainty which had troubled him since his visit to Llanddowror in August 1736. Later, he was to look back and say:

> Griffith Jones first did make my going about a Case of Conscience. Since, I have not been quite easy, but have been drawn on by earnest entreaties of godly Ministers and the cries of the People and not by some flashy zeal of my own.[63]

The uneasiness is clearly to be seen in his attitude to his conversion experience. Beginning with a realization during January

1737 that 'God's Spirit in a great Measure had left [him]',[64] he came to suspect his commission[65] and felt 'very stupid, that notwithstanding all tokens of God's love' he was still in fear and doubt.[66] Afraid that others would be brought into God's Kingdom while he was left outside,[67] he admitted in March that he had lost his 'old strictness'.[68] By September the situation had deteriorated further, to a point where Harris believed not only that he was 'short in Love to Christ' but also that there was 'no sign of being a Member of His spiritual Body'.[69] He prayed that God would by some means convince him of his calling so that 'nothing [would] disturb his Peace',[70] but by October he had come to the conclusion that he had not 'come through the narrow birth'.[71]

Although greatly encouraged by the experience he enjoyed while listening to Daniel Rowland at Gwenddwr, the collapse of his health during the spring eroded whatever progress he had made. Not allowing himself time for the meditation and reflection necessary under such circumstances, he returned to his work and travels at the earliest opportunity with the result that, by October, little had changed. Reading John Bunyan on the covenant of grace, possibly in *The Doctrine of Law and Grace Unfolded* (1659), he claimed that he knew nothing experientially of that covenant, and admitted that he was still troubled by doubts.[72] His greatest wish, as he later read Bunyan's *Jerusalem Sinner* (1688), was that he too would come to possess the enviable assurance seen 'in the Preface where he spoke assured of Grace'.[73]

Harris's position was thus, in one respect at least, similar to that of John Wesley on his return from Georgia at the beginning of 1738: both were passionately in search of assurance.[74] But the dilemma in Harris's case was rooted in the question of the relationship of faith and works within the covenant of grace, since he had initially believed that faith and obedience were both necessary for salvation. His personal theological understanding and his teachings in the society meetings had been based upon this assumption, and what disturbed him so deeply was that he had come to the conclusion that this fundamental conviction was erroneous. As with Wesley, Harris also needed to be convinced that God's grace was the initiator of the new covenant, to which human obedience was a response rather than a duty.[75] But his need also went deeper. Even when he had accepted the fact that the doctrines of election and free grace were biblical, he then faced the problem of assessing whether his own experience during the spring of 1735 conformed with them and served as an example of the objective biblical truth. During and following his conversion the emphasis had been on repentance, the reformation of his personal life and the need to evangelize; he was now able to convince himself that, prior to this activity, there had not been a valid experience of God's free grace. He feared that he had deceived himself and pondered, even if God had called him in 1735, to what extent later developments had resulted not from a submission to His sovereign will but only from a personal attempt to merit salvation through good works.

R. T. Jenkins has already pointed out that Harris's views on assurance developed in a similar way to those of John Wesley,[76] who held – for a time – not only that personal assurance of the forgiveness of sin was possible, but that it was an essential component of saving faith itself. Both men defined faith in subjective terms. Wesley, emphasizing the personal pronouns, held that it was, 'a sure trust and confidence that Christ died for *my* sins, that He loved *me*, and gave Himself for *me*'.[77] By 1744 Harris was also able to write in much the same vein.

> Last night I had a particular sight how Christ had lived for *me* and died for *me* and rose again for *me* and ascended for *me* and is glory-fy'd for *me* – so that *I* have kept the Law and satisfy'd Justice and overcome Death and Sin and am gloryfy'd.[78]

Faith was closely related to assurance and Harris was to adopt the view that they were inseparable. He declared 'that we cant be in Christ and not know it, and that tho' there is a weak faith, yet assurance is necessary'.[79] Justification was 'real ... actual ... personal';[80] he who did not possess assurance was not justified.[81]

This emphasis was characteristic of many early Evangelicals, but there were others, Dissenters in particular, who disagreed and defined faith in more objective terms. They held that assurance, although desirable, was not essential, and as a result of this difference, tension developed between Harris and others, most notably David Williams of Pwll-y-pant.[82] Being accused of denying the need for assurance, Williams argued that he had 'asserted it and proved it in the Strongest manner and urged all persons to use Diligence to attain it'. At the same time, he did not believe 'that it was ... absolutely necessary to salvation'. Many had gone to heaven 'who attained not a full Assurance thereof here, but none without being in Christ'.[83] This view infuriated Harris to such an extent that, when on a journey in Pembrokeshire in 1741, he was 'led to call such as oppose assurance dogs of Hell'.[84]

In his understanding of the doctrine Harris put great emphasis on the 'direct witness' expounded by Wesley in his sermon on 'The Witness of the Spirit'.[85] This is evidenced by the entries in his Diaries as early as the autumn of 1737. On 3 October he wrote: 'O! God, use some means to convince me ... of my effectual calling THAT NOTHING may disturb my Peace. O Christ, I lean on Thee. Give me a spiritual knowledge of Thee.'[86] Four days later, after expressing his fear that he 'never had true conversion' but rather 'a great Desire after it', he wrote, 'I know Thou canst give me the grace Thou gavest Thy Saints formerly. O! Lord, I wait. I know not what to plead. O! shew me if I am in the way or not.'[87] Not only did he believe that God through His Spirit was able to witness to his soul that he was His child, but he also believed that this was one of the ordinary graces. In November, still searching for some measure of assurance, he wrote, 'O! Lord, where art Thou. O! dear Jesus that used to visit [me], where art Thou gone?'

He also recognized the need for the 'indirect witness' – 'the result of reason, or reflection on what we feel in our own souls' – which Wesley held to be equally necessary. 'Experience', wrote Wesley, 'or inward consciousness, tells me that I have the fruit of the Spirit; and hence I rationally conclude: therefore, I am a child of God'.[88] Harris, because of what he claimed to be an indifference towards the Word of God, could not come to such a conclusion, and prayed: 'O! that Thou wouldst draw my love to Thy Word. How can I love Thee and not long for Thy Word entirely?'[89] This failure to appreciate the means of grace worried him. Two months earlier he had observed that he felt 'no longing for the Sacrament, the Sabbath, the Word &c',[90] a condition which, in the Calvinist tradition, indicated that the individual's relationship to God needed to be further investigated. While good works were, according to this school of thought, the most common proofs of both regeneration and adoption, a love of God, joy in His promises and love for one's neighbours were also recognized tokens.[91] Tension between himself, the Dissenters and churchmen, coupled with his inability to feel joy in those things which were essential to a healthy spiritual life, again led Harris to suspect the grace which he had received. Not only did he lack the 'direct witness' of the Spirit, to his mind the 'indirect witness' was also lacking. Reading *The Life and Death of Vavasor Powell* (1671), and comparing Powell's experiences with his own, further deepened his doubt, and although he continued to honour his public engagements, he secretly admitted in his Diary that he felt 'no inward Inclination, but rather a reluctancy'.[92] His greatest desire was to be assured that God had called him and given him a commission to go about to preach in order to draw others to Christ.

During the first week of December 1738, he again visited Llanddowror and there heard Griffith Jones explain what made a Christian 'conform with Christ'. It was not so much the outward knowledge of Christ, Jones declared, but rather the effectual working of inner faith. Harris was greatly encouraged by his words and felt 'some Power' that was 'healing to [him]'. However, in a private interview, Jones reiterated his disapproval of his itinerant ministry and sent him home to renew his studies, urging him to set about preparing himself once again for ordination. Diffidently, Harris did not believe that he had been sufficiently 'enlightened' to warrant making another application.[93]

If a second application was to be made, he was determined that it would be as a result of God making known His will, and although he was 'asked, pressed and urged' on all sides to apply, he saw several reasons why he should not succumb to external pressure.

> 1. I am very unacquainted with the Scriptures and too raw and slight in a matter of such moment . . .
> 2. I am not sure of my inward call.
> 3. As God bless'd me thus visibly, I fear to chain and fetter myself.
> 4. Good men are divided in their desires for me. The cry and condition of the Country seems . . . to call me on this way.[94]

As 1738 drew to a close, Harris was again unsure how to proceed. Pryce Davies, Griffith Jones and others had encouraged him to cease itinerating, but his own heart and the situation in general urged him to continue. In addition to doubt about his personal standing before God and the significance of past experiences, there now came the additional burden of having to plan for the future. Should he seek ordination or not? It was at this juncture, when so many aspects of his life were in disarray, that he received his first letter from George Whitefield.[95] This again was a momentous event in Harris's life and fraught with consequences both for his evangelistic career and his spiritual peace.

Whitefield was a young man – known as 'the boy preacher' because of his youthful looks – and thus much of an age with Harris himself. Already, he had gained a reputation as an electrifying preacher, emphasizing as he did the need for 'the new birth in Jesus Christ – that ineffable change which must pass upon our hearts before we can see God'.[96] Having undergone a conversion experience during his days at Oxford, he was ordained deacon in 1736 and began his ministry at Dummer in Hampshire. In 1737, he sailed to America as a missionary and became involved in the supervision of an orphanage at Savannah in Georgia. The visit was a brief one; less than twelve months after his departure, he returned to England.[97]

Like Harris, Whitefield believed Christ's sacrifice to be the only source of salvation, but was yet to discover the significance of the doctrine of justification by faith alone. In 1738, there was still a clear emphasis on 'duty' in his sermons and letters,[98] and it was not until the middle of 1739 that he modified his doctrine and became a Calvinist.[99]

His career as a field preacher was also yet to begin; his first excursion into the open air, on English soil, was at Kingswood, near Bristol, on 17 February 1739. Field-preaching was acceptable in Anglican circles only in circumstances such as those encountered by foreign missionaries where churches were yet to be built, and Wesley was typical of many of his contemporaries when he wrote that he 'should have thought the saving of souls almost a sin if it had not been done in a church'.[100] Seeing the Kingswood miners 'little better than heathens',[101] Whitefield believed that his irregular conduct of preaching in the open air was justified; 'Blessed be God', he wrote in his *Journal*. 'I have now broken the ice.'[102]

Élie Halévy[103] attributes this development to Whitefield's meeting with Harris on 7 March 1739, but Whitefield was by then already a field-preacher by his own admission. In the entry in his *Journal* for March 5, he wrote, 'My preaching in the fields may displease some ... but I am thoroughly persuaded it pleases God.'[104] The fact that Harris was also involved in such a ministry was certainly of great interest to him,[105] but the two men differed in that Harris was a layman, working, in Whitefield's words, 'not authoritatively, as a minister, but as a private person, exhorting his Christian brethren'.[106]

In his letter, Whitefield encouraged Harris to continue in his work and suggested that they should meet. Harris replied[107] and hinted at the possibility of Whitefield coming to Wales: this he did, and the two men met at Cardiff.[108] Following their meeting, Harris accompanied Whitefield, first to Bristol, and then to London; this was his first encounter with English Methodism and was to be the means by which he was led back towards the peace of mind and assurance of salvation he had sought for so long. At the same time, while not responsible for proving to Whitefield the efficacy of field-preaching, Harris was visible proof to the English Methodists of the success of a lay ministry. He had conducted meetings regularly in south Wales for over three years; many had been converted and nearly thirty private societies had been established.[109] Being presented with such convincing evidence that 'God [had] greatly blessed his pious endeavours',[110] it was not long before English Methodist laymen were following his example.[111]

Although Harris's stay at Bristol was brief, it offered ample opportunity for his spiritual unease to surface. He and Whitefield arrived there late on Friday 9 March, and even before breakfast on the following day, Harris had begun the quiet process of comparing himself to the other Methodists he had met. This was not an uncommon practice for him; he often compared himself to others in order to assess his own spiritual condition. In his Diary he noted how Howel Davies had progressed much further than himself while he was at Trevecka, and he also compared the insufficiency of his own experience to that of Vavasor Powell as described in his biography. Much the same reaction followed his meeting with Whitefield at Cardiff.[112] Now, having met the Bristol Methodists, he wrote in alarm, 'Alas, I want love. They are full of Joy and I am dry ... [I] have a sense of my blindness and coldness, but desire nothing in the World as much as Christ more clearly revealed in my Heart.'[113] From Friday to Monday he was in a dejected mood, seeing himself 'nothing in stature' in comparison to his English brethren, and feeling his 'soul low and longing and seeking for Christ'. Travelling to Bath on Monday, he was 'still in great doubts', and listed his reasons thus:

1. I can't say I have the indwelling of the Spirit...
2. I can't see my love inwardly working to God and burning with delight in, and zeal for, the Saints and full of concern for the Glory of God and pity to poor souls...
3. I find they [the other Methodists] feel the Spirit working every moment on their souls and 'tis Hell to be without Him a moment — alas, where am I then?
4. I am not in Spirit in every duty.
5. I can't say assuredly I am united to God in Christ — I can't set the Glory of God before my eyes.[114]

Back at Bristol on the Tuesday night, he was again 'cast down' when he heard during a society meeting 'that there must be absolutely an indwelling of the Spirit in every Christian testifying [that] he is a child of God'. This, it was said, was a God-given privilege: the believer, through the testimony of the Spirit 'knows he is a Christian'. Harris came to the conclusion that if this was true, he was 'not yet born again'.[115]

For some time, he had been eager to visit London.[116] After meeting Whitefield again on 4 April, they travelled together to the capital. Lodgings were provided by James Hutton[117] at the Bible and Sun, a bookshop in Little Wild Street, and the events which occurred during the six weeks that Harris was there were to be of paramount importance to his spiritual pilgrimage.

From the outset, he was at the centre of the religious turmoil which seethed in the nascent Evangelical movement in London at that time. On his first evening he was taken by Whitefield to a society meeting at Fetter Lane and admitted to full membership without the customary oral examination.[118] This was, presumably, because of his connection with Whitefield, and an act of courtesy which recognized his position as a spiritual leader in Wales.

The Fetter Lane society[119] was the scene of much tension during this period[120] and on the evening that Harris joined them the doctrines held by John Shaw[121] were being discussed. Shaw was of the opinion that there was no need for a priesthood in the

Christian church and that, as a layman, he had as much right as anyone to baptize and officiate at the Lord's Table.[122] As a strong churchman, Charles Wesley opposed these views, as did Whitefield, and they were supported by Harris who urged, with Whitefield,[123] that Shaw should be expelled from the society. After the meeting, far from being disheartened by the vehement arguments that he had heard, Harris thanked God for bringing him to London and into contact with 'these ripe Saints'.[124]

It must be remembered that prior to these visits to England, Harris had not had the benefit of the company of other lay Christians who were not in some way subjected to his authority as a spiritual leader. From the time of his conversion, despite all his doubts, he had always been conscious of his position as the founder of many of the Welsh societies. To his followers in Wales he had always been the authoritative voice in all matters pertaining to the faith and to the organization of the work, and he had generally viewed himself as a chosen vessel, 'comfortably and powerfully led by perpetual outpourings of [God's] love'.[125] In London he found himself forced into a new role, that of an observer rather than a leader, looking at a movement which owed nothing to his own work. During his stay, he was to see many who were accustomed to taking part in debates and arguments concerning the minutiae of Christian doctrine, arguing their point of view with conviction and force; to him they appeared sophisticated and learned, much further advanced than himself in their understanding of the faith, but his perception of the Londoners' apparent maturity was largely due to his inexperience as an evangelist.

Again, he began to compare himself to other Methodists, concluding, as before, that perhaps he had not been converted.[126] He wrote in his Diary that though he could not deny that Christ was in him, he was in great doubt that it was so, especially as it seemed to him that his love was not as deep or as genuine as that of others. Beset by feelings of inferiority, he admitted that as he listened to the Methodists who surrounded him every day, he regarded himself as unworthy to clean their shoes. In great confusion, he praised God for the 'wonderful things' he had heard since coming to London, and expressed the hope that the assurance already given to others would one day be given to him. But, while reading Romans 9, he was convinced that his salvation was based on works rather than faith. His fear about his condition increased, and as the days went by, assurance continued to elude him and he was unable to find any real satisfaction or escape from his distress.[127]

While this struggle was taking place, he was told by 'a brother in the faith' that 'working' and 'striving' for eternal life alienated sinners from Christ.[128] Justification lay in man's ability to come to the Saviour empty-handed, in the manner of a child, to allow Him to do all that was necessary. This was the doctrine of 'stillness',[129] as later taught at Fetter Lane by the Moravian, Philip Henry Molther,[130] who emphasized the need for the sinner to be spiritually still before God, and wait for Christ rather than strive for his salvation. Although both Wesleys and Whitefield opposed this doctrine, Harris was attracted by it, even though it added to his confusion and fear, not only for his own spiritual condition but also for the validity of the whole of the revival work in Wales. If his own personal experience was suspect, the same must have been true of others. If 'stillness' was the way to salvation, then the Welsh, whom he had exhorted to strive for salvation, had laboured in vain.[131]

The doctrine threw Harris into a quandary. He could think of no way forward, and later wrote:

> I did not know what to do. I was afraid to write these convictions down least [sic] it was 'working'. I was afraid to pray, though I had desires put in me, least it was 'doing' ... I went along (much humbled inwardly) fearing every step ... dreading the name of 'doing' or anything like it.[132]

On 1 May he cried in despair, 'I am lost, I am lost.' He again explained his predicament:

> I could not look at Christ, nor could I pray nor seek for Christ least it was working, because I had done so much of that already and yet [was] a stranger to Christ ... I fear I sin even in my groans, griefs and humblings, least I privately expect to be heard for my humblings. Alas, I know not how to think ... and none can give me sound, solid Peace but Jesus Christ.

He prayed, 'I throw my self at Thy feet. I can't empty myself, I can't strive, I can't believe, I can't love or long till Thou givest it, O dear Jesus.' Two days later, still tormented by his doubts, he prayed, 'O! let me hear Thee say again plain that I may be sure, "Thy sins are forgiven Thee", that I may be sure the Peace I enjoy is solid.'

Within a few days he was able to repeat yet again that he had 'solid reasons' for concluding that Christ had never come to his soul; his watching, striving, faith and love had not been the work of the Spirit but the result of his own desires and efforts. The following day, John Cotton's *Treatise of the Covenant of Grace* (1659) came into his hands, and on reading that some had faith in themselves rather than in Christ, he declared that he belonged to that category.[133] But, though he doubted his own faith, he never doubted that he was the object of God's love.[134] He prayed fervently that He would come to him, and such was his longing for Christ that he wrote the words 'O! come' twenty times in succession in his Diary on 8 May. On the same day, while meditating and praying, his Bible opened on Revelation 22:17 – 'let him who is athirst come. And whosoever will, let him take the water of life freely.' These words were to remain fixed in his mind for some time, for having read them, he wrote: 'my soul was filled with fresh longings, crying (almost) out, "All the Devils in Hell can't make me believe that this Promise is not mine".'[135]

On 16 May, Harris analysed his condition yet again and noted eight points which summarized his position:

1. I have not been convinced . . . of Unbelief.
2. I have not seen sin exceeding sinful.
3. I have not seen and felt myself groaning in spirit under the Load of sin . . .
4. Satan has not been cast out of me.
5. The Spirit of Christ does not dwell in me.
6. I never came through the Pangs of the New Birth.
7. I never was made to see and admire . . . the wonderful Love of God so as to kindle Love in me.
8. I never did anything . . . to God's glory.[136]

It is on this note that Diary 44 comes to an end. Diary 45 begins eleven days later on 27 May, and we can only speculate as to what happened between those two dates. In the final paragraph of Diary 44, Harris wrote:

All I can say of my self now is that I think and am pretty satisfied that Christ does not dwell in me ... I know, believe and am satisfied there is an Habitation of Christ in the Heart so as to be assured of His being there, to put off all fears. This I believe He gives Gratis and we don't deserve it ... This the Lord has enlightened me more and more to see since I came here to London ... I don't feel Christ in me ... but the Lord will, I hope, establish me.[137]

This visit to London, without doubt, was a traumatic part of Harris's spiritual pilgrimage. He himself realized as much. In his autobiography he said that he went to London 'about the end of March 1739', and 'received further Gospel light' while there.[138] He claimed that it was through the visit that he came to understand 'that Faith is the fundamental Grace in the spiritual work and the genuine spring of all our obedience'.[139] This was exactly what Peter Böhler had explained to John Wesley in 1738 when he was in similar circumstances.[140] Harris admitted that he had come to see his own faith as totally insufficient and learned that the only path to salvation was to rely solely 'on Christ's Blood'.[141] In 1740 he stated that it was when he met Whitefield that he came to understand the doctrine of justification by faith,[142] and in 1743 claimed it was then that he was delivered from 'Reason'.[143]

Traumatic though it was, it must be emphasized that the events which constituted the 1739 experience occurred within the boundaries of faith. It should not, despite the similarity of Harris's phraseology to what he wrote in 1735, be construed as part of a second conversion experience but rather as a quest for Christian assurance.[144] Less than twelve months after these events, Harris wrote:

I see that I have been under the Law 'till I met the Methodists, though called effectually and led by feeling before, from the time I was made to give myself to God, a little after my conversion in Talyllyn, after the first Whitsuntide, and at sacrament then, had my burden taken off and a new life entered upon.[145]

In 1740 Harris still dated his conversion experience in 1735 and would not, therefore, have regarded the experiences of March–May 1739 as part of a second conversion. But while preaching in Carmarthenshire during 1741, he said to his congregation that, there must be 2 convictions, one from the law and one from the gospel, one to believe in the Father, the other in the Son: the one faith wounds and kills, the other heals and makes alive: the one shews sin without subduing it, the other purifies it.[146]

This strongly suggests that Harris saw this experience in London as bringing with it a 'second conviction'. In a later entry in the Diary, made in January 1743, he elaborated his view of the categories of the spiritual life, describing the successive stages of the Christian rebirth in terms not dissimilar to those of Puritan clinicians of the soul before him. He divided conversion into four stages which closely resembled his own experience; the first and second corresponded to the spring of 1735, when he was initially convinced of sin, pardoned and given the Spirit of Adoption; the third was the period up to 1739 with all its uncertainty, while the fourth was reached at London after he had met Whitefield. In this final stage, Harris claimed, the Christian is 'sent to school to learn fully to know himself and Christ, and God in Christ, and himself in and out of Christ'. He is brought to see the wonders of grace, but this is 'a hard time ... 'till at last the Law has done with him and he is fully brought out of himself to Christ and lives in and on Christ'.[147]

This was his own experience; he was 'sent to school', and there began to understand 'himself and Christ, and God in Christ and himself in and out of Christ'. He began 'to see the wonders of the way of Grace'.

It must be remembered that it was primarily because of his lack of assurance, brought about by Edward Dalton's advice in 1736, that Harris had first begun to show signs of anxiety. Believing, despite all his doubts, that he had a ministry to fulfil, he persevered for three years, and following his introduction to Whitefield, travelled to London. There he met converts who were everything he himself desired to be: knowledgeable in the things of God, spiritually mature, in constant communion with their Saviour and in possession of the same enthusiastic spirit as himself. In their presence, he developed an acute sense of inferiority. However, he was unable to avoid being plunged into discussions, debates and arguments on various themes and doctrines, which led him to realize that his grasp of the faith was insufficient.

As the days went by, his understanding of the Christian faith increased. His lack of assurance led to a willingness to be taught – by friends, through books and by listening to sermons and lectures. Being in London was an educational experience which brought him further spiritual light, and, as he looked back in 1740, he admitted, 'Providence brought me ... to meet Mr Whitefield ... to bring in the Light of the Covenant of Grace.'[148] This 'light' was intellectual and doctrinal, rather than the spiritual light usually associated with the conversion experience. After returning to Wales, he reflected on his visit to the capital and noted his belief that the purpose of the journey had been 'to enlighten [him] in the Gospel'.[149] It was there that he was taught the implications of the doctrine of justification by faith, a 'gospel' which he claimed in 1740 he had never heard until he had met the English Methodists.[150]

Ten years after the visit, Harris wrote concerning the verse he had read in the final chapter of the Book of Revelation: 'this sustained me, and I felt I was willing to let God do what He pleased with me.' Yet he admitted:

> I was troubled ... 'till, at one time, a woman came to me to relate how all the night she had been in distress and perplexity, reasoning with the enemy, whether she was a child of God or not, and that she could have no rest or satisfaction, 'till it came to her mind to go to Christ as she was, and that she had, thereupon, peace and victory.[151]

It was after hearing this, according to Harris, that he was made 'to cease from reasoning' and go with all his 'complaints and fears and lay them before the Friend of Sinners'. He had learned 'to look and go directly to Christ at all times, and in all circumstances'.

There is no reference to this woman in either Diary 44 or Diary 45. We can only conclude, therefore, that the conversation between them took place during the ten days for which we have no entries, between 16 and 27 May. A very marked change of tone follows that period of silence, as can be seen in the following extract from the entry for 27 May: 'O! Lord, I acknowledge ... that Thou hast indulged me in a wonderful manner and borne with me much, and given me much demonstration of Thy Love. But still, Lord, I beg more assurance, stronger faith, more habitual Love.'[152] The reference to '*more* assurance' is striking when it is remembered that it was his total lack of assurance which had caused Harris so much grief. By 27 May, something had happened which enabled him to write with renewed confidence and hope. On the same day he wrote again:

> Sure the Lord alone did bring me here to London ... seeing every thing concurring ... to supply all my wants; His servants made to speak to my purpose, their words working on me and sending more and more to build me in faith on Christ.[153]

It is true that further passages referring to his doubts and fears are to be found from time to time in the Diaries, but that is hardly surprising considering the pressures under which Harris was labouring and the company that he kept. The revival was fraught with many kinds of difficulties throughout its history and those at the helm were in no way immune from setbacks and doubts. Even in 1743 he still remembered his loss of liberty after his encounter with Edward Dalton. He had been 'plunged in[to] Reason' until he had met Whitefield and the other Methodists, 'and from that time to this', he wrote, four years later, '[I] have been gradually delivered'. If deliverance was a gradual process, begun sometime between 16 and 27 May 1739, it is not surprising to find the occasional discordant note in his writings during the early 1740s.

Harris had been through a traumatic experience, but one that was part of his maturation as a revivalist and spiritual leader. Where his own spiritual development was concerned, Wales at that time was infertile ground for him; he was too involved in teaching to be taught. At Bristol and London he was brought face to face with the shallowness of his faith and the extent of his inexperience, while at the same time he was given an opportunity to develop and grow. Part of Harris's problem was his slowness to realize that the need for growth, development and maturity did not negate his earlier experiences or invalidate the faith which he already possessed. When he reached the position where he was prepared to go to Christ as he was, exercising faith, however weak that may have been, it was then he was given the assurance and the peace of mind that he had been seeking for so long.

Though he was now able to proceed with renewed confidence, his assurance of salvation being strengthened as the days went by, the same cannot be said of Harris's attitude towards his itinerant ministry. The advice he had received from Griffith Jones and

Pryce Davies continued to weigh heavily on his mind. He was doubtful whether it was God's will that he should continue preaching, and although his acceptance by Whitefield and the London Methodists had greatly encouraged him, he still hoped that God would in some way sanction his work.

Following his return to Wales, he undertook a journey that was to take him to Pontypool. There, after he had preached, Capel Hanbury,[154] a local magistrate, stepped forward and read the Riot Act. This was not Hanbury's first attempt at curbing the activities of the Methodists. Whitefield wrote in his *Journal* on 4 April 1739 that he had been informed, 'that Mr C— H—ry did me the honour at the last Monmouth Assizes, to make a public motion to Judge P—d, to stop me and brother Howell Harris from going about teaching the people.' The congregation at Pontypool was ordered to disperse within an hour, and, although Harris was willing to obey, Hanbury instructed the constable to take him into custody. Later, following his appearance before the bench, Harris was remanded on bail to appear at the next Great Sessions at Monmouth.[155] The day following his arrest, he and Miles Harry, the local Baptist minister,[156] 'took a Recollection' of the previous day's discourse 'to send to the publick press', and added 'some observations' on what had occurred.[157] As the hearing was not to be held until the beginning of August, there was ample time for the case to be given the maximum amount of publicity, and it seems that Miles Harry took it upon himself to arrange that aspect of the preparations. On 25 June Harris received a letter from him concerning the arrangements for the trial,[158] in which he mentioned that he had suggested to William Seward,[159] the son of an English country squire, 'that some friends in London should consult with the counsellours [sic]' who would be coming to Monmouth.

The rumour that a Methodist preacher was to face charges in a court of law quickly spread in both London and Wales. Harris received letters from Thomas Price,[160] a Justice of the Peace living at Watford near Caerphilly in Glamorgan, and Andrew Gifford,[161] minister of a Baptist church at Eagle Street, London, who both wished him well at the trial. Gifford, who was chaplain to Sir Richard Ellys[162] and an influential man, having such distinguished figures as Lord Chancellor Hardwicke, Sir Arthur Onslow, the Speaker of the House of Commons, and Lady

Huntingdon among his circle of friends, informed Harris that he had made enquiries on his behalf in London.

> I have been with counsel and some of the most Judicious too, who is a Justice of the Peace [sic], who tells me you might have refused and ought not to have gone with the Constable if he had no warrant, and have an action against him for takeing you without it. It does not appear that you have broke any Law, but as bail is given you must appear.[163]

On 2 July, following other enquiries, he wrote again saying that Sir Richard Ellys did not believe that Harris had anything to fear, but if the episode proved expensive, he would gladly assist him in that respect. Gifford had also been with Sir John Gonson[164] who believed that the jury could never find against Harris. Moreover, he thought Harris had a reasonably good case against Capel Hanbury for reading the Riot Act without sufficient cause.

Edmund Jones of Pontypool reported in another letter that the Lord Lieutenant of the county 'did put his hand in Mr Fowler Walker's hand[165] that no harm should come' to Harris.[166] Henry Davies, another Congregational minister, wrote requesting the names and addresses of the most eminent persons of piety whom Harris had met in London and during his travels around England and Wales.[167] Although he did not elaborate what use he would make of such information, it is reasonable to conclude that he also was involved in the attempt to raise support for Harris.

Another letter from London was that of Joseph Stennet,[168] the Baptist minister at Little Wild Street. On reading the contents, Harris wrote, 'I found that he had Presented my Case to Sir Robt. Walpole and had feed [= hired] a Council . . . for me and spoke to the Judges.'[169] The Dissenters were obviously bringing great pressure to bear upon certain men of influence to intervene in Harris's case. Their interest in the freedom to conduct an itinerant lay ministry was considerable, and as they had co-operated with Harris in the past, it is probable that they felt duty-bound to assist him. It may also be that the trial was regarded as a test case involving the new 'Methodist way'.[170] If so, it is not surprising that the Dissenters, with their interest in religious toleration, were so determined to see the prosecution fail.

These developments were significant from Harris's viewpoint

because he saw in them the possibility of God making known his will. On 29 July he wrote in his Diary:

> Lord, I know not what to do as to going about. Wilt Thou let me know what Thy will is? Thou seest, Lord, I don't oppose order, but if Thou callest me [I] am willing to submit ... to Thy Order. But will Thou help me this following week.

The trial was to be held on 10 August, and as the day drew closer Harris began to refer to its outcome as a sign or revelation from God which would settle his future. On 30 July he wrote that he was willing, 'to chose what God choses [sic] and to be pleased with what pleases Him'.[171] If the court found him guilty he would view its decision as a sign that his preaching and itinerating, regardless of the results he had witnessed in the past, were not according to God's will, and would have to cease immediately. On the other hand, if he was found 'not guilty', God would have shown beyond all doubt that his ministry was acceptable in His sight.

On 7 August Harris began his journey to Monmouth. 'O! Lord', he prayed as he set out, 'glorify Thy Self which way Thou pleasest.'[172] On his arrival, he was called by Sir Charles Williams Hanbury who explained that the case had been put into his hands. He informed Harris that he was at liberty to preach wherever and whenever he wished, only that he would take it kindly if he would visit the Pontypool area as seldom as possible on weekdays, most probably because it was feared that his presence would distract the workers from their duties.[173]

To Harris, the Methodist movement and the Dissenters, this was an important victory; the test case had collapsed. How, and for what reason, is not known, but it was probably due to the Dissenters applying enough pressure, especially in London, to secure that the scales of justice were sufficiently weighted in Harris's favour.

Harris believed it to have been an act of divine intervention. God had shown beyond all doubt that He wished him to continue itinerating. Over thirty years later he still remembered this as a turning-point in his career, when in a conversation with Edmund Jones he recalled how he had 'doubted [his] call [for] 4 years 'till Monmouth Assizes'.[174] But, he wrote in his autobiography,

> After my dismission, I was more established in my own soul, that my Mission was from God ... I felt no scruple ever since, but have been more and more established and confirmed ... feeling the love of Christ in my heart, I saw an absolute necessity of going about to propagate the Gospel of my dear Master and Redeemer.[175]

He claimed in 1750 that the Spirit had 'sealed' him at Monmouth with words from the Scriptures: 'thus it shall be with the man the Lord delights to honour', and 'I have set before thee an open door which no one can shut.'[176]

Harris had long recognized the usefulness of an itinerant open-air ministry and, despite occasional doubts, had believed that it was not contrary to Scripture.[177] He publicly justified the principle of a lay ministry, as did Wesley,[178] by the claim that necessity made it lawful, adding that 'there never was more necessity than now'.[179] Both men also held that the success of such ministries indicated that God approved of them,[180] but Harris had wished since 1735 that God would confirm that it was so. The dismissal of the case against him at Monmouth was sufficient proof. Now, even if he was denied an outward commission by the Church, the inward commission by God would sustain him in his efforts to bring others to Christ.

Chapter 4
God's Little Parliaments

Good organization is essential to the survival of any popular movement. In the context of a religious revival, not only are preachers needed to proclaim the message, but some form of structure must also be devised through which converts can be instilled with a sense of corporeity while simultaneously being closely regulated. Vigorous preaching may lead to conviction, but it cannot provide the constant supervision required to enable converts to persevere during difficult times. English Methodism serves as an example. Both Wesley and Whitefield were powerful and effective preachers, but while the former's flair for organization secured the survival of his branch of the Revival, the latter's lack of interest in such issues resulted in the early disintegration of his Calvinistic connexion.[1]

Though it is generally recognized that Howell Harris made a considerable contribution to the organization of Welsh Methodism,[2] the extent to which the task of structuring the movement was accomplished almost single-handed has not been sufficiently emphasized. Though he did not work in isolation, and while many of his ideas were borrowed from other sources, it was he more than anyone who assumed responsibility for enforcing order among the early Welsh Methodists, and it is difficult to see how the infant movement could have survived without his firm leadership.

Following his conversion, Harris's efforts to organize his own work among the converts were to determine the future shape of the whole Methodist movement in Wales, though it must be stressed that during the early period no vision of the final outcome existed in his mind. The course of his leadership followed no predetermined plan but was an empirical process based upon the imperatives of his own personal piety, his day-to-day experience among his followers and his belief that there was a serious lack of devotional fervour and pastoral care within the

Established Church.[3] His initial desire to bring together small groups of believers was rooted in his own need for fellowship and in the intense evangelistic zeal that had possessed him. Like many other lay preachers in the Evangelical Revival, he began by conducting meetings at his home in which he was joined by his mother, his friends and neighbours; these simple acts of devotion were an attempt to persuade those nearest to him to join him in the observance of their duty towards God, a theme foremost in his mind after his own powerful personal experience.[4] Meetings at other houses in the neighbourhood developed naturally from his efforts to conform to the teachings of books such as *The Practice of Piety* and *The Whole Duty of Man*, both of which had a profound influence upon him, not least in teaching him that it was part of his duty to visit the sick and infirm.[5] As he read extracts to them from these devotional books, he found that others gathered to listen, drawn possibly by their natural curiosity and the fact that some of them were illiterate. His activities extended further as he began to exhort those who had formerly participated with him in his youthful sins and to that end he visited other villages around Trevecka. He also arranged meetings during weekday evenings for those concerned about the welfare of their souls, and through these various gatherings laid the foundation for what were later to become known as the 'societies'.

Local opposition, particularly from Pryce Davies, the vicar of Talgarth, led to a suspension of his evangelistic labours during February 1736, but this setback was offset by the encouragement he received from Mary Parry of Llangasty Tal-y-llyn[6] and Mary Phillips of Llanfihangel Tal-y-llyn, who both allowed him the use of their houses as meeting places for the converts.[7] Though these groups had much in common with the later societies, Harris did not regard them as societies proper, claiming that they lacked the permanence that was to be a characteristic of the later meetings.[8]

It was not until October 1736 that he mentioned the founding of 'societies' in a letter to Griffith Jones of Llanddowror.[9] Many have contributed to the discussion concerning the origins of Harris's concept of such meetings,[10] but confusion still surrounds the issue because of the conflicting evidence of the Diaries, Harris making seemingly contradictory statements at various times during his career.

Anglican Religious Societies had been established in the late seventeenth century in both England and Wales, and many survived well into the eighteenth century.[11] In 1678, according to Josiah Woodward, whose *Account* of the societies did much to promote them,[12] 'several young men of the Church of England', inspired by the preaching of Dr Anthony Horneck,[13] 'began to apply themselves in a very serious manner to religious thoughts and purposes'. The societies in which they met were originally exclusively Anglican gatherings, supervised by a Church of England minister, who in the role of 'director' was responsible for spiritual guidance and the admission of new members.[14] Their aim was to promote personal and practical piety through worship, a study of practical divinity and the collection and distribution of alms. The discussion of controversial subjects was forbidden, as were matters relating to the government of either Church or state.[15]

Woodward's *Account* was published after the societies had been in existence for over thirty years, probably at the height of their effectiveness, and shows how they had developed during that time. According to his 'Specimen of the orders of the Religious Societies, copied out of that at Poplar' (where he was minister),[16] their 'sole design' was 'to promote real holiness of heart and life'; this was to be achieved through self-examination. The meetings, which were held for mutual edification and encouragement, contained a strong liturgical emphasis, but allowed for more lay participation in the proceedings than Horneck's earlier rules.[17] In the absence of an ordained clergyman, a steward, or 'any other person desired', was allowed to propose a subject for discussion, the choice being made from a list of forty topics, the remaining twelve weeks of the year being reserved for preparatory devotions prior to participation in the communion at the parish church. Laymen could also guide the members in their 'conference' and lead them in worship, and despite fears and criticisms that this would lead to schism, the societies had by the turn of the century gained the approval of the highest ecclesiastical authorities.

Attempts to assess the extent to which Harris's societies were modelled on the Religious Societies in general, and on that described by Woodward in his *Account* in particular, have been hampered by the inconsistencies of Harris's own writings. In his autobiography he declared that when he first began to organize his followers, he did so 'in imitation of the societies which Dr. Woodward gave an account of'.[18] However, while writing his Diary during February 1739, having then received a gift of two copies of Woodward's book from a society at Cardiff,[19] he claimed that he knew nothing of the author when he first began his work.[20] Ten years later, he recalled the time when 'the first societies were settled ... from Dr. Woodward's accounts of the Religious Societies', and in less than four months repeated the claim, saying that 'they were first settled by reading Woodward's account'.[21] Again in 1760 at Great Yarmouth, he mentioned Woodward's publication 'by which [he had] founded societies in Wales',[22] and in 1761, while speaking at Bideford, he 'opened of Woodward's societies' and explained 'how from these [he] took the plan of societies in Wales first'.[23]

There seems, therefore, to be ample evidence that the Welsh societies were based on Woodward's book, and even if it could be argued that Harris's memory was slipping by the end of the 1740s it is unlikely that he would have made the same error so many times. To complicate matters further, Harris also stated in his autobiography that when he first established his societies there were 'no other Societies of the kind in England or Wales'.[24] If he had taken 'the plan of societies' from Woodward's book as he claimed, could it be that he was under the impression that the societies of which Woodward had written had ceased to exist?

Harris had begun gathering his converts into small groups before he met Griffith Jones in May 1736. At that time he had no knowledge of either the Religious Societies or Woodward's treatise. If Griffith Jones, on hearing of Harris's work, drew his attention to a copy of either the book or the *Abstracts* from it published by the SPCK,[25] this would explain Harris's casual reference to the formation of societies in his letter.[26] It would also add credence to the possibility that Griffith Jones, in an attempt to strengthen Harris's application for ordination, discouraged him from itinerating and conducting an open-air ministry but at the same time encouraged him to channel his energy into establishing societies similar to those described by Woodward, in the belief that they would have been more acceptable to the ecclesiastical authorities. This would mean that while Woodward's book had not been the motivation for Harris's initial attempts to bring his converts together to devotional meetings, it was, none the less, after seeing it at Llanddowror that he had begun organizing them into permanent societies. His claim that he had not seen Woodward's book when he set out would therefore be true; it was a development that took place later, in 1736.

It is also probable that it was during his early visits to Llanddowror, when his followers had already been meeting for nearly a year, that Harris first saw the wider possibilities of his work and realized the advantage of organizing societies in different localities to cater for the needs of converts. His vision was that they should not only provide an opportunity to intensify the individual's devotional life and encourage moral excellence, but also serve as a means to examine and evaluate spiritual experiences and stimulate growth.[27] Thus, while being an 'imitation of the societies which Dr. Woodward gave an account of', they were still unique, and there were, as far as Harris knew, 'no other societies of the kind in England or Wales'.

This possibility is further strengthened by Harris's entry in his Diary on 28 December 1736, that he had been reading of August Hermann Francke,[28] who is also mentioned in Woodward's *Account*.[29] Although it is possible that he had come across his name in some other publication, or that Griffith Jones, who was well informed about developments in Germany,[30] had mentioned the work of the Pietists to him during one of his visits to Llanddowror, it is the fact that he was cognizant of their work so soon after his own conversion and so early in the development of the Methodist movement in Wales that is significant. Harris would certainly have been impressed by the Pietist emphasis on regeneration, and by their call for a congruence of profession and practice and a renewal of the church;[31] these were the themes of his own meetings during the early period. Francke, the organizational genius of Pietism, had also gathered students together at Leipzig to study and discuss the Scriptures, not as part of any academic discipline but for their personal edification, believing that such conventicles, or *ecclesiolae in ecclesia*, were the ideal means of bringing about reformation.[32] At the same time, he was involved in social work among the poor and established an orphanage and workshops to provide shelter and employment. Harris's admiration of his achievements led him to write at the end of 1736 that he also would be willing to sell all his possessions in order 'to build an Alms House and School' at Trevecka.[33]

While recognizing the existence of this pietistic element, it must be remembered that other influences could have led Harris to see the need for societies. One was the example of the Dissenters. By the spring of 1736 both the Independents and Baptists had taken an interest in his work, and it was the Independents who encouraged him to undertake his first journey to Llanddowror.[34] It was not unusual for Dissenters to conduct special meetings to instruct their people and prepare them for receiving the Sacrament,[35] and Harris's knowledge of their practices is revealed in a petition, prepared on 5 April 1737, requesting the permission of the ecclesiastical authorities to establish a society in which he and his followers would be able to converse freely about their spiritual experiences.[36] He wrote: 'We have been mov'd to throw ourselves att your feet to crave leave to meet together to read, converse about our Souls, discover our observations on self-examination, to ground the ignorant in the Principles of our Religion.' Eager to assure the authorities of his commitment to the Church, he continued:

> I am willing to sign an engagement to be true my self and to confirm all others in the Established Religion . . . The granting of this [request] will secure thousands of the ignorant sort from Dissenters who personally know many that leave the Church on the account of this Priviledge [sic] the Dissenters have of conversing &c about Sermons heard, meeting in houses and they knowing no other occasion to leave the Church but that.[37]

Harris realized the importance of such meetings in the process of educating and spiritually nurturing those who attended them. It was only natural, therefore, that he should wish to see similar gatherings within his own Church, but this could not be done without the previous consent of the local vicar and the bishop. Though they were suspicious of his motives, Harris continued to argue that it would be to the advantage of the Church to allow such meetings, and claimed there was need for a greater degree of pastoral care among the people.

Initially, the activities of his early group meetings centred on the use of devotional literature which was read aloud for the edification of those present. This exercise was also part of the activities of the Religious Societies.[38] But, as time went by, and as Harris's confidence grew, greater emphasis was put on relating spiritual experiences, exhorting and extempore prayer, and it was this, together with his public appearances at fairs at Talgarth, that led Pryce Davies to express disapproval of his conduct in a letter sent to him in February 1736.[39] It was not until May 1737 that Harris began addressing the societies without a book,[40] and it was during the same period that he established at Wernos what he later came to regard as the first 'permanent' society.[41] It may be that, as nothing came of his petition to the Anglican authorities during April, Harris decided to proceed regardless of their response, for by that time he would have been considerably heartened by the fact that others had joined him in his work, among them Joseph Saunders, the blacksmith at Trevecka,[42] and John Powell of Abergwesyn[43] who was later to join the Baptists. With them, and others of whom little is known,[44] there began a new period in the development of the Methodist organization, for the establishment of a 'permanent society' at Wernos, together with the end of the regular use of books at the meetings and the appearance of new workers, marked the end of the experimental stage in the history of the formation of the Welsh Methodist society.[45]

Though Whitefield had published his work on *The Nature and Necessity of Societies* during 1737,[46] and Peter Böhler,[47] John Wesley and James Hutton had established the society at Fetter Lane during May of the following year,[48] there is nothing to indicate that Harris had heard of either of these developments. He did not come into personal contact with the English revival until 1739 when, on meeting Whitefield in Cardiff, he accompanied him to Bristol and later to London. Developments in Wales had taken place independently of those in England[49] and appear to have been, in Harris's own territory of south-east Wales, mostly under his personal control.[50] Other than what had reached him by word of mouth or through published material such as Woodward's volume, Harris's efforts were unaffected by outside influences; whatever had been achieved was done through his own efforts though he was later to discover that in organizing his work he had been moving in a direction parallel to that of the English Methodists.

The extent of his inventiveness is difficult to ascertain. For example, the listing of society members' names according to their sex is a custom usually associated with the Moravians but which was later adopted by the Methodists. However, it is possible that

Harris had suggested this practice to his followers as early as 1738, long before he had come into contact with either the English Methodists or the Moravians.[51] But this is not to say that in adopting the practice he had acted *ex mero motu*. It is known that in the Dissenting churches of the late seventeenth and early eighteenth centuries it was not unusual for the men and women to sit apart during meetings,[52] and, as he had been fraternizing with Dissenters at an early stage in the development of the movement, it is possible that Harris had seen or heard of the custom through them. Whatever the origin, the question amply illustrates the complexity of the task of attempting to assess the extent to which Harris's ideas were his own.

During January 1737 Harris confirmed the statement made in his earlier letter to Griffith Jones by noting again in his Diary that new societies were being established.[53] Within two years of beginning his revival work he claimed to have a total of sixteen societies under his care,[54] but seems to have been equally willing to participate in the activities of societies established by others. In November 1738 he listed the places at which societies met, and included not only his own but also those of the Dissenters, the 'Heavenly Mr. Henry Davies' and the 'diligent Mr. David Williams'.[55] These were situated in the counties of Glamorgan, Brecon, Monmouth and Carmarthen. By the end of February 1739 the number had increased to twenty-seven,[56] and when Harris met Whitefield in March, he claimed that the total was then 'near thirty'.[57]

Through Whitefield, Harris was introduced to English Methodism. On 25 April 1739, he arrived for the first time in London, but before his departure had arranged for the Welsh societies to be supervised by James Roberts, a Baptist minister at Ross, Edmund Jones, the Independent from Pontypool, and Thomas James, an Anglican from Crucadarn, Breconshire.[58] The fact that they represented different denominations demonstrates that the movement, even as late as the spring of 1739, was not confined to any single denomination or to the Established Church,[59] but stimulated a renewal across the sectarian boundaries. This was also true of the early societies in England. They were regarded as meeting places for people of all denominations,[60] and in the same way as Wesley was able to meet with the Moravians and the Calvinists during the late 1730s because of a unity of spirit and a common desire to secure success in the work of the Gospel, the Welsh were also able to co-operate regardless of their differences in matters of doctrine and church polity. It was a manifestation of what Wesley and Whitefield referred to as a 'catholic spirit',[61] and what Edmund Jones neatly described as the 'Methodist way'.[62]

While in London, Harris attended numerous society meetings, at Fetter Lane, Lambeth, Westminster, St Anne's Lane and Wapping;[63] he also met the Count von Zinzendorf[64] and Charles Wesley who were also involved in revival work.[65] However, it is surprising how little effect his visit had on the development of Welsh Methodism. Other than the adoption of a few terms, 'steward' and 'band' in particular, Harris introduced into Wales very little of what he had seen in England. It may be that he was so concerned about his own spiritual condition during the visit that details of organization failed to interest him, or that the disorder and controversy he had witnessed at Fetter Lane dampened his spirit. On the other hand, since no dramatic changes were made to Harris's plans for the Welsh societies, it may be that he had seen very little to convince him that changes were necessary.

There were many similarities between the London societies and his own, and the organization at Fetter Lane would, despite the internal tensions, have enabled Harris to feel quite at ease. The meetings were held for the same purpose as their Welsh counterparts, and all were admitted regardless of denomination, provided that controversial subjects were avoided.[66] The main activities were preaching, exhorting, singing, prayer and the sharing of spiritual experiences.[67] While it is true that the society had been regulated from its founding at the Bible and Sun through agreed rules (which clearly set out the purpose of the meetings and the conditions under which newcomers were admitted),[68] it is also known that rules had been distributed in Wales since 1738, although it is difficult to determine their nature or the extent to which they had been adopted by the societies.[69] The main difference between Fetter Lane and the societies in Wales was that the Welsh societies had not as yet been divided into smaller groups or 'bands', each with its own leader, but an attempt was later made by Harris to introduce this practice among his own converts.[70] The conditions of access to the Fetter Lane society were also broader than those of the Welsh societies: there was no mention in the 'Orders' that faith or a conviction of sin were a prerequisite to membership. Wesley insisted that an Evangelical experience was not a necessary qualification,[71] while Harris always emphasized the need for such experiences,[72] to the extent that the awakening of the sinner came to be regarded as the door to the Welsh Methodist society.[73]

The visit to London proved to Harris the need for close regulation of the societies; the controversies at Fetter Lane demonstrated clearly that lack of discipline led to discord and disruption. His belief in the need for firm organization was therefore strengthened, but this is not to suggest that from 1739 the organization of Welsh Methodism was modelled on that of England.[74] On the contrary, it seems that the arrangements for the organization of the Welsh societies remained unchanged after the new links with the English revival had been forged. They continued to be largely pragmatic in nature, evolving gradually according to circumstance and need. Having been to Bristol and London, Harris did not return home with the intention of building an imitation of the English organization on the foundations he had already laid in Wales; his aim continued to be to provide the highest possible level of care for the individual societies without changing their structure, and securing overall uniformity in the oversight of Methodist activity in the various areas where he had been active.

Following his return from London, Methodism in Wales continued to prosper, and, by December 1740, Harris was able to claim that there were more than sixty-four societies in south Wales.[75] The extent of the work now demanded that further organization take place, and the adoption of an agreed set of rules for the societies seemed a natural step forward.

The earliest manuscript in the Trevecka Collection containing society rules is dated 1740.[76] Written in Welsh by an anonymous hand in a dialect similar to that found in south-east Wales,[77] it begins with a declaration that the members, who professed faith in Christ, agreed to abide by the following rules, each of which was proved biblical by references to appropriate scriptural texts:

1. That all were to regulate their lives and be honest, in obedience to the Gospel.

2. That only those who possessed faith were to be accepted into fellowship.
3. That great care was to be taken not to refuse admission to those whose faith was weak.
4. That none should dictate over the others.
5. That all were to avoid blasphemous expressions and keep all personal secrets heard during the society meetings.
6. That all should serve God in their various occupations as well as in private, and were to attend public services of worship.[78]
7. That if anyone was unable to comply with Rule 6, the society reserved the right to investigate the reasons.
8. That expulsion from the society was possible if Christian love was found wanting in any of its members.

Another manuscript containing three early society rules was discovered by M. H. Jones at Llangeitho in 1927.[79] Though the date of the volume is uncertain, it is believed to have been written sometime during the period 1741–4[80] and is mainly a collection of hymns sung by early Methodist societies.[81] The rules, which appear towards the end of the manuscript, state that members were 'to open their whole heart' to enable them to resist Satan's deceit and assess their own spiritual growth. Each was to allow an examination of his or her motives and principles by the others, and all were to regard their souls, bodies, gifts, knowledge, wealth and time as belonging primarily to God.

This manuscript is similar in both layout and vocabulary to the first part of a page attached to the entry for 13 February 1741 in Harris's Diary 69.[82] When comparing the two, it can be seen that the Llangeitho copy ends in the middle of a sentence in Harris's version; the latter goes on to list three more rules, making a total of six. Harris's version also betrays the marks of the original author at work; the beginning of the fourth rule, referring to the problem of being under the ministry of unawakened clergy, is deleted and replaced with an alternative, referring to the members' common belief in the doctrines of free grace, assurance, election and perseverance.

Though these rules may well have been used among the Cardiganshire societies during the early 1740s,[83] there is little doubt that they were originally composed by Harris. It has already been noted that he began issuing such rules to his societies as early as 1738, and when rules were formally accepted and published by the Methodist Association in 1742 the measure of Harris's contribution can be seen by the similarity between many of the expressions used in that publication and the manuscript attached to Diary 69.[84]

By the end of 1739 the increase in the number of societies had also created a need for further structural development of the movement, and Harris embarked on a process of grouping together individual societies in order to regulate their activities. On 16 January 1740, at a joint meeting of several societies at Mynydd Meio in the parish of Eglwysilan in Glamorgan, he wrote:

> I was enabled to give very strict Rules of Discipline to the Societies to examine home ... particular Rules – to meet once a week 3 or 4 societies [sic] – and once a week private and once a week to exhort and catechise the Neighbours &c.[85]

During succeeding months, other similar societies were arranged to meet at monthly and bi-monthly intervals. In the prologue to the Association Records,[86] Harris stated that

> The Brethren in Wales did meet above 2 years – once a month and once in 2 months in 1740 – before the Date of this Book, and examined many of the Exhorters and Searched to know the Place of each, but no outward settled agreement was formed till the Date of this Book.[87]

During the same period, Harris hoped not only that the societies could be better organized through special meetings but also that ministers and lay leaders could be brought closer together through a special society of their own. This possibility may have been discussed with Edmund Jones of Pontypool at Mynydd Meio in January, for Harris noted then that he was 'settling the minst [sic][88] Society – its foundation, the names and the Questions proposed'. By the beginning of September a 'Society of Ministers'[89] had indeed been arranged,[90] and was to meet at Glyn, Defynnog, on 1 October.[91]

The meeting was attended by eight ministers and ten laymen.[92] The ministers were John Oulton, the Baptist from Leominster,[93] Edmund Jones of Pontypool, Daniel Rowland of Llangeitho, David Lewis, an Anglican from Radnorshire, David Williams of

Pwll-y-Pant, John Powell, another Anglican from Aberystruth in Monmouthshire, and James Roberts, the Baptist from Ross. Also present was William Williams of Pantycelyn.[94] A native of Carmarthenshire, he had been educated at Llwyn-llwyd Academy in Breconshire and converted under Harris's ministry.[95] Ordained deacon in 1740, he was refused ordination as priest three years later because of his Methodist activities,[96] but became one of the leading figures of the Welsh Evangelical Revival and a prolific writer of hymns, poetry and prose.

Harris explained[97] that he had been moved to call them together by 'hearing of associates in Scotland and America',[98] and declared that the purpose of their meeting was 'to incite to Love and strengthen each others hands'. Rules were proposed for the Society (but not listed in the Diary), and a fast arranged for the following Tuesday; Harris then entrusted to them the care of the societies.

His sermon that evening was on the theme of 'assurance and liberty', but he soon discovered that some of his hearers were less than pleased with what they heard. The following morning, he noted that 'Edmund Jones and I lost our Love', and, though the reason for the disagreement is not given in the Diary, John Oulton, in his account to *The Christian's Amusement* reported that 'Brother Harris expressed himself about the Notion of Perfection somewhat unintelligible to some: and one Minister was so uneasy that he declared against it, and rose up to leave us.'[99] The meeting was not therefore as successful as Harris had hoped; though he had succeeded in bringing the Methodist leaders together, their conference had produced little more than ill-feeling. But after returning home to Trevecka, and despite his disappointment, Harris continued to discuss with the local exhorters the possibility of arranging monthly meetings for those involved in the supervision of societies in Glamorgan and Breconshire, and judging from the entry in his Diary, this was yet another conference aimed at improving the overall organization of the work. On 3 October he claimed that

> The Lord enabled us today, to take proper care to settle the 6 weeks societies of Ministers att Glyn – the monthly society in Glamorgan and Brecon shires, and them both to meet both together in 2 months with all the Bands of the Societies.[100]

The next 'Society of Ministers' was held on 13 November.[101] Its purpose was again to 'to knit and unite' the Methodist leaders, but on his arrival Harris discovered that some who had attended the first meeting were absent from the second, two Anglican clergymen and Edmund Jones among them. There were, however, some new faces present: Miles Harry, the Baptist from Pontypool; Phillip Morgan, Baptist minister of Trosgoed; and Lewis Rees, an Independent minister from Llanbrynmair.[102] After reading a letter he had sent to *The Christian's Amusement*,[103] emphasizing the need for unity and charity among the brethren, Harris led the Society in settling the preaching rounds. This was followed by a discussion on assurance which resulted in failure to reach any measure of agreement on the subject.[104]

While tension was developing between Harris and Edmund Jones over matters of doctrine, there was also friction with Miles Harry, but for a different reason. Even before the October meeting, at which Harris had expected Harry to be present, he had resolved: 'I shall put it home to them, if they have the faith – that I suspect Miles Harry of Covetousness and most of the Baptists of Bigotry.'[105] Relations with the Baptists had been deteriorating for some time, mainly because of John Powell's insistence on preaching believer's baptism among the converts, an act which was construed as an attempt to proselytize Methodist society members. On 14 September 1739, Harris heard that Powell had been 'indiscreet' in some of his statements, and when he met him later in the day, he admitted that he 'set upon him violently'. The next day, their arguments concerning 'externals' continued,[106] and when the two men met four months later, their talk was still 'about Disputes'.[107] In March 1740, Powell was declaring the doctrine of infant baptism to be 'a deadly poison' originating from hell;[108] he now 'challenged all to dispute with him' on the subject.[109]

The charge of covetousness levelled against Miles Harry arose from his involvement in the publication and distribution of Christian literature;[110] according to Harris, the prices charged for his books were exorbitant.[111] He responded by saying that there was nothing immoral about his activities and was supported by Oulton, Rees and Morgan. Angered by this display of solidarity by the Dissenters, Harris next accused Harry of bigotry 'in preaching and conversation', and condemned the Baptists in general for allowing others to face the dangers of preaching for the first time in certain areas before moving in to 'disturb and break love by giving songs against infant baptism' and proselytizing the new converts.

Later in the day, the Society took advantage of Harris's absence to insert a clause into the Rules, 'to keep Liberty to mention disputed Truths'. When he discovered what they had done, Harris objected strongly, claiming that it would only lead to disorder. During the bitter argument that ensued, he told Miles Harry that he suspected first his grace, and secondly his mission, angrily declaring that he had never met anyone who had been converted under his ministry. It seems, therefore, that by the latter half of 1740 relationships between Harris and the Dissenters were becoming increasingly tense, and disagreements and accusations threatened the newly formed society. Instead of bringing the leaders closer together, it led to arguments and disputes, and owing to Harris's inability to moderate his expressions and to show diplomacy in his treatment of others, men like Miles Harry and Edmund Jones were being alienated.[112] Realizing that things were not going as he had intended, Harris wrote: 'the Lord gave me help to be easy when I saw that this Society was coming to nothing and to be as contended, if it be the Lord's will, as to go on.'[113]

Though disappointed for the second time by the failure of the Society, Harris renewed his efforts to organize the societies into clusters meeting on a monthly or bi-monthly basis. On 29 December 1740 he noted that he was 'contriving for God, how to settle [the] Societies' and described a plan which was by then being formed in his mind and which involved more than local organization. By this time, he had begun to envisage the nation-wide possibilities of some kind of association of societies, and also realized that co-operation between the English and Welsh branches of the revival was not only feasible but desirable. Therefore, with regard to the societies, of which he believed there to be close to seventy in south Wales,

> every 5 or 6 [were] to meet monthly, and all the Ministers and exhorters of 2 Counties every 2 months in Llandovery,[114] 1 in Glamorganshire and 1 in Breconshire and all of all parts in 6 months – and all the Methodists and us &c. once a year.[115]

The following day his 'thoughts were employed much in overlooking [the] Master's work in Wales'. He estimated that there were thirty-two exhorters and sixteen ministers, 'eight choice ones', involved in the work. He further considered his strategy for the future; the societies were

> to meet every 6 [i.e. in groups of six] once a month with the neighbouring exhorters &c., and the exhorters in Carmarthenshire and Breconshire in Llandovery once in 2 months, and in Glamorganshire and Monmouthshire so often in Gelligaer, and in Cardiganshire and Pembrokeshire so often near Cardigan, and all the Ministers and exhorters to meet once in 6 months for a day and night and all the Methodists – thro' the Nation – once a year.[116]

By the beginning of 1741, Harris's plans for the movement were therefore well advanced. The basic structure of the organization began with a network of individual societies which were to be clustered together into groups of five or six and to meet every month. Exhorters and preachers were to attend local meetings every two months, while a general meeting of those working in Wales was to be held every six months. The annual meeting was then to be held in conjunction with the English Calvinistic Methodists.

A bi-monthly society was established at a public house in Llandovery on 13 February 1741, and attended by two clergymen, two Dissenting ministers, four exhorters and 'many more' who were to be admitted after examination on the following night.[117] It began by agreeing that it should meet every two months with the intention of 'going heart and hand after Christ', and by listening to letters being read, the first from Harris to Charles Wesley concerning their personal doctrinal differences,[118] the second from Whitefield to John Wesley.[119] All present agreed with the contents of the two letters and thus stressed the Calvinistic foundations upon which the society was to proceed.

The following day, the society met again and agreed on the adoption of six rules.[120] Arrangements were made for organizing the work, and preachers chosen to venture 'with their lives in their hands' on missionary excursions to north Wales. Harris, who had recently been mobbed during a visit to Bala in Merioneth, gave an account of what had occurred,[121] and a dispute concerning the

Methodist response to the ministry of unawakened clergy was also settled. Some suggested that more benefit would be derived from Methodists remaining at home on Sundays rather than subjecting themselves to 'carnal' ministries, but the society disagreed and decided they should attend public services of worship at parish churches regardless of the conduct of individual clergymen. If, during the services, false doctrine or 'lies' were heard preached from the pulpits, it was their duty to confront the clergyman and inform others of his unorthodoxy. As to the suggestion that society meetings should be held as an alternative form of worship in those parishes where 'carnal' clergy officiated, it was decided that Sunday worship was the prerogative of the ordained clergy, 'that there ought to be Ministers ordained to make a publick worship [sic] and that exhorting is not to fill up that Place but to give way to it.'[122]

This society displayed a far greater degree of cohesion than any other which had previously met, and marks the beginning of true Methodist organization in Wales.[123] Brought into existence through Harris's efforts as a policy-making body to which both the clergy and lay exhorters were able to contribute, it assumed the role of organizing the work locally and opted clearly for a policy of non-confrontation with the Church. It regarded public allegiance to the Church and subjection to its authority as of paramount importance, a policy which remained unchanged while the first generation of revivalists remained in control of the movement.

Similar meetings were soon established in other areas.[124] On 21 March a bi-monthly meeting was held at Watford in Glamorgan, where the issue of communicating with Dissenters was discussed. Those present were well aware of the uneasiness of the faithful who sat under 'carnal ministers' and heard the doctrines of grace controverted or ignored; they were also disturbed by strong rumours that the Methodists might soon be forcibly ejected from the Church. At the same time, they doubted the wisdom of fraternizing with the Dissenters; they were not opposed to the principle of communicating with them, but feared that such an action would bring their own cause into disrepute in the eyes of the public. Harris wrote: 'here, as at Ystradffin in Carmarthenshire, about 20 or more members agreeing to receive the Sacrament mutually with Dissenters and they with us, but not till the Lord open the way.'[125] The possibility of their actions being misunderstood was a major consideration, and the Methodist leaders were anxious to display their allegiance to the Church. However, they were careful to keep open the option of joining with the Dissenters at some later date if it was found that such a step was either desirable or forced upon them through their being denied communion at the parish churches.[126]

At Watford, rules were again adopted by the society. They were the same as those attached to Diary 69, but excluded the sixth rule which referred to the Word of God as the rule in all things and the establishment of special days for prayer and fasting. At Watford it was also decided to translate the rules into English, which suggests that they were widely used by the Methodists in Wales during this period.[127]

Other bi-monthly societies were established in Monmouthshire on 23 March and at Trevecka on 14 June,[128] but while Harris was organizing the movement in this manner he was also giving serious consideration to going to America with Whitefield. Such an undertaking would naturally have involved making arrangements for the care of the societies during his absence, and this seems to have been foremost in his mind during the meeting at Trevecka.[129] Apart from the arrangements made with the Dissenting ministers in 1739 while he was in London, this was the first time Harris had suggested that exhorters could act as supervisors over specific areas, and, though nothing came of his plans to cross the Atlantic, his arrangements were still implemented and were an important development in the organization of Welsh Methodism.

During the summer of 1741, Harris again visited London. Events in Wales were at this time overshadowed by tensions in England where John Wesley and Whitefield were at variance concerning the doctrine of predestination. Wesley had published a sermon on 'Free Grace' soon after Whitefield's departure to America in August 1739, in which he roundly condemned the Calvinistic doctrine of election because of its implied doctrine of reprobation.[130] Whitefield first saw the sermon in America and was deeply offended by the attack on what he considered to be a biblical theme, and on his return to England published a reply in which he defended his own views.[131] The controversy led to separation.[132] Harris's sympathy lay with Whitefield,[133] but his desire for union between the branches of Methodism ensured a continuing dialogue with Wesley despite their inability to agree on doctrine.[134]

Prior to his departure to London, Harris noted in his Diary that rumours were circulating that the Methodists were soon to be ejected from the Church.[135] He believed that they should remain within her communion until cast out, but on his return to Wales in October set about consolidating the societies in preparation for that eventuality. The fear of ejection also led to a deepening of the desire for union between the Methodist factions, and when Whitefield came to Wales in November[136] one of the topics of conversation was a union not only between English and Welsh Calvinists but also between Calvinists and Wesleyans. John Wesley had already shown a willingness to discuss this possibility by visiting Wales during October and meeting with Harris, Rowland, Thomas Price, Joseph Humphreys and 'many others'.[137] However, the conference was not a success;[138] though the Welsh were eager to come to some understanding, the English Calvinists remained adamant that a union was not feasible. Whitefield expressed his opposition to the plan in a conversation with Harris at Abergavenny, and though the Calvinists 'talked much of an Union', Whitefield was, according to Harris, 'utterly against it'.[139] This was made abundantly clear during a sermon that Whitefield preached nine days later at Trevecka. His advice was, 'Let Wales see to it self lest God should remove his Gospel away.'[140] In the wake of the controversy in England, Whitefield was implying that in order to protect itself from Wesley's Arminianism, Welsh Methodism should remain autonomous. Harris was horrified at this suggestion,[141] but there was little he could do to make Whitefield reconsider. His dream of a single Methodist organization uniting the English and Welsh, the Calvinists and Arminians, was for the time being shattered, but this failure did not rule out the possibility of a closer union among the Calvinists. With Whitefield's approval,[142] Harris therefore concentrated his efforts on bringing this about, confident that it could be achieved without much difficulty.

Though Harris was to visit Rowland, Howell Davies and Griffith Jones before the end of 1741, it cannot be taken for granted that the purpose of his journey was to discuss further developments in the organization of Welsh Methodism.[143] His intention in going to Llanddewibrefi on 21 November was 'to hear dear Brother Rowland',[144] and details of their conversation were not included in his Diary entry for the day. From Cardiganshire he travelled to Llanddowror where he met both Davies and Griffith Jones. The detrimental effect of the employment of Methodist exhorters as teachers upon his efforts to expand his charity school movement had led Jones to be openly critical of the Methodists;[145] he had also recently objected to Rowland's preaching at a chapel of ease at Llanlluan in Carmarthenshire and to Davies's conducting an itinerant ministry.[146] Much to his dismay, Harris had heard of his intervention during his travels, and at Llanddowror an argument occurred between them during which Harris was accused of 'self-confidence' and claiming 'infallibility' and told of 'the unlawfulness of a layman preaching'. It may be that Griffith Jones was also concerned that the societies which he had at one time encouraged as auxiliaries to the Established Church were becoming so tightly organized as to be able to survive independently of the establishment from which they had emerged. If the rumours of an ejection of Methodists from the Church had reached Llanddowror, then, in an attempt to protect his own good name, Griffith Jones would have been eager to distance himself from the leaders of the new movement. In any case, his involvement with the SPCK would have been sufficient reason for him to do so, since any semblance of collaboration between himself and the Methodists would damage his work, were there to be any form of schism from the Church.

Harris next met Rowland on 20 December at Llanddewibrefi and on this occasion the two set about 'settling a Society of Brethren Preachers to settle the cause of God'.[147] This was to meet early in the new year,[148] on 7 January 1742, at Dugoedydd, Cil-y-cwm, Carmarthenshire, the home of William Lloyd, a member of the Cil-y-cwm society. It was attended by four clergymen[149] and eighteen exhorters,[150] and Daniel Rowland most probably acted as chairman. It had been hoped that Whitefield would have been present to take the chair, but being unable to attend, he had written a letter through which he addressed the meeting.[151] Having emphasized the importance of the topics to be discussed, he turned to the organization of the movement:

> One great matter is rightly to know what particular office, and to what particular part, Jesus Christ has called each of you ... Some are called to awaken; others to establish and build up ... Those who are called to act in a publick manner, I think, ought to give themselves wholly to the work, and go out without purse or scrip ... Others, who can only visit privately, may mind their secular employ, and give their leisure time to the service of the Church.

The exhorters were encouraged to meet regularly in order to consult about their work, and it appears that Whitefield envisaged similar developments among his own people in England. With regard to the attitude of the Methodists to the Church of England, he wrote pessimistically:

> Some of you are ministers of the Church of England; but if you are faithful, I cannot think you will continue in it long. However, do not go out till you are cast out; and when cast out for Jesus Christ's sake, be not afraid to preach in the fields.

This was timely advice; there was grave concern at this time that the Conventicle Act might (quite legitimately)[152] be applied to stop field-preaching. Had such a step been taken in response to the growth of Methodism, and been effective in restricting the freedom of the preachers and exhorters, there is little doubt that the progress of the movement would have been severely impaired.[153]

There were also other problems that worried the Methodist leaders. Some of their followers were being denied communion at their parish church, but Whitefield hoped that the other Methodist clergy might partly overcome this difficulty by allowing visitors to their churches to receive communion from their hands. That, as Whitefield noted, was regarded by some as uncanonical. He therefore pleaded with the clergy:

> whilst you remain in [the Church of England], O! let not the Children of God starve for want of the Sacrament, though they may belong to another parish. The canon which forbids 'strangers' was only to prevent persons coming unprepared, without the minister's knowledge. It is regarded by none of the clergy; and nothing but the enmity of the old serpent excites them to mention it to any of you. For my own part, I should think it an honour to be put into the spiritual court, and to be excommunicated, for giving the children of God the sacrament at my Church, when they cannot

have it elsewhere. The Spirit of Christ and of glory, I am sure, would rest upon my soul.

Those who felt unease at the prospect of receiving communion from unawakened clergy and who turned to the Dissenters in order to be able to communicate with clear consciences were not, according to Whitefield (who had worked extensively with Dissenters while in America),[154] to be discouraged, even though the practice was much frowned upon by the Dissenters themselves. 'If a brother or sister has a mind to communicate among the Dissenters, and has freedom to receive in the Church too, they ought to be left at their liberty.' At the same time, care was to be taken not to separate from the Church prematurely. It was Whitefield's view that 'All this may be done without a formal separation from the Established Church, which I cannot think God calls for as yet.' These recommendations were accepted without exception. It was agreed 'not to go out of the Church until turned out' and that 'such as can't receive the sacrament in Church [were] to go to [Dissenting] Meeting to receive, only not to leave us nor go under any name but a Christian'.[155]

Whitefield's letter set out the policy of the Welsh Methodists with regard to both its attitude to the Church and its own development. The system of supervising the societies through the exhorters was formally adopted, as was the decision not to secede. Unlike John Wesley, Whitefield believed it was only a matter of time before the Methodists and the Church went their separate ways. The Methodists defended themselves from the charge of schism by blaming the clergy and the ecclesiastical authorities for any future Methodist withdrawal: if separation were to come, the fault, they claimed, lay with those who withheld the means of grace from them. And what right had the clergy to use canon law against Methodists when they themselves flagrantly ignored many canonical rules?[156] Since the Methodists had no intention of either keeping quiet or leaving the Church, it was up to the clergy to eject them. The initiative for this was placed squarely on the dignitaries of the Church, and it was in preparation for it that the Methodists were at this time being organized by Harris and the others.

The Dugoedydd meeting is usually regarded as the first Welsh Methodist Association, though the term 'Association' had not yet come into common use.[157] The significance of the assembly lies in the fact that it was regarded by the Methodist leaders not only as a place to discuss various aspects of the work and organize preaching rounds but also as a policy-making body which assumed responsibility for all Methodist activity throughout Wales. While earlier meetings at Llandovery, Watford and Trevecka had discussed policy and organization on a local basis, the Dugoedydd meeting regarded itself as a national governing body whose decisions were binding on all the societies nationwide. Decisions with regard to the Church and the partaking of the sacrament among the Dissenters, the organization of the societies and the exhorters became, through the incorporation of this body, official policy rather than the personal opinions of individual leaders. This meant that if the movement was for any reason severed from the Church, it would be capable of organizing itself efficiently in order to secure its own survival.

The second Association met on 11 February at Llwyn-y-berllan in the parish of Llandingad in Carmarthenshire. Here, a discussion was again held on the rules that were to be adopted and applied to the societies, and it was decided that they should be published and circulated. While new exhorters were examined and accepted into fellowship, discipline was also exerted; one exhorter was rejected and 'turned out'. Preaching rounds were settled and arrangements made for preachers to visit north Wales, but Harris was unwilling to undertake a journey there following the persecution he had suffered during January 1741.[158]

The society rules appeared from the press before the end of the year. Published in Welsh and printed by Felix Farley of Castle Green, Bristol, who was also John Wesley's publisher, they bore the title *Sail, Dibenion, a Rheolau'r Societies Neu'r Cyfarfodydd Neullduol a ddechreuassant ymgynnull yn ddiweddar yn Nghymru. At y rhai y chwanegwyd Rhai Hymne Yw Canu yn y Cyfarfodydd Neulltuol, gan Wyr o Eglwys Loegar* (Bristol, 1742).[159] They claimed that the societies were 'of the Church of England', and unlike Wesley's later *Rules of the United Societies*[160] noted their biblical basis – the command in Hebrews 10.25 that assemblies for the purpose of exhorting should not be forsaken, and the duty to exhort one another, as seen in Hebrews 3.13.

The aims of the societies were similar to Wesley's: to encourage love and good works; to prevent hardness of heart and backsliding; to lead to a better understanding of the work of grace in the soul and to build up faith through instruction in the Word of God and prayer. Their activities were tightly regulated.[161] After singing and prayer, members were to open their hearts to one another and relate everything, both good and bad. In order to uproot everything that hindered the increase of love, suspicions concerning each other were to be confessed by the members, and all were to show a willingness to be questioned and examined by the others.

Admission to a society was by application, and membership was granted only after the testimony of existing members concerning the suitability of the candidate had been heard. Applicants who could not satisfactorily answer questions concerning their spiritual condition were refused admission; conviction of sin, spiritual awakening through God's grace, admission of inability to do good in and of themselves, acceptance of the imputed righteousness of Christ, and an inclination through the Holy Spirit to surrender to Christ, were all necessary qualifications. There were also questions concerning the cost of discipleship, the inner witness of the Spirit, the receiving of the Spirit of Adoption and acceptance of the fundamental truths of the Trinity, Election, Original Sin, Justification by Faith and Perseverance in Grace as taught in the Thirty-nine Articles and Homilies of the Church of England. The Welsh societies were, therefore, in stark contrast to their Wesleyan counterparts, exclusive assemblies; not only was faith a condition of acceptance, but the applicant was also expected to subscribe to Calvinism.

This doctrinal emphasis in the rules formally established the Calvinistic nature of the Welsh Methodist movement, and was most probably included for three reasons. The pamphlet naturally reflected the views of the leaders; Harris, Rowland, William Williams, Howell Davies and the vast majority of the Welsh exhorters were by this time staunch Calvinists, and it is likely that they were eager to emphasize that they did not wish 'unorthodox' ideas to be promulgated within the movement which they, through the guidance of the Spirit, had established. Secondly, it must be remembered that the contents had been prepared against the background of the 'Free Grace' controversy with Wesley. Those who had been involved in the argument were eager to promote their own views; the seeming threat of Wesley's

Arminianism secured the strong Calvinist bias. Thirdly, with ejection from the Church looming large, the Welsh Methodists were eager to emphasize that their movement was not a hotbed of schismatics nor a haven for disgruntled heretics; they were for the most part devout Anglicans, and even those who did not worship at their parish church were in agreement with the biblical doctrines set out in the Articles and Homilies of the Church. Forcible ejection could not therefore be justified on doctrinal grounds.

Most of the activities of the Welsh Methodists had so far been conducted in an amicable spirit, but tension was soon to surface at one of the monthly meetings. At Glanyrafon-ddu Ganol near Talyllychau, in Carmarthenshire on 17 March,[162] the hitherto successful co-operation between Harris and Rowland was marred by disagreements concerning the nature of God's covenant with Man and assurance of salvation.[163] Harris was deeply shaken by the controversy, and the meeting demonstrated that working within the same organization was not always easy for such committed and determined men.

A half-yearly Association was held at Trevecka on 9 June.[164] Harris heard on the previous day that Rowland had refused to attend, and that he was 'complaining' to others about his conduct.[165] Under the circumstances, there was no alternative but to proceed without him. Once again, in an attempt to protect the movement from criticism, it was declared that none of its members, as yet, saw God calling them to leave either the Church or the Dissenting meeting houses. There was therefore no justification for secession; Methodists in the various parts of the country were expected to remain loyal to whichever church they belonged.

Early in July, a bi-monthly meeting was held at Watford,[166] and followed in the evening by a 'Society of Brethren of many parts' at nearby Groes-wen. Thomas Price, the host, informed Harris that he was 'for going from the Church'; he was uneasy about receiving the sacrament from the hands of unawakened clergy. Two days later Harris himself admitted that he also was willing to leave the Church as he was 'tired of the carnal Ministers sorely', but he insisted that they should wait for Divine guidance, for God to lead them out. Price, in the meantime, had been pacified, 'made easy about staying in Church', but his desire is indicative of the frustration felt by many of the Methodists during this period.[167]

During the summer Harris again attempted to assess the size of the Methodist movement in Wales, and estimated, without including the societies belonging to Howell Davies and Daniel Rowland, that mid-way through 1742 he had seventy-eight societies under his control, compared to sixty in 1740.[168] This suggests that Welsh Methodism was still in a period of expansion and growth, but a general view of the movement at this time indicates that it was not without its problems. Following the apparent success of the first Association at Dugoedydd in January 1742, tensions had later surfaced between Harris and Rowland concerning doctrine, and though the differences between them do not seem to have affected the progress of their work, the fact that Rowland had refused to attend the June meeting at Trevecka was ominous of later developments. Meanwhile, there was fear among the converts that the Methodists were soon to be ejected from the Church, and, though it had been decided to remain within its fold until forcibly ejected, some were becoming restless under the ministry of men whom they regarded as 'carnal' ministers, blind guides. Though it seemed that Methodism was prospering in 1742, the truth seems to be that its first year of central organization was far from being a happy one.

Harris had hoped since the middle of 1741 that Whitefield would have been able to join the Welsh at their Association meetings to give them the benefit of his experience and guidance. His admiration of Whitefield was immense; they were of a similar temperament, and Whitefield was, despite growing caution, more of an 'enthusiast' than most Evangelical clerics. The invitation to attend was therefore left open, and was accepted during January 1743 when the Association met at Watford. There, the English contingent comprised Whitefield, Joseph Humphreys, John Cennick and Thomas Adams,[169] while the Welsh were led by Rowland, Williams, Harris and John Powell, the Anglican clergyman.[170]

Several significant decisions were made at this meeting. Whitefield was appointed Moderator,[171] and several of the brethren public, or itinerant, exhorters. Twenty-four private exhorters were appointed to their respective society or societies, and it was agreed that none should leave the Church until 'the Lord should open a plain door for leaving her communion'. No exhorters were to be considered Methodist until examined and approved by the Association and none were to go beyond their prescribed limits without prior consent. Each private exhorter was to bring an account of his society to the next Association, together with an account of those who wished to be admitted into fellowship at their next meeting.

With the formation of this joint Anglo-Welsh Association, the organizational framework of the Welsh Methodist movement finally solidified. Order had been brought into the ranks, and the authoritative voice of a regulative body could be clearly heard. Exhorters were appointed and given their tasks; they could also be dismissed, suspended or restricted. Those wishing to be involved in Methodist activities had now to be sanctioned by the Association, and society reports were to be prepared, thus establishing a system through which the progress of the whole movement could be supervised.

The organization demanded a high level of commitment from its workers. At the next general Association held at Watford on 6-7 April, it was decided, though Rowland was absent, that William Williams should permanently leave his curacies in order to act as his assistant. Harris was appointed Superintendent over Wales, and instructed to go to England when called; Herbert Jenkins[172] was appointed his assistant, and likewise given the freedom to cross over to England when necessary. Superintendents were appointed to the various counties and the instruction issued that they were to obtain a book in which to

> write the names of each of their private Exhorters and the names of each Member of the private Societys [sic] and divide them into Married Men, Married Women, Single Men and Single Women and likewise to bring the state of each Society to the General Association.

They were also given the liberty 'to preach on their journey (if called)', provided they were of the belief that this would be the wish of the members of the Association. Superintendents were therefore made aware that their conduct and actions were the subject of constant scrutiny by the Association to which they were answerable.

The minutiae of the arrangements for the smooth operation of the new disciplinary and organizational machinery were not finalized by 1743. During succeeding months, suggestions were made as to how to improve the oversight of the societies, and fine-tuning of the system was attempted through discussions at various Association meetings. Whatever was found to be expedient or practical was adopted, while the controversial elements, such as the division of society members into groups of single, married and widowed persons, were discussed and settled.[173] As with Wesley, pragmatism was the overriding factor; the adopted system was, above all else, to be effective in regulating the movement. At the beginning of 1744, Harris seemed satisfied with the progress the Methodists had made; in the minute book of the Association he noted:

> Wonderful what subordination the Lord works in our spirits to each other, so that we are enabled to go on in faith, our outward order following the inward, and [when] we run before the Lord we have a Cross from some Quarter or other.[174]

He therefore regarded the organization which he had been instrumental in establishing as a theocracy; 'Lord', he wrote, 'this is Thy doing. Glory to Thee alone.' While attending an Association at Abergavenny he saw the gathering as 'God's little Parliament',[175] and in 1746, while explaining to the London brethren the 'order in Wales', he added 'how the Holy Spirit led us to it'.[176] The organization had not developed as a result of his own inventiveness; it was divinely ordained, a fulfilment of God's will. Yet he held that he did not look upon it as 'sacred': God may have more to reveal, and changes might be necessary in order to meet future needs.[177]

From the small beginnings in Breconshire in 1735, Methodist organization in Wales had developed steadily over the years to care for the increasing number of societies. In England, Wesley was still laying the foundations of his organization; the first edition of his *Nature, Design and General Rules of the United Societies* was dated 23 February 1743, and was therefore composed more than twelve months after its Welsh counterpart. Moreover, it was not until June 1744 that his first Annual Conference was held at the Foundry in London; the Welsh Methodists had already been participating in similar conferences for over two years. This may well have been a factor in Wesley's mind as he pondered over the future of his own societies;[178] realizing that there was a possibility of ejection from the Church, and having parted with the Moravians, the sight of the Calvinistic wing of the Revival organizing itself into an autonomous body may well have prompted him to consider anew the position of his own branch of the work.

By 1743 the structure of the Welsh Methodist movement had been erected; it was a self-regulating body which would now be able to survive alongside the Church from which it had emerged, should the need arise. It was through Harris's efforts above all others that this had been accomplished;[179] it was he who had travelled, exhorted and organized the converts and it was he who had brought the ministers together. It was he also who had kept up the momentum of development.[180] While Rowland was occasionally absent from the Association meetings, Harris was always present, acting as the driving force behind the whole movement. Whitefield was amazed at Harris's achievements,[181] and it is significant that at Watford, during April 1743, the Association accepted that in the event of Whitefield's absence, Harris was to act as Moderator; here was recognition of the colossal task he had accomplished in organizing the movement and bringing about the establishment of the Association.

Chapter 5
The Church of England

The massive institutional presence of the Church of England must provide the backcloth to any study of the eighteenth-century Revival in Wales. During the early part of the century, well over 90 per cent of the Welsh population regarded themselves as members of the Established Church, and Church and state were so closely intertwined that loyalty to one was still widely regarded as a demonstration of allegiance to the other. Most people were therefore opposed to both Dissent and the Roman Catholic church, whose members not only were disadvantaged in their citizenship rights under the Test Acts, but were also often regarded as less than loyal subjects to the Crown.

According to his own testimony, Harris was a devoted 'birthright' Anglican, nurtured within the fold of the Established Church. During his upbringing, a large measure of piety and Anglican loyalty had been instilled into him, and until the age of sixteen, he claimed that he was a regular worshipper at the parish church.[1] Though he admitted that he then began to neglect the duty of keeping the Sabbath, it was, nevertheless, at a church service that he became aware of the need to change his way of life.

During his conversion experience, Anglican literature played a prominent part in bringing him to a realization, not only of his own sin but also of the source and means of forgiveness. Two volumes seem to have come into his hands at critical moments during his spiritual pilgrimage: *The Practice of Piety* (1610), by Lewis Bayly, bishop of Bangor, and *The Whole Duty of Man* (1658), probably by Richard Allestree. The two authors in some ways represented different types of piety: Bayly, a Calvinist much admired by the Puritans, emphasized the doctrines of free grace, while Allestree represented a post-Restoration non-controversial brand of Anglicanism.[2] However, it was not for their theological contents that Harris studied them but for their guidance in practical issues, and it was through their teachings and exhortations that he came to experience forgiveness during the spring of 1735.

Harris's conversion occurred without any traceable Dissenting influence. Though Nonconformists were to help him later in his search for a theology that would reflect his own personal experiences, he had not as yet made contact with them. His conversion, therefore, served to confirm him in an inherited churchmanship, and though he was later to criticize the shortcomings of the Church, he was never to forget that it was under the ministrations of one of its clergy and during its regular Sunday services that he had come to experience forgiveness. In 1737 he set forth as his chief reason for refusing to join the Dissenters the fact that he had been converted and spiritually fed within the Anglican fold; to him its principles as laid down in the Thirty-nine Articles and Prayer Book were sound,[3] though he admitted that they were sadly ignored by many of the clergy and laity.[4] In 1740, he further claimed: 'I stay not in it because I was brought up in it, but because I see it according to God's Word.'[5] This was not to say that he dismissed his upbringing as irrelevant, but after 1735, though critical of the Church, he was determined not to leave her communion, and his resolve was rooted in the fact not that he was from birth one of the sons of the Church, but that he was through her ministrations one of the sons of God.[6]

In his autobiography Harris recalled his feelings concerning the 'general slumber' which he believed to be so widespread in the latter half of the 1730s. Allowing for exaggeration in this retrospective view, there can be no doubt that, from the time of his conversion, Harris was deeply disturbed by the low ethical standard of his fellow Anglicans and by the failure of the Church to exert salutary discipline over its members. Here he was perhaps reflecting the dismay of many churchmen at the decline of the Church's moral authority after 1689, when the Toleration Act weakened the power of the Church courts to punish moral offences and compel church attendance.[7] He did not regard popular frivolities as harmless social pastimes, but as a proof that his heedless contemporaries were exposing themselves to divine judgement and in imminent danger.[8] In what he saw as a moral crisis, the Church was inactive, 'rent in pieces by her sins and her ignorance'[9] and in need of repentance.[10]

This lack of discipline greatly perplexed him, particularly during the years immediately following his conversion. His concern was not so much for the Church as an institution as for the spiritual safety of the huge number of souls committed to its care. In 1737 he prayed that God would 'pity the poor Church of England where so many 10,000 souls starve',[11] and a few months later he wrote: 'O! will Thou hear my cry and behold my Tears for the poor Church of England – O! shall so many thousands call on Thy name and know nothing of Thee?'[12] With so many 'in entire negligence and ignorance',[13] the Church was 'poor, blind and miserable'; her bulwarks were 'taken down, her shepherds sleeping';[14] the only hope was that God, in his mercy, would intervene.

The clergy weighed heavily on Harris's mind and he often prayed that God would awaken them and send others to assist them. In September 1737, as he recorded his prayer, he wrote: 'Thou seest what spirit is crept into the Pulpit. Thou seest the condition of these poor souls. O! will Thou not hear and send labourers to Thy vineyard that will seek Thy Glory and not their own?'[15] In its deep-rooted aversion to religious 'enthusiasm', the Church had by the 1730s developed a piety based on rational theology, a close attendance on formal, disciplined public worship, and on liturgy, and the sacraments in particular.[16] The laity were encouraged to fulfil their duty towards both God and the Church by regular attendance on 'the ordinances', and little more than the regular services – matins and evensong – were offered in many parishes as practical help. It is noteworthy that, in giving an account of his upbringing, Harris does not refer to any church meeting attended by either himself or his parents other than the Sunday services, which suggests that they were deemed a sufficient contribution by the Church for the promotion of personal holiness.

A sermon heard by Harris in 1741 seems to have been typical of many of the exhortations given by the clergy during this period; he claimed that 'the sum of it was, "Do this, be good &c., and Live".'[17] Preaching in many Welsh churches was occasional and not standard, as visitation returns attest.[18] Griffith Jones of Llanddowror recognized that one of the reasons why some deserted the Church to join the Dissenters was the 'want of plain, practical and zealous preaching in a language and dialect they are able to understand'.[19] Others were also anxious, and aware that the Church was failing to cater for the spiritual needs of its members.[20]

Harris believed from the outset that it was the clergy's duty to enlighten the laity as to the real inward power of their religion, and was grieved to find that most of them had failed with, to his mind, catastrophic results. While in Pembrokeshire in 1740 he wrote in his Diary: 'Sad things do I hear of the Ministers in this Country [sic] – all dark &c. – souls perish for lack of knowledge.'[21] He did not believe the 'darkness' which had overtaken the Church to be a recent phenomenon. Like other Evangelicals, he sometimes traced it to the near-extinction of the Puritan tradition in Anglican piety, and in 1742 commented that Anglicanism had been in 'an obscure and almost utter darkness of [sic] near 80 years' – that is since 1662, the year of the Great Ejection of ministers from the Church.[22] Elsewhere he suggested that the Church had been in decline since the days of Charles I,[23] probably a reference to the advent of Laudian Arminian doctrine into the Church during the first half of the seventeenth century.

Like many former Puritans, he claimed that there were many relics of 'Popery' in the Anglican liturgy. In 1745, he noted: 'I see much legality and Judaism left in the constitution of our Church – holy days, holy places, holy persons, priest, vestments, tythes, hour and forms of prayers, and all performances, and faith lost.'[24] Harris did not let himself despair, however, but pinned his faith on further reformation, by which God would restore the Church and purge it of all 'human Invention and popish Ceremonies'.[25] Notwithstanding its faults, he declared himself 'much for the Church',[26] and though deeply offended by sights such as the people 'babbling through God's service careless'[27] and 'running over the prayers',[28] he hoped that God would one day enlighten them. He refused to allow the conduct of 'carnal' professors to detract from the institutional splendour of the Church, or from the Reformed truths for which it stood. However, he continued to fear that he would 'be prejudiced against all the Principles of the Established Church without examining them, by looking att the wicked lives of its professors and because [he] was persecuted by them'.[29] He often claimed that pity towards the members of the Church prevented him from seceding.[30] They were not to be blamed for their ignorance; it was their clerical leaders who were responsible. But since the Church was doctrinally sound there was always hope of its revival, provided that its doctrine could but be effectively applied to the lives of its members. Therefore, he was 'prodigious strict' for securing the continued membership of all that were within the Church and disapproved of any leaving her communion to join the Dissenters.[31] Reformation, not desertion, was the solution.

Assessing his own position within the Church, Harris wrote during March 1737 that he saw only three things lacking in it: the right to meet together as a society; the clergy's failure to emphasize the need for regeneration and to provide edifying 'family and public instruction'; and the absence of an intimate relationship between the pastor and his flock.[32] These faults could be easily rectified with the co-operation of a sympathetic clergyman, but many were unwilling to respond to the Methodist call to 'vital religion', which forced frustrated lay Methodist leaders to criticize the clergy as 'blind guides', and to attempt forms of religious leadership which were indignantly rebuffed as 'intrusion'. Harris himself was rebuked by his own vicar in February 1736, but was also warned not to leave the Church.[33] Therefore, while Pryce Davies was being cautious not to push Harris into the arms of the Dissenters, quite unknown to him, Harris was even more determined that he would never join them as he believed that it would hinder his work. In 1740, he claimed: 'Had I been a Dissenter, I should not have done the 20th part of the good I do.'[34] This was a major consideration when Harris was tempted to secede. Like Wesley, he realized the folly of leaving the Anglican communion, which commanded the allegiance of the huge majority through its legal and social pre-eminence, in order to throw in his lot with a small minority group such as the Baptists. At the same time, he felt highly uncomfortable within the Church, where he found so much hostility to his work, and, in an attempt to prove his loyalty, set about publicly defending her, hoping thus to pacify the opposition. None the less, he sometimes doubted whether God approved of such tactics.[35]

Repeatedly he argued that he could not fault the constitution of the Church and in 1749 stated that he 'had no objection to the present Establishment but some few expressions in the Common Prayer [and] the laziness, lordliness and pride of the bishops'.[36] This distinction between the Church, as a properly constituted establishment, and its members, allowed Harris to remain an

Anglican, despite his scruples concerning the general quality of Anglican spirituality. In a similar way to John Wesley, he argued that the validity of the Church was proved by the purity of its official doctrine,[37] and did not believe that he was being inconsistent in criticizing the Church while at the same time continuing to be a member. For all his reservations, he saw himself as divinely guided to remain loyal, and in April 1737 wrote: 'I am persuaded 'tis of God – be true to [the] Church of England – I find I am called there.'[38] Had he believed that he was called by God out of the Church, he would willingly have deserted her,[39] but this never came to pass. In his *Last Message and Dying Testimony* (1774), he declared that God had called him 'to live and die in the communion of the Established Church', and in October 1743, when there was real danger of secession, he used, as an argument to persuade his fellow workers to remain loyal, his inspired conviction that he 'had been called to Labour in this Church'.[40] From the days of his conversion he believed that he was likely to do more good if he remained than if he left.[41] He summarized his position in his autobiography and claimed:

> I find [God's] presence always in the worship and ordinances, and have great freedom to wrestle in prayer for it, and a strong confidence that God would receive, and revive this work in it, &c. However, in this faith and persuasion only I can testify that I was called to abide in it – and not on account of any prejudice against any other party, I abode in it to this day.[42]

Though he held that 'the way of the Church of England [was] right' and 'according to God's Word',[43] none the less Harris did not claim any form of church government to be infallible.[44] His concept of church government was essentially pragmatic and utilitarian; in 1748 he claimed that 'no outward form of government is compleat for all Times and Places', and the structure of the Church could 'be altered according as the Cases require [*sic*]'.[45]

The only alternative to the Anglican Church was Dissent, and in May 1748 Harris noted in his Diary that he had discussed with Herbert Jenkins, now leaving Whitefield and the London Tabernacle to become an Independent minister,

> the nature of Independency and how it appears to me contrary to the Nature of the Old and New Testament Church, contrary to the names

given the Church in the World and quite contrary to the way the Lord has led us from the beginning.[46]

Again, at an Association meeting in 1746, he declared that 'if the Independent way be strictly the true light, then all my conduct and Bro. Whitefield's conduct is wrong',[47] a conclusion at which he had arrived as early as 1741.[48] To declare against the Independent form of church government was also essential from his point of view, since recognition of its validity would undermine his authority among the societies. The concept of autonomous groups as 'gathered churches', whose collective decisions overruled the wishes of any individual member, was a threat to him,[49] and partly accounts for his refusal to entertain any notion of the validity of this form of organization. By submitting, theoretically at least, to the hierarchy of the Established Church, he defended his own position within the Methodist movement. It did not appear incongruous to Harris that, while he defended the Anglican system, he still refused to defer to the commands of those who were in authority within it and continued to exhort and itinerate while knowing that he had been ordered by his bishop to cease his irregular activities.

Contact with the Baptists had been made early in Harris's revivalist career through William Herbert, whom he had met in 1736. Together with Phillip Morgan, his minister, Herbert encouraged Harris to leave the Church, and for a while, during 1737, seemed very near to success.

With regard to baptism, Harris accepted the traditional Anglican view that the sacrament was a sign of the covenant between God and his people. He based his justification of infant baptism on 1 Corinthians 7.14,[50] and held that it had been given to the early Church in place of circumcision.[51] While in London in 1742, he declared that

> from Abraham's time to the end of the world ... believers' children (though the Baptism necessary to salvation is that of the Spirit) should be baptized on their parent's faith, because God declared so in His will, and because they'll bring them up in the nurture of the Lord.[52]

He held that, according to 1 Corinthians, 'the Apostles did baptize the children of believers when the [parents] both believed', while they refrained from administering the same baptism in families where both parents were unbelievers.[53] In 1739 he claimed that the reason for his initial attraction to the Baptists was not sympathy with the baptism of believers but their apparent piety, which appeared in contrast to 'the unruly, carnal lives and the preaching' of Anglican clergymen,[54] and also his own theological ignorance. By January 1741, having learned a little more of the difficulties surrounding the question of baptism, he had become so opposed to the Baptist position that when a treatise against infant baptism came into his hands he threw it into the fire.[55] Having decided not to throw in his lot with the Baptists in 1737, Harris was never again tempted to join them and, following some acrimonious arguments during the early 1740s, came to regard them much in the same way as they came to regard him: as bigoted and narrow-minded.

As he continued his efforts to evangelize the neighbourhood, Harris experienced considerable difficulty in understanding why any were opposed to him, since he had not 'actually done any evil but great good'.[56] He protested that he had not sown the seeds of Dissent in the hearts of any,[57] and had consorted with Dissenters only because he believed that they loved Christ.[58] Now that he had 'coolly examined both sides' and spent much time in prayer, he had come to the conclusion that he should be 'fixt in [his] Principles'.[59] He therefore advised his followers to remain faithful to the Church.[60]

Always scrupulous of conscience about his own motivation, Harris sometimes suspected that his chief motive for defending the Church was his fear of persecution.[61] At the same time, his heart was filled with envy when he heard of the successes of the Dissenters.[62] He tried to convince himself that in the sight of God denominationalism was unimportant, and that He delighted only in the fact that people drew near to Him regardless of their ecclesiastical attachments. Encouraged by the news that God had raised a 'number of true servants of Christ' within the Church that would join him in his work,[63] and having taken his momentous decision to remain faithful to the Church, he wrote: 'I had greater gifts to take away Prejudice, to ground each in his Principles, to engage love to Pastors ... I find open prophane sinners converted ... each secured from dissenting as it appears to me they should not.'[64] This proclamation of Anglican loyalty led to accusations from some Dissenters that he was 'a hypocrite and a persecutor'.[65] This was unfair; Harris was eager to befriend members on both sides of the divide, and even while considering his own position with regard to the Church had envisaged himself in the role of a mediator, labouring 'to engage the Parties to Love'.[66] But he had lost as well as gained by his public affirmation of Church principles. Rumours that he was being 'hotly pursued by the Dissenters' caused some of his followers to turn away from his meetings,[67] making him again doubtful of the wisdom of his decision publicly to praise Anglicanism.

Numerous accusations were at this time being levelled against Harris by the Dissenters: that he hindered many from attending the meeting houses, jested about full immersion at baptism, encouraged people to avoid their pastors, and that, in order to escape persecution, he was 'carnally prudent, casting a blast on Dissenters [and] taking part with the Persecutors'.[68] Harris acknowledged to William Herbert that he was not without fault, but averred that he was motivated by a concern for the welfare of the new converts. The next day he prayed: 'O! God, remember my former prayers. Help me between Tories and Dissenters, to go upright looking to Thee.'[69]

Though the Diaries for the period between the end of April and the beginning of September 1737 are missing, it is clear that by September the crisis had passed; Harris was firmly committed to the Church and hoping that God would guide her into a period of renewal.[70] Yet he still entertained hopes that it would be possible for Christians of all denominations to co-operate in the task of saving souls, and this sentiment was instrumental in moderating his attitude to the Dissenters on many occasions. He informed William Herbert that a union between the parties was his 'sincere intention',[71] and encouraged friends 'to bear Dissenters' as they had 'more of God amongst 'em'.[72] He did not forget that in the early days following his conversion they were often the only ones that encouraged him in his work,[73] and in 1740 declared himself 'a Lover of all Dissenters that love Christ', though he was firmly of the Church.[74]

The fact that Dissenters had 'more of God' did not lead Harris to encourage others to join them; on the contrary, he aimed to keep the new converts within the Church so that their presence would lead to renewal. His confidence in his own decision to remain loyal was later increased when he discovered that there were men of similar mind to himself among the clergy. Meeting Griffith Jones, Daniel Rowland, Thomas Jones of Cwm-iou and Thomas Lewis of Llanfihangel Cwmteuddwr was confirmation that God had not forsaken the Church. Whatever its shortcomings, there was still hope that it could embark on a new era of submission to God's will, provided it listened to His servants.

In 1738 many Dissenting ministers from beyond the neighbourhood of Trevecka began taking an interest in Harris's activities.[75] Of these, Edmund Jones seems to have been the most enthusiastic supporter of the Revival, and, in a letter to Harris in August 1738, invited him to visit Pontypool at the earliest opportunity.[76] Harris was impressed by the interest shown in him by the Dissenting ministers, especially in the face of renewed opposition from within his own Church. Close co-operation with the Dissenters followed, and lasted into the early 1740s.

This friendship was predicated in part on the Calvinistic views which he and the Dissenters held in common. However, theology divided Methodists from Dissenters as well as drawing them closer together. In particular, Harris emphasized the importance of assurance as an essential component of faith, while others, such as David Williams of Pwll-y-Pant, opposed the notion that it was a normal concomitant of justification. Writing to Harris during December 1740, Williams conceded that he had no objection to the doctrine itself, but objected to the use Harris made of it. He asked, 'Must we pronounce a sentence of Damnation upon those that are not absolutely assured they are in Christ?'[77] Phillip Pugh, another Dissenting minister, agreed with Williams;[78] Lewis Rees of Llanbrynmair also joined in the protest.[79] It is not surprising that by February 1741 Harris was noting in his Diary that 'the Dissenters (poor souls) much oppose assurance'.[80]

There is little doubt that, when the Dissenters realized that a religious awakening was taking place in south-east Wales, they had hoped to benefit from it by attracting new members to their churches. Harris, on the other hand, was adamant that all the Anglican converts should remain within the Church, and objected to any form of proselytizing or talk of forming a new sect. In 1742 he wrote: 'God I find does not call me to make any new party but to reform all &c. I am persuaded God called me to this and He will bless it.'[81] While in Pembrokeshire in 1740, he explained 'the dangers of leaving any Church but for Conscience sake', but at the same time defended the right of converts to attend any service where powerful preaching was to be heard. This, however, did not extend to participating in the Sacrament at different churches. In his view, 'it was all's duty to hear every intense, powerfull Sermons [sic], but to communicate where we were before.'[82]

The Dissenters did not regard the Methodist societies as a threat; on the contrary, they believed that they could serve to further their own cause. They were, after all, unofficial gatherings, open to all who were in the 'Methodist way', and it was hoped that, sooner or later, their attachment to the Church could be weakened to such an extent that they would finally secede from it. Having been critical of the Church in the past, Harris seemed the most likely person to bring this exodus about, but when they realized that he had no intention of leading his converts out of the Church, the Dissenting leaders' frustration accentuated the tension already brought about by their doctrinal differences. By 1740 both sides were accusing each other of sectarianism[83] and Harris was often infuriated by the attempts to steal his own Anglican sheep. The Baptists were the cause of greatest ill-feeling, and did little to promote their own cause by saying, to discredit the paedobaptists, 'that dogs were more proper objects of baptism than infants'.[84] By 1741, Harris was extremely critical of the 'sad, dry, dividing spirit of the Baptists',[85] whom he now regarded as bigots,[86] and remained deeply concerned that they were drawing his younger converts away from him.[87]

Harris's forceful and mercurial temperament also contributed to the deterioration of his relationship with the Dissenters. In 1740 he was accused by Evan Davies, a Dissenting minister at Haverfordwest, of being selfish and proud.[88] Ambition, coupled with a conviction that his leadership was vital to the success of the Revival, encouraged him in his autocratic style of leadership,[89] and though his overbearing manner may well have been due in part to his uncertainty about his own position and authority within the Methodist movement, and the fact that he was unordained,[90] there was also a strong element of megalomania in his personality, especially towards the end of the 1740s.

His lofty self-image led him to be severely critical of others, and early in the 1740s the Dissenters, on discovering that cooperation with him was not easy, began to distance themselves from him. Attempts were made to moderate his approach; in August 1741, when Harris had followed Whitefield's lead in being critical of the Dissenters' lukewarmness, Edmund Jones wrote to him claiming that Whitefield's rebuke had been delivered in 'a prudent and honest manner'. Harris's style was different, and Jones wrote searchingly: 'Had you, dear brother, done this with less passion and intemperance of spirit ... you might have done much good, but as it was, I fear it did but little good ... [and] ... Satan puffed us up to undue resentment.'[91] Harris always found it difficult to state his case without launching into personal attacks on his opponents. His correspondence with David Williams in 1740 serves as an example.[92] 'Mr. Williams', Harris wrote later, 'continues to be the gall of bitterness';[93] in return, Williams declared his sadness, 'that one who formerly made it his business to expose Biggottry [sic] should himself be a great example of it'.[94]

There were also considerable differences in the religious culture of Methodism and Nonconformity which made these conflicts all the more likely. Following the persecution of the seventeenth century, the Dissenters had come to enjoy their freedom of worship under the Toleration Act, and were often disinclined to attract the continuing threat of Tory mobs by provocative evangelism. Their pattern of worship was often that of their Puritan forebears; they prized learning and order in their ministers.[95] Methodism, on the other hand, was characterized by an atmosphere of urgency; its meetings often noisy with emotional outbursts. Many Evangelical itinerant preachers and exhorters were unlettered and crude, and, to the leaders of the Old Dissent, the Methodists were heavily tinctured with 'enthusiasm'. A characteristic Nonconformist view was expressed by Philip Dafydd of Penmaen, who, after hearing Thomas Saunders of Llanfaches preaching in 1774, commented that 'his way of preaching is like the Methodists, observing no order but rambling'; he also disliked others who indulged in 'screaming with some hideous noises and unbecoming gestures'.[96]

Nor was this view confined to Dissenters. Griffith Jones was also concerned about Methodist 'enthusiasm', and in 1741 cautioned Harris to be wary of extremism. In reply, Harris assured him that he had investigated the charges made against the Methodists, and wrote:

As to crying out, some I have seen and spoken to. They were so penetrated by the Word that they could not help crying out, some on seeing that they were lost, and others on seeing that they had pierced the Son of God by their sins, whom if you had seen you would have had no scruple about, but have blessed God on their account.[97]

However offensive some of their practices appeared to the 'polite' world, Harris held they could not be abandoned as they were the work of the free, sovereign Spirit of God. The Methodist response to the divine initiative was seen as the expression of souls 'enflamed with the love of God',[98] and the warmth generated by spiritual experience and evidenced by emotion was seen as an essential part of the faith: the manifestation of the inner change that was taking place in the soul.

Against this background of tension, Harris's Society of Ministers, attended by Dissenting and Methodist leaders, met towards the end of 1740. Rather than stimulating love, the meetings acted as a further catalyst in a deteriorating situation, and after they had met only twice, Harris abandoned the experiment. Thereafter, he and the Dissenters drifted apart; the gatherings had confirmed Harris's decision to remain within the Church.

After their failure to persuade Harris to secede, the Dissenters found others easier to lure, and Edmund Jones was accused of using his influence to draw some of the Methodists to the Dissenters. At Defynnog, in Breconshire (Harris's home county), the whole society left the Church without even consulting the Methodist leaders, while at Neath, in Glamorgan, a similar step was being contemplated by a society there.[99] Deeply as Harris respected the Old Prophet,[100] he wrote to him and declared that he found their 'sentiments differing so far about the ordering of the dear lambs' that they could not have 'such an outward agreement' as they had enjoyed in the past. Objecting to his attempts to proselytize Methodist society members, Harris explained his own position, saying:

> as yet 'tis not clear to any of us God calls us out [of the Church] . . . we are not persuaded the Time is come for any to leave any Sect among us. If ever it may come, we know not; we leave it to God . . . 'tis Conscience and a sense of my Duty and not Bigotry keeps me in this Communion.[101]

Harris held that the society members should be discouraged from leaving their churches to join others, God having as yet not shown this to be His will. All were to remain where they were until 'the Lord calls us on'. Like Wesley, he seemed to have been willing to follow the dictates of Providence, as it led him onwards.[102]

During his visit to London in the latter half of 1742, sectarianism was much on Harris's mind.[103] On 20 September he preached at the Tabernacle, and his sermon suggests that he had by this time subscribed, like most Evangelicals, to the belief that the Church of Christ was made up of all the regenerate of whatever terrestrial church.[104] Inviting his auditors to come to Christ, to enter within the veil and discover the paradise they had lost in Adam, he claimed that the angels within that paradise enjoyed 'full union and perfect love'. He announced:

> There is no party or division. No Church Angels, Presbyterian Angels, Independent Angels, and Baptist Angels. O! come and be plunged in love, and when you have learnt all of Christ and known Him fully, then you go back to read controversies, but not till then. In God is no division. If you are asked what religion you are of, say 'Jesus Christ'. If what name, say 'Christians'. If asked what Church you belong to – 'the Catholic Church'.[105]

Since the day that they had met at Cardiff in 1739 Harris had greatly admired George Whitefield. He, Rowland, the two Wesleys and numerous other Evangelical clergymen, through their presence within the Church, had proved to Harris that God had not forsaken it. Through Whitefield an additional ray of hope appeared. As early as the summer of 1735 he had written to John Wesley, saying:

> If you remember, Sir, in my greatest affliction last Lent, it was told me I should be a bishop, and therefore must be poor in Spirit. That thought came home upon me with so much force, and so many circumstances have since occurred to favour the temptation, that I knew not what to do.[106]

During the 1740s the hope that this would be fulfilled was still being entertained by many of Whitefield's followers and Harris himself believed the notion to have been divinely impressed upon Whitefield's mind.[107] Once he was elevated to the episcopate he could ordain Methodist lay preachers, Harris among them, but patience would have to be exercised until it came about.

From the outset, Harris had regarded his societies, though not directly under the rule of the Church, to be nevertheless attached to it. When he gathered the exhorters together into Associations he still had no intention of seceding, though he regarded their organization as a precaution lest they eventually be ejected from the Church. Others believed that secession was desirable and advocated a voluntary exodus before they were forcibly ejected. This was totally unacceptable to both Harris and Whitefield, and it was in an attempt to stem the growth of secessionism that the latter wrote his letter to the 'Brethren in Wales' in December 1741, encouraging them to stand fast within the Church.[108]

Since Harris himself had been conscious of the deficiencies of the clergy since his conversion in 1735, he had no difficulty in appreciating the feelings entertained by other Methodists with regard to the Church. He was unwilling, however, to see them leave. In 1737, while exhorting some friends, he distinguished between the ideal and the actual nature of the Church,[109] and encouraged them to remain faithful to the 'principles' even if they were disillusioned by the failure of others to adhere to them. However, it was not until the 1740s that the threat to leave the Church became a real danger, mainly because of widespread dissatisfaction among the Methodists with the conduct of the 'carnal' clergy. Harris discussed the question of receiving the Sacrament with the Dissenters at a meeting in Monmouthshire during 1741, and concluded that it was 'not right now, till God would make the way clear that 'tis His will and to His Glory'.[110] This seems to have offended his hearers, many of whom had already participated in the sacrament with the Dissenters, and, finding them uncompromising in their attitude, Harris declared that he 'had no thoughts of leaving the Church, as seeing no occasion' for taking such a step. This remained his policy throughout the period: the Methodists were to remain in the Church either until they were ejected or until God led them out.[111]

One of the most important activities of the Church for Harris was the administration of the communion by the clergy. This sacrament had been central in his own conversion experience and he never doubted its efficacy as a means of grace. Like Wesley, he was convinced of the value of frequent communion, and partook of it as often as he could, sometimes more than once on the same day.[112] Five months after that memorable Palm Sunday at Talgarth he wrote to Pryce Davies to express his wish 'of communicating oftener ... once a month'.[113] Davies refused and, although pressed on numerous occasions, it was not until 1764 that the request was granted, by Davies's successor.[114] In an attempt to curb Harris's 'enthusiasm', Pryce Davies went so far as to use the Sacrament to reprove him; in 1742 he barred Harris from communicating at the parish church.[115]

The Communion was to Harris an act of remembrance, but also a source of direct spiritual strength,[116] the Table being a meeting place with God his Saviour.[117] He did not elaborate on a sacramental theology, perhaps because participation in it was to him an intensely personal moment, surrounded by the numinous and mysterious workings of God's Holy Spirit. His experience in 1735 had impressed upon him the significance of the act of communicating; he had seen Christ bleeding on the Cross, and through that experience he had received the forgiveness of sin for which he had been searching.

As the Methodist movement grew, complaints about the clergy and their administration of the Sacrament were common. Many Methodists declared themselves unable to receive the elements from the hands of ungodly clergymen. This Harris rejected, claiming that the presence of an ungodly celebrant had not vitiated the value of the communion for him.[118] In this, he echoed the twenty-sixth Article of the Church which had expressly denied that the validity of the sacraments was in any way endangered by the evil lives of those administering them,[119] a view he shared with Wesley.[120]

Following the reading of Whitefield's letter at the Association at Dugoedydd in January 1742, it was decided that the Methodists should receive the Sacrament at the parish churches regardless of the conduct of the clergy. Not all were happy with the decision, and the society at Defynnog expressed its protest by incorporating itself into an Independent church. Harris believed their action to have harmed the Methodist cause in that it appeared to confirm the suspicion that the Methodists were, after all, forming a new party or sect. It would lead to an increase in persecution, encouraging the belief that the Methodists were hypocrites who, while claiming to be faithful to the Church, were in fact Dissenters.[121]

The balance between the Methodist movement and the Established Church was of paramount importance to Harris and not to be disturbed any further than was absolutely necessary. He realized that being 'an Anglican with a difference'[122] was to his advantage in that it offered him some protection from legal prosecution and enabled him to reach the majority of the people. It was a position that he did not want to relinquish or lose.

When considerable numbers of his followers wished to secede from the Church during the early 1740s, Harris found himself in the dilemma of not knowing whether their wishes were a sign from God. In April 1742, on hearing that some had defected, he begged that God would show him whether or not He wanted him to dissent also and was fully persuaded that he did not. His doubts thus resolved, he went on to insist that this was God's will for all Methodists everywhere, and in 1744, while listing issues and dilemmas in which God had given him especial guidance, he wrote that while trying to decide whether 'to stay in Church or to leave it' he had been 'again and again satisfied' that he was to stay.[123]

The Dissenters condemned Harris's policy of not allowing the Methodists to join them. Thomas Lewis, an exhorter, warned that he 'would fall to many errors' through implementing it,[124] and as Harris reflected further on the question, he admitted that he could be wrong. However, he claimed that 'none as yet of my Brethren [have] declared for this [i.e. allowing Methodists to join the Dissenters]. Bro. Thomas Lewis [of Llan-ddew] I hear [is] against it. Bro. [Daniel] Rowland and Bro. Howell Davies indifferent.'[125] It seems from Harris's words that, though they were ordained clergymen, he believed that neither Rowland nor Davies were as zealous for the Church as he was himself. This suggestion seems further confirmed by an entry made by Thomas Morgan of Henllan[126] in his diary on 26 May 1744, recording that he had been told by Thomas William, the Methodist exhorter from Eglwysilan, Glamorgan, that 'the Methodists had once all of 'em agreed to depart from the Church of England, excepting Mr. Howell Harris, who opposed their design with all his might'.[127]

Enforcing his policy on the movement as a whole was difficult for Harris. In August 1742 he warned Whitefield that many converts objected to going to the parish church for communion.[128] Whitefield tried to comfort him by telling him that 'dividing times generally precede settling times'. As tactfully as possible, he warned Harris that the fault might be partly his own,[129] and covertly suggested that Harris's strong emotions had perhaps led him to write an exaggerated account of the problem, whose underlying cause was that others disagreed with him. Eight days later, Whitefield sent him another letter in which he appears to have come to a decision to visit Wales to see the situation for himself.[130] That visit took place during the following January, when Whitefield was appointed Moderator of the Association at Watford. Under his prestigious chairmanship, it was decided that the Methodists 'should continue to receive in the Church, till the Lord should open a plain Door for leaving her Communion'.[131] They were thus kept, through Harris's efforts and the intervention of Whitefield, from leaving the Church during 1742–3.

The problem had not, however, been solved. There was still a great deal of discontent among the Methodists, and the danger of secession still threatened in England. During his visit to London in August 1743, Harris found himself again discussing the subject with Whitefield and the two Wesleys and noted that Whitefield was not as confident of their future within the Established Church as he had seemed six months earlier while in Wales.[132] None the less, when the 'Great Association of all the English Brethren'[133] met in London on the last day of August and set about discussing the question, it was Whitefield together with Harris who opposed the suggestion that they should secede. Harris argued that he had not set out to form a party but to carry through a general reformation, and, since Whitefield had been told by God that he was soon to be made a bishop, it was their duty to wait for that prophecy to be fulfilled. When Joseph Humphreys broached his desire to join the Dissenters and settle as an ordained minister of one of their churches, Harris declared that he was prepared to allow him the freedom to follow his own conscience but, if he seceded, he would no longer be able to have fellowship with him as a Methodist, for Methodists were 'properly Church of England, and there stay unless . . . turned out'.[134] It seems that his earlier arguments against party spirit and divisions within the Church had for a while been forgotten in order to defend the establishment. Above all things Harris was a pragmatist.

After long debate it was again decided that the Methodists

should remain loyal to the Church, but those who were already Dissenters should be allowed to receive the Sacrament from their own ministers. Furthermore, those Methodists who were refused communion by their local clergy were to be allowed to receive from any Methodist clergyman 'though against the Canons', since they denied the authority of the Canons in a matter of such importance.

The possibility that Methodism appeared to outsiders too much like Dissent, or even as a totally new sect, was viewed with concern. In April 1744 the Association at Watford, after emphasizing that Methodists were loyal members of the Church of England, entered in the minute book 'that we are not, nor should call ourselves a Church or Sect, but Societies called in the Established Church, till turned out, and that such as discourse are not, nor should they, be called ministers but exhorters'.[135] In Monmouthshire, where some had already joined the Dissenters in order to participate in the Sacrament, a similar declaration was made by a monthly Association meeting at New Inn to counteract the interest being shown by the local Methodists in Dissent. There it was decided, 'that in order to remove Stumbling Blocks, to communicate in the parish Churches, and to advise the people to do so in order to prevent our appearing as a Sect'.[136] However, the debate about separating rumbled on and, at the beginning of June, Harris found himself under attack from some Dissenters at Bristol who accused him of bigotry. In reply, he claimed that he was not opposed to Dissent: Welsh Methodism was extremely tolerant, and society rules allowed Dissenters to be members in the same way as churchmen. Howell Davies allowed them to participate in the communion at his church even though they were turned out by their own ministers for so doing, while Harris himself never encouraged any to leave the Dissenting churches but to remain where they were. Moreover, he did not stand in the way of those within the Church who, because of their conscience, felt themselves drawn to the Dissenters; neither did he himself object to the principle of receiving communion with Dissenters. He stressed that he preached at meeting houses, prayed for Dissenters, and had told Joseph Humphreys that if he was ordained a Dissenting minister he would still love him as a Christian and as a minister of Christ, and would invite him to preach in the Welsh societies if the members so desired.[137]

When Whitefield joined him from London the following day, he declared his support for Harris's stand against secession and at a society meeting spoke 'against divisions and leaving the Church or dissenting'. As a result of his words, 'there was great melting and weeping' – a sign of God's witness to the validity of the message, according to Harris.[138]

This was 'an Intricate time indeed', and by June Harris believed that the whole situation had 'come as it were to a point – either of our being turned out or received in wholly';[139] it was therefore important that the whole issue be handled with the utmost delicacy. When the question of ministers administering the Sacrament in private houses was raised at an Association meeting at Trevecka on 27 June, Harris opposed the suggestion vehemently,[140] but on realizing the depth of feeling among those present, he was finally persuaded to allow them time to meditate on the subject and to pray for guidance; the question could then be resolved when they convened at some later date.

A perennial problem in the Revival was that of anticlericalism. It was not easy to criticize the 'carnal' clergy as 'blind guides' without appearing to demean the priesthood and undermine the authority of the Church whose spokesmen they were. It was, perhaps, because of this that a charge was brought against Thomas William, one of the exhorters, at an Association meeting at Watford in September 1744,[141] that he had spoken against the gown and cassock. While attempting to defend himself, William did not deny that he had mentioned them but construed his words not as an attack upon the practice of wearing vestments, but rather upon the tendency of some to idolize them. Although a relatively unimportant issue in itself, the episode illustrates how sensitive the Methodists had become to any criticism of the Church by their own people; it was regarded as detrimental to the cause and to be avoided until the all-important question of the future of Methodism within the Church had been settled.

The campaign to keep the Welsh Methodists within the Church had to be conducted not only at the Association meetings but also in the various societies, if it was to be successful. Therefore, as he travelled the country, Harris encouraged the people to remain faithful to the Church and was disturbed at any hint of disloyalty or unrest. While passing through Glamorgan during September 1744, he heard of some who were about to dissent at Neath, the society there having complained for over two years that the local clergyman was a Deist and that they wanted an Evangelical ministry.[142] Harris had opposed their intention from the outset and continued to encourage both Dissenters and churchmen to remain where they were, suggesting that, as there were weaknesses in both camps, no one should be attracted to leave one by the outward appearances of the other. Each denomination possessed attractions for those contemplating membership, and many were driven from one camp to another by their failure to keep their eyes firmly fixed on Christ rather than on the means of grace. The means and ordinances had their vital place, but if they became prized as ends in themselves, and not as channels of grace, then there was danger of falling into the Papist error of setting mediators between God and men. As God had not withdrawn His Spirit from the ordinances in either church or meeting house, it was a duty incumbent on all Methodists, whether Anglicans or Dissenters, to remain in their respective churches while the reformation brought about through and by the Methodists continued. From a spiritual point of view, neither side was better than the other; Harris claimed that those who had left the Church to join the Dissenters had succumbed to the flesh, for 'to the flesh the sight of the Church of England is more black – the sins and ignorance more open and visible; but to faith, the flesh and the Law is as visible among the Dissenters only 'tis dressed with an Evangelical Dress.' He therefore encouraged the Anglicans: 'go among them [the Dissenters], go into the [Meeting] House and examine the inside of their souls and with all their outside order and appearance of Holiness we should find self, unbelief, the World &c within them.'[143]

Such harsh words naturally led many to believe, as at Bristol three months earlier, that Harris was opposed to the Dissenters, but this was his strategy for defending the Church and preventing the society members from deserting it. He professed a profound respect for all Dissenters from whom he had received great benefit. He did not doubt that God worked through their ministry; while attending a service at the Independent meeting house at Tredwstan near Trevecka in November 1744, he claimed that he was 'under a sweet influence and was warmed and melted and affected and cry'd for all Dissenters', especially those at Tredwstan.[144] At an Association meeting in London during

December he expressed his feelings towards the Dissenters by admitting: 'though many of them are lukewarm, and have the doctrines in their heads only, yet ... the power of God is among them, and they have the truth.'[145] During the same visit he also declared that 'there was bigotry and party spirit against the Dissenters too much in Bro. Charles Wesley',[146] and expressed his belief that God 'was offended with him for somewhat of his tenets'. It seems, therefore, that Harris only attacked the Dissenters defensively, when it was necessary for him to do so in order to keep the Methodists from going over to them. When the threat had receded he was prepared to praise them.

The technique of using harsh words to frighten and discourage Methodists from leaving the Church was not as successful as Harris had hoped. It was again brought to the fore when five Glamorgan exhorters wrote to the Association at Caeo, Carmarthenshire, in 1745 requesting, in an oblique fashion, permission to be ordained.[147] Their complaint was that the Methodist leaders were too attached to the Established Church and that the societies should encourage men other than the clergy to preach and to administer the Sacrament to them. A decision on the whole question of the ministry to the converts had been awaited by the signatories for over two years and was long overdue. They freely admitted that they believed secession to be the best policy for the Methodists; only respect towards a few Gospel clergymen who had fed their souls had prevented them from leaving earlier.

Unfortunately, the minutes of the meeting at Caeo are not included in the Association Records, but while Harris's Diary gives us some indication as to what occurred, the most interesting aspect of his entry for that day is his own personal reaction to the exhorters' letter.

After the letter was read, there followed 'a strict and long examination of the nature, evil and symptoms of Pride and self appearing in the Exhorters', and after some discussion it was decided that the Association would have to 'declare against the Dissenters, that they sleep and leave the Lord'. Such a step had not been taken before. The following morning Harris delivered a thundering message to those present on humility and spiritual poverty and by the end of the Association the revolt had been quelled. Those who advocated remaining in the Established

Church had been victorious and by the end of the month all the societies which had expressed a desire to secede had been visited by Harris personally and had been made aware that such rebellious suggestions were not to be tolerated.[148]

As the next Association drew near, this time at Watford, Harris was deeply concerned about the exhorters, believing their pride to be increasing and all poverty of spirit lost. As he travelled to the meeting, he heard rumours that further steps were being taken to break away from the Church, and was tempted to return home to Trevecka.[149] At Watford he clarified his own position even further by stating that he had never regarded the societies as churches but as branches of the Church; neither had he regarded the exhorters as ministers authorized to administer the sacraments. There were some among them whom he believed unsuitable even to preach; they were exhorters, and their duty was simply to exhort. Again, he reiterated his opinion that the Methodist movement was not a sect but a people called by God within the Church to carry through a reformation until they were either heard or turned out.

Having thus stated his view as a founder member of the movement he then proceeded to analyse the situation. The talk of secession was not the work of God but of human pride; was it likely that God would reveal the 'greater things' to the exhorters before He had revealed them to the leaders? It was only natural to expect Him, if He desired secession, to 'begin the Separation by such as He has and does give most of Himself to', that is, Harris himself and the other leaders; it was unimaginable that God could bypass him and speak directly to the exhorters. Harris was apparently unaware that this argument was inconsistent with his earlier view that there should be no mediators between God and men.

He claimed that his main reasons for refusing to leave the Church were:[150]

1. That there was no precedent. The Apostles had been turned out by the Jews and the Protestants by the Papists. The Protestants had also received the sacrament from the Papists for nearly a century before establishing a church (a reference, possibly, to the Lollards but set as an example for the Methodists).
2. To the exhorters' argument that they could not be ordained

within the Church, Harris answered that when the door was opened, it must be opened by God. It was He who would make ordination possible, either by opening the hearts of the bishops to ordain Methodists, or by allowing them to be forcibly ejected. The initiative had to be left to the Almighty.
3. He argued that ordination 'was no great thing in the Apostles' days', that one could conduct an effective ministry without being ordained. When Apollos preached, he was not charged with being unordained but with being deficient in his knowledge of Christ; so also in the case of those who went about at the time of Stephen's death in the Book of Acts. Harris admitted that it could be argued that this was at a time when Christians were being persecuted, but answered, 'So 'tis now, when we shant be ordained.' Refusal to ordain Methodists was to him a form of persecution.

To this attack on their motives, Harris joyfully noted, the exhorters were unable to reply. Pleased with his handling of the situation, he felt that they now had 'more Love, humility and Subordination', and he warned them that they would not prosper if they continued along their chosen path, but would, in fact, 'put a greater hindrance in the way of the work ... than anything that has yet happened'.

The Association 'reasoned the matter over and over' and three of the exhorters agreed to stay within the Church to see how the situation would develop, while a fourth decided to dissent. It was then agreed that, if secession should occur, the stewards from all the societies would speak to the clergymen of their respective parishes and the Methodists' case would be presented to the bishops; as children of God, they would not leave, as others had done before them, 'in a bad spirit'. William Williams of Pantycelyn was in agreement with Harris that this should be the procedure if the day came for them to leave the Church; if they went, they should go with dignity.

After the great conflict in 1745 between the leaders and the exhorters, a period of calm followed. Those in favour of remaining within the Church had established their authority over the movement and had succeeded in convincing most of the exhorters that secession was not the way forward. During the tumult Harris had been the staunchest defender of the Church and it is beyond doubt that, of all the leaders, he was the most conservative in his view. Even when faced by a swelling tide of opinion in favour of secession he refused to capitulate but insisted that the Methodists should remain faithful until they were ejected or led out by God.

Few problems concerning Methodist adherence to the Church arose between 1745 and 1750, the battle having already been won by Harris. However, two Glamorgan societies did become Independent churches, Groes-wen in 1745 and Aberthin in 1749. The society at New Inn, Monmouthshire, followed in 1751, but these were the areas which had displayed the greatest element of discontent, and each secession was opposed by Harris. Towards the end of the 1740s problems appeared in north Wales following the success of Methodist preachers there. At the Association meeting at Cil-y-cwm during July 1747, a letter was received from William Jones of Trefollwyn, Anglesey,[151] 'giving an account of the good reception of Bro. Peter Williams and Bro. David Jones and other Brethren in North Wales',[152] but warning that, since the Methodist organization was still in its infancy in that part of the country, there was a danger that all the new converts might join the Dissenters. At a later Association at Trevecka another letter from Anglesey was read which contained a plea to the Methodists in the south to take the souls in the north into their care. As a result, it was agreed 'that Bro. Harris go there now immediately and exhort them to abide in the Church of England and settle them in private societies'.[153] Harris championed the Anglican cause, but owing to his inability to remain in the north for any length of time it was also agreed at the Association 'that some brethren from South Wales ... be there continually to succeed each other'. It was hoped that this arrangement would prevent a rush of new Methodist converts from the Church to the Dissenters.

Harris's intervention in the north led to the Dissenters being 'exceeding bitter and angry',[154] but he was by this time less concerned with their response to his Anglican zeal, and during subsequent visits preached the same message: that there was no justification for leaving the Church.[155]

Since Methodists were usually denied the use of ecclesiastical buildings in which they could conduct their meetings, Harris supported the idea of obtaining, even building, other premises for their use. The first was constructed at Groes-wen, near

Caerphilly, as early as 1742[156] and Harris encouraged other societies which faced difficulties to consider building an appropriate house. At Cefn-y-fedwast, Clyro, Radnorshire, in November 1746 he explained 'that building a House would be as nothing to them', while at Pen-y-bont, Llandeglau, in the same county, he rebuked the society members at the beginning of 1747 because they did not have a house in which to meet.[157]

Many buildings were adapted for use as society meeting houses during the 1740s, and in the towns many individual rooms were hired for the same purpose. It appears that Harris was unconcerned that their use of separate buildings could undermine the Methodists' claim to be loyal churchmen. It must be remembered, however, that he was familiar since 1739 with the Methodist buildings and meeting places at London and Bristol; furthermore, he refused to license the buildings as places of worship which he saw as a mark of separation or Dissent.[158] As with Wesley's connexion, so in Wales, the Methodists tried to avoid describing their buildings as 'meeting houses' for fear of being regarded as Dissenters. Their buildings were 'society houses', 'New Houses', 'New Rooms', 'preaching houses' or 'a house ... for religious uses'.[159]

To the end of his life, Harris remained opposed to any suggestion that the Methodists should leave the Church. His reasons for this inflexible resolve were summed up by him in 1760, when he attended John Wesley's seventeenth conference at Bristol. There, he claimed, 'When I met Charles Wesley, I told him I came 600 miles in purpose to [i.e. specifically to attend] their Conference, and that if they went out of the Church now, the work was stopped.'[160] It was this fear that kept him so intransigent; God had blessed them within the Church and there was no guarantee that if they left that they could take His blessing with them. On the contrary, if the Methodists seceded, it was possible that they would be leaving God behind. John Wesley agreed, and said, 'Let this be well observed. I fear, when the Methodists leave the Church, God will leave them. But if they are thrust out of it they will be guiltless.'[161] Moreover, Harris regarded himself as involved not only in the task of saving souls but also in the reformation of the Church itself; his aim was not only to convert individuals, but to transform the establishment. His vision was a combination of revival and reformation; regeneration and rejuvenation. In her old age, the Church had become lethargic, and nothing but the Spirit of God could restore her to her rightful state as the young and beautiful Bride of the Saviour. If the Methodists seceded, the Church would be left to languish in her own sin, deprived of hope. But firm in his conviction that she was, despite her failings, the Church of God, and that he had been called through her and to serve God within her, Harris stood fast against those who derided her virtues. He prevented the Welsh movement from yielding to the temptation of isolating itself from the majority of the population by joining the ranks of Dissent. Since the Methodists had all been called by God, Harris insisted that it was His choice whether or not they were to remain in the Church; throughout his life he maintained that 'God must do it'.[162] Until the door was opened, it was a duty incumbent on all Methodists to remain as they were.

Chapter 6
The Opposition to Methodism

Opposition to Harris's lay ministry and to his particular brand of Christianity appeared as soon as his attempts at evangelism in the neighbourhood of Trevecka became public knowledge. Having gathered a small group of people to establish devotional meetings at his home, and having also ventured out on his own initiative to visit the housebound sick, he says that he was encouraged by some of his neighbours during the winter of 1735–6 to go from house to house to speak of religion, not only in his own parish but also in the parishes of Llan-gors and Llangasty. This he continued to do 'until persecution became too hot', but as he did not include in his account of the period a description of the nature of the persecution, it seems reasonable to conclude that it was verbal rather than violent opposition. Thus Harris's public denunciation at the fairs at Talgarth of swearers and cursers, the gentry and the 'carnal' clergy, and his preaching there of 'terrors and threatenings ... death and judgement', resulted in a haughty letter being sent to him by the vicar, and a Justice of the Peace advising him to beware of puritanical zeal and threatening those who heard him that they would be fined if they admitted him into their homes.[1]

The vicar's letter[2] is an interesting expression of a clergyman's objections and fears during the early days of the Revival. Pryce Davies admitted that he did not object to Harris having taken upon himself to instruct his neighbours at Trevecka 'on a particular occasion'; he was well aware that he intended to apply for ordination and allowed that his actions, if somewhat premature, 'proceeded from a pious and charitable disposition'. It was his itinerating to which he strongly objected, the 'public lectures from house to house, and even within the limits of the Church'.[3] The purpose of his letter was to inform him of the sin that he was committing by his breach of Church order.

Davies was not alone in his opposition; magistrates and clergy in the surrounding parishes also objected to Harris's activities,[4] and he found great difficulty in understanding such an adverse response to his efforts to bring about a reformation in the lives and conduct of others, and for a while suspected that their condemnation was indicative of God's disapproval of his actions.[5] During March 1736 he complained to his brother that his successes had resulted in 'the Envy of some mean, narrow thinking Parsons' who opposed him only because of their fear that he would expose their shortcomings as men of the cloth.[6] He failed to appreciate that a layman's concern for the welfare of their souls could be construed by the clergy as an attack upon their vocation, and that they most probably regarded his words as both impertinent and offensive since Harris had provocatively denounced some of them publicly.

The clergy's opposition was soon sanctioned by the bishop of St David's, who during the summer of 1736 refused to ordain Harris because of his failure to promise 'not [to] go to the fields or about'.[7] Clerical attitudes from then on were generally hostile. They were soon preaching against Harris from their pulpits, and while on his way to Tal-y-llyn during the spring he was present at a service where one of these sermons was delivered.[8] Many years later, while travelling through north Wales, he again found himself in a similar situation. John Owen, the vicar of Llannor and Deneio in Caernarfonshire,[9] had heard that he was about to visit his parish and set out to warn the people that he was 'a minister of the devil, an enemy to God, and to the Church, and to all mankind'.[10]

As the awakening around Trevecka became more widespread, several of the local clergy realized the folly of an unthinking and choleric reaction to Harris's work. The problem was a difficult one. To do nothing was unwise, but to oppose too vehemently would encourage schism and drive many serious-minded Anglicans into the arms of Dissent. It may also be that their initial opposition was not as deep-rooted as Harris at first believed – more a spontaneous reaction to what was happening in their parishes and to Harris's criticism of their spiritual leadership than a display of enmity towards his efforts to achieve reformation and promote the Gospel in the area. It is probable that they perceived his actions as a threat to the Church, to the unity of their congregations and to their personal authority, but that later, having seen that he was encouraging regular attendance at the parish churches, they came to realize that his efforts might prove to be to their advantage, and moderated their views towards him.[11] After all, Harris had been able to ask in 1736: 'What have I taken from them, or what have I gained? Their churches are fuller, and they are revered more than before.'[12] The spread of the Revival, however, meant that a wider circle of clergy were to feel themselves and their Church threatened. During an eight-day period in 1739, while travelling through Monmouthshire and Glamorgan, Harris noted that nine clergymen had opposed him in his work,[13] and during the same year an attempt was made, on clerical initiative, to obtain a warrant against him in order to prevent him and others from conducting an itinerant ministry. The warrant was issued as Harris undertook his first journey to London, but Edmund Jones of Pontypool was able to contact him in the capital and inform him 'that the warrant given out ... is come to nothing'.[14] Here, as elsewhere in the Revival, the interposition of lay magistrates friendly to the Revival counterbalanced clerical attempts at legal prosecution.[15]

During August 1739, while Harris was at Llandinam in Montgomeryshire, he received a letter from the local vicar, John Tilsley, echoing Pryce Davies's earlier criticisms, and enquiring by what authority he came to his parish to preach. 'We have a regular ministry among us in the Church Established', he argued, '... examined and approved by their Diocesans.' He would, therefore,

> be glad to know by what authority you take upon you to preach within my district ... Your ascending your unhallowed rostrums in the highways, and in open fields, and your asserting that every place, suppose a dunghill or stable, is equally consecrated with the Church for the service of God, can be with no other design but to trample upon the sacred altar, and to unravel the whole Scripture concerning the publick places of divine worship ... Your rigid way of exhorting, and of pouring out the vials of God's wrath so peremptorily upon the ignorant hearers with your extempore effusions, has not only seduced several in mine and the neighbouring parishes to live, and end their days it is to be feared, under the guilt of schism, but what I can't mention without horror, you have left several in a state of despair or with little hopes of mercy.[16]

Other clergy wrote angrily to Harris, similarly challenging both his conduct and his ministry.[17] David Lloyd of Llandyfalle, one-time opposer, then friend, returned to the ranks of the opposition by sending Harris a lengthy letter in April 1741, posing seven questions to which he demanded an answer:

1. Is a commission (or mission) necessary for preaching the word of God, and for administering the Sacrament, or is it not?
2. Who have authority to give this commission in the ordinary way?
3. Was ever a commission given in an ordinary way without the power of working miracles?
4. Was there ever a false teacher that did not pretend to more than ordinary holiness?
5. What is schism?
6. Who is the father of lies?
7. Whose children are liars?[18]

In his first reply to Lloyd, Harris declined to answer the questions on account of more pressing duties,[19] but promised a fuller response in due course. A month later Lloyd contacted Harris again to demand the promised reply.[20] He cautioned Harris about heresy, and claimed that for Harris to issue a blanket condemnation of the clergy for failing to preach the Articles and Homilies of the Church was unfair, and that it would be 'more like a Christian to detect real offenders and have them punished'. He also attacked Harris's ministry, asking: 'By what authority do you do these things? Is it divine or human? No man taketh this honour unto himself.'[21] In his reply,[22] Harris attempted to explain his attacks upon the conduct of the clergy:

> The laborious, experimental, pious, and successful among them I respect and honour and value in my heart for their work's sake; but the scandalous lives and bitter persecuting spirit of many of them should make every sober thinking person rather mourn for them than endeavour to justify them.[23]

These men, while accusing Harris and others of harming the Church, were themselves guilty of the same charge. Their indulgence of sin and their persecution of devout Methodists was deplorable:

> Many of them patronize sin, calling the vanities of the world – cock fighting, gaming, dancing – by the name of harmless recreations, and the meeting in societies to pray and edify each other in the ways of God is to bring the Church into danger, as if the Church is to be supported by ignorance; and when their drunkenness, swearing, pride and malice are exposed, it is exposing the Church. God forbid that these should be the Church.

It was not Gospel preaching but the unfaithfulness of the clergy that was 'the greatest, if not the only, cause of separation from [the] Church'; they moved among their parishioners, not as ambassadors of God but 'as heedless as if they had been in a market'. And not only were their lives unworthy of their high calling, but their preaching was also ineffectual: Harris asked, 'How many scores of parishes may you go to, and not find one man as much as reformed, much less inwardly changed by all the preaching; and yet the cry is, "What need is there that you should go about?"' He concluded with the cry, 'Shall I see this dreadful evil and not speak? ... While I see the country dead in sin I must speak out; and let those that are resolved to oppose look to themselves lest they be found fighting against God.'

After this apologia, Harris proceeded to answer the questions which David Lloyd had sent him. He began by conceding that a divine commission was indeed 'absolutely necessary', but a human commission, while necessary to administer the Sacraments, was not 'absolutely necessary towards preaching and exhorting and opening the Scriptures'. In this he was following much the same line of defence as Wesley, who also defended the custom of lay-preaching by distinguishing between the office of priest and that of the roving evangelist, which, he believed, was sanctioned by the primitive church.[24] Wesley, however, was adamant that the Methodists did not allow 'the most ignorant' to preach on the mere whim of an 'inward call', but only authorized those whose credentials were well attested by both their spiritual experience and their ability to save souls.[25]

Again like Wesley, Harris held that in the case of lay-preaching 'necessity makes it lawful';[26] this time of spiritual crisis was not one in which the minutiae of canonical rules should be strictly applied. He claimed that it was not his intention to undermine or discredit the established system of ordaining preachers within the

Church, and reminded David Lloyd that he respected Anglican ordination sufficiently highly to have applied for it.

In response to the second question, Harris expressed his allegiance to the Church of England. He argued that, 'My refusing to accept of ordination often by the Dissenters, and offering myself so often to the Bishops, answers for me that it appears to me Episcopacy is the right form of Church Government.' During the early years of the revival he had given much thought to joining the Dissenters,[27] but fearing that such a move would isolate him from the majority of the population, and seeing that he could not fault the Articles of the Church, he finally decided to remain within its fold and attempt a reformation from within.

Lloyd's third question demanded an 'extraordinary' call to be validated by the working of miracles. This argument was a commonplace in the copious literature produced against 'enthusiasm', and had been used by Locke.[28] Harris parried this attack by claiming that a calling 'in the extraordinary way' was possible without the power of working miracles. John the Baptist was adduced as a clear example, of whom it was expressly said that he did not perform miracles.

In reply to the question whether there was ever a false teacher that did not pretend to more than ordinary holiness, Harris declared that he could not answer, as he did not know all the false teachers or what their pretences might be. Even if this assertion was correct, however, it was not a reason for neglecting the duty of aspiring to holiness. He personally did not claim more than ordinary holiness; on the contrary, he was far behind others who had set out on their spiritual pilgrimage after him.

Harris accepted that 'schism' – which he defined as 'to divide or make a rent in the Church of Christ' – was a sin.[29] However, he denied that he was himself a schismatic, nor were those serious Christians who refused to accept the Sacrament from the hands of a priestly drunkard or swearer. The schism of which he warned his hearers to beware was that which cut them off from union with Christ, and behind Harris's defence lay the assumption, latent here but patent in other evangelical writings, that in the final analysis a Christian's loyalty was not to any terrestrial church, but to the church of Christ – the invisible body of the regenerate – to whom alone the adjectives 'one, holy and catholic' should be applied.[30]

To the sixth and seventh questions, Harris replied that the father of lies is the devil, and it is the devil's children who are liars.

It was not long before Harris encountered more than verbal opposition. War with Spain had broken out in 1739, and in the atmosphere of wartime hysteria – intensified by fears of a French invasion, Roman Catholic infiltration and Jacobite rising – Harris found himself under close scrutiny from the magistrates, often egged on by local clergymen. While the Conventicle Act stood on the statute book, apparently outlawing religious assemblies and condemning field-preaching, it was not surprising that the Methodists should lay themselves open to legal attack. They could have covered themselves under the terms of the Toleration Act,[31] but at the cost of registering their meetings and preachers as Nonconformists, a step which they were as yet reluctant to take.

On 11 February 1740, Harris was arrested in the parish of Cemais, Montgomeryshire, following a meeting in which he had been the preacher;[32] he was taken before the bench and found himself being questioned by three men – two Justices and a clergyman.[33] It was suggested that he was a Papist, though, paradoxically, he was also accused of being a mixture of Presbyterian and Quaker, and thus identified with Protestant opponents of the Church. He retorted by insisting that he had never spoken a word against the Articles of the Church, to which he devoutly subscribed; he also roundly denied the clergyman's charge that he was bringing about a schism and driving people mad. When told that his activities were contrary to law, he claimed that he was not in breach of the Conventicle Act[34] and that enquiries had been made in London as to the legality of his actions, which had cleared him of any unlawful activity.[35] Earlier attempts by some of the clergy in Breconshire to secure a warrant from a judge in order to ensure his arrest had been overturned by the judge when Marmaduke Gwynne of Garth[36] had explained the circumstances to him.

Here again time was given to an examination of Harris's view of his own personal holiness, and he defended himself by declaring that he did not pretend 'to holiness above others'. He solemnly avowed his loyalty to both Protestantism and the Hanoverian dynasty, and when the bench remarked that all his work could none the less be some form of disguise, Harris countered by claiming that for the past four years he had been itinerating with no ill consequences, and would continue until convinced that his work was illegal. If the court, in the King's name, commanded him to give up itinerating, he would be willing to obey, but this was more than the Justices were prepared to do, and they declined to issue such a command. However, enquiries were to be made in order to determine whether Harris had violated the law; if it was found that an offence had indeed been committed, he would have to pay a fine of £20. In conclusion, the Justice told Harris that he considered him sadly deluded, but undoubtedly sincere.

Later in the same year, returning home from north Wales, Harris had a further encounter with a clergyman[37] at Llanbrynmair in Montgomeryshire. When told that the people did not want to hear his exhortations, Harris replied that such an attitude was ample proof that they were in need of being exhorted. He brushed aside the parson's claim that he was better qualified for the task since he had been educated at Oxford: 'I said I was there', he wrote, 'but that was no help to me unless I should have God's spirit to enlighten me.'[38] He was then charged with running down the clergy and described as a wolf in sheep's clothing, but notwithstanding he went on to speak to those who had gathered to hear him.

In January 1741, while on his way to Bala, Merioneth, with Jenkin Morgan, one of Griffith Jones's itinerant teachers,[39] Harris was confronted by a local clergyman, Robert Jones of Llanycil, who, with his brother, had summoned the men of the parish to Llanycil that morning to waylay Harris and prevent him from preaching.[40] When they had all gathered, they marched under the leadership of the clergyman, 'like an army', into town. On their way they met their adversaries and, according to Harris, Robert Jones took advantage of the opportunity to challenge them.

> He asked me what was my name. I said 'My name is Harris'. He then said – what did I come this way for? I said 'to exhort the people'. He asked who gave me authority. I said I hoped by the success given me it was God. He asked me in what University was I educated. I said I was entered at Oxford. He asked 'In what colledge [sic]?' I said in St. Mary Hall. He told me not to discourse in that Parish ... I said I was

a member of the Established Church and if he pleased to come and hear, if I should say anything contrary to the Articles of our Church, he was welcome to hinder me. He then called me a 'Rascal' – looking angry and rising [sic] his staff – 'Scoundrel' or some such despicable name. I then replied he was welcome to call me what he pleased, that I had learnt not to revile again, but that I would pray for him. He said, 'So you ought'. I then rode away with Bro. Jenkin Morgan singing the hymn – 'Shall I for fear of feeble men' &c.[41]

There is ample evidence in Harris's writings to show the general clerical consensus on Methodist preachers and preaching. Their opposition was, as a rule, principled: very few opposed the new movement purely as a form of amusement. Clearly, most of the clergy regarded Harris's work, and that of other Methodist preachers and exhorters, as a challenge to their professional status. As beneficed priests of a Church by law established, they had been ordained by a bishop and appointed to care for the souls within their parishes, with the exception, possibly, of a few misguided Dissenters. They did not anticipate external interference with their pastoral work, save by the lawfully constituted ecclesiastical authorities; neither should there be any challenge from the laity within the parish, whose duty was to listen and obey.

Harris and the Methodists, by their intrusion into the parish community, appeared to invade the clerical office. The clergy demanded, therefore, to be told by what authority the Methodists acted, being unordained and formally untrained for the work they had undertaken. Uncommissioned by any congregation or church, they had simply announced themselves to be preachers and exhorters without any independent, extrinsic evaluation of their abilities to perform such awesome and momentous responsibilities.

When dealing with the question of qualifications, it is interesting that Harris frequently claimed to have been to Oxford. By implication he seems to have recognized a need for external qualifications to corroborate the 'inward call', though in his view the primary validation rested on authentic spiritual experiences and God-given ability to convert others. Nevertheless, Harris felt the need to fall back on the reputation of Oxford University to justify himself, though fully aware that his stay there was so brief as to be totally insignificant. He had received no training for the work he had undertaken, and his only justification for preaching and exhorting was that he believed that he had been called by God. The clergy had no way of determining the genuine nature of that call. What was to prevent madmen or impostors from making the same claim? Harris could offer as proof of his calling the remarkable success which he enjoyed, but this was no proof at all to the clergyman, to whom the effects of his ministry seemed not admirable but deeply suspect.

From their own pastoral perspectives, the clergy believed that Harris's actions led to fanaticism, enthusiasm and hypocrisy in himself and his auditors. Pryce Davies, John Tilsley, John Owen and the bench at Cemais all expressed the fear that Harris unbalanced his hearers, led them astray and even drove some mad. His extremism appeared mysteriously contagious; enthusiasm was a collective as well as an individual malady; ignorant people were easily led to adopt his views and follow his example. Unwilling to accept Harris's claim to an 'inward call' as genuine, the clergy quickly concluded that the phenomenon which the Methodists claimed to be a reformation or revival, was perhaps the work of the devil.

Underlying the fear of Methodism was the belief that Harris was guilty of 'enthusiasm', which implied a misguided belief in a personal revelation from God.[42] As Harris could not validate his revelation by visible or logical proof, he was regarded as a false prophet.[43] Underlying this fear of enthusiasm and fanaticism was the memory of the Civil War of the previous century during which many enthusiasts had claimed themselves to be prophets and messengers, in possession of a special revelation and a particularly close communion with God: their misconception of inspiration was responsible for the execution of the king and undermining of law and order.

The intrusion of itinerant preachers and exhorters into the parish was regarded as a threat to social order as well as to the Established Church – not surprisingly since early eighteenth-century Welsh rural society was relatively static, and the movement of population and the workforce less noticeable than in the period of heavy industrialization that followed. The peace of the parish was of great significance to the inhabitants who felt territorial loyalty to the legally defined space in which they lived and to which they belonged. The parish clergyman was a figure of stature, with official status as *ex officio* chairman of the vestry: he did not take kindly to itinerant Methodist teachers who undermined his authority, whether by attacks on 'blind guides' and 'hireling shepherds', or by teaching a version of Protestantism which diverged sharply from his own. The itinerants encouraged his parishioners to look for guidance outside the parish; they split the unity and homogeneity of the parish as a social and spiritual unit. Their practice of open-air preaching compromised the claim of the parish churches to be the acknowledged House of God. John Tilsley's views were representative of many others when he complained that Harris, in ascending his 'unhallowed rostrums in the highways and in the open fields', and asserting 'that every place, suppose a dunghill or a stable, is equally consecrate with the Church for the service of God', could have no other design in mind but 'to trample upon the sacred altar and to unravel the whole Scripture concerning the publick [*sic*] places of divine worship'.[44] John Owen went so far as to declare that Harris was 'an enemy to God, and to the Church and to all mankind',[45] while David Lloyd insinuated that he was a schismatic who by his actions did great harm to the Church. The magistrates at Cemais concurred.

Harris was also accused of undermining the doctrines of the Church and of bypassing her liturgy. Extempore prayers 'with repetitions, tautologies, &c' were, according to Pryce Davies, a 'heavy crime'. John Tilsley condemned his 'rigid way of exhorting' and his 'pouring out of the vials of God's wrath' through extempore effusions. This, he believed, led not only to others becoming schismatics and deserting the Church but also to some being reduced 'to a state of despair with little hopes of mercy'.

Harris emphatically denied that he was guilty of schism or of preaching false doctrine. He claimed that he had never preached anything contrary to the Articles of the Church and invited Robert Jones of Llanycil 'to come and hear'. In fact, he regarded himself as a defender of the doctrines of the Church who subscribed to her reformed formularies *ex animo*; he accused the clergy themselves of having forsaken the traditional beliefs.[46] The essence of a true church lay far more in the purity of her teachings than in a prickly devotion to the rules of church order, which were always subordinate to the work of saving souls, which was the primary function of the Church. The contrary view was well expressed by David Lloyd, who wrote, 'Irregular motions lead to confusion. God is a God of order, not of confusion.'[47] In this perspective, doctrine and order were inseparable. Methodist irregularity might achieve spectacular results of a kind, but at the expense of that order which held the Church together as a visible society, and without which it could not long continue.

In conclusion, it must be admitted that the clergy's fears were, from their point of view, reasonable. Fanaticism and enthusiasm, as opposed to healthy zeal, are rarely constructive, and it could be argued that their fear of the harm being done to the Church was fully justified by later events in Wales when the dramatic increase in the numbers of Dissenters led to the disestablishment of the Church. On the other hand, Harris and the Methodists also had a powerful case. Had the Church been capable of responding to the spiritual needs of the people, and had the clergy performed their duties more faithfully and diligently, the need for itinerant lay preachers and exhorters might never have arisen. Methodism filled a felt need: a sense of spiritual vacuum. Given the fact that the Church failed to respond in a positive way, and given the determination of the Methodists to put the salvation of souls before the preservation of the external structures of the Church, the conflict was unavoidable. It is noticeable that, where the local clergy accepted the Methodist priority of salvation over structure and truth over tradition, the representatives of the two camps were able to cohabit and co-operate. Where these priorities were not recognized, there was often tension, misunderstanding and opposition.

The clergy were not alone in their attempts to curb the growth of the new movement. In many areas the gentry, landowners and magistrates stood with them, for they also came to regard Methodism as a threat. The 1740s was a period of acute political tension, and private meetings and itinerants were viewed with deep suspicion; the possibility of covert political activities taking place under the guise of religion aroused deep feelings of anxiety, especially since the Jacobite cause was so closely linked with Rome in the popular mind. It was widely rumoured that the Methodists were Jacobite agents or Jesuits in disguise travelling the country, mobilizing their supporters in meetings behind closed doors.[48]

As Harris travelled around, it was natural that he, above all other Welsh Methodists, should be suspected of subversive activities. In Montgomery in 1740, a rumour was circulating that he was in league with the Spaniards, preparing men in order to help them with their invasion, and that a £40 reward had been offered for his capture.[49] As he travelled through north Wales, again in 1740, he recorded in his Diary:

> towards Llanymowddwy [sic]. I was hooted along as I went by, the children and others crying and running after me, 'Down with the Rumps' &c ... when I came near the Church there was a Crowd of grown Persons and Boys met together. As soon as I came to sight they hallow'd 'Down with the Rumps' &c – and got the Dogs together to run them att us.[50]

The familiar Tory election cry, 'Down with the Rump', served well to express the popular political affiliation, and to suggest that Harris and the Methodists were rebels similar to those who had beheaded the king a century earlier.

Harris combated these misconceptions by publicly emphasizing his loyalty to Church and Crown. In May 1741, his 'heart drawn out for the King and for Liberty',[51] he was led to pray 'for the King and the Royal Family'.[52] Again in April 1744, he was praying for the king and the nation, but against the French,[53] while in 1745 he spoke in his sermon 'of our present danger and approaching tryal from the Pretender'.[54] This included 'shewing King George is our lawful king' and warning that if the people turned to the Papist Pretender, they left 'the Light and Truth and the Lord', and as a result could not be saved. At an Association meeting at Erwood on 3 October 1745, the 'present tryal' was discussed by the exhorters. Harris 'opened and showed how King George is our only lawful King', and all present, he wrote, 'were loyal'.[55]

Even when the true nature of the Methodist activities was understood, the gentry still found cause for concern in their fear that their social position would be undermined by the work of 'hedge preachers': like the clergy, they too were accustomed to the exercise of a paternalist authority in their locality. The invasion of their territory by outsiders threatened their position, especially when an itinerant preacher such as Harris, who delighted in criticizing genteel iniquity, pronounced them reprobates in front of their tenantry.

The Methodist teaching on conversion implied that a peasant could be regarded as saved while the landowner was lost. Thus, by creating a 'spiritual' difference between the social classes, based not on wealth or lineage but on the individual's relationship to God, a gulf could be opened between the different ranks of society with the result that the labourers or tenants could regard themselves as spiritually and morally superior to the gentry. Harris's preaching was certainly calculated to instil this belief. At Monmouth about twelve months after he had appeared in court there, he described how he

> went with Bro. Seward on the Table in the publick street before the Hall windows where the Gent [the Duke of Beaufort] dined and began with a Hymn before Sermon. Began on – 'if you have the Son, you have Life &c.' By and by, they sent the Drum out to beat by our sides – I felt power now home and the Lord did now exalt my voice and enabled me to bear my testimony home against their Balls – Plays – assemblies – Horse Races – Whoredoms – Drunkenness &c – that these sins did draw a Curse on our heads – asking who will go to Hell for you? There will be no Grandeur or Liverymen in the last day when all, rich and poor, shall stand naked before God.[56]

Not all the gentry were opposed to the Revival. Some were indifferent; others were themselves converted, with the result that they took a keen and protective interest in Harris's activities. Marmaduke Gwynne of Garth was one notable example: in 1737 he had set out to silence Harris while he was preaching in the Llangamarch district, was converted through his ministry, and thereafter became a staunch supporter of the Methodist cause and its defender when they found themselves threatened by the law.

Robert Jones[57] of Fonmon Castle in Glamorgan was another supporter who always welcomed Harris to his house. It is said[58] that he also went out with the intention of persecuting him but was converted through what he heard. According to Henry Davies, the Independent minister, he became 'truly inclin'd to piety, and very loving to assist that come together [sic] to keep Religious Societies',[59] but he preferred Wesley's Arminian doctrines and entertained both John and Charles at his home.[60] He died in 1742 at the age of thirty-six, and in his death Welsh Methodism lost a valuable benefactor.

Such protectors were the exception rather than the rule. Many of the gentry not only opposed the revival but also persecuted the Methodists with surprising ferocity and attempted to silence them through intimidation and prosecution in the courts. Harris himself stood before a bench on several occasions. His first appearance at Monmouth followed his arrest on 15 June 1739[61] at Pontypool, where Capel Hanbury,[62] the owner of the local ironworks, read the Riot Act at one of his open-air meetings.[63] As the first prosecution of a Methodist itinerant preacher, it was widely regarded as a test case which the Methodists and their supporters could not afford to lose. If Harris had been either fined or imprisoned, many other cases would in all probability have come to the courts, the persecutors spurred into action by the success at Monmouth. The effort to secure his release was, however, effective; the case was dismissed.

It was seven months later, during February 1740, that Harris appeared before the bench at Cemais. In October of the same year he was in court at Presteigne in Radnorshire following a scuffle in the parish of Llandeglau.[64] He wrote in his Diary: 'they lay, I hear, many things to my charge – vizt, drawing people idle, making Disturbance, Riots and all the ill behaviour of the people they would lay on me.'[65] The formal charge was one of riotous assault, and due to the seriousness of the offence, the case was referred to the next Quarter Sessions.

The hearing took place on 14 January 1741 at Knighton. Harris derived great comfort from hearing that Marmaduke Gwynne had arrived there to support him, and sought his advice. He was instructed to find himself an attorney, but flatly refused, saying that he did not need the help of the ungodly. The charge was read,

> that we, (9 of us) came to Llandegle by force of arms and did beat, wound and abuse William John (Mr. Burton's man who had the blow from Thomas Jones) and broke the Peace &c in a riotous manner so that his life was despair'd of &c.[66]

An examination of the accused followed and, in response to his testimony, the court declared that they found great difficulty in understanding how Harris could claim that he had entered Llandeglau peaceably. Did not his conduct disturb the peace, and disturb the Church of England by drawing people away from her? Harris explained that he had never preached during the time of church services nor attempted to draw people from them; he himself was an Anglican, and was not only a regular communicant, but had applied for ordination on four occasions. Even though he had been refused he was still unwilling to become a licensed Dissenting preacher; he was determined to remain faithful to the Established Church.

He defended himself vigorously; he had not struck anyone or contributed to the affray. However, if the bench believed him to be in any way guilty, he publicly asked their pardon; but despite his plea, it was announced that the case could not proceed as the prosecutor was absent. Thomas Jones, who admitted that he had delivered the blow, came forward and said that he had approached the victim and that they had now come to an understanding. The case was then adjourned until the following morning.

Harris was advised by his friends to bring the issue to a speedy conclusion by pleading guilty, but this he was unwilling to do; he claimed that it was not right to 'ask pardon when [he] had not offended'. 'Then again', he reasoned, 'if I would plead "not guilty" then I must go and try it [at] another Quarter Session or High Session.'[67] Marmaduke Gwynne believed that, though he had been wronged, God would justify him, and a lawyer whom Harris consulted was of a similar opinion. At the end of the day, when all the other cases had been heard, Harris decided to submit: 'we agreed to pay 11/6d a piece and 6d fine.'

Though these were the only cases in which Harris stood as a defendant, there were others in which he was indirectly involved, for example the cases of Morgan Hughes, an exhorter, who was imprisoned in Cardigan in 1743, and Lewis Evan, imprisoned at Dolgellau in 1746. In assisting them, Harris was convinced (probably erroneously) that neither his own nor the other Methodists' actions were in any way illegal and that the laws concerning religious meetings and preaching were aimed at those who were not members of the Church of England. This belief originated in the advice that was given him by Andrew Gifford, the Baptist minister at London, prior to the dismissal of his case at Monmouth in 1739, when he had reported that he had 'been with Counsel and some of the most Judicious too' and that they had assured him that 'it does not appear that you have broke any law'.[68] When the case was dismissed, it had served not only to confirm Harris's belief that he had not acted illegally but also that it was actually legal for an Anglican to preach and conduct religious meetings. At Knighton, however, the charge against him was not that he had been preaching or conducting illegal religious meetings, but rather that he had been involved in an affray. There his argument concerning the legality of his activities was not relevant.

Some of the Breconshire gentry attempted to curb Harris's activities by applying to a judge for a court order. In their presentment they stated that there were

> several ... illegal Field and other meetings of persons styl'd Methodists, whose preachers pretend to expound the Holy Scriptures by virtue of Inspiration, by which means they collect together great numbers of disorderly persons, very much endangering the peace of our Sovereign Lord the King: which proceedings, unless timely suppressed, may endanger the Peace of the Kingdom in general.

Their fear was that the Methodists

> very much confound and disorder the minds of great numbers of His Majesty's good subjects, which in time may prove of dangerous tendency, even to the confusion of our Established Religion and consequently the overthrowing [of] our good government, both in Church and State.[69]

As plaintiffs, they named the houses of John Watkins in the parish of Bronllys and 'Howell Harris in Trevecka in the parish of Talgarth ... as places entertaining and encouraging such dangerous assemblies' and begged the judge, if the authority of the court was not sufficient to halt this subversive activity, to apply to some 'Superior Authority'. This attempt to suppress the Revival was again to fail; nothing came of the presentment.

The provocative nature of Methodist preaching made it likely that ineffectual legal checks would be supplemented by others. There were several ways of counter-attack open to the gentry who wished to preserve their parish from Methodist contamination. Some punished their tenants by eviction,[70] or dismissal. Sir Watkin Williams Wynne, Member of Parliament for Denbighshire,[71] continuously harassed Methodists in his area throughout the 1740s, and was, in Harris's view, finally punished by Providence when he was killed in a riding accident in 1749.[72]

These were more violent and unofficial forms of local control. Another well-tried method was raising 'the mob' against the interloping preacher. Some of these were hired by the gentry or clergy, bribed with beer or money, but not all mobs were composed of mercenaries: the Methodist collision with popular culture – its critique of local recreations and customs – roused a good deal of plebeian support behind gentry-inspired mobs.

Much interest has been generated in the 'mob' as a social phenomenon, its actions, leaders, members and techniques.[73] According to Wesley, the mob comprised of 'many of the baser sort', but in his *Brief Account of a Trial at Gloucester* he noted that they were 'privately encouraged by some of higher rank'.[74] This was certainly Harris's experience. While at Machynlleth, Montgomeryshire, in February 1740, he was set upon by a mob, having been previously threatened at Bala in Merioneth where, he said, a gun had been shot twice by his side.[75] On Thursday 14 February, on his way home, he came to Machynlleth where four friends had arranged for him to preach from a loft door opening on to the street. After taking up his position, he began his sermon, but claimed that 'they were so enraged, they would not hear'.[76] The leaders were evidently local notables: 'a minister (Mr. Griffiths of Penegoes – a Dissenter's son from Cardiganshire) and an attorney, Lewis Hughes, and a Gent, Mr. Thomas Owens, seemed to be set on fire of Hell [sic] by Satan.' Most of the other mobs that Harris faced also had their leaders and seem to have been far more organized in their activities than has been previously supposed: premeditation rather than spontaneity characterizes most such disturbances. At Newport, Monmouthshire, on 9 September 1740, the mob was stirred up by 'one James Pettingall',[77] while at Monmouth two days later 'many Gent' were among the leaders. At Bala on 11 February 1741, the mob was led, as has been already noted, by Robert Jones, a clergyman who had supplied 'a Barrel of Drink' in order to secure the support of his followers.

Under their local leaders, the mobs set out to harass the Methodists. They nearly always began by shouting abuse which was intended not only to frighten the preacher but also to prevent him from being heard. At Machynlleth, Harris found that, when he began his sermon, he was competing with the minister and the attorney, both 'roaring' and 'threatening'. At

Newport, the crowd not only 'hallow'd and cry'd' but were 'lifting up their hats', while at Monmouth, the gentry sent out a drummer to stand beside the preacher to make him inaudible. At Bala, some were laughing, others shouted abuse while others again 'hallow'd "Down with the Rumps"'. Diversionary tactics were often used: at Swindon on 25 June 1741, they 'did ring a Bell all the while – blow a Horn – Hallow'd – played att Cudgels'.[78] A horn was also used at Cemais when Harris was arrested, the intention being to show disapproval of the preacher and his message, and communal resentment at the fact that he had dared come to their parish.

Coupled with intimidating noise was a display of threatening behaviour. When the disturbance began at Newport under the leadership of James Pettingall, according to Harris, he 'made to us as to drag us down – but he could not come near us'. As the crowd increased in size, 'they raged and came near us – crying out ... and aiming to reach Bro. Seward and me but could not yet come near us.' As he preached, 'they kept the greater noise still and raged more horribly and drew nearer most violently.' At Monmouth, 'one came up to drag us down and lay hold of my arm, but the Lord found means of stopping him among themselves', and when a drunkard appeared 'the Lord stirred up some among them to hinder him.' When he arrived in Bala in 1741, Harris found a man approaching him wielding 'a great stick in his hand, rising it on the man of the house' who was desperately trying to calm the people. When Harris later retired to a house to preach, 'one broke the glass in the window with a staff', and the building was surrounded by shouting, threatening, unruly people who called on Harris to come out to face them. They smashed all the windows and climbed on to the roof to taunt and threaten those who were inside.

A similar pattern was seen at Machynlleth. When Harris left the upper room from which he had attempted to preach, he was escorted by friends 'to a private room', which was immediately surrounded by the mob. 'They came about the window then roared again', he wrote, and as he attempted to leave he was again abused, 'they in ridicule calling me "Parson"' (a sneering reference to his usurpaticn of the clerical role), so that he was forced to seek refuge yet again.

Threats not infrequently led to assaults upon the person. It was a common occurrence for missiles to be thrown at the preacher, as at Machynlleth where 'the mob enrag'd, and did fling stones, earth and old bones'. At Bala, dirt was thrown, while at Newport it was apples, dirt and stones. When Harris and Seward reached Caerleon after leaving Newport, the same pattern was again followed: 'they began to roar most horribly... they did pelter us with dung and dirt and some with eggs, and threw dirt in our faces and hallow'd home so as to drown my voice.'[79] At Monmouth, the crowd attacked with apples, pears, stones, dirt and a dead dog, while at Swindon they not only threw eggs and 'dust', but also used a 'Water Engine' to drench the preacher and his companions 'with water for near 2 hours till our shirts were all wet'. The mob then 'poured the stinking water of the Ditch on us till we were all mud and dirt'.[80]

Physical attacks were not uncommon, as at Newport when the mob 'came with double fury... stirring up each other to the utmost rage', tearing the sleeves from Harris's coat and stealing his peruke. He also received 'a great Blow' on his forehead 'which caused a rising and some little blood', and at Caerleon he said that Seward was 'knocked by an apple in his eye most furiously'.[81] During the attack at Machynlleth, he wrote: 'I went out intending to go away but in the Crowd I found my Life in danger, expecting to be stabbed privately in the Crowd, having already [had] two private kicks.' He retreated indoors and bolted the door. When he finally managed to reach his horse, stones were flung at him as he rode away.

The worst physical attack took place at Bala in 1741, when the house was surrounded by the crowd. After some time, Harris was persuaded by a constable to come out, his safe passage through the furious mob being guaranteed. He was, however, immediately set upon in the street by a woman who took hold of a handkerchief tied around his neck; another delivered a 'great Blow' to his ear. Harris attempted to turn back to seek refuge in the house, but there was no escape.

> They came about me like Bees... they ran after me and the rest [of the hearers] and we judged it best to run for our lives, they running (many scores of men, women and children with staves and stones with unutterable fury followed us) as fast as they could. [They] gave me several blows with all their might on my back and on my head till I could hardly see with my eyes – another struck me on my eye furiously –

some with great stones and some with their great sticks – I running for my life – expecting to be slain.

Then, one assailant struck him to the ground and, according to Harris, 'they came about me with their sticks, going to lay on me to kill me. I told them, "O! don't kill me" ... then I had help to resolve to dye [sic] and to commit my Soul to God in Christ.'

Threats from firearms, usually intended to frighten rather than injure the victim, were a common occurrence. When a gentleman rushed up to the upper room from which Harris was preaching at Machynlleth, he held a pistol in his hand and, as he entered, fired a shot. At Swindon, Harris claimed that 'they shot from 2 Blunderbuss [sic]' and 'from a Musket, about 12 or 15 times each over our heads'.

Incidents like these were intended to instil into the victim the fear that he was in imminent danger of life and limb from a crowd that appeared largely out of control and baying for blood. However, this was probably an illusion, more often than not, for the activity of the 'mob' was governed by unspoken conventions of behaviour – what E. P. Thompson termed 'the moral economy' of the crowd.[82] Mobs usually knew how far they were prepared to go: they did not, whatever impression they gave, usually intend more than a ritualized degradation and humiliation of their victim. Fatalities occurred only when the control occasionally broke down or a sudden and unexpected accident happened.[83] The shootings that took place during the attacks on Harris suggest the restraints of this 'moral economy'; notwithstanding all the shots fired at him, he was not hit once; even the blunderbusses at Swindon missed their mark. Though brutal, mob violence seems to have been regulated by those who led the crowds, and who decided what form the ill-treatment of the victim should take and when it should begin and end. The Newport mob was led by James Pettingall, and, although Harris's coat was torn and his peruke stolen, the only injury that he suffered was a blow to his head. At Monmouth, he and Seward were approached by one who intended to drag them down, but he was restrained by his own companions. When a local drunkard appeared, he also was prevented from interrupting. Later in the day, they were to be abused by the same crowd, but harassment was always collective, rather than individual. Mobbing was a group activity and the safety of the individual from possible future prosecution lay in the fact that he was an anonymous member of a large group.

It must be admitted, however, that there was often an element of hooliganism in the activities of the mob. Many undoubtedly joined the demonstration purely for the pleasure of being part of a disturbance and seeing the humiliation of another person. Mobbing was a convenient outlet for tensions and emotions and gave the participant a feeling of importance in that he or she was allowed to voice an opinion.

At Machynlleth Harris had been forced to retire 'to a private room', and on attempting to reach his horse was pushed back by the crowd. Afraid that he was about to be murdered, he asked for peace in the King's name and announced that he was willing to leave the town. Immediately, one of his persecutors assured him that he would not be harmed, while another attempted to calm the crowd by reminding them that Harris was 'a fellow creature'. This sudden change of attitude suggests that the mob's activities had succeeded in reaching their goal: the leaders had effectively shown Harris that the people of Machynlleth did not approve of his arrival in their town, or accept the message that he had attempted to preach to them. The victory was theirs and Harris had been taught a lesson.

Lastly, when Harris appeared from the besieged house at Bala he was chased along the road and finally caught. After beating him violently, his pursuers 'reasoned among themselves and said "Don't kill him – he shant be killed"'. They asked him whether he had any intention of returning to their town. Harris replied that he had not, and was then allowed to leave. Here again, the mob believed it had reached its objective in wringing from Harris the admission that the Methodists were not welcome in Bala.

To some extent popular hostility to Harris and his allies reflected the desire of parishioners to please their social superiors and show the quasi-feudal deference expected of tenants to landlords. But plebeian opposition had other roots too. There was a strong sense of outraged territorialism against 'intruders' who violated the cultural space of the parish. Thus Harris was asked at Swindon, 'Why don't you stay in your own parish?' Some feared that interloping preachers – who seldom had visible means of support – might try to gain a legal settlement in the parish and come on to the poor rate.

Methodism also had socially divisive effects on parish life which were often feared. Its teaching of conversion disrupted family life, dividing 'father against son and son against father'. Evangelical piety emphasized the separation of sheep from goats, the spiritual from the carnal, and so split the parish into discordant halves. Sons and daughters began obeying Methodist exhorters instead of their parents. Wives were said to squander their husbands' earnings by contributing their housekeeping money towards the upkeep of itinerating mountebanks. Methodists were therefore regarded as a threat to the stability of the family and to the authority of the husband or father. The mob, thus, often saw itself as the defender of traditional family ties.[84]

The religious basis for opposing the Methodists was closely tied to the popular attitude towards the Church of England. The vast majority of the population regarded themselves as members of the Church even though their attendance at worship might be lax, and many saw it as their duty to defend the Church when threatened. Methodism seemed designed to wean villagers away from the religion of their ancestors. The Swindon mob, according to Harris, had 'heard [that] we came to bring some new Religion, and to deny them Baptism, to [baptismally] plunge them'.[85] John Evans,[86] later to become a Methodist preacher, noted how at Bala in 1741 the parson had sent for the parishioners in order 'to defend the Church', and on his arrival in the town 'called on all those that loved the Church to come to defend her ... On hearing this, many townfolk came and joined his army.'[87]

There were other reasons for mob disturbance as Methodism continued to spread. Several trades lost money through the new habits of sobriety which it inculcated. Innkeepers protested that their trade was being hampered through the conversion of their customers. Thus, in February 1740, Harris received 'a message from the woman of the Ale House of Cwmteuddwr [Radnorshire]', asking him not to go there 'to spoil her sport' and charging him with 'being a Traytor to the King and in correspondence with the King of Spain'.[88]

This threat to popular leisure activities aroused much resentment. The Methodists, it was said, did not allow people to enjoy themselves or spend their money in the tavern. Fiddlers and other musicians realized that, if Methodism flourished in their parish, their employment would cease. Harris regarded dancing as evil and said that it was 'worshipping the devil';[89] he often spoke and preached against it and thus became unpopular among those who enjoyed an occasional dance. Cock fights and races, fairs and wakes were also criticized by him;[90] all were very popular recreations.[91]

Attempts were made to ridicule Methodism and its leaders, and some anti-Methodist literature was published, either in Wales or by Welshmen. A brief sample will suffice. As Harris and the other preachers travelled the country, local poets began composing derogatory ballads and songs,[92] and through these some of the accusations made against the itinerant preachers have been preserved. For example, in a poem written by Harry Parry[93] from Montgomeryshire, the doctrine of regeneration is ridiculed and the Methodists accused of being self-righteous and condemnatory 'false prophets', 'Dissenters' and 'rebels'. The poet says that he would never listen to them:

> Nid a Harri Parri pêr, i wrando
> Ar Roundiaid na Chwacer,
> Y dynion sydd o dan y sêr,
> Yn peidio dweud eu Pader.[94]

In an *anterliwt*,[95] written by William Roberts of Llannor[96] and published in 1745, not only are Harris, Rowland and Jenkin Morgan among the list of characters, but they are also accompanied by 'Chwitffild' – George Whitefield. Here Harris is accused of blasphemy, hypocrisy and preaching false doctrine; the poet encourages women to draw near him – perhaps suggesting, by innuendo, that Harris was using society meetings to seduce the women who attended.

Another poet, Ned Lloyd, composed a poem about Harris's visit to Bala and Llanuwchllyn. Although called an 'elegy' in its title, it is rather a bugle call to draw the Churchmen of the area together to drive out the 'round-heads', 'Shenkun' [Jenkin Morgan] and 'Harish' [Howell Harris]. If the brave men of the neighbourhood failed to drive them out, the Justices of the Peace would use the power of the law to send them on their way.[97]

During wartime, mobbing as a means of persecution was occasionally augmented by a more legal form of violence: the press gang. In time of national emergency, those without visible means of support, vagrants and vagabonds, were eligible to be pressed, and since many Methodist itinerants seemed not to have regular employment, 'the press' proved to be a serious threat. Two exhorters, Jenkin Morgan and Richard Tibbott, were arrested in north Wales in 1742 and escorted back to the south by constables.[98] Later, towards the mid-1740s, the classification of vagrants and vagabonds became useful to gentry who were opposed to Methodism since, as magistrates, they were able to issue warrants for the arrest of troublesome preachers. Hugh Griffiths of Aberdaron in Caernarfonshire was arrested early in the 1740s but managed to escape to Anglesey, and, in May 1744, James Ingram, Howell Harris's assistant, was taken. He was held briefly in the cells at Brecon while Harris endeavoured to secure his release, with the assistance of Marmaduke Gwynne, James Erskine[99] and the Countess of Huntingdon.[100] At the same time, another exhorter, Roger Williams, was pressed and, although Ingram was finally released, Williams wrote to Harris in September 1745 giving an account of his experiences as a soldier at Gloucester.[101]

These developments in the persecution of itinerants soon had a depressing effect on the exhorters. Richard Tibbott wrote in his diary on 16 April 1744 that he feared the press gang,[102] and in May two brothers, Thomas and Edward Bowen, wrote to Harris explaining that the reason for their absence from the Association was fear of meeting the press gang on their way there.[103] In July 1745 the Association at Glyn received letters from both Tibbott and John Richard expressing their concern at the possibility of being pressed as they conducted their itinerant ministries, and asking whether the time had not come for them to take out a licence as Dissenting preachers. It was decided that the exhorters should not be allowed to take advantage of the provisions of the Toleration Act.[104] This confirmed an earlier decision taken at Abergorlech in May 1745 when 'there were Press Warrants out ... We examined each other about our willingness to go to the war and each was willing.'[105] Exhorters were not to seek refuge by becoming Dissenters; if sent by Providence to war, it was their duty to serve.

Harris himself often worried about the activities of the press gangs. In June 1739 he wrote in his Diary, 'Today I heard that if

I had staid [sic] in Cardiff Thursday night I should be press'd next morning, that some were actually in the house where I was, looking for me to that purpose.'[106] Soon there were rumours circulating that he actually had been pressed. On 19 June, he received a letter from James Erskine giving an account of how he had heard that Harris had been taken.[107] In fact, Harris was never pressed; perhaps it was due to the influence of people like Marmaduke Gwynne, James Erskine and the Countess of Huntingdon that the effort to use the press gangs to persecute the Methodists was thwarted.

The opposition to Methodism in Wales seems to have been strongest during the first ten years of the revival, between 1735 and 1745. The Methodists' courage and perseverance proved stronger than many of their opposers expected, and as the 'new sect' held its ground in the face of adversity, the opposition lost its momentum and weakened. The intention had been to stop the spread of Methodism before it gained a foothold in the various parishes; in this the opposition failed, and the Methodist message took root in the hearts of many ordinary folk. Persecution served only to give the society members a sense of unity which otherwise would have been more difficult to achieve: under attack, they drew closer together, nurturing in each other a spirit and a faith capable of withstanding the hardships which opposition entailed.

During 1739 Harris declared that it was an honour to suffer for what he believed. He wrote in his Diary: 'O! how sweet it is to suffer persecutions for our Dear Lord. I could count it now Joy to have my name set at nought for my Master's sake.'[108] Later, in 1744, while in Monmouthshire, he heard that he had been indicted and was to be prosecuted for conducting illegal religious meetings at his home at Trevecka; but, he claimed,

> in hearing this, the Lord made good His promise and was present indeed with me and I was made to rejoice with being made willing to give up the house and all I had to Him, thanking God that He had counted me worthy to be first indicted [at Monmouth in 1739].[109]

He often expressed a sense of honour when persecuted and was filled with joy in that he 'was thought worthy to be ridiculed for Christ's sake'.[110] In 1742, he not only 'rejoyced for the honour of suffering for Christ', but also 'thought of going to prison sweet beyond expression'.[111]

He firmly believed that all opposition and persecution was the work of Satan. At an Association meeting at Glanyrafon-ddu in 1744, he told the exhorters that Satan was 'trying all means to hinder this work by the mob, gentry and clergy'.[112] On his way to Machynlleth in 1740, he observed that 'hitherto Satan [had] been let loose a little',[113] but when he entered the town, the people seemed to him 'to be set on fire of Hell [sic]'. Such opposition was to be expected: 'Satan is offended att every new step we take in God's way', he wrote, 'being willing we should go on in the old [preaching] Rounds and not advance on. But when we advance one fresh step on, then he rages in us, opposing, and in all his servants.'[114] He was a formidable enemy, a threat to the individual and to the Revival in general, and much feared. Harris recorded that, even in the safety of his home, 'One night, the Lord suffered one's coming to the House to be a means of frightening me, as believing it either the noise of a thief or of the Devil.'[115]

Satan could not persecute without first being allowed to do so by God, and God allowed His people to undergo such trials in order to lead them to a stricter discipline. Persecution was 'a father's rod to Scourge Pride and bring them down';[116] when the sleeves of his coat were torn off at Newport, Harris said that it had been done 'justly for my Pride in my cloaths'.[117] Again, while being opposed by a gentleman in Pembrokeshire in 1743, Harris commented that he 'could not help admiring the many ways and means God makes use of, to reach and humble and empty' him, and to make him realize his unworthiness of receiving the least of His mercies.[118] But, having said this, Harris also believed that it was possible for him to bring persecution upon himself; following the disturbance at Machynlleth in 1740, he came to the conclusion that the attack had taken place due to his own failure to 'seek the Lord' before delivering his sermon. It was a judgement on his own pride in regarding himself capable of preaching without God's assistance.

Persecution was also regarded by Harris as a means, in the hand of God, to separate the sheep from the goats within the Methodist fold. While staying in Montgomeryshire in 1740, he wrote, 'discous'd att Lodge [Llandinam] ... shewing the great good of Persecution to Saints and Hypocrites, it being to winnow'.[119] Though these words were written before he had experienced the violent attacks at Bala and Machynlleth, his belief remained unchanged eight years later. Again in Montgomeryshire, he wrote: 'as to this storm of Persecution, because it tries the Hearts of many, I can't help blessing God for it – 'tis God's fan to winnow.'[120]

The numerous accounts of persecution entered into the Diary confirm that he was convinced that God was in control of each situation. In March 1739, at Caerleon, although '3 clergyman came there to persecute, God did wonderfully send them away',[121] and, as the mob threw stones and earth at him at Machynlleth, he said that 'the Lord did not suffer one' to touch him.[122] Later, while making his escape 'thro' the middle of them', 'the Lord saved me and none touched me'. His horse, though tired after a long journey, was providentially enabled to gallop away. Thus, it was through divine intervention that he was able to escape; the friends whom he left behind to face the hostile crowd were also saved in a similar manner. At Newport[123] the mob threw apples, stones and dirt, 'but God did not see fit to let them strike me but once on my forehead'. At Bala, 'the Lord did rise one of the most violent' to defend him, and also saved Jenkin Morgan in such a way that Harris commented that 'never did the Providence of God appear more visibly'.[124] But though Harris believed that God could, and did, intervene to deliver him and others from the hands of His enemies, he did not expect Him to perform miracles in order to save them. While on his way to Llandyfaelog, Carmarthenshire, in March 1740, he heard that he was to meet 'great opposition', and that a cock fight had been arranged, and guns obtained, to create a disturbance. He admitted that he 'felt nature to fail, but I was taught one lesson – viz. that we are not to expect God to come to help us but in a rational manner'.[125]

When he and other Methodists were attacked, little effort was made to retaliate. William Seward, referring to the disturbance at Newport at which he was present, wrote in a letter to *The Christian's Amusement*: 'We had Christian friends enough out of the country to over-power the Mob if they had been so minded; but we charged them not to resist, but to return blessing for cursing, which accordingly they did.'[126] It was, therefore, a matter of policy that they be prepared to suffer, for the Methodists believed that they did not suffer for their own sakes but for the sake of the Christ who had forewarned his followers that persecution would come. When the mob, again at Newport, advanced towards the Methodists who had come there to listen, Harris told them 'not to lift up a hand or make any opposition, but to suffer calmly'.[127] Retaliation was avoided not only because it would lead to a mêlée but also because of the Scriptural command that Christians were to love their enemies. God had saved them from the wrath to come but called upon them to suffer for His sake. Many Methodists would have been prepared, in the face of persecution, to repeat Seward's words, 'Better endure this than Hell.'[128]

Since Harris and the other itinerants proclaimed themselves to be messengers sent by God, they came to regard opposition as directed not against them but against God Himself. At Bristol on 31 May 1744, Harris wrote:

> when I see wise men, great men, and many too, against us, I am wonderfully animated by seeing we and this work are of God and that He is on our side, nay, that all the opposition is against Him. Therefore, His superior Wisdom and Power shall, after all the opposition, prevail and be glorify'd.[129]

His belief remained unchanged six years later when he wrote: 'I feel God is on my side and all the opposition against me is against the Lord and I see all conquered and I pity the opposers.'[130] By that time, however, his opposers were the other Methodists who objected to both his doctrines and his conduct, but Harris was convinced that God was with him as he separated himself from their 'carnal' views. Opposition to Harris was construed as a rebellion against God; it was a sin, whether it came from outside or inside the Methodist camp. Harris expressed this belief even more clearly when he wrote: '[I] saw myself a beloved child of God and a favourite, and so favoured that none could go against me without going against the Lord too.'[131]

This view of persecution was developed further to include the belief that when the persecutor opposed the Methodists he was liable to be struck by providential judgements. Harris heard in July 1739 that, when Jenkin Morgan was arrested in Montgomeryshire, 'a mare to the Persecutor, about the time of his being taken, dy'd, and another persecutor in New Town [sic] giving money to the Mob was taken ill.'[132] In the same area, claimed Harris, 'when I was there last, after I had been that moment to warn them – the feast day – 2 horses dy'd, att which the fiddler ran away and the Dance broke up in a confusion ... Thus the enemies of the Lord are scattered.'[133] In his sermon at Bala in 1741, when the mob was attacking the house in which the meeting was held, Harris explained to his congregation 'that a time is coming on when all as persecute now shall be called to an account by Christ Himself' and declared that God was with them, 'a wall of fire'.[134] When the account of the events of that day later appeared in his autobiography, it was accompanied by a lengthy footnote containing 'a true account given by men of veracity, of the Judgement of God upon some of the most cruel persecutors at that time'. One of the most violent 'fell from his horse, and broke his back, and died'. Another collapsed and died, while a third again fell from his horse, 'fractured his skull, and instantly died'.[135] Several others also met their end in similar terrifying circumstances.

Time and tradition have heightened the popular belief that the Methodist leaders were all superhuman men of iron will and constitution, who stood before multitudes of violent persecutors without any fear or doubt. But a study of the writings of such men reveals that such scenes belong only to the realms of imagination. Howell Harris was never without fear, and part of his greatness lies in the fact that he disciplined himself to venture out to face his persecutors in the name of God.

The ill-treatment he suffered at Bala and Machynlleth engendered within him a great fear of returning to either of the two towns, or even to the whole of north Wales,[136] and his unwillingness to go there did not pass unnoticed by some of his contemporaries. Daniel Rowland 'checked' him for his lack of faith, and asked what had become of his assurance.[137] Harris was ashamed, but in his view, mankind could hardly sink lower than the 'brutes' of the north,[138] and it was indicative of Christ's greatness that His rule extended over such people. On 3 February 1742 he wrote: 'Christ has overcomed [sic] all the Devils and Sin and Death and reigns above and has all under Him. He rules Bala People and the North Wales Lyons. He over-rules all the wars. He has all power given to Him.'[139] Yet, 'on thinking of North Wales', he wrote in January 1743, 'I felt I could not go there';[140] when it was reported at an Association meeting during July that 'the Door is open'd in Anglesey, Merioneth and

Caernarfonshires', he still felt that he had 'not yet [been] freed from fear to go'. It was therefore decided that Daniel Rowland should undertake the journey in his stead.[141]

At an Association meeting at Trevecka in November 1746, Harris encouraged the exhorters 'to undertake a battle with the North Wales Devil'.[142] In 1747, he reluctantly directed his steps towards Bala, but not before making a will and ensuring that all his affairs were in order.[143] As he set out on his journey he earnestly believed that he was going to his death, expecting 'to be murthered'.[144] Even in 1751, after he had been to Bala and returned home safely, he again wrote in his Diary, 'I am going to sure death in the North.'[145]

His resolve to master his fear of travelling through north Wales and to visit those places where he was once persecuted remained undiminished until he had succeeded. As a result, he was able to announce during a visit to Caernarfonshire in 1749 that

> all opposition is come to the ground in South Wales and must come here ... there is no law against us ... the Pretender is conquered and King George reigns ... it has been openly proved ... there is no law against our going to exhort people to repent.[146]

He therefore set out to exhort and to build up the societies. As early as 1741, he had recognized that facing persecution would be an integral part of that process but believed that there were distinct advantages in having to undergo severe trials. Through persecution, he wrote,

> 1. we are tried to see what is in us ...
> 2. we come to have more pity to others.
> 3. we come to rely more on Christ.
> 4. we come to be more earnest in Prayer, more diligent in self-examination.
> 5. By tryals we come to know our heart's deceit and helplessness.
> 6. ... we come to be poor in spirit and ... strengthen our selves ... in the Grace that is in Christ.
> 7. It brings us out of our selves to Christ ... all persecutors are God's dogs.
> 8. it makes way to have more Joy, Comfort and enjoyment of God than ever – the spirit of Glory shall then rest upon us in particular.
> 9. this makes room too for the strength of Christ in us.[147]

Persecution could therefore be regarded as a blessing in disguise. Being by his own confession weak and fearful, Harris was to experience that inner strength that he attributed to the workings of God's spirit in his soul. He persevered through all the opposition that he encountered; he was abused, criticized, prosecuted, persecuted, beaten and kicked, but his constant testimony was that God gave him strength, to exhort and preach, both in the north and in the south. It was due to his valiant efforts, and those of others like him, that yet another opposer was able to comment at the beginning of the following century, 'North Wales is now as Methodistical as South Wales, and South Wales as Hell.'[148]

Chapter 7
Controversy and Division

Howell Harris first met Daniel Rowland during the summer of 1737. After hearing him preach at Defynnog, and witnessing the power and authority with which he spoke and the effect of his words upon his congregation, Harris declared that a friendship began which was to last to all eternity.[1] Years of co-operation followed as the Methodist movement expanded, but by the end of the 1740s the relationship between them had deteriorated to such an extent that they were unable to continue working together. In 1750 they finally parted, and Welsh Methodists were forced to decide which of the two commanded their allegiance and was to be recognized as their leader.

The result was a divided movement; two parties were formed – 'Harris's people' and 'Rowland's people'.[2] Both claimed to be the sole representative of the true spirit of Methodism and, through their respective Association meetings, to have authority over the exhorters and societies. In the confusion that ensued,[3] individuals and societies aligned themselves with whichever leader they held to be representative of their own beliefs and interests, and the inevitable polarization of opinions led to much tension and ill-feeling. Some opted to secede from the movement and join the Dissenters,[4] while others were lost to various denominations and sects.[5] David Jones, an exhorter from Pembrokeshire, joined the Baptists, while John Sparks, of the same county, went to the Moravians.[6] Thomas Bowen, of Builth, opted for independence from all parties, and such was his influence that he was able to take several of the Breconshire societies and group them together to form an independent body.[7] John and James Relly,[8] in association with John Harris of St Kenox, established their own sect, but James, having become a universalist during the 1750s, later migrated to London, where he further promulgated his views.

The most significant outcome of the division was Harris's early retirement from public life. Following an unsuccessful attempt to rally his supporters, he realized that events had slipped beyond his control and that he did not command the allegiance of the majority. Unwilling to submit to his clerical adversaries, he retired to Trevecka with a small number of supporters to establish a religious community.[9] His withdrawal from the Revival was total, and it was not until 1762 that he was persuaded to return.[10]

The erosion of the relationship between Harris and Rowland has yet to be satisfactorily explained. Given the fact that it was Harris who was mainly responsible for the organization of Welsh Methodism, and bearing in mind that he had devoted himself to the task of expanding the movement, how was it possible for him, within a period of fifteen years, not only to put Methodism on a firm foundation, but also to bring all that he had achieved to the brink of destruction?

The Roots of Controversy

It has been suggested that the initial co-operation between Harris and Rowland was possible only because they were so heavily involved in activities in their respective areas.[11] This is to imply that they were incompatible from the beginning, but were denied the opportunity to realize that fact through not being in constant fellowship. Certainly, working independently allowed both men freedom to operate as they wished, while working together would of necessity have involved a close scrutiny of each other's ideas and actions, a process which would have resulted in a certain amount of friction. But this does not mean that co-operation was impossible, and in order to understand the evolution of the separation it is necessary to differentiate between the temporary friction resulting from such close co-operation and the more deep-rooted differences which were responsible for the breach.

Because of a lack of source materials, it is extremely difficult to obtain a clear picture of Rowland's character; even so, there is little doubt that he was as stubborn and determined as was Harris. Both possessed an indomitable will and explosive tempers.[12] They were also young and inexperienced: in 1740, Rowland was only twenty-seven; Harris was twenty-six.

The Diaries make possible a far more detailed assessment of

Harris's character. He was a severe person, with little humour;[13] as early as 1737, John Games, the music teacher, observed that he had 'no feeling in the least with bad Parsons and light people'.[14] He believed that as he was involved in 'soul's work, eternity work and God's work', there should be no levity. 'There is', he said, 'no jesting with God.'[15] On more than one occasion he rebuked Rowland for his 'lightness',[16] and this lack of humour, coupled with his strong convictions and fiery zeal, gave the impression of an overcritical attitude evinced by excessive harshness. On different occasions, he was accused of being 'selfish and proud',[17] of possessing 'a spirit of contradiction',[18] and of being 'too censorious'.[19] As the pressure of the work mounted and the situation within the Welsh Methodist camp became more tense, these deficiencies in his character became more evident. Harris defended himself by saying, 'What they think is harshness in me is not my sin or anger, but my created nature, a rough voice and a rough appearance is created to me – my soul is love [and] I speak in love.'[20]

Others could only judge by what they heard and saw.[21] Morgan John Lewis,[22] speaking on behalf of the exhorters, said that Harris 'imposed on them and kept them in bondage',[23] while a certain Sister Jeffreys in London told him that his 'common character' was that he 'wanted to rule and to be heard'.[24] It is also significant that he was known as 'the Bishop' in London in 1743–4, and as 'Pope' in Bristol in 1747.[25]

Whitefield also recognized in Harris what he described as a 'desire for power'.[26] In part, this probably stemmed from Harris's obsession with the fact that he was the first of the Methodist leaders to be called by God; he described himself as 'the first of all the Brethren'[27] and 'the first to sound the Trumpet about the Country'.[28] Unable to claim the overall leadership of the movement owing to his unordained status, he stressed his precedence in time, especially after 1745, to secure for himself a prominent position among the other, mostly clerical, leaders.[29] Always intent on proving himself a helmsman of the movement, he often did so through displays of stubbornness, an autocratic manner and criticism of others.[30] Though it could be argued that firmness was necessary to ensure tight discipline within the societies, it was generally accepted by the late 1740s that he was overbearing and dictatorial.[31]

In comparison, the early years of the Revival were happy ones for Rowland and Harris. After their first meeting, while the former confined himself, for the most part, to the Llangeitho area, the latter began his itinerant ministry in earnest. By 1739 they had between them established over thirty societies in south Wales,[32] and the steady growth of the movement revealed a need for better organization. The responsibility for this fell on both men for, through their powerful preaching and their claim to precedence, they were recognized as the natural leaders.

Meeting occasionally as they did, they knew little of each other's faults and weaknesses; Rowland was a 'Valiant Champion of the Lord'[33] and a 'laborious minister of Christ'.[34] They found that they were in agreement on most relevant issues[35] and, of all the brethren, Harris felt 'the closest love to Bro. Rowland'.[36] He would not allow anyone to speak ill of him, and protested to Griffith Jones when he heard that he had been critical of Rowland's conduct.[37] Harris admitted that he was not without fault, and prayed, 'As for dear, dear Rowland, oh! set him free from all chains, slavish fear, self, darkness, rashness, and imprudences, and everything that may keep him from honouring Thee.'[38] Such sentiments were typical of the relationship between them throughout 1740 and 1741 and, when they met at Llanddewibrefi in Cardiganshire in December,[39] there was nothing to indicate that anything but the closest co-operation would follow in 1742.[40]

The first meeting of the new year was a happy one. On 7 January, four ordained ministers and eighteen exhorters met at Dugoedydd, near Cil-y-Cwm in Carmarthenshire.[41] Harris felt such union as he had 'never felt with any before' and, remembering his previous disappointments with the Society of Ministers at Glyn, believed that his prayers had at last been answered.[42] From Dugoedydd he travelled to Llangeitho, where he enjoyed more of Rowland's company in 'pleasant conversation', and on 10 January he wrote that the union between himself and 'the associate Brethren' was deeper than ever before.[43] But two days later, as he prayed for Rowland, he wrote, 'O Lord, destroy his lightness and unbelief and make him to shine in Grace.'[44]

There is nothing in the Diary to indicate what Harris had in mind as he offered this prayer. In an entry three days previously he noted that he felt a strong cry within him 'for the Lambs that are scattered around the Country having no Shepherd (being now turned away by Bro. Rowland)'.[45] This was a reference to Rowland's reluctance to allow visiting Methodists to communicate at Llangeitho, presumably because of his fear of the ecclesiastical authorities, but it is difficult to see how this could be construed as evidence of 'unbelief'.

At another Association held at Glanyrafon-ddu Ganol, Talyllychau, on 17 March, a controversy erupted between them concerning the nature of God's covenant. Rowland argued that the covenant was made between God and Man, while Harris held that it was between God and His Son, as Man's representative.[46] This was their first public disagreement, and Harris later regretted contradicting Rowland in the presence of others.[47] Such was the intensity of the confrontation, that he wrote that he would have been 'pleased to divide from [Rowland] without any consideration of the consequences to others'. He retired full of anger and admitted that the love he had once felt towards Rowland had now totally evaporated.

When the Association reconvened on the following morning at Llwyn-y-berllan, the tension continued; Harris was rebuked for wasting time in writing his Diaries, and Rowland raised difficulties concerning the rules of procedure.[48] Prayer, repentance and tears led to reconciliation, but then another argument arose, this time concerning assurance.

Harris believed that assurance was essential to salvation, while Rowland argued that it was possible for a believer to be in Christ without being fully assured of the fact. Harris wrote:

> Some were for me, and some for him, and some were confounded. I . . . said I could not join in Society with him nor invite him to us because we could not build up the same people. What I was afraid in him was his feeding hypocrites and what he feared in me was my overthrowing weak ones.[49]

Harris was here at variance with his own experience;[50] from 1736 to 1739 he lacked the subjective assurance which he now demanded of others. But by 1742, having overcome his former doubts, he had adopted the view that lack of assurance – the positive conviction of forgiveness of sin and salvation – evinced the absence of true faith.[51] Assurance therefore belonged to the essence of faith, a view shared by Wesley following his Aldersgate experience in 1738.[52] In a letter dated 1745,[53] Wesley claimed that 'it cannot be ... that a man should be filled with this peace, and joy and love by the inspiration of the Holy Spirit without perceiving it as clearly as he does the light of the sun'; this, he said, was 'the main doctrine of the Methodists ... the substance of what we all preach', and it was his firm belief that 'none is a true Christian till he experiences it'.

This doctrine was rooted in the teachings of the Reformation, and both Calvin and Luther held that personal assurance was an essential component of saving faith.[54] By the time of the Westminster Assembly (1643), the Calvinists had adopted a more moderate view, which recognized that those who possessed real faith could frequently be oppressed by doubts and not always sensible of the assurance of salvation.[55] However, Puritans of all parties were united in their belief that the witness of the Spirit was primarily 'that we are the children of God',[56] and it was this which Wesley and Harris were at pains to stress. In both his sermons on 'The witness of the Spirit' (1746, 1767),[57] Wesley declared that 'the testimony of the Spirit is an inward impression on the soul, whereby the Spirit of God directly witnesses to my spirit, that I am a child of God', and, although twenty years separated their publication, he saw no reason to retract his words when the second sermon appeared in 1767. However, by 1768 he had slightly modified his position and, like the early Reformers, had reconsidered because of pragmatic considerations.[58] He wrote:

> I do not affirm, there are no exceptions to this general rule. Possibly some may be in the favour of God, and yet go mourning all the day long. But I believe this is usually owing either to disorder of body or ignorance of the gospel promises.[59]

Lack of assurance did not, therefore, invariably evince the absence of justifying faith, and Wesley no longer regarded 'a consciousness of acceptance to be essential',[60] but he maintained that, under normal circumstances, a consciousness of being in the favour of God – which he admitted could be weakened, even interrupted, by the return of doubt or fear – was the common privilege of Christians.

Whitefield had exercised caution in expressing a view on this subject as early as 1741. Having previously regarded assurance as essential to saving faith, he wrote:

As for assurance, I cannot but think, all who are truly converted must know that there was a time in which they closed with Christ. But then, as so many have died only with a humble hope, and have been under doubts and fears, though they could not be looked upon as Christians, I am less positive than once I was, lest haply I should condemn some of God's dear children.[61]

Rowland objected to Harris's views at Glanyrafon-ddu and Llwyn-y-berllan because he believed, like most later Evangelical clergymen – including Whitefield and Wesley – that although assurance was desirable, it was not always in evidence among those who possessed weak faith. Harris remained adamant that such an approach was unscriptural, but within two years he also had reconsidered and moderated his view. When Cennick claimed at the Tabernacle that 'no faith is without assurance', Harris approached him to challenge his teaching.[62]

Disappointed that the unity of the Association at Llwyn-y-berllan had been disrupted, Harris again felt like 'giving up all'. In a dejected mood he made another attempt to persuade the exhorters to accept his point of view and, when opposed, threatened to leave, believing they would submit rather than risk losing him. The following morning, the exhorters, in response to his intransigence, expressed a willingness to go on without him and, realizing that he was in danger of being ostracized by his own movement, Harris accepted that he would have to apologize to Rowland. Following an emotional plea for forgiveness, the tension again eased; the two men retired to discuss their differences, and agreed on a statement of the doctrine: 'that when the man is effectually called – he knows he has something but does not know 'tis justification or faith by name 'till he hears it explained'.[63]

Harris realized that things had gone too far at this Association,[64] but was convinced that Rowland was wrong 'when he [was] dabling [sic] so much with saying we may be in Christ and not know it'.[65] He was also uneasy about other aspects of his conduct, and during April noted the reasons for his dissatisfaction:

1. . . . he is not clear about assurance.
2. can't admit mixed communion.
3. does not walk close enough [to God].[66]

Co-operation continued, however, and on 23 May Harris called at Llangeitho and stayed the night at Rowland's house. Despite their differences, they were apparently still able to plan for the future, but a fortnight later the situation had again deteriorated. Rowland had now been critical of Harris's conduct and had announced that he would not be attending an Association meeting at Trevecka on 10 June.[67] This was probably because he had heard of Harris's comments following his last visit to Breconshire; on 27 April Thomas Price of Watford,[68] one of Rowland's closest friends, had written to Harris accusing him of possessing an imperious spirit and rebuking him for saying that he had not benefited from listening to Rowland preaching any more than if a ballad had been read.[69]

Since 1739, the year of his first visit to London, Harris had been a regular visitor to the capital. During the autumn of 1742 he was there again, assisting John Cennick[70] at the Tabernacle while Whitefield was in Scotland.[71] By this time, his visits to England were beginning to irritate Rowland; they had become annual events, lasting for weeks, sometimes for months.[72] In October, he wrote to Harris and pleaded for his return home.

> Don't you hear, all the brethren in Wales crying out loudly, Help! help! help! help! Brother Harris, thou bold champion, where art thou? What, in London now in the day of battle! What, has not London champions enough to fight for her? Where are the great Wesleys, and Cennick? Must poor Wales afford assistance to England? Oh, poor Wales![73]

By the end of the year, the discord of the earlier Association meetings appeared, for the time being, forgotten. Harris again visited Llangeitho during December, and as he listened to Rowland preach he was aware of the influence of the Spirit upon him. The conversation between them was also edifying as they talked of the London brethren and the future of the societies in Wales, and Harris noted that neither he nor Rowland could do without the other.[74]

From Llangeitho, Harris wrote to Whitefield to confirm the arrangements for his visit to Wales for the Association meeting at Watford in the new year. His letter reflects his harmonious relationship with Rowland.

This day, I heard Dear Bro. Rowland, and such a sight mine eyes never saw. I can send you no true idea thereof. Such light and Power there was in the congregation as can't be expressed ... I believe that we shall have a joyful Meeting. I trust we are all of one Mind.[75]

It has been suggested that Whitefield was invited to the Association, and to a position of leadership among the Welsh, because Rowland and Harris were unwilling to allow each other to become the outright leader of the movement;[76] his presence also reinforced Harris's vulnerable position as a layman, threatened by the Methodist clergymen, who because of their higher social standing commanded greater influence among the converts.[77] It must be borne in mind, however, that Rowland had, in his letter to London three months earlier, expressed his profound need for Harris's co-operation in the work; had he wished to assume control of Welsh Methodism, Harris's absence in England would have been propitious. Moreover, it is likely that Harris's invitation to Whitefield was motivated, not by a desire to hinder Rowland, but by a belief that Whitefield would bring prestige to the movement. The entries in his Diaries suggest that he profoundly admired Whitefield's power and now wished to harness his vigour to the Association by making him its Moderator.[78] If parochial duties and family ties prevented Rowland from conducting an itinerant ministry, and if he was unwilling to take his position as a national leader seriously,[79] and if Harris, because of his unordained status, felt himself lacking in the outward authority necessary to lead the Methodist clergy, it was natural for him to look for the most suitably qualified man to fill the position. Whitefield would then have been a reasonable choice.

It is highly unlikely that Whitefield would have allowed himself to be used to prop up Harris's position. The fact that Harris was given the position of 'General Visitor' at Watford, and 'Superintendent' a few months later,[80] does not necessarily suggest a conspiracy, but probably reflects his qualifications for the post. He was unordained, free from parochial responsibilities, unmarried, a keen traveller and willing to undertake the hardships of the itinerant's life. He was the obvious, perhaps the only, candidate.

The absence of tension between Harris and Rowland during

1743 has led to further suggestions that Whitefield acted as a buffer between them,[81] a view which presupposes that their relationship was marred by continual animosity. However, Harris's references to Rowland during this period show little ill-feeling; on the contrary, Rowland is seen as an extremely powerful preacher, intellectually enlightened and spiritually gifted.[82] It appears, therefore, that the disagreements of 1742 had not permanently weakened the bond of friendship that existed between them. Although there had been quarrels and misunderstandings, they had been the result of rash words and differences of opinion rather than deep-rooted divisions. Close co-operation had led to the friction that is often experienced by those working within the same organization.

Nevertheless, Harris's Diaries offer ample proof that changes were taking place during 1744 that were to contribute to the heightening of tension between himself and Rowland. These affected two aspects of his work – his teaching concerning the Person of Christ, and his view of his role within the Methodist movement. Though they may not at once have been apparent to his contemporaries, Harris's honesty in his self-revelation betrays beyond doubt that they were taking place.

Most other Methodist leaders in both England and Wales were Anglican clergymen who, through their ordination, had been invested with a form of authority which had been denied to Harris. However, Harris was able to claim for himself a place among the leaders; it was through him, although he was a layman, that the Revival had begun.[83] Periodically, he found it necessary to remind himself and others of this fact,[84] and, after the establishment of the Association meetings and his appointment as 'General Visitor'[85] in January 1743, he soon became aware of the 'high place' he occupied within the organization.[86] Taking upon himself the care of Whitefield's London Tabernacle in 1745[87] further added to his responsibilities, and intensified his belief that he was especially blessed of God and an important figure among the Methodists. But as his responsibilities increased so also did the number of references to his position, and, while it would be possible to overlook occasional allusions to his high status, the number of instances of Harris giving praise to God for elevating him suggest that, even by the end of 1744, he was becoming obsessed with the idea. This may have been due to

Harris's belief that, having been opposed and vilified for many years, his efforts were at last being rewarded; he was suddenly in the forefront of a national, even international, movement.[88]

During the same period, changes were taking place in his theology. Since 1738, he had emphasized the atoning death of Christ as the means of salvation; this was not only a fundamental Christian doctrine but also part of his own conversion experience, to see 'Christ bleeding on the Cross'.[89] But in 1739, when he first visited London, he came into contact with the Moravian Brethren;[90] he was deeply impressed with the warmth of their piety and the apparent strength of their faith.[91]

Care must be taken, however, not to exaggerate Harris's admiration of the Brethren. Though he could write in 1741 that he saw much of the power of godliness among them, this was 'notwithstanding their Errors',[92] and in 1742, having noted their simplicity and willingness to be sacrificed in the service of God, he admitted that he could not find the Lord among them.[93] His admiration was therefore intertwined with criticism of what he believed to be their shortcomings, and throughout the 1740s he denounced various aspects of their teachings.[94] In December 1745 he condemned their practice of preaching but one message – the Person of Christ – and their 'implied' doctrine that there were no degrees of faith;[95] he also rejected their belief in universal salvation and claimed that there was 'somewhat very human and bad in their discipline and way'. 'They don't feed the weak', he complained, 'nor preach the Law for convictions [of sin], and also their cunning I think is not right.'[96] Yet, he held that they were a true branch of the Church, 'more erroneous in expression than in meaning'.[97] He claimed that he loved them for their knowledge of the Saviour; whatever deficiencies were to be found in their doctrine, he held that they loved God 'and set Christ as the foundation'. He was therefore willing to defend those aspects of their doctrine which were acceptable to him, but it was unfortunate that his defence coincided with an increase of opposition to Moravianism, and with the 'Sifting Time', a period during which the continental Brethren sentimentalized their beliefs, yielded themselves to many antinomian excesses and overemphasized the 'blood and wounds' theology.[98]

While in London during December 1744, Harris was dissatisfied with Cennick's teachings at the Tabernacle, in particular with his declarations that 'no faith is without assurance' and 'that the Law and graces are to have no place at all, that there is no duty nor wants, but to believe'.[99] Having by this time moderated his own views on assurance, and perturbed by Cennick's antinomian tendencies,[100] Harris decided to approach him, but, in response to his criticism, Cennick declared that Harris knew only the baptism of John and was like Apollos, who needed to be taught 'privately' the ways of God. He also claimed triumphantly that he was 'in liberty and walked in God's will and conversed with Christ continually and was always happy, and had power over every sin'.[101]

A few hours later, Harris attended a Moravian 'Letter Day',[102] in which correspondents related their 'experiences of the Blood of Christ', and, as he listened, he considered that they had advanced much further than himself in the life of faith. Still remembering his earlier confrontation with Cennick, he concluded that the spiritual benefits others had experienced from the knowledge and application of the 'Blood' was wanting in his own life and, as it was this that gave the Moravians their strength, he believed that a clearer emphasis should be put on that doctrine.

This was a turning-point, not only for Harris, but for Welsh Methodism in general. His preaching of the 'Blood', his defence of various aspects of Moravianism and his use of their terminology led many to suspect that he had become one of them.[103] This Harris denied; he argued that he had not adopted any of their teachings, and that the suffering and death of Christ and the significance of the Blood had been part of his message years before he knew the other Methodists.[104] He admitted that he had failed to see it in a 'clear light' until 1744, and that the Moravians had been used by God to enlighten him,[105] but his debt to them went no further. This may well have been true. Though he made extensive use of Moravian terms and phrases during the latter half of the 1740s, it does not seem that he was tempted to join them. He continued to be as critical of many of their teachings and practices as he had ever been.

However, the sudden emergence of the 'Blood' as the main theme in his preaching was so dramatic that it could not fail to arouse suspicion that he had been influenced by the Moravians during his visits to London. He now claimed that his eyes were constantly kept on the Blood of Christ, and that he was made to love all who preached it.[106] He could no longer bear to be 'unwashed in the Blood of the Lamb', and he 'had faith to set [himself] in Christ's wounds'.[107] But, in his eagerness to explore and expound the significance of Christ's death, Harris was soon to find himself in difficulties with the doctrine of the Trinity, and, as the Church had already witnessed a Trinitarian controversy earlier in the century following the publication of Samuel Clarke's *Scripture Doctrine of the Trinity* (1712),[108] Harris's failure to present a clear statement of the doctrine was to lead to accusations of unorthodoxy.[109]

The doctrine of the Trinity has always teemed with difficulties and has been a constant subject of debate since New Testament times. The Council of Nicaea in the fourth century asserted the consubstantiality of the Son with the Father, while it was left to the later Council of Constantinople to assert the deity of the Holy Spirit. As to the interrelation of the three, the church professed that the Son was generated by the Father, and that the Holy Spirit proceeded from the Father and the Son.[110] These were the *opera ad intra*, works within the divine Being which did not terminate on the creature.[111] In some of his statements, Harris seems to have lost sight of these personal attributes by which the Trinity of persons were distinguished, and when he declared, as he was later to do, that all the Godhead was in Jesus, he could claim to be orthodox only if he was referring to the divine essence which belongs wholly, equally and undivided to each of the three persons within the Godhead. His critics did not believe this to be the case; they complained that his teaching was confused and suggested that both God the Father and God the Son had suffered when Jesus died on the Cross.[112]

Following his return from London, and while preaching at Erwood during January 1745, Harris referred for the first time to 'the Blood of Christ ... as the Blood of God'.[113] The use of this phrase, with its Patripassian undertones, must be viewed against the background of Harris's words during an Association meeting in London a month earlier, where he argued against the notion 'that God, who is a spirit, can bleed'.[114] As he defended the doctrine of the Trinity, he refuted the Monarchian[115] heresies by saying:

> I believe the Word made flesh means the Word manifested in the flesh, and not that the man became God [Adoptionist Monarchianism] or

God man [Patripassianism], and when His Blood is called the Blood of God it implies that 'tis the Blood of one really united to the Godhead ... I believe that He is still God and man in one Person – two natures perfectly unconfounded and yet mysteriously united – so that God is still God and the man still man, and yet the two one Person.[116]

But, however orthodox Harris's doctrine may have been at the end of 1744, his reference to 'the Blood of God' indicated that his theology was beginning to change. It was not long before he used the phrase in the presence of the exhorters, and, at a meeting at Trevecka on 16 February, he noted that he 'had more power than ever to show of the Blood of Christ ... I never had such liberty to preach Blood – Wounds – the Blood of God – Blood, Blood and Blood again.'[117]

When he and Rowland met at the end of January, Harris was careful not to draw attention to this development; he totally avoided the use of Moravian phraseology and made no reference to the 'Blood'.[118] But the rumour that there had been a significant change of emphasis in his preaching did not take long to circulate, and, when they met a month later, Rowland warned him to be more guarded in his expressions.[119] Harris accepted the admonition without protest, and during the following weeks was more restrained in his preaching.[120]

Coincident with the fresh zeal that Harris experienced in preaching the 'Blood' was a fear among the Methodist leaders that the Revival was coming to an end. Rather as Whitefield had expressed concern in 1742, that 'the awakening [seemed], in some measure, to be over',[121] so Harris believed at the beginning of 1745 that the 'power' had been lost.[122] During April he heard Rowland express concern that God seemed to be leaving the exhorters,[123] and Harris took it upon himself to warn them that they were falling from grace.[124] The fear stemmed not only from a failure to win new converts but also from the general attitude of the exhorters; by 1745, many of them had been involved in revival activity for a number of years, and were by then sufficiently mature to think and act independently of the leadership. On 30 May, Harris complained that there was 'a spirit which is not the Spirit of the Lord gone out amongst us; it has not the humility, meekness, love, forgiveness or fellow feeling of Christ, but is haughty, rash, censuring, stiff &c.'[125] Harris also believed that there was another more significant reason for the spiritual declension: something was lacking in the Revival; the preachers were omitting some important aspect of God's truth. The missing element, he declared, was the preaching of the Person and Blood of Christ, and it was because these doctrines had been neglected that the 'power' had been withdrawn.[126] He therefore set out to remedy the situation, firm in the belief that, if the 'Blood' was preached, God would return with power.

As the months went by, Harris took less heed of Rowland's warning to be more guarded in his doctrine, and in April wrote that 'the Glory of this Blood is but beginning to come in sight'.[127] He claimed that he experienced unusual freedom in speaking of it to the converts,[128] and saw 'the Blood, Wounds and Nail holes of Christ as all in all, and everything else nothing'. God, he claimed, was revealing new things to him, opening his eyes to glimpse at His greatest mysteries. Among these were

1. the Word made flesh.
2. the 3 in one.
3. the reality of the Union between us and Christ.

All three were 'summed up in viewing the Blood', 'and as we grow in faith, we see all in the Blood, and will want to hear of nothing else but that, and that alone will feed our souls'.[129] He insisted that this was not self-deception; God was removing the veil from his eyes to show him 'the reality of spiritual things'.[130] He therefore rejected as the work of his enemies any suggestion that he was unsound in doctrine,[131] and failed to appreciate that even his friends were becoming uneasy about his teachings. Rowland was soon joined by Wesley in expressing concern,[132] and, by August, Harris was aware that he was 'set forth as very black everywhere'.[133] He defended himself by claiming that he had been given 'a glympse of the great mystery of the God-man, and [of] the Blood as the Blood of God',[134] and was so confident that no one could convince him he had slipped into error. He now saw 'all Wisdom, Doctrines and Knowledge in Heaven and Earth meeting together in Christ, in His Blood and Wounds'.[135]

Having been denied ordination, Harris held fast to a belief that he had been divinely invested with patriarchal authority which was to be exercised within the societies to enforce discipline and to ensure that the work was conducted according to God's will. This was to be done in conjunction with the other, mostly clerical, leaders, but, since Rowland was reluctant to accept that he also had been placed as a 'father' among the Methodists,[136] Harris assumed it was his duty to shoulder the burden alone. During 1745 he found himself in difficulties while attempting to perform the task.

In order to overcome the 'bad spirit' which had crept into the movement, he embarked on a process of purification within the societies, by which he hoped to remove the elements which, in his opinion, hindered their progress and obstructed the free movement of the Spirit. He declared that he would expel anyone who had fallen into sin, regardless of their position or status; he claimed that it was better for the societies to be small and spiritual, rather than large and carnal.[137]

The enforcement of discipline had always been part of Harris's ministry,[138] but he now devoted himself more vigorously to the task. The Calvinists were at this time concerned at the lack of organization within their branch of the Revival,[139] and in a letter to the Tabernacle society, published in the *Weekly History*, Harris drew attention to the decay of love and general drowsiness among the professors, and to the confusion and disorder within God's house.[140] There was need for action, and Harris was convinced that the only possible remedy was a clearer proclamation of the means of salvation. His method of purifying the movement was, therefore, two-pronged: the denunciation of sin and the elevation of the 'Blood'.

His sternness while attempting to implement his plan led to widespread ill-feeling. He became increasingly critical of those around him, verbally lashing them at the least opportunity. At Llwyn-y-berllan during April, he admitted that he censured one convert for no reason at all; 'I could not help it,' he wrote, 'but was led to it'.[141] Such conduct did little to promote his popularity, but he was resolute; his aim was to ensure complete and utter submission to God's will, as he himself saw and understood it.

The exhorters were naturally open to repeated attacks, and at Association meetings Harris admitted that he was often 'cutting and searching' in his exhortations.[142] The societies were also subjected to the same treatment and severely rebuked for their lukewarmness, indifference and loss of first love.[143] Harris enjoyed 'much liberty in the reproving and awakening way', but his attempt to save the movement was in fact contributing to its destruction. Though firmly of the belief that his actions would lead the converts to aim for moral and spiritual excellence, he unfortunately failed to realize that this could not be done by creating an atmosphere of fear. Constant threats and repeated verbal attacks strained their continued loyalty; his method was undermining, rather than reinforcing, his authority.

By the end of the year, Harris's departure from orthodoxy had become common knowledge, and many were suspicious of his talk of 'Divine Blood'[144] and his emphasis on the mystery of the union of the two natures in Christ's Person. Reports were circulating that he was so engrossed in the wonders of the Incarnation that he advocated worshipping Christ as a man rather than as the Son of God, and, although these were unfounded, the rumours demonstrate how sceptical some had become about his teachings. It was probably because he realized that his doctrine was frowned upon that Harris expressed concern at the prospect of attending the first Association meeting of 1746; he suspected that he would be criticized,[145] and that Christ would be 'stabbed' among his friends.[146]

At the meeting, there was no sign of the hostility which Harris had expected. After listening to him speak, those present admitted that they had done him an injustice.

> The Brethren acknowledged their mistaking me ... in starting up carnal questions about worshipping Christ's manhood, having raised carnal ideas, as if His manhood was separated from His Godhead in suffering &c., and so not to be worshipped ... On their acknowledging their fault, I had freedom ... to speak of the Mystery of Christ and how it was first revealed to me after I had seen a veil on my Heart.[147]

Rowland was present at this meeting and heard Harris speak, and it is noteworthy that he did not take advantage of the opportunity to condemn his doctrine.

By the beginning of 1746, Harris had taken upon himself the care of Whitefield's London Tabernacle. Cennick, who had been entrusted with the responsibility following Whitefield's departure to America in August 1744, had long been attracted to the Moravians, and by the end of 1745 had become 'more of a Moravian than a Whitefieldian'.[148] It was, however, the burden of responsibility rather than party spirit that finally drove him to the Moravian camp in December. While at an Association meeting at Gloucester on 11 September, he shared with Harris the acute sense of inadequacy that he felt while attempting to fill Whitefield's place at the Tabernacle. The misbehaviour of some members had profoundly upset him and when he sought the advice of the Moravians they suggested that he should share his responsibilities with Harris.[149] When Harris arrived in London in November, he discovered that Cennick had by then decided to join the Moravians, leaving him in charge of the Tabernacle.[150] Finding himself a leader, not only among his own people but also called 'to the Head of the work in England',[151] he firmly believed that this was yet another honour bestowed upon him by God. He had been 'exalted, honoured in all Respects'.[152]

Another factor which contributed to the heightening of tension between Rowland and Harris was the latter's defence of James Beaumont.[153] A native of Radnorshire, he was initially a member of the Independent congregation at Gore but, after hearing Harris during the early years of the Revival, began to preach. At the Association meeting at Watford in 1743 he was appointed a public, or itinerant, exhorter, and it is clear from the evidence of Harris's Diaries that there was a close bond of friendship between them. In 1741 Harris admitted that he experienced warmth and light while listening to him preach,[154] and a year later reported to Whitefield that he walked 'solidly with God'.[155] This admiration led to Beaumont becoming 'like a right arm and a pillar' to Harris;[156] 'what strength and guard Bro. Beaumont is made to me', he wrote in December, 'to tell me of my faults.'[157] But, by this time, Beaumont was showing strong antinomian and Moravian tendencies,[158] and, when Harris heard him preach during March 1745, he observed that his sermon contained many 'Mysterious deep things'.[159] By the summer Harris believed that he had yielded to selfishness and pride, and in June 1746 warned him that, unless he modified his doctrine, he would 'declare against him and his mystic nonsense'.[160]

The Welsh Methodists decided in April 1746 that they should discuss Beaumont's teachings, but the occasion offered his critics an opportunity to condemn not only Beaumont's doctrine but also the activities of the Moravians.[161] They were at that time eager to secure a better foothold in Wales, particularly in

Pembrokeshire, an enterprise for which they would need additional workers. It was suspected that they were attempting to proselytize Methodist society members and exhorters,[162] and the Association was, therefore, bitterly critical of them. Harris took it upon himself to speak in their defence, but his reward was to be 'shot at, wounded and grieved'. He wrote:

> I declared my mind that I thought there was too much self and Bigotry on their [the Moravians] and our side, and that would give an advantage to Satan if we should not be humbled. [I declared] that I was as much as they against their errors ... and against their coming here to make a division ... But whilst I endeavoured to set a loving construction on the Moravians' erroneous expressions, I was judged an Antinomian, Moravian, &c.[163]

Being openly accused among his own people deeply shocked Harris; he was also shaken and saddened by Rowland's bitter opposition to the Moravians.[164] But the chief significance of this Association was that it was the turning-point in the relationship between Harris and Rowland. Until April 1746, Rowland had been remarkably reticent in his response to Harris's doctrinal anomalies; apart from the friendly caution delivered early in 1745, he had avoided confrontation and adopted a policy of restraint in the hope that Harris would reconsider the theological implications of his own statements.

At Watford, though Rowland knew Harris to be critical of some of the Moravian teachings, his defence of them at a time when they were believed to be encroaching on Welsh Methodism seems to have finally tipped the scales against him, and, though there is no evidence that Rowland took an active part in the debate, there is ample evidence that he came to the conclusion on that day that Harris was in much the same position as Cennick a few months earlier – very near entering, if not already in, the Moravian camp. It was the exhorters, rather than Rowland, who first accused Harris of unorthodoxy but, once their unease had surfaced, Rowland, as if following their lead, ceased to allow Harris the benefit of any doubt that may have remained in his mind. He realized that Harris had been exposed and that it was his duty to oppose him in order to defend Welsh Calvinistic Methodism.[165] To remain silent was impossible; the exhorters had forced his hand. Consequently, though Harris notes that he was approached on the following morning by Howell Davies and William Williams, both 'in a loving, humble and meek spirit', there is no mention of a similar approach by Rowland.[166] Where repentance and tears had dissipated tension in the past, this time it was allowed to remain.

The Great Separation

Discontent about Moravian activities continued among the Welsh Methodists notwithstanding Harris's attempts to moderate their opposition to them, but, as he laboured to dampen the nascent hostility, others seemed eager to fan the flames of strife. While Harris undertook a journey through Pembrokeshire during April 1746, Daniel Rowland and William Williams attended an Association at Caeo in Carmarthenshire where, according to the minutes, 'all [were] stirred up against the Moravian Errors'.[167] With Harris absent, Rowland was given free rein to express his opposition to their doctrines and to secure the support of a number of exhorters.

At the next quarterly Association, held at Trevecka on 27 [26] June, the differences between Harris and Rowland became apparent to all; for the first time, they publicly argued about the issues which now divided them.[168] Harris had recently returned home from London, and had heard on his way that Rowland was determined to oppose the preaching of the 'Blood', but, as he had been away for seven weeks, he had not yet been able to assess either the extent or the effect of his campaign. While in the capital, he found rumours were circulating that he was soon to join the Moravians,[169] and, when he preached at the Tabernacle on 26 May, some of the congregation were so offended by what they heard that they left.[170] As he prepared to journey home in time to attend the Association, he prayed for the success of the meeting and praised God for the forbearance and love that He had 'planted in the great Rowland'.[171] He hoped, no doubt, that Rowland's attitude had mellowed during his absence.

He was to be disappointed. Even before the meeting began, an argument erupted between them. Harris denied that he was a Moravian: not only had he opposed their doctrines in private, he had also preached against them in London. He resented the suggestion, made at Watford during April, that his doctrine had changed; it was the same now as it had been for the past nine or ten years. He held, however, that the accusations against him were an answer to prayer, that God would use some means to prevent him from being exalted in the eyes of the brethren. This was the providential way God had chosen to humble him.

Rowland was not impressed. He again accused Harris of being a Moravian, and reminded him of his use of such terms as 'the Blood', 'the Lamb' and 'worshipping that Man'. Harris riposted that he had been struck by the glory of Christ's Person before he had come into contact with the Moravians; if they preached the Mystery of Christ, he would not deny that he was in agreement with them, but that did not mean that they were the origin of his beliefs. He had received them directly from God. He went on: 'I also said that I know no God out of Christ – out of that Man – that I see (according to the measure of my faith) all the Godhead in that Man – the Father and the Son being one.'[172]

Finding the charge of Patripassianism fully justified by Harris's own words, Rowland angrily ridiculed his use of the word 'mystery'. Harris responded by explaining that the attempt to foster peace, love and moderation was central to his ministry,[173] thereby suggesting that his phraseology was designed to appeal to all the various factions within the Revival. He regarded the Moravian Brethren as a true branch of the Church, and wished them to be included within the bond of unity that he strove to secure.

Rowland rejected this approach as naive, and held that the differences between himself and Harris went much deeper. Had he not heard him preaching antinomianism? Harris challenged him to quote some of the expressions he had used and, when Rowland failed, refuted the charge; 'I do not hold one branch of it', he said, 'and declare to all, "I am no antinomian."' He warned Rowland that if he continued 'in entertaining surmises from the Enemy', he would commit all to the Lord and leave the Welsh Methodists to fend for themselves. Secretly, he saw little hope for their continued co-operation; Rowland was 'so stiff' that Harris believed only God Himself could prevent a breach.

Representatives from nine Welsh counties were present at this Association. News of any developments within the movement would, therefore, travel quickly to all parts of the country, and, as Harris joined the conference, he confessed that he was nervous owing to his fear that they would see that all was not well. Rowland, the Moderator, seemed unconcerned, and at an early stage in the proceedings criticized the exhortations given on the previous evening by Harris and others.[174]

He then invited those present to express an opinion on Harris's recent work, and some gave voice to their fear that he was leaning too heavily towards antinomianism and Moravianism. Harris was again quick to deny that his doctrine had changed, but was fiercely attacked by Rowland as a changeling, a self-contradicting liar and an antinomian. Harris realized that both his position and his ministry were now directly threatened and defended himself by emphasizing that he had received his ministry directly from God and was, therefore, answerable only to Him. Though he loved and honoured Rowland as a preacher, meeting him outside his pulpit he saw his pride and, from his 'dark, witty, cutting, carnal way of speaking', knew beyond doubt that his was not the work of the Spirit of God.

His attempt to convince the members of the Association of his innocence was unsuccessful, and they displayed their displeasure by condemning his emphasis on the 'Blood', declaring their opposition to the Patripassian heresy, and criticizing the preaching of 'mysteries' which remained unexplained. Again Harris replied: 'I had this from God and not from man, and would preach; and God would cut my way through men and devils, and if they would all stand against it, it was no more to me than to see butterflies.' In response to their denial that God had suffered on the Cross, he declared his belief that

> God did not and could not suffer, but God-man did suffer. Neither the man nor God separately but the two natures in one Person suffered. I never saw Him a man and not God too – and declared that that man is God [sic]. If I had seen Him in the Cradle, in the manger, I would have worshipped, and so the Dead Sacred Body in the Grave was in God and united to the Godhead as well as His Soul in Paradise – and this, through Grace, I would seal with my Blood.

This confrontation shows the extent to which the relationship between Harris and Rowland had indeed soured, and highlights the general belief that Harris was very nearly, if not actually, a Moravian. His confusion over the doctrine of the Person of Christ and his denial that there had been any change of emphasis in his teaching appeared to some, and to Rowland in particular, as a deliberate attempt to mislead. There seems little doubt that ostracism of Harris by the exhorters was sanctioned by Rowland, and the fierce attack upon his orthodoxy and integrity could only have been with the intention of precipitating a crisis which would permit Rowland to demote, if not remove, Harris from the leadership of the movement.

The struggle for that leadership had now begun in earnest. The following morning, before parting, the bickering continued as Harris warned Rowland against preaching 'from Books and not from the heart'. This, to an extent, summarized the nature of the tension between them; while Rowland emphasized the need for a rational understanding and presentation of the Gospel, Harris's approach had always been dominated by his enthusiastic spirit. He was suspicious of academic study as a means of ascertaining divine truths, and preferred to submit himself to the direct guidance of God's Spirit.

Less than a fortnight later, the two men met again in Carmarthenshire and, as Rowland preached, there was so much 'Power and Love and Presence of the Lord and crying out'[175] that even Harris, who had been 'despised, disparaged and trampled upon by him', was made thankful. As they travelled together to the village of Talyllychau, they openly discussed their differences, and Rowland assured Harris that he recognized that he had been called by God, but reiterated his opposition to the Moravians; he also expressed disappointment that Harris had decided to defend James Beaumont at the Association meetings. Glad that they were still able to converse, Harris hoped that the storm which had raged between them was now blowing over, but he failed to realize that, even if Rowland seemed to have mellowed, there were many others within the movement who were still suspicious of his emphasis on the 'Blood' and critical of his attitude towards the societies.

This was to become apparent to him during the autumn. Throughout August and September he was in London attending to the affairs of the Tabernacle, but during his absence alarming developments were taking place in Wales. On hearing of the fracas at Trevecka, a process of polarization had begun among the exhorters, and Harris, on his return, found that many of them had deserted him. He suspected that this was part of a conspiracy to topple him from his position of authority,[176] and at an Association meeting at Gellidochlaethe on 1 October his worst fears were confirmed. There he heard that the Methodists had decided at an earlier Association, and in his absence, that Rowland should replace him as leader and have authority over all the exhorters, including himself. This was totally unacceptable to Harris: if they believed that he would be willing to yield his position to Rowland, they were making a serious error of judgement. Passive acceptance of their decision would amount to a betrayal of the honour God had bestowed upon him, and, rather than allow himself to be dismissed in such an undignified manner, Harris again threatened to withdraw from the work and leave Wales.

Rowland was not present at this Association, but even in his absence the argument with Harris continued throughout the day. He was not only asked to explain his use of expressions such as 'the Blood' and 'the mysteries', but also to divulge the contents of his Diaries and the names of his correspondents, presumably since these would confirm that he had become a Moravian. The next morning his humiliation continued, but by then some of the exhorters had decided that the inquisition had gone too far. They began to speak in his defence, and their words, coupled with Harris's threat to retire to England, kindled a measure of sympathy towards him. Morgan John Lewis, one of the most influential exhorters, declared himself in favour of having Harris as leader of the movement, and was immediately supported by others. He was therefore reinstated, but with the recommendation that he and Rowland should meet a fortnight later to discuss their differences.[177]

The meeting took place at Watford on 16 October.[178] Feeling insecure and threatened, Harris immediately set about defending his ministry, but Rowland was now willing to admit that he had been unjust in his treatment of him, and explained that he had received some misleading letters of complaint about Harris's conduct. He was now willing to forget the whole issue, on condition that Harris denied the validity of the Moravian teachings. This Harris was willing to do; he also admitted that he was guilty of making some careless statements while preaching. This mutual confession led to a desire for reconciliation on both sides, and, grateful for the victory.they had won over Satan, Harris wrote in his Diary:

> I see by our late tryals we are led more to see each his place and to study more on Church Government. I see 'tis my place to be free and to look after the Societies I was the means of gathering together, unless they reject me. Many of the Brethren, I find, despise me more and more on my infirmities [sic] and I am enabled to commit it all to God to see to keep me in my Place and to suit me with all Grace and Gifts.[179]

Here, Harris was using the phrase 'Church Government' in its widest sense, realizing that he and Rowland needed to define more clearly their respective roles within the movement if harmony was to be fully restored. However, he was determined not to allow Rowland to gain overall control; there was to be no higher authority than his own, since he was answerable only to God, and, though aware of the rising tide of his own unpopularity among the converts, Harris did not allow this to dampen his spirit. It was, after all, God's answer to his prayer for means to keep him humble, and undoubtedly a means by which he subconsciously insulated himself from criticism.

Due to the opposition he had encountered within his own movement, Harris now saw the need to re-establish himself among the societies; this he did by emphasizing his position. During a visit to New Inn, Monmouthshire on 21 October, he was led 'to declare [his] office and place', and the Diaries during this period abound with references to the powerful and often fierce preaching which he hoped would lead the Methodists to submit to his authority. He was often led to 'thunder and cut and lash and condemn and wound and denounce woes', and was aware of the 'vast authority and Power' which accompanied his efforts. 'To thunder most dreadfully' was, to him, to recapture his 'old authority',[180] but, though it was a powerful way of convincing some and building up others, it was a technique that should have been used wisely and in moderation. The sight of a preacher thundering through his sermon may, in the short term, have been acceptable to the societies, but as time went by they soon tired of being under constant attack. Too much aggressive preaching was unlikely to win the affection of the people or increase Harris's popularity, and the Methodists soon began to complain that he had become too dogmatic and bad-tempered.[181]

After a brief lull, the tension between Harris and Rowland began mounting again. Not only did the rumours of a rift between the two leaders make it difficult for the Watford spirit of reconciliation to survive,[182] but Harris's continued fascination with his belief that he had been given a special 'glimpse' of the significance of Christ's suffering and death was also an important factor. It became his main spiritual interest and the constant theme of his conversation, and was expressed through repeated references to the 'Blood'. This suggested to his auditors that there was still little difference between his doctrine and that of the Moravians, but Harris insisted that it was of paramount importance. He wrote:

> I saw deeper into the Mystery of Christ's Blood, [and saw] how 'tis from this Blood (and not from my obedience) flows all the mercies, spiritual and temporal, that I enjoy. My inmost soul was made thankful for that Blood, crying, O! blessed Calvary, O! amazing wounds – hereby, in this Blood, I am justified – hereby, in this Blood, I am washed and am raised when I fall and am brought near to God. O! Glorious Blood, O! Mysterious Streams. O! [Lord] bring all Thy children to view these Glories.[183]

Heartened by the birth of his daughter, Anne,[184] and the dawning of a new year, Harris hoped for happier days during 1747; 'sure some great things are coming after these storms and Tryals which I trust are near over', he wrote on 8 January.[185] As he travelled around the societies, he was confident that his ministry was richly blessed and continued to emphasize the need for discipline.[186] He instructed that none were to be admitted into fellowship without the society members first consulting with the leaders;[187] 'such as would not obey should be turned out.'[188] Meanwhile, his purge of the disruptive elements continued. At an Association meeting at Little Newcastle in Pembrokeshire on 7 January, he examined and turned out 'many';[189] twelve days later, finding his teachings opposed by an exhorter at Groes-wen in Glamorgan, he 'was obliged to cut him off'.[190] The following day, at New Inn, he was again 'home about discipline', 'about their not receiving any [preachers] among them without consulting', and about his own position within the movement, announcing that he had sinned by not exerting the authority given him as a Methodist 'father', and that he now felt that it was his duty to enforce discipline as he was the 'eldest' among them – the first to be called.

Morgan John Lewis, who had defended him at Gellidochlaethe, on hearing this, raised his voice in protest. He and another exhorter objected to Harris's approach, and claimed that he imposed upon them.[191] Why, they asked, should anyone who contradicted Harris be regarded as spiritually blind or evil? When John Powell, the clergyman from Llanmartin, added his voice to the protest by accusing Harris of being prejudiced against Edmund Jones of Pontypool, the meeting deteriorated into confusion. Later, Harris claimed, they continued in a more dignified manner, discussing those aspects of the work that needed their attention, but this was no more than an attempt to paper over the cracks which had appeared. At New Inn, he had again been given another clear indication of the exhorters' feelings towards him.[192]

The responsibility for Whitefield's Tabernacle still rested with Harris, though he found it difficult to devote much time to the work in England. His responsibilities in Wales, the problems with Rowland and the birth of his daughter forced him to remain at home during much of 1746, but arrangements were made for others to minister at the Tabernacle during his absence. Thomas Adams, James Beaumont, James Relly and Herbert Jenkins took to the preaching, but neither their experience nor influence was sufficient to allow any of them to fill Whitefield's place.

Consequently Harris was in England for much of 1747,[193] and, while he maintained that his responsibilities at the Tabernacle kept him from returning to Wales, it is possible that there was also a desire to escape the swell of dissatisfaction among the Welsh Methodists. His absence naturally resulted in less friction within the movement, but this was not as a result of any change in Harris's doctrine or in his view of his own position. He still held that 'the Person that Bled was God',[194] and continued to emphasize his right to exercise total authority among the Methodists; God, Whitefield, the preachers and the people had all chosen him to oversee the work in hand.[195]

Co-operation with him had, by this time, become extremely difficult. Believing himself placed by God among the Methodist leaders, and constantly guided by Him in all matters, both spiritual and temporal, he felt little need for the advice of others. But the situation was further complicated by a development during May which Harris believed vindicated his position, and which certainly boosted his confidence. While in Montgomeryshire, he attended a society meeting at Llanfair (Caereinion?);[196] there was a 'triumphant spirit' among those present, and Harris wrote that he and others could only cry 'the Blood, the Blood, the Blood, the Blood, the Blood, the Blood for a long time', evidently overcome by some form of ecstatic excitement or hysteria. This was the first time that such an incident had occurred, and Harris interpreted it as a particular form of divine confirmation that his work – and doctrine – pleased God. Two days later a similar scene was enacted at Tyddyn, Llandinam. As Harris preached, he announced: 'I'll go out as far as I can to declare this fountain, this Blood: crying Blood, Blood, Blood, Blood, and the Spirit came down like a mighty shower.'[197]

Following these experiences, Harris reasoned that if God displayed His satisfaction with his ministry in such a convincing manner, there was no reason why he should be reticent in his dealings with those who had been critical of him in the past. He therefore became more outspoken in his own criticism of others, and even the Methodist clergy were not excepted. On 20 May Harris met William Williams of Pantycelyn at Merthyr Cynog in Breconshire, and invited him to travel with him to his home. Upon their arrival, Williams preached on the parable of the wise and foolish virgins, but Harris was so disappointed with his sermon that he informed him that his 'legal' expressions were neither acceptable nor welcomed at Trevecka. Williams was naturally offended, but the situation deteriorated further when Harris informed him that, in his opinion, Williams's Gospel zeal and purity had declined. He replied that Harris was in no position to pass judgement on anyone's doctrine, when his restless eclecticism tried to reconcile incompatible positions in ways that could only lead to confusion.[198]

Following a calmer than usual Association meeting at Cil-y-cwm two months later, Harris again travelled home to Trevecka with William Williams. On their way, they stopped to preach, and Harris took his text from 1 John 1:17: 'the blood of Jesus Christ his Son cleanseth us from all sin.' In his Diary he wrote:

I called on them to return to the Blood of Christ. [I was] Cutting to such as pray and preach and love and obey and profess without feeling the Blood of Christ in and thro' all – 'tis by the Blood God comes down to us and we go up to Him – O! precious Blood! O! Blood of the Lamb &c. On crying out this, the Lord came down, as well as in cutting and reproving carnal professors. I had much authority to show what the Blood does.[199]

Since Williams was there listening to Harris preach, it is probable that much of what was said was later repeated to Rowland.

Harris spent the remainder of the summer travelling through south Wales, preaching and organizing the societies. During September he began showing a renewed interest in the doctrine of the Trinity and was spiritually refreshed through meditating on 'the Eternal and Co-equal Three-one God'. He now claimed that he saw God as he had never seen Him before, and, though he had always known Him to be a Trinity of persons, he had not realized the three persons were co-equal as well as co-eternal.[200] He also declared that he saw 'the whole Godhead in the Word become Incarnate' and claimed to have 'a deeper sight of the Glory of Christ's Priesthood and Blood and Sacrifice'.[201] He now held that 'all the Godhead is in the Man. Tho' 'tis the Word only become flesh, yet the 3 is undivided in Essence ... what the one does, all the 3 does [sic].'[202]

Harris's words strongly suggest that he failed to comprehend the immense complexity of the doctrine of the Trinity, and did not appreciate that such statements, though seeming rational, suggested Patripassianism.[203] Orthodox Protestantism held that the personal distinctions within the Trinity were to be understood as existing within the divine essence,[204] yet the essence was undivided. The whole essence belonged equally to the three persons, but there were also personal attributes by which they were distinguished, the *opera ad intra*. The *opera ad extra*, activities by which the Trinity was manifested outwardly, were, as Harris affirmed, never the works of one person exclusively but of the Divine Being as a whole. At the same time, in the economical order of God's works, some of the *opera ad extra* were ascribed more particularly to one person; creation to the Father, redemption to the Son, sanctification to the Holy Spirit. Harris's confusion stemmed from his failure to differentiate between the 'essence' and the '*opera*', and, since his statements suggested that he had adopted a modalistic concept of God, it is hardly surprising that Rowland and others became uneasy.[205]

Harris was not the only person under suspicion. At an Association meeting at Trevecka during October, one of those invited to preach was James Beaumont. According to Harris, his message contained many dark expressions concerning the Incarnation, 'as if our Saviour had a sinful body because all our sin was imputed to him'. Such an antinomian view, held in opposition to the Reformed doctrine which stated that the guilt rather than the culpability of sin was imputed to Christ, was hardly likely to gain a sympathetic ear among the clergy. His declaration that God was present not only in the Church of England but also in the church of Rome and in every other sect 'which walked humble with Jesus', was also totally unacceptable; it was a typically Moravian concept, not dissimilar to Zinzendorf's notion that each denomination or tradition had in its possession a unique spiritual 'jewel'.[206] Beaumont concluded with a reference to the 'Church of the Methodists', which because of its separatist implications angered Harris, who was campaigning diligently against secession and who rejected any suggestion that the Methodists had formed themselves into a separate church. When Beaumont had finished, Harris hurried to protect him from the onslaught that he believed would follow; he attempted to calm those who had been offended, but found that despite his efforts they remained 'stiff'.

Beaumont's comments might easily have been ignored had Harris refrained, on the following morning, from praising him and saying that he believed that God had been with him as he preached on the previous day. The subject broached, one of the exhorters declared that he was for separating from such teachers as Beaumont, and the clergy showed themselves to have been deeply offended.[207] In their view, Harris had failed in his duty to defend the Methodist movement from doctrinal errors; he had even aligned himself with Beaumont, whom they regarded as a threat. But, whatever objections the clerical party may have had to Beaumont's doctrines, Harris believed that they could be countered by support from among the societies. He therefore began to explain Beaumont's teachings to the societies as he itinerated,[208] but was at the same time secretly critical of him, accusing him of pride, lack of tenderness, and stirring up a bad spirit.[209]

The application of discipline continued to be a topic of discussion among the Methodist leaders, and, as Harris continued with the task of bringing order to the movement, his constant claim that lukewarmness had reached scandalous proportions[210] led to the subject being raised at a meeting at Lampeter during February 1748. The difficulty lay in agreeing on the most effective way of assessing the spiritual condition of individuals within the societies. Rowland and William Williams held that the only possible criterion was their outward conduct, while Harris pressed for a process of discernment of spirits, claiming that there was always 'an Eye in the Body' to fulfil the task.[211] In his view, judgement was to be reached by an assessment of the individual's spiritual condition, and he declared sternly that even in the absence of gross sins, if there was evidence of lukewarmness, society members should be turned out unless they repented. This meant that discipline and expulsion would become a subjective process, a matter of opinion rather than the enforcement of recognized rules. Such a policy would not only have led to widespread feelings of injustice among those expelled, but also to uneasiness and fear among those who remained.

This issue had been the subject of much discussion during the previous century, and, in common with many Puritan divines, Rowland and Williams held that the primary judge and touchstone for the discerning of spirits was the Scriptures.[212] Harris, on the other hand, adopted the 'enthusiastic' notion of a spiritual perception through which the work of the Spirit could be detected. The difference of opinion therefore went far deeper than an inability to agree on a method of assessment; it was rooted in the question of the extent to which individuals could depend solely on the guidance of the Spirit.

The tension therefore continued, and Rowland still claimed that Harris denied the Trinity through his Patripassian teachings. When they met at Carmarthen on 4 May, a heated argument erupted between them concerning the equality of persons within the Trinity, and Harris told Rowland that he feared that he 'did not know the Lord'; Rowland responded by accusing Harris of being ignorant of the Scriptures.[213] This was a new development in that they had not before cast doubt upon each other's integrity as preachers. Now, even this was being eroded. Harris also claimed that Rowland was deliberately undermining his efforts to bring discipline to the societies, and, on his way to an English Association in Gloucestershire on 17 May, complained to William Williams that Rowland was admitting into communion those whom Harris had turned out of the societies.[214] Though it is impossible to ascertain whether Rowland had resorted to this particular course of action in a deliberate attempt to isolate Harris, it must be borne in mind that, by administering communion to those whom Harris had openly humiliated, Rowland did appear to be more compassionate and understanding. As a result, dissatisfaction with Harris's methods of applying discipline increased, and society members became more outspoken in their criticism of his sternness and peevishness. Rowland, on the other hand, was making new friends and gaining support among the converts.

On 30 June 1748, George Whitefield arrived back in England, having been in America for four years.[215] Harris was in London to greet him on his return,[216] and gave him an account of the progress of the work and the tensions that existed within the Methodist camp.[217] The two men met again at an Association meeting at Watford on 3 August; there, Harris was shown a letter written to Whitefield by the Dissenter, David Williams of Pwll-y-pant, in which he complained of Harris's pride, stubbornness, despotic spirit, doctrinal errors and enmity towards the Dissenters.[218] Harris was deeply offended, and conscious of the threat which the letter posed.

He was naturally eager to ensure that Whitefield did not side with Rowland in the controversy which existed between them. Since his first visit to the Welsh Association in 1743, Whitefield had been a powerful and influential ally who had shown his confidence in Harris by allowing him to participate in caring for the Tabernacle during his absence. In order to protect himself, Harris would have to prevent him from making common cause with the other clergy, and it was in this context that he regarded Williams's letter as a threat. Moreover, much to Harris's discomfort, Whitefield, in his sermon to the Association, was critical of those who claimed to have received divine revelations, and declared himself opposed to such phenomena and to the following of impulses purporting to be part of God's guidance to his people. To Harris, this was a surprising change of tack by one who, prior to his departure from England, had been telling him that God had impressed upon his soul that he would one day become a bishop.[219] But while he was in America Whitefield had realized that the Great Awakening had gone woefully out of control through the antics of 'enthusiasts',[220] and he himself had been the object of many scurrilous literary attacks accusing him of yielding to impulses and impressions, and encouraging others to do the same.[221]

Feeling himself threatened by Whitefield's comments, and fearing that Whitefield was about to be wooed by the clergy, Harris considered it expedient to warn him about them, and advised him to be cautious, especially with regard to such topics as 'lightness, answers to prayers and the Moravians'. He then rebuked the whole Association for their trifling spirit and time-wasting, warning them that, unless they changed their ways, he would have no choice but to leave. Daniel Rowland and Thomas Price were further rebuked in private for their lightness during the two days they had been together, and, before leaving, Harris read to the Association the letter which Whitefield had received from David Williams. While claiming that the letter showed the absolute necessity of having Christ as a Saviour, there is little doubt that he hoped that, by making the charges public knowledge himself, he would diminish their impact.

He was by now becoming increasingly isolated, and during the summer of 1748 his concern about the groundswell of discontent among the Methodists becomes apparent. On 17 August he reflected upon the accusations made against him and wrote:

> It came to me that because all the Professors are so terribly angry with me so as to write and speak all bitter things of me, and since this terrible corruption has been so long let loose on me, whether 'tis not a voice to me, that in somewhat I may be wilfully out of God's way in the work, in staying in the Church. And so I had faith to ask the Lord, and He came to my soul and assured me to the contrary, that these things are to other ends and that I am where He has plac'd me.[222]

He therefore saw no reason to change his ways, and threw himself with renewed confidence into the work.[223] As he travelled through Caernarfonshire during October, he met Sidney Griffith of Cefnamwlch for the first time, and accompanied her to Penllech, probably to her home, where he gave an account of his conversion experience. This fateful encounter was to begin an intense relationship with the wife of another man, the profound consequences of which played an important part in the separation of 1750.[224]

During the latter half of 1748, possibly in response to criticism of his teachings, but probably because of his fear that he was losing a powerful ally in George Whitefield, Harris preached less of the 'Blood' and concentrated on other themes such as the means of salvation, the ability of Christ to save and the nature of sin.[225] But, by the end of the year, Rowland was complaining, not so much about his doctrine, but about his autocratic spirit, and accusing him of being 'self seeking and aspiring'.[226] This criticism, and the fear of isolation, worried Harris, and, as he meditated on his position in the movement, he was convinced that Rowland was deliberately undermining his authority.[227] He prayed that God would enlighten him as to how he should proceed; was the coolness in the relationship with Rowland sent by God to test his own faith or a providential intervention intended to prevent Harris from mixing and co-operating with the other, mostly clerical, leaders? Was it a sign that he was too strict in his discipline in the societies, and of divine displeasure? These questions preyed on his mind and caused him much anxiety.

Meanwhile, James Beaumont continued to be a thorn in his flesh. At the end of October, Harris again spoke to him about his doctrine, but to no avail.[228] Several of the exhorters were determined that he should be ejected from the movement,[229] but, while Harris admitted that he possessed a proud spirit, he declared that he did not doubt his sincerity or see any justification for his expulsion.[230] This unwavering loyalty, though laudable in some respects, acted as a wedge between Harris and the clergy; it infuriated Rowland, and, as Beaumont's errors were so widely recognized, there was little hope of them overcoming their differences until the issue of Beaumont's membership was resolved.

At a quarterly Association at Erwood on 1 February 1749, another attempt was made to settle the problem: 'certain Queries that had been sent to [Beaumont] about the Trinity and the use of the Law and Sanctification, were read', and he was asked to respond. He declared that he firmly believed in the Trinity but denied the eternal generation of the Son; he also admitted making use of the term 'person' only to please others, since he regarded it as unscriptural and of little significance in the Christian vocabulary.

The Association now seemed ready to expel him, but, on realizing this, Harris announced that he could not be part of any such action, and that if Beaumont was turned out he would go with him. He reminded them that Beaumont was a preacher sent of God, and though he may have been guilty of a sin, he was no more so than those who were about to pass judgement upon him. Despite all he had heard, Harris still believed him to be 'sound at Heart', and was determined that he should not be ejected for what he regarded as a harmless difference of opinion with the clergy.[231]

With the dawning of 1749, Harris hoped that the disagreements between himself and Rowland would quietly recede into the past. Though there was still tension, he was sure that, given time, it would ease, and on 27 January referred to the disputes as 'our past confusions'. Meeting Rowland at Erwood in February, he 'felt a oneness with him',[232] and this renewed feeling of friendship led to a visit to Llangeitho in March, the first for three years. An invitation was also issued to Rowland to visit Breconshire, as he had not preached there for some time. Generally speaking, there was, therefore, during the first quarter of 1749, a faint glimmer of hope that the situation could be remedied without further acrimony, but this sudden softening in Rowland's approach may have been due to the restraining effect of Whitefield's return upon Harris and the fact that Harris had lost a daughter during January.[233] There is no evidence to suggest that the bitterness of the past had in any way receded, and, while Harris now hoped for a lasting reconciliation, Rowland was still reluctant to respond. It was, after all, Harris's doctrine that was suspect: Rowland regarded himself an orthodox churchman; there was no reason why he should compromise.

Following his return to England, Whitefield was eager to free himself from his responsibilities at the Tabernacle in order to conduct an itinerant ministry.[234] Harris was again invited to take care of the London society,[235] but, conscious of the burden of his own problems in Wales, wisely hesitated. He did, however, attend a meeting of the English Calvinistic Methodists at Gloucester on 26 January, in the hope that they would be able 'to come to some order, all as yet being in confusion'.[236] Whitefield explained that he did not believe himself called to labour in one place, but to itinerate on both sides of the Atlantic. His absence for such lengthy periods had in the past led to uncertainty about the future of the Calvinistic branch of the English revival, and it was agreed at the meeting that the converts should receive the highest possible standard of care and be properly organized. The problem was that no one seemed willing or able to take Whitefield's place; Harris was the first choice, but Whitefield argued that his duties in Wales prevented him from taking on additional responsibilities in England. There is room to believe that he by now lacked confidence in Harris's ability to cope; he knew that the Tabernacle had not flourished under his ministry between 1745 and 1748. In a letter to John Wesley in September 1748, he explained that it would not be possible for him to establish more societies in England as he did not have 'proper assistants to take care of them'.[237] He therefore did not believe that Harris would be able to shoulder the burden.

Others were also reluctant to step into Whitefield's shoes. When issued with an invitation, James Relly and Thomas Adams both refused, declaring that they did not consider themselves suitably qualified to lead the movement.[238] Harris was then asked to reconsider, and decided to accept. He held that the revival in Wales had by this time regained some of its lost momentum;[239] this allowed him more freedom to work in England. It did not, however, justify any relaxation of the high standards which he had set in Wales; the revivification of the movement was an encouragement to be even more diligent, and those who were unwilling to be disciplined, or were in any way unruly, would still be ejected from the societies.

Appointed leader of the Calvinistic Methodists in his own right, and not as a result of Whitefield's absence, Harris returned to London in April 1749, hoping that through his visit he would be able to bring about some measure of union between the various factions involved in the Revival. For many years he had entertained the belief that God had appointed him to act as mediator between the different parties,[240] and, realizing the significance of his new position, he pressed for preliminary discussions between the Calvinists and Wesleyans, with a view to coming to an arrangement which would make greater co-operation possible. He argued that a union was essential; unless it was achieved, everything was 'like to go to Pieces'.[241] Whitefield was not convinced, and his opposition to the Moravians, and criticism of the Wesleys, greatly worried Harris, who on more than one occasion found it necessary to speak to him about his prejudiced views.[242] But, while Harris attempted to pressure him into discussing the possibility of a union, Whitefield held fast to the belief that in time both the Wesleyan and Moravian branches would wither and die.[243] He did, however, allow himself to be persuaded 'to have a Conference with Mr John Wesley about terms of some union',[244] but, although this was done with the best of intentions, Harris's friendship with the Wesleys and dialogue with the Moravians did not please many who objected to their doctrines and teachings.[245]

While Harris attempted to secure closer co-operation between the brethren in England, his own relationship with the brethren in Wales continued to deteriorate. At an Association meeting at Watford on 25 May, where another futile attempt was made to expel Beaumont, Harris's criticism of his opponents was more scathing than ever, and he displayed exceptional bitterness towards Thomas Price, who he declared had fallen from God and lost his former love and simplicity.[246] Within a few days, Rowland was also denounced for moving from the strong meat of the Gospel to worldly philosophy gleaned from books.[247] In Harris's view, he was diluting experiential religion by overemphasizing the need for doctrinal purity, with the result that the spiritual springs of the Revival were drying up. Harris also complained that 'many live on knowledge instead of Christ, others on past experiences';[248] no benefit would come from seeking 'light in the Understanding instead of the Eye of Faith'. There was also harsh criticism of Rowland's ministry; he was 'under the veil', incapable of appreciating the true nature of God's glory, grace and love.[249]

Visiting north Wales in July, Harris again met Sidney Griffith, and travelled with her to an Association meeting at Llangeitho. This journey south was one of the high points of Harris's life.[250] Arriving full of renewed zeal and seeing so much 'lightness' among those present, he claimed that he rediscovered his 'old authority', and began to 'cut and lash and reprove'.[251] Two days later he claimed that his commission was renewed, and noted that, with Sidney Griffith, the 'old divine taste and favour' was given him once more. Romantic joy had restored his flagging spirits.

Sidney Griffith's appearance precipitated a crisis in Harris's family. Seeing her husband with another woman, Harris's wife, Anne, felt somewhat insecure, and approached her husband.[252] He assured her that his love towards her was growing rather than diminishing, but eleven days later confessed in his Diary that he was aware of a 'coldness and indifference' towards his wife and child.[253]

This crisis affected the whole of the Methodist movement in Wales, and Harris's frankness in his Diaries helps explain why Rowland and others reacted so strongly against Sidney Griffith. Whatever the other differences between them, there was now a suggestion that Harris was involved in an immoral association; the Methodist clergymen could not allow themselves to appear to be turning a blind eye to such a development, neither could they allow Harris to go on unchecked. By the end of August, he was claiming that a great change had taken place in him since meeting Sidney Griffith; he had experienced 'new life', and regarded her as his 'nearest counsellor friend'.[254] At the same time, Beaumont was his 'nearest brother and fellow labourer', notwithstanding 'the rashness of his spirit and judgement'.[255]

However, reaction to the situation was delayed by Harris's absence from Wales during much of August and September; he had again been called to London to attend to the affairs of the Tabernacle. Not everyone there was pleased with his appointment,[256] but, since no one else was qualified to fill Whitefield's place, there was little that could be done. When he returned home, Harris interpreted the rumours about himself and Mrs Griffith as opposition to God's work; to him, it was yet another providential way of testing his faith.[257]

It was Howell Davies who first suggested to him that his friendship with Sidney Griffith was arousing widespread public interest. When the two men met at St Nicholas, Glamorgan, during October, Davies told him that reports of his association with her had reached Carmarthen and that derogatory songs were being sung about them. Harris was deeply perturbed at hearing this news, but his concern did not lead him to consider terminating the friendship; on the contrary, he declared that he could not bear the thought of being without her.[258]

Coincident with the 'new life' that Harris experienced during this period was a return of the emphasis on the 'Blood' into his preaching, together with many of the Moravian phrases which he had previously used. By the middle of October,[259] he was again referring to the 'mangled Body of God' and to 'the Bloody Mangled Body', and, although such expressions were initially used only in private, he was soon repeating them in the presence of the preachers and exhorters. He also began referring to Sidney Griffith as an 'eye', claiming that she possessed the gifts of discernment and prophecy;[260] he was being taught by God through her,[261] and he confided in Beaumont that she was given not only to him, but also to 'the whole body' of Methodists.

Harris undertook another journey to London during December, and was accompanied by his wife and Sidney Griffith, but, unlike other times when he had arrived at the capital, he was not extended the usual invitation to preach at the Tabernacle. After three days he decided to enquire why the invitation was not forthcoming,[262] and was informed that the London Methodists did not approve of his friendship with Sidney Griffith. The opposition to the relationship was therefore increasing; the 'rage', as Harris described it, was in evidence everywhere. As a result, he decided, on 6 January 1750, to give up his rooms at the Tabernacle, and declared that he would never preach there again. This, he believed, was God's will; it was 'a reproof on Mr. Whitefield and the people' of the Tabernacle.[263]

He returned to Wales in time for the Association meeting at New Inn on 31 January. There, Rowland again charged him with 'changing continually', and domineering over the preachers and the society members.[264] Harris responded by saying that, as his efforts were not appreciated, he would leave the movement. Such drastic action was unnecessary, Rowland claimed; unless Beaumont was expelled, he himself would leave. As a compromise, it was decided that the issue of Beaumont's membership should again be left until the next quarterly Association meeting.

The following day Rowland, Howell Davies and Thomas Price informed Harris that Whitefield had at last openly declared his opposition to him.[265] Harris was unimpressed. Though he noted in his Diary that he was aware of a deep-rooted enmity among the clergy towards Beaumont and Sidney Griffith, he had by now become accustomed to their criticisms. His wife, his mother, his former friends, his fellow labourers and the populace in general also roundly condemned his conduct, but he was determined not to yield. He firmly believed that he was being led by God,[266] and, even though his marriage was on the verge of collapse and his relationship with the other Methodist leaders virtually at an end, he could see no reason for reconsidering his position. He comforted himself by saying it was he, rather than his rivals, who was 'within the veil' and nearest to God.[267]

By the beginning of March, Harris was visiting the societies, not to minister to their needs, but to secure support for himself in the struggle with the clergy. He claimed that the Welsh Methodist movement had fallen victim to selfishness and pride, and described his opponents as Jews and Pharisees, enemies of Christ, in possession of 'a little light in the head and gentle touches on the affections'.[268] He also accused Rowland of being responsible for all the tension that had developed between them,[269] and said at Llanbrynmair, Montgomeryshire, that he now found himself having to oppose Satan within the Methodist flock, in much the same way as he had formerly opposed him in the 'world'.[270]

He was now desperate to rally what support he could among the converts; the clergy had totally isolated him. On the last day of March 1750, during a conversation with William Powell,[271] an exhorter, he suggested that God was about to unite some of the brethren, notwithstanding the fact that most of them were so carnal and blind as to be incapable of taking part in any form of meaningful Christian fellowship. He warned that great opposition was to be expected to this work from the clergy, who because of their 'legal', 'carnal' spirit could not see it was the work of God. On the same day, he mentioned to Thomas William[272] the possibility of calling a private meeting to discuss the way in which they believed God wished them to proceed, and 'to consult about gathering the souls together, and to see among the people who grow up into the knowledge of Christ Crucified'.[273] The meeting was to be attended by Harris, Thomas William, William Powell, Thomas Jones,[274] John Richard,[275] James Beaumont and a few others; its purpose was to prepare the way for separating from the clergy.

Harris now lost no opportunity to belittle his clerical adversaries, and, in order to elevate himself, attempted to undermine their authority within the movement. At Aberthaw in Glamorgan he asked whether being called a clergyman, having a bishop's hand upon the head and wearing a gown, was anything in the sight of God. He expressed doubt about the clergy's godliness and sincerity, and taught that they should be respected, not because of their position, but as a result of their work. He said: 'If there is more of God with a Clergyman than a Layman, then let him have more honour, but not because he wears a Band.'[276]

His attacks upon them were bitter. When he met Thomas Price of Watford at Cardiff during April, Harris immediately set about criticizing Rowland for his love of money and ineffective preaching; his sermons, he claimed, were 'only milk for Babes and some witty turns', resulting in superficial 'outward Gales' of emotion. Since Price was one of Rowland's staunchest supporters, it is not surprising that a heated argument developed between them on the following morning, Harris having expelled some stewards from the Aberthin society after they had criticized William Powell's work.[277] Angered by Price's criticism of his own labours, Harris left, declaring as he went that Price had trampled upon his ministry, and was both immature and ignorant.

The clergy and their supporters were by now as one in their opposition to Harris. On 23 April he heard not only that Howell Davies had deserted him, but also that he, Rowland and William Williams intended to be present at the next Association meeting to lead an attack upon him.[278] Harris claimed that he felt no fear; 'I can't bow down to their flesh', he wrote, 'and they can't come down except the Lord bows them.' The separation was now imminent.

The Association met at Llanidloes, in Montgomeryshire, on 9 May. Howell Davies was not present, but Harris claimed that 'Rowland and Williams were so full of enmity ... and self and pride' that he felt obliged to tell Rowland that, though he could accept him as a brother, he could not regard him as one vested with the authority of an archbishop, nor submit to him, as he was answerable only to God. This seems to have been the only direct exchange between them, and, as the Association was not to meet again as a united body, Harris's words seem a fitting farewell. He, Rowland and Williams left Llanidloes to go their separate ways, Harris returning to Trevecka, and a week later setting out on a journey through Glamorgan and Monmouth to rally his supporters.

The formal decision to separate was taken at the meeting which

Harris had earlier suggested to Thomas William, and which took place at Trevecka on 7 June. Harris began by emphasizing the need for those present to submit to God's will, and then explained that he was of the opinion that the clergy, through their conduct and doctrine, had already separated from them. Sidney Griffith suggested that Harris's people should, therefore, publicly declare themselves opposed to the clerical party, but, unhappy with the sectarian connotations of such an action, Harris retired to pray for guidance. He insisted that he was not leaving the movement in the hands of the erroneous clergymen, and claimed:

> We are the Body and Centre of the work of the Methodists. Here in this Body [we have] the mind, spirit, truth, Blood and Glory of the Lord ... God is in the midst of us to supply us with all Graces, Gifts &c ... all that He wills will be added to us.

After he had rejoined the others, the meeting continued and, having 'opened everything to the brethren', Harris retired again, this time to allow his followers an opportunity 'to consider and see whether they have faith to go on against all the opposition and are united, or else go on as before'. It was a definitive moment for Welsh Methodism.

> We parted again to weigh things before the Lord. All seemed to see we must separate before we can be united, and we saw how they [the Methodist clergy] really preach Grace in the place of Christ, and grow more and more selfish and proud and opposing.[279]

Harris believed that clerical criticism of his doctrine, and their denial that he was guided by the Spirit of God, amounted to rebellion against God Himself. Again, he wrote in his Diary: "'tis against God the other Brethren are fighting and against the Blood of Christ and the Authority of God in me.'[280] It was a deeply ironic situation: though he had seen himself for some time as a mediator between the various factions within the Revival movement, Harris now found himself leading his followers into a separation. He could not accept that he was in any way responsible for the breach, and his 'enthusiastic' spirit, his belief that he was being directly guided by God, and the myriad of revelations he had received,[281] while being the main reasons for the tension between him and the other Methodist leaders, also served to protect him from their criticisms; their condemnation of his doctrines and practices was itself a revelation and part of God's guidance, designed to prevent him from succumbing to pride. He thus managed to insulate himself from his critics, and, while they were convinced he had fallen to error, he was equally convinced that it was they who had erred, while he had remained faithful to both God and the Gospel. On 25 June, he summarized the situation by saying, 'there is somewhat in me they can't bear – they call it the Devil and I say 'tis God.'[282]

This seems to have been a fair assessment. The underlying reason for the separation was the tension between the spirit of enthusiasm, as embodied in Harris, and the more moderate spirit of Anglican Calvinism, with its reliance on the revealed will of God in the Scriptures, as represented by Rowland. Rowland believed that Harris's deviation from orthodox doctrine was sufficient proof that he had either misunderstood God's revelation, or been deceived by Satan through the guidance he claimed to have received. Their attempts to correct his errors were blocked by Harris's insurmountable conviction that the beliefs which he held had been directly revealed to him by God. As a result, he expected other Methodists to bow to his own understanding of the faith, and experienced considerable difficulty in accepting that he could be mistaken, or that fellow labourers could be at variance with him in their understanding of the Gospel. As early as 1741, following an interview with John Wesley, he noted that their 'differences seem[ed] to be in words';[283] the same naive approach led to his failure to understand how Rowland could disagree with him on the question of assurance in 1742. All too often, those who expressed an opinion contrary to his own were charged with insubordination or undermining his authority, and his heavy-handed approach, coupled with his determination to establish better discipline during the second half of the 1740s, and the peevishness of his nature, which was probably aggravated by exhaustion and the lack of outward authority comparable to that of the clergy, led to his popularity diminishing among the converts as the years went by.

Harris's defence of James Beaumont contributed more to undermining his relationship with the other leaders. He and Beaumont were kindred spirits, and the untiring loyalty which Harris showed to him demonstrates that they had much in common. Though he disagreed with some of his views, the bond of friendship was so strong that Harris was unwilling to see him victimized. His constant refusal to allow the clergy to expel him therefore served only to isolate Harris even further; Rowland's determination, and his constant condemnation of Beaumont's doctrine, together with his anger towards Harris because of the latter's intransigence, ensured that all the ingredients necessary to bring about a division were present within Welsh Methodism by the end of the 1740s.

Even if Sidney Griffith had not appeared as she did in 1748, the separation would still have taken place sooner or later. Her role in the deterioration of Harris's relationship with the other Methodists was that she enabled him to give a clearer expression to his 'enthusiastic' spirit. Being herself an enthusiast, albeit an un-experienced one, she inspired Harris to stand by his principles regardless of the views of others. A woman of strong character, she gave him new confidence, based on the belief that God was revealing to them that He was about to do even greater things than they had hitherto witnessed. It was that belief in direct guidance which proved to be Harris's final undoing.

Chapter 8
The Prophetess

Sidney Griffith has earned herself a place in the annals of Welsh history solely on account of her association with Howell Harris. Though their relationship has in the past been the subject of much discussion in religious circles in Wales, the story of its development remains largely untold, partly because of the difficulty of transcribing Harris's Diaries, but also because research into the episode has not been encouraged, probably through fear of discovering unfavourable material concerning one of the founding fathers of Welsh Calvinistic Methodism.

The encounter of Harris and Mrs Griffith is of great interest as romantic drama, yet it has a much wider significance that justifies its treatment at some length. Harris's entanglement at a critical stage of his career with the wife of another man was an important element in the great disruption of Welsh Methodism in 1750; it was not a private affair, but a public scandal which affected the course of the whole Welsh Revival. Sidney Griffith's presence among the Methodist leaders acted as a catalyst in an already tense situation; the relationship between Harris and Rowland had been deteriorating since 1746, but in 1748 – the year that Harris first met Mrs Griffith – though it was well known that there was friction between them, a separation was not seen as either imminent or inevitable. Despite the disagreements that existed between him and Harris, Rowland still believed that he could be persuaded to change his views, and recognized that his talents as an organizer and his effectiveness as an itinerant made him an indispensable asset.

Following the appearance of Sidney Griffith, and after her role in the movement had become apparent, Rowland was forced to reassess the situation. She thus became an important factor in the development of the rift between the two men, and as time went by her presence led to a willingness in Rowland to allow a separation to occur. At the same time, her presence influenced Harris in a similar way; his belief that Sidney Griffith was divinely appointed to assist him in his work partly accounts for his conclusion that a separation was necessary. He reasoned that, if the clergy and their supporters were unable to accept her, he had no choice but to leave them.

The relationship brought many aspects of Harris's character to the fore; his 'enthusiastic' spirit, his imperviousness to argument, his unwillingness to listen to reason or to accept criticism, and a disturbing ability to justify to himself what was patently unacceptable to others. These tendencies were intensified by what can only be described as symptoms of a disturbed personality, for there is little doubt that by the end of the 1740s Harris was suffering from extreme mental and physical exhaustion. His 'enthusiasm' and his desire to be recognized as a leader fulfilling God's will in a selfless manner, coupled with the appearance of Sidney Griffith, who possessed a similar spirit to his own, and the fatigue which resulted from years of itinerating and preaching, led to his inability to see the dangers of his actions. The failure of others to convince him of his folly was finally to lead to his alienation from the main body of Methodists in both England and Wales and to his early retirement to Trevecka, at the age of thirty-eight.

The daughter of Cadwaladr Wynne of Plas y Foelas near Ysbyty Ifan in Denbighshire, Sidney was married in the early 1740s to William Griffith, the squire of Cefnamwlch in Caernarfonshire.[1] At that time, Griffith's estate was beset by financial problems, and this may have contributed to the difficulties that they experienced in their marriage and to their final estrangement towards the end of the decade.[2] Having been converted in 1747, most probably through the ministry of Peter Williams,[3] a Methodist clergyman who had visited Llŷn[4] during that year,[5] Sidney Griffith and her husband[6] began taking an active interest in the Methodist movement by attending their meetings, a rare occurrence among the gentry of 'poor dark North Wales'.[7]

Harris first met her while on a preaching tour in the north during October 1748. Having arrived at Rhosddu in Caernarfonshire on 7 October, he found thousands of people gathered to hear him preach.[8] After the meeting he went 'with a Lady, lately called, to Penllech', where, in private, he spoke to her of his conversion and 'of improving every Talent to the utmost'. This 'Lady' was Mrs Griffith. The following morning he saw her again and his mouth, he says, was 'suitably opened to direct her against carnal and for spiritual prudence'. After his return to Trevecka he sent her a volume of Whitefield's sermons and some 'papers' which he believed could be of use to her 'to scatter among friends'. In a note that accompanied the package, he wrote: 'my prayers are for you, that you may stand fast believing in the Lord, going on from faith to faith, devoting yourself continually to Him whose you justly are by Creation and Redemption and Choice.'[9]

Four months later, on 1 February 1749, their paths crossed again at a quarterly Association at Erwood in Radnorshire. Sidney Griffith had travelled to Llangeitho during January and had come to the meeting with Daniel Rowland. In his account of his conversation with her, Harris wrote: 'the Lord opened my mouth indeed to speak home about being faithful to Him and continuing to live by faith, and of the honour of waiting on the Infinite Majesty and of being despised for Him.'[10] A few days later Sidney Griffith, travelling with her maid, arrived without warning at Trevecka, and stayed as Harris's guest for two nights. Much of the time was spent in private conversation, during which Harris felt that his words were more effective than they had been 'for many years'.[11] Mrs Griffith's response, as one of the gentry, greatly pleased him, as did the fact that she decided to accompany him to a preaching engagement at nearby Bronllys. After their return to Trevecka, they sat together in conversation until the early hours of the morning, and continued their discussion the next day with Harris experiencing 'much Light, Liberty and Love' in her company. As she began her journey home on Thursday 9 February, he escorted her as far as Erwood before setting out to honour other preaching engagements which he had arranged in the area.

These meetings with Sidney Griffith contained nothing to indicate that the relationship would develop any further. Harris had met a convert from among the gentry while on his travels, had instructed her in spiritual matters and encouraged her to continue in the life of faith despite opposition from those of her own rank. It may be that he was impressed by her character and conviction, and flattered when she appeared at his home, but there was nothing unusual or untoward in his conduct towards her. He and his wife welcomed her into their home; she responded with similar courtesy by accompanying Harris to Bronllys to hear him preach. In recognition of her social status, Harris then escorted her on the first few miles of her journey home. All would have been well had the story ended there; unfortunately, during the latter half of 1749, the relationship developed at an astounding pace, and it was then that Harris's wife, Rowland and many other Methodists began to feel uneasy.

The turning-point came in July 1749. Harris was again on a preaching tour in north Wales, and on Tuesday 18 July[12] he came to Tre-garnedd, near Rhosddu where he had first met Sidney Griffith. There he met her again, and during the society meeting was 'made faithfull to God, crying to Mrs Griffiths [sic] that she should mind the Lord alone and be as if there was none here but the Lord and her'. That night he accepted an invitation to dine at Cefnamwlch, and after another society meeting at Tre-garnedd he stayed the night at nearby Tŷ-mawr. No suggestion is made as to why the courtesy he and his wife had extended to Sidney Griffith at Trevecka was not reciprocated at Cefnamwlch. It may be that by then her husband's initial interest in the Methodists had already evaporated, for it is known that by 1750 he was totally opposed to Methodism, as John Wesley discovered at Holyhead. While on board a ship bound for Ireland, Wesley was disturbed by Griffith who 'tumbled in and poured out such a volley of ribaldry, obscenity, and blasphemy, every second or third word being an oath, as was scarce ever heard at Billingsgate'.[13]

Two days later, on 20 July, en route to an Association meeting at Llangeitho, Harris came to Pwllheli and there met Sidney Griffith yet again. In the account of their meeting in his Diary, he included an interesting note: 'fearing her coming with me least the Lord did not send her.' Judging from these words, it can only be assumed that Sidney Griffith had suggested the possibility of travelling with Harris to Llangeitho[14] and that he did not feel entirely at ease at the prospect of being seen journeying through the country with another's wife, even though chaperoned by her maid. And yet, he argued with himself, no harm would come from such an arrangement. Unable to decide on what answer to give, the question was taken to God in prayer; Harris was duly assured that 'it was right, and that He would wash her and [their] conversation in His Blood'. Before nightfall they set off, and this was to be a journey that Harris would never forget.

For some unknown reason, they first travelled to Plas y Foelas in Denbighshire, Sidney Griffith's home prior to her marriage. Then, turning south, they travelled through Bala and Llanidloes towards Llangeitho, and, as they passed through mid-Wales, they related to each other their past religious experiences. Harris was convinced that his companion was a particularly devout and sincere Christian and was attracted to her, but, as his religious principles prevented him from expressing his feelings in sexual terms, he endeavoured to do so through his spiritual vocabulary. Even so, it was impossible for him to disguise the fact that a deep attachment or bond was in the process of being formed, and as the days went by, even though he was careful that no improper term should be used to describe his emotions, he could not avoid betraying the great excitement that he felt through being in her company. He claimed that, during their conversations, he had 'never had so much freedom'; 'the Lord came down' and gave him 'freedom of heart such as words can't express'.[15] This warmth was not confined to isolated incidents but was the result of a prolonged experience which lasted for many days. The journey took nearly a week to complete and as they progressed the relationship deepened to such an extent that, as they neared their destination, Harris saw himself richly blessed. He wrote: 'I never felt the like before. For 6 days the Lord has filled my heart and mouth. If the discourses I have had these 6 days with Mrs. Griffith were all written down, it would make a volume of pure, clear, strong relating.'[16]

They arrived late on Tuesday 25 July, with Harris in an ecstatic mood. Even after the long tiring journey, he could say: 'yet was neither my spirits low, my heart and love and zeal marred or cooled, my body tired or argument failed or mouth stopped or gifts failing.'[17] He also wrote: '[I was] willing I should indeed be forgotten for ever that God alone may be exalted in Mrs. Griffith. Soul crying that I may indeed never stand between her and any of God's Commands, Threats, Promises or Glories &c.' Sidney Griffith felt similarly blessed during the journey and declared that she saw 'the honour of having friendship with a father in God's house'.

The Association meeting was uneventful apart from one of

Harris's attacks on the exhorters. The following day, as if eager to deny to himself that there was any sexual attraction between him and Sidney Griffith, he noted that the Lord was using 'several means to cut off what [was] nature' in their relationship. He also believed that he had received 'fuller Confirmation' that 'the Lord undertakes it [the relationship] all Himself, to guard both sides from error, blinding nature, self, &c.'[18] This suggests that Harris was again aware of the need for caution if he was to protect his good name. But now the need was greater than ever. Since leaving Caernarfonshire, their casual acquaintance had developed into an intimate friendship, and the possibility of corruption by nature had increased dramatically. The situation could easily have got out of hand unless great care was taken by both parties, and, while it would have been wiser for them to have separated at this time, Harris was confident that he would be kept from succumbing to temptation. His commitment to the relationship could not be shaken by fears of what might be; he 'had faith to give it all up to Him and so rested'.

Following the meeting at Llangeitho, the pair began another journey which took them through Carmarthenshire to Laugharne and Llanddowror. In all, they were to spend three weeks together,[19] during which Harris recorded his thoughts in his Diary. It was as if new life had been breathed into his ministry; he claimed that he was 'feeling now my Commission again renewed, and my old Authority restored ... In being with Mrs. Griffith I felt the old Divine Taste and favour, which I had a little lost, restored again and saw things in the spirit I never saw before.'[20] By Saturday 29 July, their relationship had developed to such a degree that he could say that he 'felt we had but one soul, one heart, one will, one judgement, one affections and that here [with Mrs Griffith] I could open my whole heart and no where else'.[21] He was 'now raised up into God so as I never was before and such purity and love like cloathing my soul [sic], that nothing can come near me – all my care is that the Lord may be exalted.' He still feared lest some 'nature secretly mixed' with the spiritual element that formed the basis of their union. Fearing that this could occur unconsciously, he depended on God's grace to protect the purity of the friendship, 'because 'tis so ordered that if God Himself should not carry it all Himself and guard it against the motions of Nature, it may prove of bad consequence'.[22]

Harris realized the power of the emotions involved and that the intimate nature of the relationship could lead some to believe that it was an adulterous relationship conducted under the guise of spiritual fellowship. However, this realistic assessment did not hold him back; he utterly failed to realize that his emotional entanglement had already progressed too far and that, not only as a public figure but also as a married man and a father, he had become too involved with Sidney Griffith. Since God had apparently shown that it was His will that they should be together, Harris assured himself that He would therefore supervise the development of the relationship, thus comforting himself that it was not his own but God's will that was being fulfilled. Although as an experienced pastor Harris had often advised young people on sexual relationships, he failed to see that he was as much at risk as any of his young converts, and could himself be caught in the web of spiritual deception that often accompanies the stirring of deep emotional feelings. On the contrary, he was so thoroughly intoxicated by Sidney Griffith that he wrote:

> I see [the] friendship I am now called to great and glorious, and a Step of Honour I am called to above all I ever knew before, it being ... out of and above nature, to be so spiritually great and glorious that it can't have the least stain of Nature to mix with it or stain it, it being begun and carryd on in and by the Lord and founded only to exalt the Lord.[23]

He attempted to explain the attraction that he felt towards Sidney Griffith in his Diary on 30 July 1749. The 'peculiar views' he had of her were due to three facts: that she was the first of the gentry openly to confess the Lord,[24] that she was given so much spiritual growth in so short a time, and that she had so publicly shown her allegiance to the Methodist movement.

While these statements are acceptable as a basis for respecting Sidney Griffith's public stand as a Methodist convert, they hardly explain the depth of feeling in Harris's other references to her in his Diary. The attraction was based on reasons far more personal than he cared to admit even to himself, and the binding ingredient in their relationship was evidently one of romantic love. She was attracted to him, possibly by the charisma that he possessed, and he was so infatuated with her as to be unwilling or unable to detach himself from the relationship.

When a messenger arrived at Carmarthen to call Harris to Bristol to attend a meeting between the Calvinist and Wesleyan leaders, he expressed a desire to have Sidney Griffith accompany him on his journey but was concerned that it would appear improper to others. He 'prayed in private for Directions' and, after 'consulting and considering the Consequences',[25] he set out with Sidney Griffith on the first stage of the journey to Trevecka. God had again given His blessing to their travelling together and was, in Harris's view, responsible if the nature of their friendship was misunderstood. He was convinced that 'nothing should ever be able to sully [the relationship] or hinder it, because God had taken the whole care of it Himself both to Prevent, wash, heal, carry on and complete it'.[26]

As they travelled, he explained to Sidney Griffith the place that he believed God gave her in the work. On her return to Caernarfonshire she should visit the societies around her home and build up the saints. She was also to settle her affairs concerning her family, and, as we know that her marriage was in difficulties, Harris's words must have been intended as an encouragement to come to some form of understanding with her husband. But, regardless of what was happening to her marriage, he was delighted to be in her company; he again 'felt light and strength communicated' to him by the new friendship that he had been 'called' into, and wrote: 'I see my reasoning Power enlarged, my faith increased, my Soul enlarged, Nature dying, my Soul like raised out of Sin, self, uncleanness &c into God.'[27]

The meeting between Whitefield and Wesley took place over a period of three days, and Harris and Sidney Griffith began their journey back to Wales on Sunday 5 August. Though the parting with the English leaders had been 'sweet', Harris did mention 'some sore stabs from the spiritual Pride of Mr. Whitefield', and on the next day noted that 'a home, cutting battle' had taken place 'about Pride, self and their fruits'.[28] Could it be that Whitefield had expressed his disapproval of Harris's travelling companion? Though the Diaries offer no explanation for the quarrel, Whitefield's later attitude to Sidney Griffith makes this a distinct possibility.

There is no indication in Harris's writings as to how Sidney Griffith intended to explain to her husband her prolonged absence from home; neither is it known how William Griffith responded, at this time, to his wife's association with Harris. However, it is reasonable to assume that the fact that she and Harris were being seen so often together in public may well have led to further pressure upon the Griffith marriage; it may also account for William Griffith's later opposition to Methodism. Convinced that his friendship with Sidney Griffith was wholly spiritual, Harris does not seem to have considered her husband's response; not only was he overwhelmed by her presence, but Cefnamwlch was also too far away for William Griffith to take any action. Moreover, Harris knew that the relationship was platonic; he probably thought William Griffith had no reason to feel that he had been in any way wronged.

Anne Harris was nearer to the situation and realized what was happening. As she raised her voice in protest, Harris wrote:

> My dear + [signifying Anne Harris] having been somewhat tempted that I did not love her ... The Lord came down and I had much freedom indeed to give up all family Care and management to her, declaring my Confidence in her Grace to consult the Lord and her Judgement and Prudence to manage, and my place is to supply all her wants and to make her easy, declaring how my love grows instead of decaying.[29]

By this time, Anne Harris must have been extremely concerned about her husband's involvement with Sidney Griffith, but he seems to have given very little thought to her feelings, and was unaware of how desperately unhappy she was.[30] But, after she had made her suspicions known, Sidney Griffith was on her way home within twenty-four hours. Whether her departure was directly connected to what Anne had said is a matter of conjecture, for on the evening prior to her departure, Harris had been making arrangements to visit London with James Beaumont. When he and Sidney Griffith set out for Builth (where Harris was to preach and Mrs Griffith was to start her journey home), it is unclear whether she was leaving Trevecka because of Anne's protest or because Harris was going to London. All that can be said is that on the day after her departure Harris set off for London without his wife and child, and remained there for six weeks, until the end of September.

The parting at Builth sheds further light on the situation as it was after Anne had spoken to Harris. Though he could say that he had faith to commit his 'dear friend ... to the Lord', 'to make her a match for all her enemies, equal to her work and Place, to adorn her with all Christian Graces and Gifts suitable to the place she fills in life',[31] he also forbade her to see him or write to him again. It would seem, therefore, that he was now attempting to free himself from the relationship, but, though the future of his own marriage appeared to have been his primary concern, it is open to speculation whether this was because of a genuine desire to see his wife's happiness restored or because of his fear that Anne would leave him. Harris did not really wish to bring his friendship with Sidney Griffith to an end, for on the day that they parted at Builth he mentioned for the first time his conviction that God 'intended [them] to live together'.[32]

Six weeks later, on 22 September, Harris returned home from London to find his wife ill and his 'dearest friend', Sidney Griffith, waiting for him.[33] She was to stay for a fortnight, during which time there were to be further significant developments in their relationship.

Realizing the potentially explosive nature of the situation in which he now found himself, both women being again under the same roof, Harris began to hope that his wife could be brought into the spiritual union that existed between himself and Sidney Griffith, thus creating a *ménage à trois*. It would certainly have solved his problem if 'Mrs. Griffith, my wife and I may be made as 3 cords in one'.[34] He was, therefore, optimistic that Sidney Griffith and Anne would be able to establish a friendship, and prayed for a 'Union' which would bring them together as 'as two poor sisters'.[35] In an attempt to remove their prejudices against each another, he spoke to them about his marriage and his 'friendship and freedom' with Sidney Griffith,[36] but the prospect for a lasting peace was not good, as Anne showed little intention of sharing her husband with another woman. Clashes between Harris and his wife were inevitable, and took place regularly while Sidney Griffith was at Trevecka.

Since her domestic problems remained unsolved, Harris suggested the possibility of writing to her brother, Watkin Wynne,[37] to make proposals under which she would be willing to return to her husband.[38] A draft copy was prepared setting out the terms, but even as he composed the letter Harris secretly wished that she would not only stay at Trevecka but also make it her permanent home. He claimed that 'oft on asking [God] if I should propose to her about coming to Trevecka, I was answered home'.[39]

His view of Sidney Griffith's spiritual qualities remained unchanged despite his wife's disapproval. He believed that as a result of their friendship God's 'light' was being communicated to him, to set him on his guard against the legal spirit which had crept in among the other Methodists, the clergy and their followers in particular. The 'light' also enabled him to lead his own followers in a more effective manner, to a fuller knowledge of the crucified Christ.[40] Sidney Griffith had been brought to Trevecka in order that he might be spiritually strengthened but at the same time to derive spiritual benefit herself, for Harris saw himself in the role of her protector, chosen by God to guard her from antinomianism and Moravianism. She, in turn, recognized the benefit that she had received from being with Harris, and claimed to have experienced more of God in listening to him than to anyone else.[41]

Though he regarded her as an intensely spiritual person, Harris did not for one moment believe Sidney Griffith to be perfect or infallible.[42] In fact, during the times they were together they often argued and quarrelled,[43] but Harris hoped that, given time, she would 'grow up out of all nature, self, delusion &c, that she may indeed be a Pillar and a Publick blessing'.[44] Hostile rumours concerning the relationship had by now begun to circulate. Harris satisfied himself that this hostility was directed against God rather than himself; when told that many were critical of him, he 'felt no rising against them but was easy'.[45] This attitude made it increasingly difficult to communicate to him that his conduct was seriously threatening the credibility of the whole Methodist movement. He refused even to listen to those who were nearest to him; while speaking to his family, who he knew were totally opposed to Sidney Griffith, he informed them that he regarded her as a gift from God, and anyone who did not see her in the same light, and who objected to her presence, was guilty of resisting God's will.[46] This was to become his general attitude to his opposers: failure to appreciate the greatness of the relationship betrayed deplorable lack of faith; the more people objected, the more he 'saw the Greatness of the Relationship'.[47] Patronizingly, he felt no surprise that the weak were staggered by such strong manifestations of the divine will,[48] and announced that he had come to see that 'the friendship [was] the first thing to be considered and every thing else [was] subservient'.[49] Outside his own family circle Harris considered all criticism of the relationship as a threat to his leadership. While at a private society at Llywel, Breconshire, he told his hearers that they were his spiritual children and that he could not allow them 'to Judge and censure' him. He and his companion attempted to serve them in a spirit of love, and it was their duty to respond through simple obedience.[50]

Secretly, Harris wished to be able to invite Sidney Griffith to make her home at Trevecka, and by the end of September he was confident that there would be nothing improper in issuing such an invitation. By now he had also come to see himself in the almost blasphemous position of being to Sidney Griffith 'what Christ is to His Church, a King, Priest and Prophet and a Treasure of Wisdom ...' When his wife heard the suggestion that Sidney Griffith should make her home with them 'there was a positive Denyal given', and Harris, 'shaken to the bottom', attempted to reconcile her attitude with the guidance he had received from God. Though concluding that these checks were means by which God overcame the element of 'nature' in the relationship, he was honest enough to admit that he was staggered by the ferocity of Anne's opposition to the proposal.[51]

The next day he was to witness an even worse scene. According to his account of the incident, he had been led to 'see more and more Glory, and more of the Lord' in his friendship with Sidney Griffith, but also saw 'Satan opposing it' within his own home. He therefore decided to take decisive action. He said that he 'felt Authority to cut and lash and defend myself, and to shew the Greatness of my office ... shewed my dear Anne how she stays behind'.[52] John Cennick had called at Trevecka on that day and had probably heard Harris speak. Both men had later gone out to preach and, on returning at about two in the morning, found Anne waiting for them. 'O! what scenes', wrote Harris. 'What tongue can express what of Satan was let lose [sic], endeavouring to overturn all indeed of the work and my friendship &c ... O! what a storm ... with opposition that none but God could go against! Satan himself was there indeed in Anne.'[53] He retired feeling 'inexpressible distress', and could wish only for death as a means of escape from the circumstances in which he now found himself trapped.

The possibility of this latest attack by Anne being the voice of God speaking to him did occur to Harris, but did not shift the counter-argument that he had never shown any desire to have Sidney Griffith as a friend, and that it was Providence which had brought them together. But, if God was now speaking through Anne, what was His message? Did He now wish him to bring the friendship with Sidney Griffith to an end, or was it a test of their faith in the face of adversity? The prayer was answered, and Harris wrote: 'I was confirmed in the latter and I felt inexpressible Love to my dear Anne, seeing her as torn by Devils.'

This view of his wife meant that she would never be able to convince him of his folly; all her protests would be dismissed as irrelevant. However, Anne Harris showed remarkable determination and resilience in the face of immeasurable pressure to capitulate. Her position was virtually impossible because of the intensity of the obsession that had possessed her husband, and, although his wife, she found herself relegated to second place owing to the alleged superiority of Sidney Griffith's 'light'. Unable to claim the possession of similar spiritual gifts or talents, the possibility of dethroning her rival was negligible, but it is a credit to her that she did not yield. Despite her degradation, she fought to protect her marriage, even though her husband could write of Sidney Griffith: 'I have not one that walks in the Light with me to see all spiritually in God's Light as she does and I find I am strengthened in the Light and led to see things clearer.'[54]

Harris's involvement was deepening as the days went by. By mid-October he was prepared to admit: 'I love Mrs. Griffith above Anne and all because I love more of God in her and she has more faith and Light and views of God than any I know.'[55] On another occasion he wrote of the two women:

> I felt a superior love to Mrs. Griffith over all, even Anne. I examined what if Anne had the same degree of Light and faith as she, would I then love, honour and Esteem her the same? ... then I saw them both in the Light and saw my dear Anne as given me of and by the Lord and so loved and honoured her indeed in the Lord, and saw Mrs. Griffith as given me of the Lord to comfort and strengthen me &c., and so felt I could converse with and write to them both together, having no flesh in it.[56]

Harris not only held that Sidney Griffith communicated new 'light' to him from God; he also claimed that she had experienced 'many Revelations',[57] and, though there seems to be little evidence of these up to the end of September 1749, it was certainly a phenomenon that was to develop later. However, there were many references to the 'light' after the memorable journey from Pwllheli to Llangeitho, but most of the observations made by Sidney Griffith merely confirmed what Harris already knew. It was his mental condition that led him to think her words to be of particular significance; in reality it seems that he derived great pleasure from having his beliefs confirmed in this particular way.

His inability to make balanced assessments also explains the reason for his uncompromising response to his wife's objections to his conduct. Harris had come to regard Anne as representative of the whole Methodist movement which, in his view, was 'Legal, Dark, under the veil' and 'carnal in conversation'. Like his family, many society members were rapidly losing sight of him in spiritual matters; while he had moved closer to God, there were no indications that they had made any progress.[58] All the opposition to his conduct, he claimed, was part of a pattern; while Daniel Rowland opposed the knowledge of God's will through the Spirit, and his followers opposed the preaching of the mystery of Christ's Godhead and death, Anne, in a similar manner, objected to the presence of Sidney Griffith. It was Harris's belief that she, like the other Methodists, needed to be raised into the light of the Spirit, and this was to be achieved not only because he wanted her support but also because he was afraid of losing Sidney Griffith. She had already mentioned that she felt an attraction towards the Moravians, and Cennick's visit had heightened her interest in them.[59] If the opposition to her at Trevecka continued, Harris feared that she would sooner or later be 'sinned away', and fall into the arms of the Moravian Brethren.

Anne was adamant that she should go. On 6 October another argument occurred which Harris described as a 'contest with Satan in Anne'. He noted in his Diary that he was obliged to declare to her that 'she had sinned me away and had sinned against the Christian, the friend, the father and the Preacher in me and stabbed the Lord and opposed His Glory and I never saw such sin go unpunished'.

Harris had always believed that it was possible for a Christian to attain knowledge of God's will through prayer and through the inner workings of the Spirit upon the soul. While speaking to some preachers on 24 September 1749, he expressed regret that there were so few spiritual 'fathers' among them 'to see of the Urim and the Thummim',[60] to convey to the society members the directly revealed will of God. On 3 October he returned to the subject while speaking to his family, saying that God had some within his Church who were nearer to Him than others, a form of 'Privy Council', to which He 'opens His secrets and Mysteries and gives the Urim and Thummim'. This He did through the use of natural 'means', through God 'giving His mind by the spirit . . . in searching the Word, minding Providence, consulting His Children, reason &c.'[61] But, by insisting that this was given only to a few, Harris was now creating a spiritual hierarchy among the converts: it was a theme that was to gain prominence as his relationship with Sidney Griffith developed.

His wife's sustained opposition to Sidney Griffith's intrusion into their home led Harris to decide that she should return to Cefnamwlch. But, much to Anne Harris's alarm, he gave the impression that he was leaving with her, and claimed that he had been sinned away, and that his home was overrun by Satan. When, in their fear, his family begged them to stay, Harris said that he would not allow Sidney Griffith to remain 'where every spirit trampled on her'.[62] He then left, but, while Sidney Griffith returned to the north, he set off towards Glamorgan. This journey forced him to realize the extent of the opposition to the relationship which he valued so much.

At St Nicholas he met Howell Davies, who told him 'how the Devil roared at Carmarthen and Dygoed [sic]'. Songs were being sung about him and both he and Sidney Griffith were becoming the laughing stock of the country. This news briefly brought Harris back to his senses. Realizing the harm that was being done to his prestige as a leader, he began to think that it would be to his advantage if Sidney Griffith stayed permanently in north Wales.[63] The measure of his concern is shown by the fact that he sent her a letter 'to intreat [sic] her to stay' there;[64] if God should wish them to be reunited, He would arrange the circumstances so that her return appeared 'right to all'.[65] The news from Carmarthen had shaken him, and it was his sincere hope that Sidney Griffith would complete her journey home and remain at Cefnamwlch with her husband.

Conscious that there were many Methodists who were opposed

to him, Harris was sometimes tempted to give up his position as General Superintendent. When he met Thomas Price of Watford in early October, he mentioned that he was considering this possibility, as it would clear the way for Whitefield to be the leader in England, for Rowland to take charge in Wales, and for John Wesley to assume authority 'over them both'. Intensive negotiations were taking place at this time between Whitefield and Wesley in an attempt to unify the English Methodists,[66] and Harris, having been accused of keeping Wales out of the union,[67] believed that by relinquishing his position he would be able to show beyond all doubt that he supported the effort, though he emphasized that he would continue working among the Methodists without his title.[68]

Price doubted that Rowland would be prepared to take over Harris's responsibilities; neither did he believe that he would wish Harris to relinquish his position. Rowland still honoured Harris and envied his many gifts, but held that he did not think things through before acting, choosing rather to 'follow impulses'. Price assured Harris that, despite all they had been through, he also wanted him to stay. It appears, therefore, that, whatever disagreements there had been, both Price and Rowland recognized the talents which Harris possessed and realized that it would have been foolish for them to force him out of the movement. Had it been possible for them to persuade him to act in a more reasonable manner and moderate some of his expressions, they would have been more than happy to see him continue as a leader.

When Price relayed the news of Harris's intentions to Rowland at an Association meeting in November, Rowland attempted to clarify the position. Harris heard

> how Mr. Rowland sent to me as thinking I was going to leave them &c, that [I thought] they did not receive me in my place, and that I would have him to be head, that he would not be and that they all did choose me to be their head as before and if I would not be that he would go back to the Church as att first.[69]

While regarding this as good news, Harris remained unconvinced that Rowland was sincere. Because of the bitter exchanges that had taken place between them in the past, he believed that Rowland still secretly opposed him by suggesting that he had become a Moravian in all but name.[70] It seems, however, that Harris was misinformed and that neither Rowland nor many of the other Methodists wished to see him alienated from the movement.

Having come across Sidney Griffith at Bolgoed on 20 October 1749 while on his way home from Glamorgan, Harris took her home with him to Trevecka, and, though he noted in his Diary on the following day that she was to stay only for three days, she in fact stayed for nearly four weeks. During that time their relationship reached its zenith.

Anne Harris had mellowed considerably since the departure of her husband a fortnight earlier. Shocked by the fact that he had walked out with Sidney Griffith, she had probably decided that uncompromising opposition served only to complicate matters even further. So, when Harris returned, he sensed at once the change of atmosphere and was heartened to see that the 'clouds' were beginning to vanish. But Anne still experienced difficulty in accepting Sidney Griffith without protest, and she and Harris were soon arguing again over her presence in their home. Harris continued to believe that her opposition was due to the evil influences of the Devil, and regarded his 'spiritual' relationship with Sidney Griffith as far superior to the natural sexual relationship that had previously existed within his marriage. Such was his conviction of the Devil's involvement in his wife's attitude that he reacted to her intransigence by becoming critical of the notion of her romantic love, claiming that 'to be beloved in Nature', as he was by Anne, was an experience comparable to having the Devil's arms around him.

A 'General Society' was held at Trevecka on 22 October during which Harris claimed to have 'had vast Authority to bring down the Mangled Body of Christ'. Conscious of the glory that had descended among them, he wrote: 'I saw Mrs. Griffith was given me for an Eye and God teaches me by her.'[71] This was the first time he had used this particular term to describe Sidney Griffith.[72] His concept of her role was that through her ability to recognize God's will she would enable him, and the Church in general, to fulfil their duty towards God by communicating to them whatever was revealed to her.[73] Her contribution to his spiritual pilgrimage had already been immense; he had been 'so raised to the Light, so strengthened, so taught, so drawn up to God and so enlightened in the spiritual Kingdom of Jesus Christ by means of her' that, if he was called to suffer for what he had already received, he would be content. She was 'continually abiding in God and viewing His glory'; the light that came down through her words was 'inexpressible'. Even when Harris fell for one moment from the 'light', she felt her spirit wounded 'and could bear a limb rather [to be] cut off'.[74] Indeed, Harris found it 'hard to come up with her pace [sic]'; everything was changing, 'a new life, a new World, a new state, a new view of all things' were beginning to appear.[75]

Within a few days this ecstatic outlook was shattered. On Wednesday 25 October a disagreement developed between them which escalated to such a height that Sidney Griffith announced that she would be leaving at once. Harris did not enter into his Diary the reason for this sudden discord, saying only that it was a 'great storm' that led to their separation.[76] Broken-hearted and believing that he had lost his 'Eyes', he decided to go after her and, accompanied by his wife, travelled towards Builth, 'groaning audibly' as he went, and in as much pain 'as a Woman in Childbirth'. After he had caught up with her at Erwood, they talked until five in the morning, 'opening the mutual views [they] had of each other'. This suggests that the disagreement involved the question of her role, in relation to both Harris and the Methodist movement, for during their conversation she seemed determined to assert herself as 'a Mother in Israel'.[77] Harris agreed that she was suitably qualified for such a position and was relieved that their friendship was now restored. Their differences overcome, he wrote in his Diary: 'I see such a oneness between Sidney Griffith and Christ, and between me and her too, that I can call her by His names, being my Light and Life.'[78] But if Sidney Griffith was to be proclaimed a 'Mother', it was but a small step for Harris to suggest that he was a 'Father'. This he did before leaving Erwood; warning his wife to beware of Satan's insinuations against him, he referred to himself as a 'Father in Israel' and reminded her that he was 'at the head of this Reformation'.

These titles were to lose much of their grandeur during yet another quarrel which erupted between Harris and Sidney Griffith later in the day. Tension arose when she made the astonishing announcement that in communicating 'light' or messages from God, she 'could not mistake or err, but was infallible'; she did not believe that it was necessary to pray for herself, only to join with others and assist them in their devotions. It was her belief that she was now 'Perfect in the Blood of Christ'.

Harris was shaken by these claims. He strove against her 'infallibility' by reminding her of the errors of the Ranters[79] and the French Prophets.[80] As to not having to pray for herself, had Christ Himself not taught his disciples to pray that they would not be led to temptation? Praying for oneself was scriptural, as any study of the 'Examples and Precepts of the Bible' would demonstrate. If she claimed to be perfect, he would have no choice but to separate from her. He insisted on having unfettered freedom to examine the 'light' that was communicated to him through her, and to 'try it by the Word'; if this was denied him, their association would end. He was prepared to accept that she possessed the spirit of discernment[81] and the gift of prophecy, but no more. Many who had been given spiritual gifts in the past had been 'over-turned by self or [by] leaving the Word'. It was in her best interest that he warned her, and 'she should be more careful that her Light [was] not ... marred and that Delusions [did] not come in.'[82] Sidney Griffith was unwilling to accept his advice, and Harris wrote: 'on her rejecting all I said as being dark and [saying] that she was confirmed in all she had said, I then agreed to part with her and felt now peace in it, which I never did before.' On asking God whether He was pleased with what he had done, he was assured that it was so.

His resolve did not last long. Within hours he felt that he 'could not bear to lose her' and went after her again. But how was he to reconcile her beliefs to his own? The temptation was to search for a way out of the predicament, and he wrote in the Diary:

> A Light came to me that I never saw before. First, I saw she was my Eye and I was the mouth to speak to others. This she was not. The eye sees for the Whole Body, and sees before the Body comes to it, and I was to digest and express to others, and not her. And so her Blunders in conceiving and expressing some things confusedly I should bear with, as she ought to bear with me in explaining and communicating &c some things. Also [saw], the Mystery of the Union between her, my Eye, and me, the Head, so as I can't express ... One can't do without the other, and hence one feels the need of the other, and I should be tender to the Eye and not rough to it.[83]

Having thus found a way of excusing her errors, he found no difficulty in accepting her back. Seeing her as the 'Eye' and himself as the 'Head' also gave him a clearer view of their combined role within the Methodist movement. While God gave her the 'light' or the prophetic utterance, it was his task to evaluate and interpret what she had received by comparing it with the Scriptures. Having done this, he could then communicate the message to others.

Their combined role having been revealed to him, Harris was eager to tell his closest friends the news. First to be told were James Beaumont and Thomas Jones of Llanfeugan,[84] who were at Erwood at that time. Others were informed as Harris, Anne and Sidney Griffith travelled together to north Wales.

The journey north was not uneventful. On leaving Erwood on 28 October they travelled to Llansanffraid-yn-Elfael where Sidney Griffith 'had strong agitations in her body and cried out'. She was unwell and unable to continue the journey,[85] so it was decided that she should remain at Bryn-melys, in the parish of Betws Diserth in Radnorshire, until she had recovered, while Harris and his wife went on.[86] Before leaving, Harris retired to pray and asked whether some prophesies made by Sidney Griffith were a true revelation of God's will. She had predicted that John Wesley, John Cennick and the Calvinists were to be united and that Harris was to be at 'the Head' of this union; she was to be his 'Eye', while he was to be her guide. In answer to his prayer, Harris noted that 'the Lord did shine' upon him, a clear indication that all Sidney Griffith had predicted would be fulfilled.[87]

On arriving at Mochdre, three miles from Newtown, Harris was met by a messenger urging him to return at once to Bryn-melys. Realizing that his wife would not be prepared to obey the summons, he decided not to tell her of his intention, and as they rounded through Llandinam and Llanidloes, she was unaware that they were travelling in a full circle. On the last stage of the journey, she realized that their final destination was Bryn-melys, and this led to what Harris described as 'another Combat with Satan in Anne'.

The call to return naturally suggested to Harris that Sidney Griffith was about to die, and, while he feared being greeted with bad news on his arrival, Anne relished the prospect of being rid of her. But not only was Sidney Griffith alive when they reached Bryn-melys, she was also prophesying energetically. She predicted that Harris would not attend the next Association meeting, that James Beaumont would visit Trevecka on the following Sunday, that both Anne Harris and William Griffith (her husband) would soon die, that Harris would become 'outwardly a Bishop' and wealthy, and that she would marry him and have three children. The previously predicted union between Wesley, Cennick and Harris would still take place, but Daniel Rowland would not join until later, after initially opposing the plan. The Moravians would not join at all; they were too selfish, according to prophetic utterance.[88]

Harris was staggered by 'the greatness and strength of the Revelation' and on his return to Trevecka excitedly considered the implications of himself and Sidney Griffith 'coming together'. As 'father' and 'mother' in Israel, they could organize and discipline the converts, build them up spiritually and lead them in the 'light' that they would receive from God. Perhaps this work could be done at Trevecka? Harris began thinking of erecting additional buildings to accommodate the converts, and dreamed of his home becoming an even greater centre of Christian activity. While the idea was to recur often in his mind during the succeeding months, the dream was not realized until the establishment of the 'Trevecka Family' in 1752.

To his own immediate family, Harris's dream was a nightmare. Finding Sidney Griffith back with them again led Harris's mother to threaten to leave; Anne was 'still under the Devil', and there were rumours that William Griffith was on his way to Trevecka 'to stab and wound' Harris.[89] Meanwhile, Sidney Griffith continued prophesying, with predictions whose fulfilment was dangerously imminent. Anne would become ill on the following Sunday; Harris was to see 'vast things in a weeks time [sic]'; he would suffer, and be 'new born in Soul and Body'.[90] When Sunday came and the prediction concerning Anne was not fulfilled, Harris was 'set to reason', but did not for one moment doubt the gift that he believed had been given to Sidney Griffith. On the contrary, his view of her greatness increased as the spiritual union between them gained an almost apocalyptic intensity. He wrote:

> the Lord did shine upon me and I felt that oneness that I never knew before, seeing us both in the same Robe, in the same Kingdom, in the same Love, eating the same food, united together out of and above Nature and Death in the Light, to view together the Eternal Kingdom and to be one in spreading the fame of Jesus.[91]

Later in the month,[92] Harris began to recognize the possibility that Sidney Griffith might at times misinterpret the 'light' that was given to her; she was so young and inexperienced,[93] and the 'light' was 'coming fast'. But, if disappointed in the outcome of the prediction concerning Anne's health, he was to be satisfied in another. On asking God whether he was to go to the next Association meeting, he was assured, though he felt a great desire to attend, that he was to stay at home. Sidney Griffith's prediction was, therefore, correct, and Harris's absence was due not to his own wishes but to his unwavering obedience to God.

By now, Harris was showing clear signs of a serious personality disorder; his megalomania, though clothed in spiritual terms, had reached proportions suggesting a loss of mental balance. Sidney Griffith, he claimed, was 'the highest visible token of Especial Love and favourite Grace' that God had bestowed upon him, and his belief was that "tis not by the Law of common Love [through which God] deals with His Children [that] He deals with me, but by the Law of especial Love, distinguishing Love, favourite Love'.[94] He was 'God's child and favourite': Sidney Griffith had been given to enable him to overcome 'self' and yield to the Spirit, so that he might be able to live, not for himself, but for God.

On 16 November, Sidney Griffith began a journey north to her parental home at Ysbyty Ifan in order to attend to some personal business, but arrangements were made that she would meet Harris and his wife at Gloucester on 1 December[95] in order that they might proceed together to London. Before her departure, she mentioned the sufferings her husband had inflicted upon her and claimed to have been beaten and driven out of her home.[96]

During her absence Harris gave further thought to her prophecies. His greatest burden was the predicted death of his wife;[97] he realized that her demise would be opportune, but shrank from wishing her to die. He wrote in his Diary:

> My Heart [was] kept ... right toward Anne, not once desiring her Death but the reverse, feeling such love that I could not bear the thought of parting with her, judiciously longing, if He wills it, that I may have her and her alone whilst I live, desiring nothing indeed from Sidney Griffith but that I may love what God has to bestow on me spiritually to strengthen my faith.[98]

Though the thought of his wife's death led him to use such loving terms, it is evident that there was still tension within him. He claimed that the thought of parting with her was 'intolerable', but still noted in his Diary that he believed 'that she should die before half a year or June 18'.[99] Troubled by pangs of conscience at entertaining such a callous thought, he consulted God for confirmation, and 'again and again' was told that the prophecy was correct. He comforted himself with the thought that his wife's death was 'her going home, the Lord taking her and pitying her as she [was] too weak for her place and for the Glory that [was] coming'.

Sidney Griffith arrived at Gloucester as arranged on 2 December, and two days later moved on towards London with Harris and his wife. Upon their arrival, Elizabeth Whitefield refused to allow Harris the use of his usual rooms at the Tabernacle,[100] while her husband offended him further by not inviting him to make use of his pulpit. Puzzled by Whitefield's reticence and infuriated at being left idle after travelling such a long way,[101] Harris decided to tell Whitefield all that he believed to be amiss in his conduct towards him. A few days later, angry at his hesitation in accepting an offer to take care of the Tabernacle while Whitefield was away in America, he demanded an explanation, and was told that Sidney Griffith's presence as his companion was unacceptable not only to Whitefield but to many others who had complained to him about her.[102] At the end of the month, still without an invitation to preach, Harris declared that the door of the Tabernacle had been shut to him. He had been 'turned out'.[103] On 6 January he decided to leave his lodgings, as he could not expect the society to pay for the rooms while he did nothing to justify their generosity.[104] The parting with Whitefield was amicable, though a little tense, and Harris continued to work at the Tabernacle even though he was not staying there. When he again offered to take care of the society during Whitefield's absence, Whitefield himself explained that he did not feel free to entrust the Tabernacle into his care, for he had been led to understand that, if Harris took charge, the lease would not be renewed.[105] Harris's conduct had, therefore, led many of his old friends to distance themselves from him; his doctrine, his manner and his association with Sidney Griffith had made him an embarrassment to the Calvinists, and the prospect of having him as leader in both England and Wales led many to feel concern about the future of the movement.

Harris returned to Wales in time for the Association meeting at New Inn, Monmouthshire, on 31 January 1750. There he heard Rowland preach, but regarded his views on the Trinity 'carnal' and objected to his portrayal of the 'Father, as it were, by Himself creating, the Son as separate, Redeeming'. Rowland was also critical of Harris and accused him of 'changing continually with all opinions', and of 'domineering over all' that would not submit to his authority.[106] Both charges were met with a firm denial. However, Harris conceded that if Rowland, in making these accusations, represented the views of the Methodists in general, he would be prepared to withdraw from the work, give up his position, and preach only to those who expressed a desire to hear him.

Underlying these exchanges was the tension caused by Sidney Griffith. While talking to Howell Davies, Harris commented on the enmity he had witnessed towards her at the meeting, and observed that the brethren not only despised her personally but also every word he had said in her praise.[107] It is more than likely that the relationship reminded the Welsh Methodists of other recent and similar 'spiritual' attachments which had soon deteriorated into debauchery, most notably the case of Westley Hall, John Wesley's brother-in-law, who a few years previously had taken advantage of the female members of his society at Salisbury, 'telling them this was Christian fellowship and a part of the communion of saints'.[108] It would also partly account for the accelerated deterioration of Harris's relationship with Daniel Rowland during 1749–50; when they met at Llandeilo on 9 February, Harris found that 'no Christian Brotherly fellowship' was possible between them,[109] which to his mind only confirmed Sidney Griffith's prophecy that Rowland would be the last to join in any union between the various groups involved in the Revival.[110] Rowland, he held, was 'legal' and 'carnal', unable to grow up in Christ, growing only 'in self'; his sermons were intellectual rather than spiritual and led the people to be more 'worldly, sensual, selfish, trifling and wise in their own eyes'.[111] He was also careless in matters of personal holiness, 'looking on it as indifferent and no matter of Conscience to spend 6d or 1s on snuff or Ale if a man has it without doing injustice to any, or to spend hours idle if he does not neglect some Immediate Business

&c.'[112] Harris also feared that Rowland was influenced by love of money when deciding where he should go to preach. He saw no indication that the people were advancing in faith, or growing in love or humility, under his or any other clergyman's ministry.

The tension between the Methodist leaders led to confusion in many parts of the country.[113] Now that he had been rejected by Whitefield and his other English friends, Harris saw that it was his responsibility to act.

> I see it [is] time for me to come to Wales and to leave England, and to stand against the self &c that is come in and I must expect to be sorely judged &c. All the people are like wicked little children ready to reject every yoke and Authority, going to rest in the flesh ... taking nature for Grace.[114]

Now, he concluded, was the time to bring to an end the constant idolization of the name and gown of the clergy;[115] he would not allow them to assume control of the movement which he had founded.[116]

Though absent, Sidney Griffith continued to be a source of strength to him. When Harris was 'dry', God brought the remembrance of her to his mind and 'in it did bring Life'.[117] During the period following his departure from London he received several letters from her[118] and through her exhortations felt encouraged to persevere.[119] Feeling that she was with him in spirit,[120] he wrote:

> I had still fellowship with Sidney Griffith, which I can't comprehend or explain, but is somewhat I never knew before, and I know is of God and is a means of filling me with God and is carried on by Him and He keeps my will out of it and all carnality and flesh [so] that I have no will to see her.[121]

Coupled with his efforts to bring stricter discipline into the societies was an attempt by Harris to create an inner circle of Methodists whose loyalty to him was beyond doubt. A few had already been entrusted with the secret of the future that he envisaged for Sidney Griffith and himself, but Harris was now eager to add to their number. More were taken into his confidence, among them John Sparks,[122] Thomas William,[123] William Powell[124] and John Richard;[125] all were 'a little staggered', but still submissive.

They were, therefore, regarded by Harris as friends who had grown 'into the Light', and it was his wish that they should soon meet 'to consult together about gathering the Souls ... to see among the People who grow up into the Knowledge of Christ Crucified and the Life of faith'.[126]

Also high on Harris's list of priorities at this time was his search for a home for Sidney Griffith somewhere in south Wales. While in Pembrokeshire during February, he mentioned to John Sparks the possibility of her settling in that part of the country, the opposition to her being so strong at Trevecka that he believed it would have been unwise for her to return there.[127] Another possibility, slightly nearer home, was Glyn in the parish of Defynnog,[128] but towards the end of March Harris decided to give up the search, having been shown in spirit that Sidney Griffith was, after all, to settle at Trevecka.[129]

Throughout this period, he continued to emphasize the need to enforce discipline within the societies, and, as he had foreseen, his efforts met with considerable opposition.[130] He therefore restricted his activities to a minimum in Cardiganshire and Carmarthenshire, realizing that both counties were by then firmly held by Rowland, who was opposed to his manner of 'settling outward things'. Total obedience was expected of all society members, and failure was met with fierce condemnation. Those who did not approve of his methods were subjected to strong verbal attacks, as Harris was led 'to wound, cut, lash, and reprove those that [were] against rough work and reproving'. The rule was simple: society members who would not submit to the law and discipline of Christ would be turned out, a policy hardly likely to increase Harris's popularity among the societies, but seen by him as necessary to lift the people on to a higher spiritual plane.

During April 1750, Harris felt himself prompted in spirit to travel to Bristol in order to meet Sidney Griffith, whom he had believed until then to have been in London. Three days later he and Thomas Jones of Llanfeugan set out on their journey, the latter also believing, through reading Acts 10.20,[131] that God sent him there. When Sidney Griffith failed to appear, Harris wrote:

> O! what distress was I in ... not seeing Sidney Griffith and being mistaken in my light. Almost resolved never to ask about anything to

the Lord lest I should mistake ... I saw myself more blind and ignorant of God and of His mind than ever ... I felt I was willing to be despised and laughed at for mistaking God's mind.[132]

His attempt at following the 'light' had not been a success.

Throughout the first half of 1750, Anne Harris kept up her opposition to her husband's relationship with Sidney Griffith, with the result that he sometimes feared to return home.[133] He therefore decided to remain there only as long as his presence was essential to the work,[134] and his itinerant ministry became a form of escape from the pressures to which he was subjected by both his wife and his mother.[135] Not only was he awakened in the morning by the 'dreadful voice of Satan from Anne [sic]',[136] but his early evening slumbers were also disturbed in a similar manner:

> After resting about 7 o'clock very sweet, I was awakened by a dreadful voice of scolding by Anne, where I soon heard my self and Sidney Griffith condemned in the blackest manner, and especially Sidney Griffith, and she [Anne] had got mother to join her too. Sure Sidney Griffith's light is right that I am not Head in my House ... I was charged with all that the fire of jealousy, when let loose, could suggest ... my enemies are they of my own Household ... and such a bold and strong and unbroken, cruel spirit I felt going in every word that my flesh trembled.[137]

As the months went by, Harris's opinion of his wife deteriorated even further. By the middle of May he could say to Morgan John Lewis, the Monmouthshire exhorter, that she did not know God and was in danger of being eternally lost; when Lewis demurred, he was told to leave the house.[138] Harris came to believe that his earlier relationship with his wife had been superficial and sentimental; their talk had been 'of outward matters, what our Saviour had done for us, of our courtship and how we came together'; he had never found her spirit equal to his, neither had he been able to confer with her about religious subjects or discuss various topics in depth. He now regarded her as given to him only 'for a Time', and believed that she, like Saul, had 'lost her place by abiding in the flesh'. She had opposed the Blood of Christ and had forfeited all that had once been within her grasp.[139]

He was still convinced that her death was imminent, and that she and William Griffith were soon to be removed[140] as hindrances to God's work.[141] But, by the middle of 1750, his own health was also deteriorating. Years of itinerating had taken their toll and there is little doubt that he was by this time nearing mental and physical exhaustion. The symptoms appeared early in the spring. On 16 March, being in great pain, he was forced to rest at Llanbrynmair;[142] he also failed to preach at Carno the next day. A 'most acute pain' worried him on 18 March, and on the following day he suffered a 'most violent pain' in his face as he travelled towards Rhayader, though, by disregarding his physical discomfort, he was able to preach 'with much freedom and Power and Life' at nearby Newbridge on Wye. More illness troubled him during May.[143]

On 24 April, Harris heard that Sidney Griffith had returned to Trevecka. After travelling home, he explained to her how he had been led to see the future of the work; this involved laying a firm foundation on the more reliable and spiritually mature converts, 'having conferences and laying the stones together' according to the measure and extent of their gifts, their wisdom and fatherly spirit. He then proposed to her a programme of two or three months' activity, in which they should not travel together but should meet at convenient locations 'to see and speak to particular persons'. When they met, she would be able to communicate to him whatever 'light' she would have received,[144] and would thus become more involved in the general supervision of the societies, and use her gifts not only at Trevecka for the benefit of Harris, but also around the country for the benefit of others. In June, having met his inner circle of Methodists, Harris wrote of her:[145]

> Sidney Griffith is not only the Eye of this Body, to be as a private Sister with me to bless me as a Christian with her superior light &c, ... she is [also] to be in this Knot of Brethren to hear, judge, taste, see, speak &c, [and] to be in all private matters with me where discerning of spirits is wanting.[146]

She was more than willing to co-operate as Harris's perpetual 'eye'. Both believed that God had confirmed through the inner workings of His Spirit that their respective roles were 'fixed in the work' and that, through their spiritual union, they were virtually married to one another.[147] As they recollected and discussed their past on 20 May, they saw that they had not previously realized what it was to be truly married; now they were as 'one to Eternity'.[148] Harris envisaged them both growing together in the 'Heart of God'; just as the divine love there was unfathomable, so the wisdom, love and bliss that existed between them would also be endless.[149]

Against this background, the separation between Harris and Daniel Rowland took place. The story of his involvement with Sidney Griffith demonstrates clearly the nature of Harris's character during the two years leading up to the event and explains why the clergy and the other Methodists found it impossible to accept him as they had done before. Harris's conduct, doctrine, style of leadership and mental condition all made the separation inevitable, and, while it could be said that the burden of Revival work had very nearly destroyed the man, it can also be said that the man came very near to destroying the Revival. The impact of the separation was huge: 'the greatest setback suffered by the Great Awakening in Wales'.[150]

The extent of Sidney Griffith's contribution to the separation has been the subject of debate for many years. Some have suggested that she was a major contributory factor,[151] thus rejecting Harris's own claim that 'the separation began ... before Madam Griffith was heard of'.[152] It must be said, however, that Harris's claim seems from the evidence of his Diaries to be true: even if Sidney Griffith had not appeared as she did, his doctrinal views and his autocratic manner while working among the societies, together with his mental instability, would most probably have brought the separation about, not perhaps as early as 1750 but quite soon afterwards. Prior to June 1750, when the decision to separate was taken by Harris and his inner circle of friends, it seems that Daniel Rowland had said very little in opposition to his relationship with her. That is not to say that he approved of his conduct, but it is fair to assume that the other shortcomings of Harris's ministry were, as far as Rowland was concerned, the real reasons for the tension that existed between them. If these made co-operation with Harris difficult, Sidney Griffith's presence served only to make the situation more complex and intensify the crisis. Many believed the relationship to be adulterous, and Rowland could not allow the impression to be given that such behaviour was acceptable within the Methodist movement and at such a high level. Though it can be safely assumed that neither Rowland nor William Williams suspected Harris of actually committing adultery, as leaders they could not turn a deaf ear to the rumours that were circulating both within and outside the movement. They realized that, whatever motives Harris may have had in continuing with the relationship, his conduct was wide open to misunderstanding.[153]

The appearance of Sidney Griffith made separating from Harris a much easier task for Rowland;[154] everyone not directly involved in the confrontation would assume that the separation was justified and that Harris had been expelled because of an immoral association with Sidney Griffith. On 22 June Harris heard that the Methodists had publicly declared themselves opposed to him 'on account of —— [Sidney Griffith], and because I hold Perfection and falling from Grace'.[155] However, when he met Rowland and William Williams at Llwyn-y-berllan on 28 June, Rowland insisted that their opposition to him was due only to his doctrinal anomalies, his harsh treatment of the converts and the fact that he and his followers had decided to separate from the other Methodists.[156] Moreover, according to Harris, both Rowland and Williams 'deny'd all they had said reproachfully of —— [Sidney Griffith] and me, and said they did not believe there was no harm between us, but carnal love [*sic*]'. It seems from Harris's account of the events of 1749–50 that Rowland was reluctant to see him publicly humiliated solely on the grounds of theological differences, possibly because of his fear that Harris would create a rival movement. However, the general assumption that he had been isolated on moral grounds minimized the risk and alienated Harris from many of his former supporters.

It is generally agreed that the episode was an unnecessary blemish on Harris's career. Few people outside his immediate circle of friends have ever attempted to defend his actions; he has been accused of making 'a grave error of judgement',[157] and of being foolish[158] and 'unwise'.[159] In his defence it can be said that his health had deteriorated to such an extent by the second half of 1749 that he had become mentally unstable, and was possibly undergoing a serious nervous breakdown. A man of his experience might otherwise have seen the dangers well in advance and acted to protect himself from being compromised by a situation in which his authority and status as a religious leader was undermined and destroyed.

It is possible that Sidney Griffith fulfilled a need in Harris for a helpmeet to assist him in his work. Anne, his wife, had never participated in her husband's public ministry, and the birth of their daughters in 1746 and 1748 must have greatly restricted her freedom to accompany him on his journeys. The appearance of Sidney Griffith, who, though the mother of a seven-year-old boy, was willing to travel and assist him in his work, may well have appeared to Harris – at this time increasingly isolated by the Methodists through his doctrinal aberrations – as a gift from God, a heaven-sent companion and confidante.

In fairness to Harris, Sidney Griffith's motives must also be examined. There seems to be no reason to suspect that, when she and Harris first met, her interest in Methodism was other than genuine and sincere. There was no compulsion upon her to be present at the society meetings in Caernarfonshire, or at the Association meeting at Erwood in February 1749. It may be argued that, owing to her domestic problems, she saw in Harris a man whom she could use to her advantage; her eagerness to travel with him to Llangeitho in July might suggest that she was, even then, running away from her husband and her problems. The evidence available allows no conclusive judgement here. However, many new converts travelled long distances to hear Rowland and Harris preach; Rowland drew congregations of over 2,000 to Llangeitho as early as 1739.[160] Sidney Griffith may well have been initially motivated by her newly acquired faith, and her interest was probably in the activities of the Methodist movement in general rather than any of the individual leaders with whom she was later to become acquainted.[161]

The journey to Llangeitho during July 1749 marked the beginning of the relationship; Harris fell deeply and madly in love with Sidney Griffith and, although there is but scant evidence of her feelings for him, there is no reason to suspect that she did not reciprocate. Both were totally besotted,[162] and, although it is probable that she derived immense satisfaction from the attention, adoration and care she received from Harris, this does not mean that her commitment to the relationship was merely self-interested. It is possible that her circumstances led her to seek happiness in a relationship outside her marriage; such a desire would account for her lengthy visits to Trevecka, during which her position within, and spiritual contribution to, the Methodist movement were established. Harris's desire for a gifted partner encouraged her participation in activities similar to his own; he realized during the journey to Llangeitho in July that they were kindred spirits, and by September had found her a niche in the organization. Her main disadvantage at that time was that she lacked experience and understanding in spiritual matters; her claim to infallibility and perfection, which put her into a category of delusion that was plainly extreme and blatantly heretical, very nearly proved to be her undoing, as Harris insisted on testing her utterances against the revealed will of God in the Scriptures. However, once informed of her error, and having had time to consider Harris's response, she made no further attempt to establish herself as an infallible oracle. Through Harris's refusal to accept her claims, she soon discovered both the extent of her own powers and the nature of the role which Harris envisaged for her in the Methodist movement. Meanwhile, Harris found himself having to compensate for her mistakes, but accepted that this was understandable and not an indication that her gifts were suspect.

The claim to infallibility suggests that Sidney Griffith, like Harris, was an 'enthusiast'. She did not make general predictions which could be fulfilled through natural coincidences; her prophetic utterances, as described by Harris, were highly specific, concerning people and events in the immediate future, and included names and dates. Had she been making fraudulent claims, it is unlikely that she would have made such exact predictions, since the validity of her prophetic powers could be tested by the fulfilment or otherwise of her words within a few days. She evidently believed in her own gifts, and it is highly unlikely that she was deliberately misleading Harris to secure accommodation for herself and her maid after their ejection from Cefnamwlch.

Since they held similar views concerning the reality of direct divine guidance, it is not surprising that she and Harris often found cohabitation and co-operation difficult. Their quarrels were more often than not the result of attempts to establish their roles in relation to one another, and their disagreements arose from an inability to agree how the prophecies were to be verified as genuine communications from God. The uneasiness in the relationship, which led Sidney Griffith to show an interest in the Moravians,[163] was due not to a failure to agree on the fundamental principle of divine guidance, but on the process of verification, and, once Harris had declared that Sidney Griffith was the receiver and he the communicator of the messages, the relationship seems to have become more settled and to have assumed an air of permanency.

It has been suggested that Sidney Griffith was a hypocrite who took advantage of Harris and used him to her own ends,[164] but this view fails to explain many aspects of their relationship, and seems to have been put forward with the sole intention of portraying Harris as the innocent victim of circumstance and Sidney Griffith as a ruthless predator. He cannot be so easily exonerated; anyone endowed with common sense would have realized that the relationship was undermining his marriage. Both his wife and his mother frequently expressed their opposition to Sidney Griffith with abundant clarity, but Harris was able to dismiss their views on the grounds that they were unreasonable, unchristian and unkind.

At the same time, it is an indication of Sidney Griffith's remarkable resilience that she was able to remain with Harris despite repeated attempts by those around her to have her removed; all the members of Harris's immediate and extended family opposed her, yet she continued to visit Trevecka. It must be remembered, however, that during October 1749 she had been turned out of her home, and, if she was unwilling or forbidden to return to her parental home, it is possible that she could have looked on Trevecka as a haven.

But why Trevecka? Sidney Griffith was one of the gentry; while it would have been possible for her to have gone to London to join others belonging to the same social class, she chose to remain in rural Breconshire among people of rigid religious beliefs. She was not without money, and did not attach herself to Harris because she was thrifty. During her visit to the capital in January 1750, Harris complained that she 'did not have the cause of God at heart in the least, but [spent] all her money on herself and living high'.[165]

The only logical reason for her continued interest in Trevecka, and in Harris, is that she was sincere in her convictions, devout in her belief that she possessed prophetic gifts and 'enthusiastic' in her spirit. She was also in love. As a result of her association with

Harris, she was forced to endure many hardships: she was denied many of the luxuries to which she was accustomed, made aware of the strong opposition to her presence in Harris's home and conscious of the uneasiness that existed among the Methodists concerning her role in the movement. Vulgar insinuations were made about her character, while many of her own rank frowned upon her association with inferior and fanatical people. Such pressures and criticisms would have driven many to seek refuge by retracing their steps and lapsing into anonymity; Sidney Griffith persevered and remained loyal to Harris until her death in 1752.

It is difficult to accept the view that Sidney Griffith was not sincere in her claim to possess the gifts of discernment and prophetic utterance. Harris had for nearly fifteen years been involved in the daily assessment of the spiritual condition of Methodist converts; his experience, even when the emotional aspect of the episode is taken into consideration, renders unlikely the possibility that he had been deceived. The relationship was not based on occasional meetings and infrequent conversations, but on prolonged periods of fellowship and intimate discussions. He accepted Sidney Griffith for what she was, a recent convert to Methodism and an intensely spiritual person. Though later generations have been embarrassed by his association with her, and have attempted to portray her as a deceiver, such a depiction cannot be justified through the evidence currently available. Harris regarded Sidney Griffith as 'the Greatest Woman in Wales';[166] her appearance among the Methodists certainly makes her the most intriguing.

Chapter 9
Postscript

Though 1750 marks a definite watershed in Harris's life, his career was by no means over and he was to live for another twenty-three years. Not until the study of his whole life has been completed can a full appraisal be made of Harris's role in the history of Wales.

Following the decision to separate from the clergy and their party, Harris's primary concern was to rally his supporters in every part of the country; he therefore set out on a series of journeys which were, during the latter half of 1750 and 1751, to take him to each of the thirteen Welsh counties.[1] As he travelled, he attempted to explain to the converts how the separation had evolved.[2] It was Rowland and his followers who were at fault, and he claimed: 'God is on my side, and all the opposition against me is against the Lord.'[3]

On 11 October 1750, he noted in his Diary what he believed to have been the reasons for the separation. Again, Rowland was depicted as the instigator of all the ill feeling, while he himself was portrayed as the innocent victim of a plot. Had not the clerical party clandestinely searched for all his infirmities, 'and then in a wicked light spread them to weaken [his] hands'? Had they not despised the Blood of Christ and trampled on his authority as a leader? They had in his view 'left the teaching of the Spirit to lean on, and study, books, so by the testimony of all, it was not only their private conversation [that] was void of God and corrupting, but also their public preaching', which was 'darkening the Glory of our Saviour' and leading to 'deadness, pride, self and lightness' among the converts.[4]

Harris was confident that he would be able to continue in the work of the Revival, and was persuaded that the 'spirit and Blessing of the Reformation' were to be found among his own people.[5] He therefore held his own Association meetings[6] at which he attempted to lay the foundation of his branch of the movement; exhorters were assessed as to the extent to which they had 'come to the light',[7] and doubts concerning the role of Sidney Griffith were overcome.[8] Harris warned his followers:

> if they have not spiritual views of me in God as being washed from all my Sins in the Blood of Christ, they can't come with me – if they don't see me there, they'll go and dispute about my morality in the flesh and not in Christ, and so be stumbled.[9]

During a journey through north Wales in November 1750, Harris saw for the first time the tract written by Daniel Rowland to condemn his doctrine.[10] *Ymddiddan rhwng Methodist Uniawn-gred ac un Camsyniol* (1750)[11] accused him of rejecting the doctrine of the Trinity and of preaching Patripassianism; it also suggested that he had been deceived through his 'enthusiastic' claims to divine guidance, and had become an Antinomian, a Sabellian, a Ubiquitarian and a Eutychian[12] through his failure to examine in the light of the Scriptures the revelations he alleged to have received.

Harris was deeply offended by this public attack upon his integrity but, on considering each charge 'before the Lord', believed himself acquitted. However, the publication contributed to undermining the support which he enjoyed among the exhorters and, as time went by, Harris realized that they were deserting him.[13]

The reasons for his failure to secure their continued loyalty in many ways replicated those which had led to his separation from Rowland: his autocratic spirit, his heavy-handed treatment of the exhorters,[14] the setting of unreasonably high spiritual standards, his insistence on Sidney Griffith's being accepted as a 'Mother in Israel', and the condemnation of his doctrine by the clerical party, all contributed to isolating him for the second time in less than two and a half years. By the summer of 1751, he was beginning to realize that he was not as successful as he had hoped in establishing a firm foundation on which to build for the future. On 16 August, having received progress reports on the work in various parts of the country, he wrote: 'I see I am alone, or myself ... against all, my own brethren especially.'[15] In October, while on his way to Pembrokeshire, he was told 'of the fewness of the people coming to hear the brethren in these parts and in other places',[16] while in March 1752 he noted that he 'saw ... all [his] labour for 16 years lost' as the people stayed behind in the spiritual wilderness.[17]

Harris had not forgotten his earlier dream of making Trevecka into a centre of activity at which he and Sidney Griffith would serve God by ministering to the faithful,[18] but by this time it could be that there were other ulterior motives for creating such an establishment. Since he had been separated from the 'world' by his conversion in 1735, from his Church by its unwillingness to listen to his calls for reform, and then from his former friends in 1750, would not a community at Trevecka serve as a safe haven in which he would be free to exercise his authority, express his views and yield to the direct guidance given him by God, without fear of condemnation or recrimination? He therefore set about making the necessary arrangements, firm in the belief that this was, yet again, God's will. The first task was to erect a suitable building in which to house the converts; on 14 April 1752, the old house was partly demolished and the foundation of the new laid. From then on, converts arrived to make Trevecka their home.[19]

These developments seemed to ratify the validity of the prophecies Sidney Griffith had made. Rowland had renounced Harris, Trevecka was becoming a haven for broken sinners, William Griffith, Cefnamwlch, had met with an accident and died,[20] and it was, presumably, but a matter of time until Providence removed Anne, thus making it possible for Harris and Sidney Griffith to be married. But this was not to be. Sidney Griffith had for some time been showing signs of ill health; she died during a visit to London on 31 May, the victim of tuberculosis.

To Harris, whose own health had also been deteriorating,[21] her demise was a great blow. The bereavement, coming as it did on top of extreme mental and physical exhaustion, finally precipitated a severe nervous breakdown which, though he continued with the oversight of the building project at Trevecka, confined him to his room for the best part of two years.[22] His withdrawal from public life was, therefore, total, but his retirement allowed him time to rest and to meditate on the events of recent years. As his health improved, his commitments at Trevecka continued to keep him at home, and though he ventured out after 1755, it was not until 1756 that he became involved in extramural religious activities by attending society meetings at Brecon.[23]

During 1756, the outbreak of the Seven Years War brought renewed fears of foreign invasion, and the following year an Act of Parliament reorganized the various county militias.[24] Harris was invited to accept a commission as ensign in the Breconshire militia and, though at first hesitant, finally decided to accept on condition that he be allowed to preach. He claimed that his acceptance of the commission was not only in response to divine guidance, but also a clear test of his faith, to determine whether he was willing to risk life and limb on the command of the Almighty.[25] It was also regarded by him as public proof of his loyalty to both Church and state. He claimed that 'God's glory and love of the Gospel and of our King and country [which were all threatened by a Catholic enemy] is dearer to me and the People [of Trevecka] than anything besides'.[26] Military service took him no further than Great Yarmouth on the Norfolk coast and, as no invasion occurred, Harris was not called upon to use violence. When the regiment was disbanded at the end of 1762, he returned to Trevecka.

During May of that year a letter had been sent to him by Rowland and William Williams, inviting him to return to his former position in the Welsh Methodist movement.[27] Having now fully recovered, Harris accepted, and for the first time in a decade an Association meeting was held at Trevecka in May 1763.[28]

By that time, a new Revival had begun in Wales,[29] centring on Llangeitho. Following his reinstatement, Harris resumed itinerating,[30] but, despite his valiant efforts, it could hardly be said that he was as successful during these years as during the period 1735–50. He was an older man; a new generation had emerged during his absence who had to a certain extent taken the reins of the movement into their own hands, and, as Harris moved among them, emphasizing the need for discipline and organization, there was friction.[31] There were also Harris's responsibilities at Trevecka; with over a hundred people to provide for, and the Countess of Huntingdon eager to establish a college at a nearby building,[32] he was yet again in danger of stretching himself beyond his capabilities.

Following the death of his wife on 9 March 1770, Harris often complained of agonizing bouts of pain and sleepless nights, which restricted his involvement in the Revival work. He attended to his

Diary with less vigour than in previous years, and memories of the past interested him to a greater degree than current events.[33]

He died at his home on 21 July 1773, aged fifty-nine, and was buried at the parish church at Talgarth three days later. His funeral was attended by an estimated crowd of 20,000 people, and, as they interred his body, one clergyman after the other was so overwhelmed by grief that they were unable to read the service.[34] Howell Harris, the first and most eloquent of the Welsh Methodists, was buried in total silence.

He was by nature an extremely powerful and stubborn man. Following his conversion in 1735, these characteristics were to enable him to persevere during difficult times; his fearlessness in the face of opposition and criticism, and his determination to succeed despite many disappointments and setbacks, made him a powerful preacher, an effective exhorter and an efficient organizer. When the movement he had brought into existence threatened to leave the Church from which it had emerged, Harris stood steadfastly against secession, resolute that forcible ejection would be the only justification for departure from the Anglican fold. His intransigence served to protect the movement from becoming a minority sect, and ensured its unity until the separation in 1750.

During the latter half of the 1740s, when he began to deviate from the orthodoxy which his fellow labourers expected of him, his forceful character became a disadvantage in that it was to make him impervious to criticism and deaf to advice. The problem was compounded by his 'enthusiasm': Harris believed that what others claimed to be stubbornness was in reality his submission to the directly revealed will of God. While his opponents were unable to prove to him that he was mistaken in his interpretation of that guidance, there was no way in which he could be convinced that he had slipped into error. His dependence on divine guidance made him not only spiritually powerful but also insensitive: when others disagreed with him, their words were construed as an act of rebellion against God.

Harris's 'enthusiasm' was both his strength and his weakness; it made him a man of vision, but at the same time blinded him. Through his 'enthusiasm' he was enabled to bring the Welsh Methodist movement into existence, to build it up through powerful sermons and exhortations, and to organize it through the various society and Association meetings. But it was also because of his 'enthusiasm' that Welsh Methodism was brought to the brink of destruction, and the obstinacy which sometimes accompanies deep convictions of divine guidance acted as a wedge between him and the other Methodist leaders. 'Enthusiasm' proved to be both his making and his undoing.

Notes

Howell Harris the Diarist

1. These are deposited at the National Library of Wales, Aberystwyth.
2. HHLE, p. 4.
3. For J. H. Davies (1871–1926), see DWB.
4. D. Ben Rees, *Haneswyr yr Hen Gorff* (Lerpwl a Llanddewi Brefi, 1981), p. 23. The remark was made in a letter, dated 17 January 1912, to M. H. Jones, a Methodist historian.
5. For E. O. Davies (1864–1936), see DWB.
6. JHS, XX, 14.
7. HHDR, p. 8.
8. Rees, *Haneswyr yr Hen Gorff*, p. 23.
9. Trevecka Letter 15: 15 August 1730; JHS (August 1917), 18. (Note the discrepancy between the front cover which is dated 'June 1917' and the title page which is dated 'August 1917'.)
10. TL, p. 8.
11. Diary 54a: 30 March 1740.
12. Diary 1: 25 May 1735.
13. Owen C. Watkins, *The Puritan Experience* (London, 1972), p. 18. Also, Keith Thomas, *Religion and the Decline of Magic* (London, 1978), pp. 187–8.
14. Watkins, *The Puritan Experience*, p. 21, 'the definition of the debit and credit sides may have been sharpened by its relevance to the doctrine of justification by faith: a man could bring to God nothing but the debt of his sin, while on the other hand God offered him nothing but grace.'
15. Ibid., p. 18; cf. Diary 22: 14 February 1737, 'I ... write these Blessings down to be a perpetual Memorandum of Thy goodness and to convince me of my Ingratitude ...'
16. Watkins, *The Puritan Experience*, p. 18.
17. Diary 18: 11 January 1737; Diary 23a: 30 March 1737.
18. Cf. Thomas, *Religion and the Decline of Magic*, pp. 109–12.
19. Derec Ll. Morgan, *Y Diwygiad Mawr* (Llandysul, 1981), p. 75; JHS, XXVI, 460, 'I lose many observations internal and external for want of time to write.'

NOTES

20. Ibid., p. 75, 'Harris was totally dependent upon the guidance of the Spirit.'
21. HHDR, p. 51.
22. Diary 25: 7 October 1737.
23. Diary 112: 1 August 1744.
24. Diary 110: 6 June 1744.
25. Diary 123: July 6 [5] 1746.
26. Diary 118: 4 September 1745.
27. HHLE, p. 3, 'no one could mistake Harris for anything but an enthusiast.' Also, R. T. Jenkins, *Yr Apêl at Hanes* (Wrecsam, 1930), pp. 36–8. For a broader discussion on 'enthusiasm', see W. Stephen Gunter, *The Limits of 'Love Divine'* (Nashville, 1989), pp. 13–26. Also, R. A. Knox, *Enthusiasm* (London, 1987), passim.
28. George Whitefield, *Journals* (Edinburgh, 1960). This edition includes the seven journals first published separately, 1738–41.
29. HHLE, pp. 53–4.
30. For the rational approach to Christianity during the eighteenth century, see C. J. Abbey and J. H. Overton, *The English Church in the Eighteenth Century* (London, 1878), I, pp. 178–9.
31. BA, pp. 10, 16.
32. For the quietist emphasis on passivity, see Knox, *Enthusiasm*, pp. 350–1.
33. BA, p. 33.
34. Ibid., p. 17.
35. HHLE, p. 53.
36. Ibid., p. 14; Eifion Evans, *Howel Harris: Evangelist* (Cardiff, 1974), p. 14; HHRS, p. 184: 22 July 1763, 'Declared I could never call myself a preacher, but an exhorter, my gifts being so.'
37. BA, p. 22, 'the people now began to assemble in vast numbers, so that the houses wherein we met, could not contain them.'
38. BA, pp. 20, 25, 27; TM, I, p. 338. Also, LHH, p. 109.
39. J. Dyfnallt Owen (ed.), *Rhad Ras: Ioan Thomas* (Caerdydd, 1949), pp. 28–9.
40. Edgar Phillips, *Edmund Jones: The Old Prophet* (London, 1959), p. 51.
41. E.g., HHDR, p. 42; Diary 73: 19 May 1741, 'Uncommon Power ... to cut most terribly'; Diary 85: 17 February 1742, 'words like Bullets & Thunder'; Diary 113: 17 October 1744, 'Made home to Thunder & cut & search & condemn'; Diary 115b: 25 January 1745, 'cutting and thundering'; HHVP, p. 97.
42. E.g., HHVP, p. 80: 14 December 1742. For the problem of smuggling, see W. A. Speck, *Stability and Strife* (London, 1977), pp. 126–7.
43. HHVP, pp. 97, 110, 132–3.

NOTES

44 Diary 54: 26 March 1740, 'I hear that this Country is overrun with Cards, cockfighting, dancing . . . I had help to expose home.'
45 HHVP, p. 50: 2 March 1741. Harris believed in the early 1740s 'that Dancing &c is worshipping the Devil', see Diary 89: 17 April 1742. In 1750 (Diary 142: 18 March) he was 'cutting to such as come to the Sacrament [on] Easter Sunday and go to dance on Easter Monday, there presenting their souls and bodies to the Lord and then partake of the Table of Devils'.
46 HHVL, p. 68: 15 May 1745, 'Called first, sent out first'. Ibid., p. 104.
47 Diary 123: July 15 [14] 1746, 'He has given me the Honour of beginning this work'; Diary 122: 1 April 1746, 'I went out by my self 11 years ago'.
48 Diary 12: 30 March 1736, 'after I had waited long . . . did the Spirit . . . descend.' This was interpreted by Harris as God showing His approval of whatever he had brought up in prayer.
49 Diary 132: 14 September 1748, 'God has placed me as a father among you and speaks now through me.'
50 Diary 18a: 25 January 1737, 'hearing I was called the Great Reformer . . .'
51 Diary 34: 1 November 1738.
52 For Griffith Jones (1683–1761), Anglican clergyman and founder of the Welsh circulating schools, see DWB and DEB. Harris often turned to him for advice during the early years of the Revival.
53 HHVP, p. 20: 9 September 1739; cf., LHH, pp. 285, 289.
54 HHVP, p. 69: 10 December 1741.
55 HHVL, p. 49: 16 February 1744.
56 Diary 130: 29 March 1748.
57 Diary 34: 13 November 1738.
58 Watkins, *The Puritan Experience*, p. 22.
59 HHLE, p. 5.
60 HHRS, p. 1.
61 Diary 1: 25 May 1735 begins with the words, 'The Life of a certain unspeakable sinner.'
62 Watkins, *The Puritan Experience*, p. 20, '. . . we do not get a full picture of a man from notes of this kind any more than we can judge a garden by looking through the contents of the incinerator.' Also, MTU, p. 105.
63 HHLE, p. 5.
64 TL, p. 7.
65 Gomer M. Roberts (ed.), *Selected Trevecka Letters 1742–47* (Caernarfon, 1956), and *Selected Trevecka Letters 1747–94* (Caernarfon, 1962).

NOTES

The Making of a Revivalist

1. Talgarth Parish Registers; HHDR, p. 12; JHS, IX, 36. It has been suggested that the surname 'Powell' is a clerical error but it is more likely to be a normal Welsh patronymic, representing 'Ap Howell' (the son of Howell [Harris]).
2. JHS, IX, 35–6.
3. Talgarth Parish Records. A certificate bearing the name of Howell Powell, alias Harris, declaring that the parish of Llangadog would be responsible for his upkeep if ever he needed to be supported by the parish at his new home. See HHDR, p. 12.
4. Trevecka MS 3296; HHDR, p. 12; JHS, IX, 35; HHL, p. 10. The document is dated 1 April 1706.
5. 'Trefeca Fach' can be translated 'Little Trevecka'. 'Trevecka' is the Anglicized form of 'Trefeca'. The spelling 'Trevecca' is also used occasionally.
6. For Joseph (1704–64) and Thomas Harris (1707–1782), see DWB. Also, HHL, pp. 9–39. Note, however, that Thomas was born in 1707, not in 1705 as stated in DWB and HHL.
7. This classification is based on the analysis of Gregory King (1648–1712), the leading demographer of the late seventeenth century. For King, see DNB. For an assessment of his analysis, see Speck, *Stability and Strife*, pp. 31–61.
8. Thomas Nichols, *Annals and Antiquities of the Counties and County Families of Wales* (London, 1872), vol. 1, p. 106.
9. HHVL, p. 177.
10. For an account of the development of the project, see TL, pp. 185–206; HMGC, pp. 356–77; Alun Wynne Owen, 'A study of Howell Harris and the Trevecka "Family" (1752–1760)', MA thesis, University of Wales, 1957. Also, M. H. Jones, 'Howell Harris, citizen and patriot', *Transactions of the Honourable Society of Cymmrodorion* (1908–9).
11. Harris became a member on 12 May 1756. Among the original subscribing members were Charles Powel of Castlemadoc, Penry Williams of Penpont and Sir Edward Williams of Gwernyfed. See Henry Edmunds, 'History of the Brecknockshire Agricultural Society, 1755–1955', *Brycheiniog* (Journal of the Brecknock Society), vol. 2, 32.
12. For an account of Harris's upbringing, see HHDR, pp. 11–18; JHS (August 1917), Part 2 ; POD, pp. 9–17.
13. Trevecka Letter 18: 13 October 1730. JHS (August 1917), 19–20; HHDR, p. 15.
14. Llwyn-llwyd is in the parish of Llanigon, Breconshire, and the school

was maintained by David Price (fl. 1700–42; see DWB), the Dissenting minister of Maesyronnen. Harris was later to speak appreciatively of the education provided. Llwyn-llwyd was in the tradition of the Dissenting Academies. G. Dyfnallt Owen, *Ysgolion a Cholegau yr Annibynwyr* (Abertawe, 1939), pp. 26–7; H. P. Roberts, 'Nonconformist academies in Wales (1662–1862)', *Transactions of the Honourable Society of Cymmrodorion* (1928–9), 19–20.

15 John Beadle, *The Journal or Diary of a Thankful Christian* (1656); Watkins, *The Puritan Experience*, p. 23.
16 See Watkins, *The Puritan Experience*, pp. 18, 232.
17 Ibid., p. 37.
18 Diary 1: 25 May 1735.
19 John Walsh, 'Origins of the Evangelical Revival', in G. V. Bennett and J. D. Walsh (eds.), *Essays in Modern English Church History in Memory of Norman Sykes* (London, 1966), pp. 132–62.
20 For Pryce Davies, vicar of Talgarth from 1733 to his death on 24 October 1761, see JHS, XXXIX, 27; according to H. Elvet Lewis, *Howell Harris and the Welsh Revivalists* (London, n.d.), p. 10, he was, 'as clergymen went in the early part of the eighteenth century . . . probably better than the average'.
21 BA, p. 10.
22 Diary 41: 24 March 1739.
23 BA, p. 10.
24 Diary 41: 24 March 1739.
25 BA, pp. 10–11.
26 Diary 71: 22 March 1741.
27 BA, p. 11; Diary 54a: 30 March 1740.
28 Diary 99: 6 April 1743.
29 BA, pp. 11–12.
30 Diary 1: 22 May 1735.
31 BA, p. 12; Diary 54a: 30 March 1740.
32 Diary 99: 20 April 1743. He lodged with Lewis Jones, 'a Gent'. Diary 81: 19 November 1741.
33 Richard Allestree (?), *The Whole Duty of Man Laid Down in a Plain and Familiar Way for the Use of All, but especially the Meanest Reader* (1658). For Whitefield's criticism of this volume, see Luke Tyerman, *The Life and Times of the Rev. George Whitefield*, 2 vols. (London, 1876), I, p. 360. In 1741 Harris also criticized the book, and 'said that there was an error in it . . . in its Preface . . . saying that God made a Second Covenant with Adam. That was not true.' Diary 63a: 5 November 1740. Also Henry D. Rack, *Reasonable Enthusiast: John Wesley and the Rise of Methodism* (London, 1989), pp. 21–2.
34 John Spurr, 'Anglican apologetic and the Restoration Church',

D.Phil. thesis, University of Oxford, 1985, pp. 190–1. This book was 'regarded as one of the few essential works required by a devout Anglican', ibid., p. 192. See Dyfnallt Morgan (ed.), *Y Ferch o Ddolwar Fach* (Caernarfon, 1977), p. 17, where it is described as the most influential devotional book in the eighteenth century.

35 Michael R. Watts, *The Dissenters* (Oxford, 1978), p. 426.
36 BA, p. 12; see also, Diary 46: 12 July 1739; Diary 1: 22 May 1735, '[it pleased] the Almighty, out of his inmost pity, to call [me] from death to life through the reading of that most excellent book The Whole Duty of Man.'
37 BA, p. 12; Diary 54a: 30 March 1740.
38 BA, pp. 12–13.
39 HHDR, p. 23; cf. John Bunyan, *Grace Abounding to the Chief of Sinners* (1666; Reprinted: Grand Rapids, 1978), p. 20, 'I thought no man in England could please God better than I. But, poor wretch as I was, I was all this time ignorant of Jesus Christ.'
40 Diary 46: 12 July 1739.
41 BA, pp. 12–13.
42 Ibid., p. 13; POD, p. 19; HHDR, p. 24.
43 Diary 74: 29 June 1741.
44 Ibid.
45 BA, p. 13.
46 These accounts use terms representative of Harris's later predestinarian views, e.g., 'irresistible', 'effectually called' etc. This, however, does not detract from the value of the accounts, as the interpretation offered does not alter the nature of the events themselves.
47 Diary 74: 29 June 1741.
48 Ibid.; cf. Watkins, *The Puritan Experience*, p. 130, where it is stated that both John Bunyan and Richard Baxter had experienced great storms of temptation after their conversions. John Wesley also faced strong temptations following his Aldersgate experience in May 1738. See JWJ, I, pp. 476–7.
49 BA, p. 13.
50 Diary 72: 17 May 1741.
51 BA, p. 13. See also, Diary 41: 24 March 1739, 'I had one sore temptation, to deny the being of God to Whitsuntide. Then reading Practice of Piety ... Now I saw there that whatever temptation conquered us, if we believe in the Sacrament we should be rid of it. On that I was full of hopes.'
52 Bayly, *The Practice of Piety*, p. 513.
53 John Nelson, a Methodist preacher, had a similar experience: 'Jesus Christ was as evidently set before the eye of my mind, as crucified for my sins, as if I had seen Him with my bodily eyes.' See Thomas

NOTES

Jackson (ed.), *The Lives of Early Methodist Preachers*, 6 vols. (London, 1865–6), I, p. 18.
54 BA, p. 13; Diary 41: 24 March 1739.
55 Note the similarity to Wesley's words. See JWJ, I, pp. 475–6, 'I felt my heart strangely warmed.'
56 BA, pp. 15–16.
57 Diary 74: 29 June 1741.
58 Diary 54a: 30 March 1740.
59 Diary 74: 29 June 1741; see also, Diary 70: 17 March 1741; Watkins, *The Puritan Experience*, p. 42, states that 'temptations to suicide are recorded quite frequently' in Puritan biographies.
60 BA, p. 16; Diary 54a: 30 March 1740.
61 BA, p. 17.
62 Diary 1: 25 May 1735.
63 Spurr, 'Anglican apologetic', 213.
64 Cf. D. L. Watson, 'Methodist Spirituality', in F. C. Senn (ed.), *Protestant Spiritual Traditions* (New York, 1986), p. 220. John Wesley encountered a similar difficulty with William Law's mysticism. See Richard P. Heitzenrater, *Wesley and the People Called Methodists* (Nashville, 1995), pp. 52–3.
65 This echoes Wesley's distinction between two levels of saving faith, the faith of a servant who fears God and obeys His commandments, and the faith of a son who obeys out of filial love. See Thomas Jackson (ed.), *The Works of the Rev. John Wesley, A. M.*, 14 vols. (London, 1829–31), VII, pp. 199–200. Also, 'Minutes of third annual conference', in Albert C. Outler (ed.), *John Wesley* (Oxford, 1964), p. 157.
66 BA, p. 17, 'I was ... a total stranger to all the controversies about Religion.' Also HHDR, p. 28.
67 BA, p. 17. Lack of fellowship was typical of contemporary Anglicanism. John Walsh, 'Religious societies: Methodist and Evangelical 1738–1800', in W. J. Sheils and D. Wood (eds.), *Voluntary Religion* (London, 1986), pp. 281–2.
68 HHDR, p. 29. Also, Trevecka Letters 45, 46, 48: 2, 23 May and 6 June 1735.
69 HHDR, p. 23.
70 Ibid., p. 31; BA, p. 20.
71 Trevecka Letter 57: 27 September 1735.
72 BA, p. 17.
73 Ibid., pp. 18–19. Harris declared that he was determined to trust God 'for [his] temporal blessings'. While employed as a teacher he received an income, but following his dismissal he lived 'a life of faith', depending on God to provide for his needs through the generosity of others.

NOTES

74 Ibid., p. 19, 'The generality of people spent the Lord's day contrary to the Laws of God and man ... neither had any one, whom I knew, the true knowledge of that God whom we pretend to worship.'
75 This was a common claim among 'enthusiasts'. Knox, *Enthusiasm*, pp. 1–2.
76 Even Anglican Religious Societies fell foul of this charge. Walsh, 'Religious societies', pp. 285–6.
77 BA, p. 20.
78 Ibid.
79 Cf. John Weborg, 'Pietism', in Senn, *Protestant Spiritual Traditions*, p. 183. While Pietism 'was preoccupied with the regeneration of persons it occupied itself with the renewal of the Church'.
80 Trevecka Letter 54; LHH, p. 24.
81 Harris was entered at St Mary's Hall (see Joseph Foster (ed.), *Alumni Oxonienses* (London, 1888), II; cf. HHDR, p. 36, which says St Margaret's Hall), but was unable to settle in the city. Having left Trevecka on 20 November 1735, he matriculated on 25 November and was back home on 28 November. It was intended that he should return in 1736, as is seen from Trevecka Letters 59, 61, 62, 67 and 71. However, he did not return there as a student. HHDR, pp. 36–40.
82 BA, p. 22.
83 Trevecka Letter 65; LHH, p. 29.
84 William Williams, in his elegy to Harris, described how he first saw him preaching by the porch of Talgarth church. See Thomas Levi (ed.), *Casgliad o Hen Farwnadau Cymreig* (Wrexham, [1872]), p. 30.
85 BA, pp. 22–3.
86 HHDR, p. 45; Trevecka Letter 70. Harris was ill during February 1736.
87 BA, p. 23.
88 For Harris's relationship with William Herbert and the mid-Wales Baptists, see D. D. Morgan, 'The development of the Baptist movement in Wales between 1714 and 1815 with special reference to the Evangelical Revival', D.Phil. thesis, University of Oxford, 1986, chapter 5.
89 Diary 12: 30 March 1736.
90 Ibid.
91 A common claim among 'enthusiasts'; see Umphrey Lee, *The Historical Backgrounds of Early Methodist Enthusiasm* (New York, 1967), p. 119.
92 Diary 49: 13 September 1739.
93 Diary 130: 19 April 1748.
94 Diary 109: 19 April 1744.
95 Diary 118: 10 September 1745.

[96] Diary 73: 30 May 1741.
[97] HHVL, pp. 275, 278.
[98] HHLE, pp. 8–9. For Harris's dreams, see also, POD, pp. 45–9.
[99] HHVP, p. 171, 'God reveals His will, – by Dreams.'
[100] Diary 113: 20 September 1744.
[101] Diary 25: 17 January 1738.
[102] Diary 70: 12 March 1741.
[103] Diary 113: 18 October 1744.
[104] For a discussion of this issue during the Puritan era, see G. F. Nuttall, *The Holy Spirit in Puritan Faith and Experience* (Oxford, 1946), pp. 20–33.
[105] For the response to Whitefield's Journal, see Tyerman, *Life of Whitefield*, I, pp. 151–3.
[106] George Whitefield, *Works*, 6 vols. (London and Edinburgh, 1771), II, p. 144.
[107] For example, G. Nesta Evans, *Religion and Politics in Mid-Eighteenth Century Anglesey* (Cardiff, 1953), pp. 28–67.
[108] For the French Prophets, see Hillel Schwartz, *The French Prophets* (London, 1980).
[109] Diary 25: 8 September 1737.
[110] HHVP, p. 63: 10 May 1741.
[111] Whitefield, *Works*, I, p. 144.
[112] Diary 131b: 4 August 1748.
[113] Diary 133: 5 January 1749. See TM, I, p. 358.
[114] A. M. Lyles, *Methodism Mocked* (London, 1960), p. 39. Opposers often demanded that Methodists prove that they were called of God through the performance of miracles. See Henry Stebbing, *A Sermon on the New Birth* (London, 1739), pp. 9–10.
[115] HHDR, p. 53.
[116] Diary 54a: 30 March 1740. Harris recalled that Mary Perrott had sunk 'very bad to despair'. Also, Diary 16: October 1736. It is difficult to deduce what exactly occurred.
[117] Diary 12: 30 March 1736.
[118] Trevecka Letter 68: 10 May 1736.
[119] Trevecka Letter 73: 22 May 1736. Harris wrote: 'If I can come to be known to [Griffith Jones] it must be through the Dissenters for the Clergy hate him for his singular Piety and Charity to the Dissenters.'
[120] For Thomas Jones (1689–1772), see JHS, vol. 8, new series (1984), 24–30.
[121] Trevecka Letter 73.
[122] For Griffith Jones (1683–1761), see DWB and DEB. In 1720 he married Margaret, the sister of his patron, Sir John Philipps. For his life and work, see F. A. Cavenagh, *The Life and Work of Griffith*

NOTES

Jones (Cardiff, 1930); Thomas Kelly, *Griffith Jones, Llanddowror: Pioneer in Adult Education* (Cardiff, 1950); David Jones, *Life and Times of Griffith Jones* (London, 1902). For his contribution to the development of education in Wales, see Geraint H. Jenkins, *The Foundations of Modern Wales: Wales 1642–1780* (Oxford/Cardiff, 1987), pp. 370–81; *idem*, 'An old and much honoured soldier: Griffith Jones, Llanddowror', *Welsh History Review*, 2 (1983), 449–68.

123 For Sir John Philipps (1666?–1737), moral, religious and educational reformer, Member of Parliament for Pembroke and later for Haverfordwest, see DWB and DEB.

124 The words of Adam Ottley, bishop of St Davids (1713–23), quoted in DWB.

125 HMGC, p. 81.

126 William Williams (not to be confused with William Williams of Pantycelyn) was the Independent minister of Tredwstan (1729–62).

127 Trevecka Letter 76: June 1736. It is fortunate that Harris wrote this letter, as the Diary for the period 24 May to 10 June 1736 is missing from the Trevecka Collection.

128 The nephew was David Jones: TL, p. 85n.

129 For Bridget Bevan (1698–1779), see DWB and DEB.

130 For the SPCK, see W. O. B. Allen and E. McClure, *Two Hundred Years: The History of the Society for Promoting Christian Knowledge, 1698–1898* (London, 1898). For the SPCK in Wales, see Mary Clement, *The SPCK and Wales, 1699–1740* (London, 1954); *idem* (ed.), *Correspondence and Minutes of the SPCK relating to Wales 1699–1740* (Cardiff, 1952).

131 For an assessment of Francke and Boehm's influence on the British religious scene, see D. L. Brunner, 'The role of Halle Pietists in England (c.1700–c.1740) with special reference to the SPCK', D.Phil. thesis, University of Oxford, 1988; G. F. Nuttall, 'Continental Pietism and the Evangelical movement in Britain', in J. van den Berg and J. P. van Dooren (eds.), *Pietismus und Réveil* (Leiden, 1978).

132 HHDR, pp. 85–6.

133 Trevecka Letter 78: 27 June 1736.

134 Harris's next letter to Griffith Jones was dated 31 July 1736. It opens with the words, 'I had the happiness of your affectionate Epistle ...' Jones must, therefore, have written to Harris between 27 June, the date of Harris's first letter, and his application before the bishop sometime during July. The letter is not to be found in the Trevecka Collection but much of its contents can be deduced from Harris's letter of 31 July, which also mentions a visit by Harris to Cwm-iou to see Thomas Jones.

NOTES

[135] Trevecka Letter 80: 31 July 1736.
[136] Nicholas Claggett was bishop of St David's from 1732 to 1743. Harris again applied for ordination in both May and August 1739, but was refused.
[137] Trevecka Letter 80.
[138] For Edward Dalton (d. 1761), see HHDR, p. 73n. Also, Mary Clement, 'Teulu'r Daltoniaid, Penbre, Sir Gaerfyrddin', JHS, XXIX, 1.
[139] HHDR, pp. 73–4.
[140] Ibid.
[141] The crisis is not mentioned in POD, HMGC or LHH.
[142] BA, p. 17.
[143] HHDR, p. 75.
[144] Trevecka Letter 87: 8 October 1736.
[145] HHVP, p. 42; HHDR, p. 74.
[146] This Harris claims in BA, p. 24.
[147] Little is known of Games. See TL, p. 222n.
[148] For similar work in Anglesey during the same period, see Evans, *Religion and Politics*, p. 24.
[149] HHDR, p. 83. Harris recalled in 1739 that this 'was the origin of many permanent societies'.
[150] Diary 34: 13, 15 November 1738; HMGC, p. 162. Harris regarded his earlier attempts at forming societies to have failed. See HHDR, p. 86.
[151] Diary 116: 15 April 1745; HHDR, p. 86.
[152] Trevecka Letter 92: 8 January 1737.
[153] For the 'gathered church' principle, see G. F. Nuttall, *Visible Saints* (Oxford, 1957), pp. 43–69; R. Tudur Jones, *Congregationalism in England, 1662–1962* (London, 1962), pp. 13–32, 37–8.
[154] Diary 22: 9 February, 3 March 1737. Pryce Davies rebuked Harris for continuing with his work among the societies and charged him with failing to live canonically.
[155] Diary 18: 8 January 1737.
[156] Diary 18a: 11 February 1737.
[157] Diary 20: 27 February 1737.
[158] Diary 22: 22 February 1737.
[159] A note dated 11 March 1737 found between the pages of Diary 22.
[160] Diary 23: 9 March 1737; Diary 23a: 24, 27 March 1737.
[161] Diary 22: 13 February 1737.
[162] Diary 23: 9 March 1737.
[163] Diary 23a: 25 March 1736.
[164] Ibid., 27 March.
[165] Diary 23: 18 March 1737.

NOTES

[166] John Walsh, 'Religious societies', p. 281. Even some of the Methodist critics recognized that the Church was defective in this respect. Stebbing, *A Sermon on the New Birth*, pp. 18–19.
[167] Diary 22: 3 March 1737.
[168] Ibid., 23 February.
[169] Diary 22: 2 March 1737.
[170] Diary 23: 13 March 1737.
[171] Ibid., 20 March.
[172] Diary 23a: 30 March 1737.
[173] Diary 22: 20 February 1737.
[174] Ibid., note found between pages.
[175] Diary 23: 17 March 1737.
[176] Diary 22: 13 February 1737. Griffith Jones 'cautioned' Harris against the Dissenters.
[177] Diary 23a: 6 April 1737.
[178] Ibid., 2 April.
[179] Frank Baker in R. E. Davies and E. G. Rupp (eds.), *The History of the Methodist Church in Great Britain* (London, 1965), I, pp. 213–14, 'Wesley was not concerned about the source [of an idea], so long as the projected method of furthering the purpose of God in Methodism met his own peculiar brand of churchmanship – and worked!' The same was true of Harris.
[180] Diary 25: 8 September 1737.
[181] Diary 23a: 9 April 1737.
[182] David Lowes Watson, *The Early Methodist Class Meeting* (Nashville, 1985), p. 6, quoting Frank Baker, 'John Wesley's churchmanship', in *London Holborn and Quarterly Review*, 185 (1960), 210, 'His avowed purpose was not "to form the plan of a new church", but to reform the old one.'
[183] Diary 23a: 8 April 1737; cf. Watson, *The Early Methodist Class Meeting*, pp. 5, 16, 32–3.
[184] Diary 23a: 8 April 1737.

A Mission from God

[1] E.g., HHDR, p. 28. Bennett says of Harris: 'When he began to think of matters theologically, he was a rank Arminian.' See also, HMGC, p. 103.
[2] Trevecka Letter 80: 31 July 1736.
[3] HHDR, pp. 114–15.
[4] Diary 54a: 30 March 1740. Harris admitted that he was 'full of ignorance ... and yet amazingly led about'.

NOTES

5   Eifion Evans, *Howel Harris*, p. 15.
6   Diary 54a: 30 March 1740; Richard Morris, 'Howell Harris: theologian, ecclesiastical statesman and saint', JHS, XX, 3.
7   Diary 22: 1 March 1737. At Wernos, 'speaking about Predestination &c, I angered the Dissenters and had a hot Dispute.'
8   HHDR, p. 115.
9   JHS, XX, 4.
10 Diary 54a: 30 June 1740.
11 Diary 41: 24 March 1739.
12 For Thomas Lewis (dates unknown), see HHDR, p. 130; HMGC, p. 106. He was the son of David Lewis, incumbent of Llansanffraid Cwmteuddwr, Radnorshire. In 1741, Thomas moved to Llan-ddew, near Brecon, and remained a Methodist supporter throughout his ministry.
13 Diary 43: 29 April 1739; Diary 70: 17 March 1741; HHDR, p. 134.
14 Diary 41: 24 March 1739.
15 The Diary for 10 April–31 August 1737 is missing. Details are taken from other Diaries and letters.
16 HMGC, p. 103; HHDR, p. 125.
17 Diary 41: 24 March 1739, 'I began to discourse publickly'; HHDR, p. 125, 'I began to speak publicly'.
18 For Howel Davies (*c*.1716–70), see DWB; DEB; TM, I, pp. 128–40; HMGC, pp. 104–5; JHS, III, 96–106, XX, 74–80.
19 The reason behind the setting up of this school is not known. Neither is it known how the two schools came to be united, although Richard Bennett's theory in HHDR, p. 128, seems plausible.
20 *Pace* A. Brown-Lawson, *John Wesley and the Anglican Evangelicals of the Eighteenth Century* (Durham, 1994), p. 19.
21 Diary 25: 14 September 1737.
22 For covenants, see R. C. Monk, *John Wesley: His Puritan Heritage* (London, 1966), pp. 216–18. For another early Evangelical making several covenants, see Frank Baker, *William Grimshaw 1708–63* (London, 1963), pp. 79–89; Faith Cook, *William Grimshaw of Haworth* (Edinburgh, 1997), pp. 73–4, 177–80, 186–7. For Wesley's later Covenant Service for which he drew material from Joseph and Richard Alleine, the two most widely circulated Puritan authors who advocated personal covenanting, see Watson, *The Early Methodist Class Meeting*, pp. 35–6.
23 Diary 25: 15 November 1737.
24 Ibid., 21 November.
25 For the Welsh circulating schools, see Jenkins, *The Foundations of Modern Wales*, pp. 370–81; Mary Clement, *The SPCK and Wales*; Thomas Rees, *History of Protestant Nonconformity in Wales*

[26] HHDR, p. 129.
[27] Diary 25: 21, 30 November 1737.
[28] Ibid., 9 January 1738.
[29] BA, p. 24.
[30] For Daniel Rowland (1713–90), see DWB; DEB; Eifion Evans, *Daniel Rowland* (Edinburgh, 1985); D. Worthington, *Cofiant y Parch. Daniel Rowland* (Caerfyrddin, 1923); D. J. Odwyn Jones, *Daniel Rowland* (Llandysul, 1938).
[31] For Phillip Pugh (1679–1760), see DWB and DEB.
[32] DR, p. 39.
[33] It was 'by Providence' according to Harris in 1744. See DR, p. 52.
[34] M. H. Jones, 'The Itinerary of Howell Harris', JHS, VIII, No. 3, p. 17. As Eifion Evans noted in DR, p. 52n., the source of this information is not clear. The day was a Saturday. For further details of Harris's itinerary, see JHS, X, No. 3 and XII, No. 4.
[35] DR, p. 51. This does, however, raise a problem. If Griffith Jones knew of Daniel Rowland, how is it that he had not mentioned him to Harris? Had he done so, Harris would certainly have written of him in his Diary. Is it possible that Harris first heard of Rowland from Griffith Jones while at Llanddowror during July 1737 (the Diary for that period is missing) and that he went to Defynnog in order to hear him? See HHDR, p. 132. 'Providence' would still have a hand in their meeting, having brought Rowland to that part of the country where Harris, due to its proximity to his home, would have no difficulty in attending the service.
[36] Trevecka MS 3186; HMGC, p. 106; LHH, pp. 46–7; DR, p. 52.
[37] HHRS, p. 187.
[38] Trevecka MS 3186.
[39] John Williams was High Sheriff of Radnorshire in 1736. HMGC, pp. 103–4.
[40] HHDR, p. 139.
[41] He travelled to Llanddowror on 11 September, 16 October and 4 December.
[42] Harris called at Llangeitho to see Daniel Rowland on 6 December.
[43] HHDR, p. 142.
[44] BA, p. 25.
[45] Diary 25: 8 February 1738.
[46] HHDR, p. 134.
[47] For Rees Davies (1694?–1767), see DWB; HHDR, p. 156.
[48] Trevecka Letter 100: 20 August 1737.
[49] R. Tudur Jones, *Hanes Annibynwyr Cymru* (Abertawe, 1966), p. 143; R. T. Jenkins, *Yng Nghysgod Trefeca* (Caernarfon, 1968), p. 14.

NOTES

[50] Edmund Jones (1702–93) was ordained in 1734. As already mentioned, he showed a curious mixture of Calvinism and folkloristic beliefs. To Harris (Diary 90: 29 May 1742) he was 'a Saint and a true Minister of Christ'. R. Tudur Jones (*Hanes Annibynwyr Cymru*, p. 144) claims that he was the most influential force in favour of the Revival among the Independents of his day and was as near to being a bishop as a Dissenting minister could be. For his career, see DWB; DEB. Also, Edgar Phillips, *Edmund Jones* (London, 1959).

[51] For James Davies (d. 1760), Henry Davies (1696–1766) and Phillip Pugh (1679–1760), see DWB.

[52] For Miles Harry (1700–76) see DWB; DEB. For Enoch Francis (1688?–1740), see DWB. Also T. M. Bassett, *Bedyddwyr Cymru* (Abertawe, 1977), pp. 63–5, 79.

[53] For James Roberts, see HMGC, p. 166.

[54] Diary 63a: 11 November 1740; Trevecka Letter 362: 7 August 1742.

[55] David Williams (1709–84), an Independent minister, was ordained minister of Trinity Church, Cardiff, in 1734 but was also the pastor of the Independents scattered around the parish of Eglwysilan who met in private houses until the erection of their chapel on Caerphilly mountain in 1739. See DWB.

[56] Trevecka Letter 110: 17 May 1738.

[57] Trevecka Letter 111: 9 June 1738.

[58] Examples of other letters welcoming Harris and encouraging him to continue in his work are Trevecka Letters 119, 122, 138, 218. An undated letter from Henry Palmer, the Independent minister of Henllan Amgoed, Carmarthenshire, is published in *Y Cofiadur* (The Journal of the Historical Society of the Welsh Independents) (1957), 4.

[59] The Diary for the period 26 February to 14 June 1738 is missing from the Trevecka Collection. Detailed accounts and dates of events are not therefore possible.

[60] Trevecka Letter 112: 12 June 1738. Rees, *History of Protestant Nonconformity*, p. 371.

[61] For the relationship between the Methodists and the Dissenters, see R. T. Jenkins, 'Yr Annibynwyr Cymreig a Hywel Harris', *Y Cofiadur* (1935), republished in *Yng Nghysgod Trefeca*; idem., 'Yr Annibynwyr Cymreig a Methodistiaeth', in anon. (ed.), *Hanes ac Egwyddorion Annibynwyr Cymru* (Abertawe, 1939), p. 129; R. Tudur Jones, *Hanes Annibynwyr Cymru*, pp. 145–8. For the influence of Methodism on eighteenth-century Dissent in Wales, see idem., 'Dylanwad y Mudiad Methodistaidd ar Ymneilltuaeth Cymru yn y Ddeunawfed Ganrif', JHS, XLVII, 52–70.

[62] I think this a likely explanation for Harris's action. Cf. HHDR,

p. 161, which does not suggest a reason for the composition of the Rules. Harris must have been anxious for the societies during his illness. The nature of the illness is not known.

63 Diary 41: 24 March 1739.
64 Diary 18: 1 January 1737.
65 Diary 22: 10 February 1737.
66 Ibid., 12 February.
67 Ibid., 22 February.
68 Diary 23: 20 March 1737.
69 Diary 25: 5 September 1737.
70 Ibid., 3 October.
71 Ibid., 7 October.
72 Diary 34: 17 October 1738.
73 Ibid., 14 November.
74 JWJ, I, p. 424; Heitzenrater, *Wesley and the People called Methodists*, pp. 77f.
75 I owe this sentence to Watson, *The Early Methodist Class Meeting*, p. 46.
76 R. T. Jenkins, *Yng Nghysgod Trefeca*, p. 23.
77 Edward H. Sugden (ed.), *Wesley's Standard Sermons*, 2 vols. (London, 1921), I, p. 125.
78 Diary 115b: 31 December 1744.
79 Diary 70: 12 March 1740. Also Diary 62: 6 September 1740; HHVP, p. 54.
80 Diary 121: 20 January 1746, 'I also opened ... – real Justification from Eternity – actual when Christ dy'd and personal when they first had a seeing [sic].'
81 Diary 71: 22 March 1741. Harris wrote: 'seeing that since my Justification I could never fear falling away ... Those who hold this are not Justified, never knew Christ.'
82 Jenkins, *Yng Nghysgod Trefeca*, p. 24. Also, R. Buick Knox, 'Howell Harris and his doctrine of the Church', JHS, XLVII, 77.
83 Trevecka Letter 303: no date, but inscribed by Harris, 'Recd. 10br 25, 1740'.
84 HHVP, p. 49: 28 February 1741.
85 Sugden (ed.), *Wesley's Standard Sermons*, I, p. 208.
86 Diary 25: 3 October 1737.
87 Ibid., 7 October.
88 J. Wesley, *Works*, V, pp. 123–34; Outler (ed.), *John Wesley*, pp. 209–20.
89 Diary 25: 24 November 1737.
90 Ibid., 24 September 1737.
91 M. M. Knappen, *Tudor Puritanism* (London, 1939), p. 394.

NOTES

92 Diary 25: 19 October 1737.
93 Diary 35: 2–3 December 1738.
94 Ibid., 4 December 1738.
95 Trevecka Letter 133; Tyerman, *Life of Whitefield*, I, p. 170; BA, p. 110.
96 Whitefield (letter to the inhabitants of Savannah, 2 October 1738), in Tyerman, *Life of Whitefield*, I, p. 143.
97 There were several reasons for his return. See ibid., pp. 140–2.
98 Ibid., p. 143.
99 Ibid., pp. 274–5.
100 JWJ, II, p. 167.
101 Whitefield, *Journals*, p. 222; Tyerman, *Life of Whitefield*, I, pp. 182–3.
102 Whitefield, *Journals*, p. 216.
103 Élie Halévy (tr. Bernard Semmel), *The Birth of Methodism in England* (London, 1971), p. 61.
104 Whitefield, *Journals*, p. 229.
105 Ibid., p. 227.
106 Ibid., p. 229.
107 Trevecka Letter 136: 8 January 1739.
108 For Harris's and Whitefield's accounts of their meeting, see Diary 41: 7 March 1739 and Whitefield, *Journals*, pp. 229–30. Also, *Weekly History*, printed by J. Lewis (London), Issue 27.
109 Whitefield, *Journals*, p. 229.
110 Ibid.
111 Tyerman, *Life of Whitefield*, I, pp. 223–6.
112 LHH, p. 82.
113 Diary 41: 10 March 1739.
114 Ibid., 11 March; Cf. JWJ, II, p. 91. Also, R. P. Heitzenrater, *Mirror and Memory* (Nashville, 1989), pp. 127–31.
115 Diary 41: 13–15 March.
116 This can be seen from his prayers. Diary 41: 14 March, 18 March, 23 March 1739.
117 For James Hutton (1715–95), see DNB; DEB. Also, C. Podmore, *The Moravian Church in England, 1728–1760* (Oxford, 1998), pp. 34–6; Arnold Dallimore, *George Whitefield*, 2 vols. (London and Edinburgh, 1970–80), I, pp. 112–13. It was at the 'Bible and Sun' that the Fetter Lane society was originally founded. See C. W. Towlson, *Moravian and Methodist* (London, 1957), p. 62; Podmore, *The Moravian Church*, pp. 29ff.
118 HHL, pp. 180–1.
119 For the Fetter Lane society, see Podmore, *The Moravian Church*, pp. 29ff.; idem, 'The Fetter Lane Society, 1738', *Proceedings of Wesley*

NOTES

Historical Society, 46, pp. 125–53; *idem*, 'The Fetter Lane Society, 1739–40', ibid., vol. 47, pp. 156–86; HHL, p. 67f; Towlson, *Moravian and Methodist*, passim; Griffith T. Roberts, *Dadleuon Methodistiaeth Gynnar* (Abertawe, 1970), p. 15.

120 John Wesley was in Bristol at the time but was called back to London during June to intervene in the crisis. JWJ, II, p. 216.

121 For John Shaw, see Podmore, *The Moravian Church*, pp. 52–3, 55; HHL, pp. 73, 76; Roberts, *Dadleuon Methodistiaeth Gynnar*, pp. 27–9.

122 Charles Wesley, *The Journal of the Rev. Charles Wesley, M.A.* (ed. John Telford: London, 1909), p. 228.

123 Ibid., p. 229.

124 HHL, p. 179. Also Diary 43: 25 April 1739.

125 HHDR, p. 3.

126 HHL, p. 184.

127 Ibid., p. 187.

128 Diary 44: 30 April 1739. Also, HHL, p. 195.

129 For 'stillness', see Podmore, *The Moravian Church*, p. 59f. Though very popular among the Moravians from 1739, it was 'never the official teaching of their church'. R. T. Jenkins, *The Moravian Brethren in North Wales* (London, 1938), p. 5; John and Charles Wesley opposed the doctrine. Roberts, *Dadleuon Methodistiaeth Gynnar*, p. 52; Knox, *Enthusiasm*, p. 475; Towlson, *Moravian and Methodist*, pp. 84–104.

130 For Philip Henry Molther, see DEB; Podmore, *The Moravian Church*, p. 59; L. Tyerman, *The Life and Times of the Rev. John Wesley, M.A.*, 3 vols. (London, 1870), I, p. 297.

131 Diary 44: 30 April 1739.

132 Ibid.

133 HHL, p. 205.

134 Diary 44: 1 May 1739.

135 Ibid., 8 May 1739.

136 Ibid., 44: 16 May 1739.

137 Ibid.

138 BA, p. 31.

139 Ibid., p. 33.

140 JWJ, I, p. 454.

141 BA, p. 33.

142 Diary 56: 25 May 1740.

143 Diary 97: 2 [1] February 1743.

144 See HHL, p. 210, where it states that Harris became a Christian on 8 May 1739 ('Heddiw y cychwyn Harris fod yn Gristion'). While this statement is open to interpretation in light of twentieth-century

theological thinking, its implication in the context of eighteenth-century Calvinistic Methodist theology is that Harris had undergone a (second) conversion experience. See also B. G. Evans, *Ymneilltuaeth Cymru ac Apocrypha'r Diwygiad* (Treffynnon, 1901), p. 5.

145 HHVP, p. 25: 11 March 1740.
146 Ibid., p. 47: 23 February 1741.
147 Diary 97: 2 January 1743.
148 Diary 54a: 30 March 1740.
149 Diary 47a: 25 June 1739.
150 Diary 52 (Part 2): 8 February 1740.
151 BA, p. 34.
152 Diary 45: 27 May 1739.
153 Ibid.
154 For Capel Hanbury (1707–65), son and heir of John Hanbury, MP for Monmouth from 1720 to 1734, and the owner of the ironworks at Pontypool, see A. A. Locke, *The Hanbury Family* (London, 1916).
155 BA, pp. 37–8. Also, Diary 47a: 15 June 1739 (not autograph but undoubtedly a copy of an original Diary by Harris).
156 For Miles Harry's part in this incident, see R. Jones, 'Miles Harri', *Trafodion Cymdeithas Hanes Bedyddwyr Cymru* (Proceedings of the Welsh Baptist Historical Society) (1926), 36. It was he who arranged bail for Harris.
157 Diary 47a: 16 June 1739.
158 Trevecka Letter 165: 23 June 1739.
159 For William Seward (1711–40), from Badsey in the Vale of Evesham, who had joined the Fetter Lane society in 1738, see DEB; Tyerman, *Life of Whitefield*, I, pp. 164–8.
160 For Thomas Price (1712–83), a leading Methodist who first met Harris during 1738, see HMGC, pp. 234–5; JHS, XXXIX, 55–62 and LVI, 3–7. The letter was Trevecka Letter 168, JHS, IX, No. 2, pp. 182–3.
161 For Andrew Gifford (1700–84), minister at Eagle Street from 1730 to his death, see DNB; DEB; HHL, pp. 112–13; JHS, IX, 181.
162 For Sir Richard Ellys (1688?–1742), MP for Boston, Lincolnshire, see DNB.
163 Trevecka Letter 169, JHS, IX, 182.
164 For Sir John Gonson, the London magistrate, see *Proceedings of Wesley Historical Society*, 12 (1919–20), 23.
165 Fowler Walker was the Congregational minister at Abergavenny. He succeeded Thomas Coke in 1718. See Rees, *History of Protestant Nonconformity*, p. 271.
166 Trevecka Letter 173: 13 July 1739.
167 Trevecka Letter 174.

NOTES

[168] For Joseph Stennet (1692–1758), see DNB.
[169] Diary 47: 26 July 1739.
[170] A term used by Edmund Jones in *Some Account of the Life and Death of Mr Evan Williams*, p. 122; quoted by Jenkins in *Yng Nghysgod Trefeca*, p. 11.
[171] Diary 47: 30 July 1739.
[172] Ibid., 7 August 1739.
[173] Diary 47a: 10 August. In Diary 47, Harris's autograph version of the events of this period, the entries for 9 August and the succeeding days have been removed.
[174] HHVL, p. 4.
[175] BA, p. 41.
[176] Diary 145: 25 June 1750.
[177] Eifion Evans, *Howell Harris*, pp. 13–14; TM, I, p. 374.
[178] John Wesley, *The Letters of John Wesley, A. M.*, 8 vols. (ed. John Telford: London, 1931), III, pp. 149–59.
[179] Trevecka Letter 343; LHH, p. 165; BA, p. 41.
[180] Roberts, *Dadleuon Methodistiaeth Gynnar*, p. 38; Outler, *John Wesley*, p. 174. At Wesley's fourth Annual Conference, held in June 1747, it was declared that field-preaching was justified 'Because we have always found a greater blessing in field-preaching than in any other preaching whatever'. Harris wrote (Diary 18: 3 February 1737): 'How shall I convince the World, but by the success of my work, that I am divinely constrained.'

God's Little Parliaments

[1] Tyerman, *Life of Whitefield*, II, p. 630; Michael R. Watts, *The Dissenters*, pp. 399f.
[2] This has been the view of most Welsh Methodist historians. See, for example, LHH, pp. 255–6; HMGC, pp. 162, 178; POD, p. 34; TL, p. 216; Eifion Evans, *Howel Harris*, p. 20.
[3] Harris wrote on 18 March 1737 (Diary 23) that one of the things he considered wanting in the Church was 'a Priviledge [*sic*] of meeting together as a Society to consult about Points of Salvation, [and] self examination'.
[4] BA, pp. 20–1.
[5] HHDR, p. 31.
[6] Mary Parry was the widow of James Parry (d. 1732). She was the patroness of the ecclesiastical living at Llangasty. Richard Bennett suggested that she was also Harris's fiancée, a possibility which is supported by Diary 53: 27 February 1740. See HHDR, pp. 34–5.

NOTES

7 W. G. Hughes-Edwards, 'The development and organisation of the Methodist Society in Wales, 1735–50', MA thesis, University of Wales, 1966, pp. 71–2; HMGC, p. 100; HHDR, p. 65. Bennett states that 'we are not at all sure but that it was there [at Mary Parry's house] that the first Methodist society was established'. This was not Harris's view, as will be seen later. If Bennett was referring to the first 'group meeting' rather than 'permanent society', then surely Trevecka was the venue where the first such meeting was held. In Diary 34 (13 November 1738), referring to his use of the two houses mentioned, Harris wrote, 'This was the beginning only. We met att Tal-y-llyn and I had been in our own Parish and att Madam Phillips in Llanfihangel before – but nothing worked there.'

8 TL, p. 220, 'With the death of Mrs. Parry in 1738, they seem to have perished.'

9 The term 'society' became part of Harris's vocabulary after he had met Griffith Jones during May 1736. The letter (Trevecka Letter 87) states that 'private societies' were being established. They were 'private' because only those who were members were allowed to attend. See HMGC, p. 167.

10 TL, p. 216; Hughes-Edwards, 'Development and organisation', 65; HMGC, p. 163; HHDR, p. 79; R. W. Evans, 'The eighteenth century Welsh awakening with its relationships to the contemporary English Evangelical Revival', Ph.D. thesis, University of Edinburgh, 1956, 63; R. T. Jenkins, *Hanes Cymru yn y Ddeunawfed Ganrif* (Caerdydd, 1931), p. 38; HHLE, p. 27; D. E. Jenkins (ed.), *Religious Societies* (Liverpool, 1935), pp. 15–16.

11 Michael R. Watts, *The Dissenters*, pp. 423–4; Brunner, 'The role of the Halle Pietists in England', 15–21; Heitzenrater, *Mirror and Memory*, pp. 33ff.

12 Josiah Woodward, *An Account of the Religious Societies in the City of London* (1697). The fourth edition (1712) was republished in D. E. Jenkins, *Religious Societies*, pp. 21–88.

13 For Anthony Horneck (1641–97), a Lutheran minister educated at Heidelberg and Wittenberg, who came to England in 1661, and settled as the preacher at the Savoy, see DNB; Watson, *The Early Methodist Class Meeting*, p. 68, n.3; Richard B. Hone, *Lives of Eminent Christians* (3 vols., London, 1837–9), II, pp. 287ff. Also, G. V. Portus, *Caritas Anglicana* (London, 1912).

14 Watson, *The Early Methodist Class Meeting*, p. 68. Horneck's rules for the Religious Societies are published in this volume as Appendix A, pp. 188–9.

15 J. S. Simon, *John Wesley and the Religious Societies* (London, 1921), pp. 19–20; Watson, *The Early Methodist Class Meeting*, pp. 68–9.

[16] For the 'Specimen of the Orders', see ibid., Appendix B, p. 190; Jenkins, *Religious Societies*, p. 79; Simon, *John Wesley*, pp. 12–14.
[17] Watson, *The Early Methodist Class Meeting*, pp. 68–70.
[18] BA, p. 24, quoted in LHH, p. 35. Harris began writing his autobiography in 1744. See Diary 106: 4 January 1744; HHVL, p. 50. It was not published until 1791, nearly twenty years after his death.
[19] Trevecka Letter 142.
[20] Diary 41: 20–1 February 1739. Cf. Evans, 'The eighteenth century Welsh awakening', 63; Morgan, *Y Diwygiad Mawr*, p. 95.
[21] Diary 134: 2 March 1749 and Diary 135a: 21 June 1749. A similar claim was made on 28 June 1750.
[22] HHRS, p. 90.
[23] Ibid., p. 130.
[24] BA, p. 24.
[25] Jenkins, *Religious Societies*, p. 16.
[26] Trevecka Letter 87; HHDR, p. 79.
[27] Morgan, *Y Diwygiad Mawr*, p. 94.
[28] For August Hermann Francke (1663–1727), German Lutheran minister, professor and early advocate of Pietism, see Erich Beyreuther, *August Hermann Francke 1663–1727* (Hamburg, 1958); Peter C. Erb, *Pietists: Selected Writings* (London, 1983), pp. 9–10, 99–166; Dale Brown, *Understanding Pietism* (Grand Rapids, 1978), passim; Senn, *Protestant Spiritual Traditions*, pp. 199f; Brunner, 'The role of Halle Pietists', pp. 45–8.
[29] Woodward, *Religious Societies*, p. 25.
[30] HHLE, pp. 27–8; Jenkins, *Hanes Cymru*, p. 39; Mary Clement, *Correspondence and Minutes*, pp. 39, 125n. Griffith Jones was in correspondence with A. W. Boehm. For Boehm, see DNB; Brunner, 'The role of Halle Pietists', 59–69, 176–93. For the significance of eighteenth-century Protestant international communications, see J. D. Walsh, '"Methodism" and the origins of English-speaking Evangelicalism', in M. A. Noll, D. W. Bebbington and G. A. Rawlyk (eds.), *Evangelicalism* (Oxford, 1994), pp. 19–22. For the influence of continental Pietism, see G. F. Nuttall, 'Continental Pietism and the Evangelical movement in Britain', in van der Berg and van Dooren (eds.), *Pietismus und Réveil* (Leiden, 1978).
[31] John Weborg, 'Pietism' in Senn, *Protestant Spiritual Traditions*, pp. 183f; see also, Brown, *Understanding Pietism*, pp. 35–64, 83–102; extracts from Philipp Jakob Spener's *Pia Desideria* in Erb, *Pietists*, pp. 31f, which came to be regarded as a pietist manifesto and contained the emphases noted.
[32] Senn, *Protestant Spiritual Traditions*, p. 200.
[33] Diary 18: 28 December 1736; TL, p. 189.

NOTES

[34] Diary 34: 13 November 1738.
[35] TL, p. 219.
[36] This document is listed as Diary 24 in the Trevecka Collection. The identity of the recipient is not disclosed but the contents of the petition suggests that it was the bishop. See HHDR, p. 80.
[37] Diary 24: 5 April 1737.
[38] Simon, *John Wesley and the Religious Societies*, pp. 14–16; Jenkins, *Religious Societies*, p. 81.
[39] Trevecka Letter 65.
[40] HHDR, p. 125.
[41] Diary 116: 15 April 1745. Wernos was 'the place where all this great work began over eight years ago'.
[42] HMGC, p. 219.
[43] For John Powell (d. 1743), see DWB.
[44] Some of the names mentioned by Harris are William Llewelyn, William Phillip and Evan Rice.
[45] Hughes-Edwards, 'Development and organisation', 69. The exhorters assisted Harris in caring for the increasing number of societies. They were responsible for leading the various groups in their devotions and expounding the Scriptures. The role of the exhorter was later clearly set out in the rules of the societies (see below) and by William Williams of Pantycelyn in *Drws y Society Profiad* (Aberhonddu, 1777), translated by Bethan Lloyd-Jones, *The Experience Meeting: An Introduction to the Welsh Societies of the Evangelical Awakening* (London, 1973).
[46] Tyerman, *Life of Whitefield*, I, p. 95.
[47] Peter Böhler or Boehler (1712–75), a Moravian missionary born at Frankfurt-am-Main, who studied at Frankfurt Gymnasium (1722) and Jena University (1731) where he was influenced by Spangenberg and Zinzendorf. He was created a Moravian bishop in 1748. Podmore, *The Moravian Church in England*, pp. 30ff; Towlson, *Moravian and Methodist*, pp. 47ff.
[48] JWJ, I, p. 458n.
[49] HMGC, p. 165; TL, p. 229.
[50] Diary 34: 13 November 1738. Harris notes that at least one society was organized by the Dissenters.
[51] HMGC, p. 165, and TL, p. 227. Diary 37 contains an undated list of society members at Llangynidr, Breconshire, signed by 'William Watkins'. It is set out in two columns, the first listing seventeen males, the second eighteen females. M. H. Jones believed the list must have been compiled soon after 16 January 1738, but does not state his reasons for coming to such a conclusion. Other than the fact that, according to Harris's Itinerary, he was with Watkins on that date,

and that the list was written on the same piece of paper as sermon notes dated between 1736 and 1738, there is no reason to suppose that the list was compiled at such an early date. However, the date may be correct. Even so, there is still no reason to assume that the use of columns was due to Harris's influence. It could be argued that it was natural for anyone compiling a list of thirty-five names to have done so according to sex in order to simplify the task. On the other hand, the possibility remains that columns were used at Harris's instigation.

52 Watts, *The Dissenters*, pp. 319–20.
53 Diary 18: 4 January 1737.
54 Hughes-Edwards, 'Development and organisation', 77.
55 For Henry Davies (1696?–1766) and David Williams (1709–84), see DWB. Whether the establishment of these societies was unconnected with Harris's activities is not known, but Harris regarded them as 'under the ministry' of Dissenting ministers. See Diary 34: 13 November 1738.
56 Hughes-Edwards, 'Development and organisation', 79. By counting the number of society meetings mentioned by Harris on 13 November 1738, a total of twenty-six is reached. Harris does claim that there were others which he had not named. He does not say whether he has included the societies held by the Dissenters in his total.
57 Trevecka Letter 148: William Seward to Daniel Abbott, quoted in TL, p. 232; Whitefield, *Journals*, p. 229.
58 Letters in the Trevecka Collection from this period include: (i) Trevecka Letter 154, dated 17 April 1739, a circular letter from James Roberts to the societies at Longtown, Llandyfalle, Crucadarn and Gwenddwr, informing them of his intention to visit them at Harris's request. See TL, pp. 234–5. (ii) Trevecka Letter 155, dated 24 April 1739, from Howell Harris (at Oxford) to Thomas James, Crucadarn, requesting a report of the societies' progress. (iii) Trevecka Letter 162, dated 21 May 1739, from Edmund Jones, Pontypool, to Howell Harris, giving a full report of the progress of the societies entrusted to his care.
59 A. Skevington Wood, *The Inextinguishable Blaze* (Exeter, 1960), pp. 129–30, 162; TL, p. 234.
60 John Walsh, 'Religious societies: Methodist and Evangelical 1738–1800', in W. J. Sheils and Diana Wood (eds.), *Voluntary Religion*, p. 290.
61 J. Wesley's sermon on this theme in *Sermons on Several Occasions* (4th edn; 8 vols., 1787–8), III, pp. 181–201; Outler, *John Wesley*, p. 103. For Whitefield's emphasis on the theme, see Whitefield, *Journals*, pp. 457–8.

NOTES

[62] R. T. Jenkins, *Yng Nghysgod Trefeca*, p. 11.
[63] HHL, p. 242.
[64] For Count Nicholas Ludvig von Zinzendorf, Moravian leader, see DEB; A. J. Lewis, *Zinzendorf the Ecumenical Pioneer* (London, 1962). He was visiting England while on a journey from the West Indies. Podmore, *The Moravian Church in England*, p. 52.
[65] Harris did not meet John Wesley as stated in HMGC, p. 166, and TL, p. 233. They met later, on 18 June 1739, at Bristol. JWJ, II, p. 223. Harris met the Countess of Huntingdon in August 1743. For Selina, Countess of Huntingdon (1707–91), see DNB; A. C. H. Seymour, *Life and Times of the Countess of Huntingdon* (2 vols., London, 1840); Edwin Welch, *Spiritual Pilgrim: A Reassessment of the Life of the Countess of Huntingdon* (Cardiff, 1995).
[66] Simon, *John Wesley and the Religious Societies*, p. 198. Though this may have been due to Moravian influences, as Simon suggests, that was not the case in Wales.
[67] I cannot agree with TL, p. 238, that Harris's societies 'were far more primitive and less elaborate than the English ones'. The similarities between them are striking.
[68] JWJ, I, pp. 458–9; see also, Daniel Benham, *Memoirs of James Hutton* (London, 1856), pp. 29–32, which states that the founders originally agreed on only two rules for the new society: that they should meet once a week and that newcomers would be welcomed provided that they were vouched for by an existing member. Other rules were added later, on 29 May and 20 September, to make a final total of thirty-three rules or 'Orders'. See also, Towlson, *Moravian and Methodist*, p. 63; HHL, pp. 69–70; Simon, *John Wesley and the Religious Societies*, pp. 195–6.
[69] HMGC, p. 165. A letter (Trevecka Letter 120: 15 August 1738) was sent to Harris by Phillip Prosser requesting an English copy of the 'Rules of the Society' as some members of Longtown society were unable to understand the Welsh version that had been sent to them.
[70] Diary 63: 28 September 1740, 'was led to set the congregation in Bands and to desire the Leaders to come to Mr. Rowland. Showed of the order of the English Societies.' Also, HMGC, p. 168. Such 'bands' had been a feature of the Fetter Lane society from the outset in 1738. Rules 3 and 4 of the 'Orders' governing the society stated that those attending the meetings would 'be divided into several Bands, or little Societies', and that 'none of these [should] consist of fewer than five, or more than ten Persons'. Simon, *John Wesley and the Religious Societies*, p. 196.
[71] Wood, *The Burning Heart*, p. 168; JWJ, I, p. 459, Rule 5 and appended footnote by the editor.

[72] TL, p. 239.

[73] Trevecka MS 3178, the earliest manuscript containing society rules, emphasizes that only those who had accepted Christ, and who professed faith in Him, were to be admitted into the societies. See HMGC, p. 174.

[74] Of the English terms, 'band', 'leader' and 'steward' introduced by Harris, only 'steward' seems to have gained any foothold in the Welsh societies.

[75] Diary 67: 30 December 1740, '... 10 and above in Glamorganshire, about so many in Monmouthshire, about 15 in Breconshire, about 10 in Carmarthenshire, and so many in Cardiganshire. 5 in Pembrokeshire, 4 in Radnorshire and Herefordshire.' For an analysis of the development and nature of Methodist societies located in south-west Wales between 1737 and 1750, see Eryn M. White, *Praidd Bach y Bugail Mawr* (Llandysul, 1995).

[76] Trevecka MS 3178, which is entitled 'Rheola'r Socyaty [sic] Neilltuol 1740'.

[77] For the original Welsh version, see HMGC, p. 174.

[78] This rule did not insist on worship at a parish churches.

[79] *Welsh Bibliographical Society Journal*, III, 191–2. A copy is kept at the National Library of Wales, Aberystwyth (NLW MS 5984B).

[80] HMGC, p. 175.

[81] Gomer M. Roberts, *Y Pêr Ganiedydd* (2 vols.: Aberystwyth, 1949, 1958), II, pp. 36–7; HMGC, p. 175.

[82] Diary 69: undated. The similarity between these two documents is not discussed in HMGC. Cf. MTU, pp. 34–5, and his reference to 'half a dozen rules'.

[83] As suggested in HMGC, p. 174.

[84] This fact is also recognized by Gomer M. Roberts in HMGC, p. 175.

[85] Diary 51: 16 January 1740. This meeting is not mentioned in HMGC.

[86] Trevecka MS 2945, a volume containing records of Associations dating from January 1743 to August 1745, published in JHS, XLVIII, 29–49, 69–80; XLIX, 21–8, 84–90; L, 27–32.

[87] Trevecka MS 2945. See also JHS, XLVIII, 29.

[88] Diary 51: 16 January 1740. The word 'minst' is barely legible in the MS. It is possibly an abbreviation for 'ministers'.

[89] Though called a 'Society of Ministers', it was a meeting of both ordained and lay leaders.

[90] Diary 62: 7 September 1740, 'crying O! Lord, bless ... our intended Society of Ministers to Thy glory'. Also 11 September, at Trelleck, Monmouthshire, 'I said of our intended Society of Ministers ...'

[91] The meetings began on Wednesday 1 October 1740, and not on 2 October as in HMGC, p. 168.

NOTES

[92] Diary 63: 1 October 1740. For an account of the occasion, see HMGC, p. 168; TL, pp. 262–4. Edward Godwin was not present as claimed in HMGC, p. 168. The fact that Harris arrived there in the company of a certain Mrs Godwin may account for the error.

[93] An account of the meeting was sent by Oulton to *The Christian's Amusement* (No. 6).

[94] For William Williams (1717–91), often referred to as 'Williams of Pantycelyn', Pantycelyn being his home in Carmarthenshire, see DWB; DEB; Gomer M. Roberts, *Y Pêr Ganiedydd*. For a selective English translation of 'Theomemphus', one of his epic Welsh poems, see Eifion Evans, *Pursued by God* (Bridgend, 1996).

[95] Gomer Roberts, *Y Pêr Ganiedydd*, I, pp. 32f.

[96] Ibid., p. 65; Trevecka Letter 1815. *Account of the Progress of the Gospel*, IV, No. 1, pp. 76–7.

[97] For an edited account of the proceedings, see Jenkins, *Calvinistic Methodist Holy Orders*, pp. 17–20.

[98] Probably through Whitefield. Tyerman, *Life of Whitefield*, I, pp. 497f. In 1733, Ebenezer Erskine and three others suspended by the Synod of the Church of Scotland constituted the 'Associate Presbytery', which later became the Secession Church. Whitefield had been in correspondence with the Erskines since 1739. Dallimore, *George Whitefield*, I, p. 85; Tyerman, *Life of Whitefield*, I, p. 504. Harris's visits to England would also have brought him within earshot of news from both countries.

[99] *The Christian's Amusement* (London, 1740), No. 6; cf. Diary 63: 3 October 1740. Harris noted that Edmund Jones had responded to his teaching on assurance by saying that he would oppose it 'all he could'. Harris held that assurance was necessary for salvation, an assertion which Jones denied.

[100] Diary 63–4: 3 October 1740. This conference is not mentioned in HMGC.

[101] Diary 65: 13 November 1740. This conference is not mentioned in HMGC. See p. 169, where it is stated that 'nothing came of the meeting at Glyn'.

[102] For Lewis Rees (1710–1800), see DWB; DEB.

[103] Trevecka Letter 272. *The Christian's Amusement* first appeared about the beginning of September 1740. For the history, and an analysis of the contents, of these publications, see JHS, III–IV.

[104] Harris did not elaborate on the nature of the discussion but noted that 'many would not agree'.

[105] Diary 62: 11 September 1740.

[106] Diary 49: 14 September 1739; HHVP, pp. 21–2.

[107] Diary 51: 25 January 1740.

[108] HHVP, p. 24.
[109] Ibid., p. 25. See also, JHS, XX, No. 3 (September 1935), 282. Trevecka Letter 220: anon. to Howell Harris, 10 February 1740: 'John Powell has dun A deal of mischief hear [sic] . . .'
[110] Trevecka Letters 165 and 167: 23 and 27 June 1739. Miles Harry to Howell Harris. In the first of these letters Harry arranges for the sale of 100 sermons, and, in the second, for the sale of 600 sermons. In 1740 he was involved in the setting up of a printing press at Pontypool in Monmouthshire. HMGC, pp. 404–6; T. M. Bassett, *Bedyddwyr Cymru* (Llandysul, 1977), p. 64; R. Jones, 'Miles Harri', in *Trafodion Cymdeithas Hanes Bedyddwyr Cymru* (Proceedings of the Welsh Baptist Historical Society) (1926), 39–40.
[111] Diary 65: 13 November 1740.
[112] Harris did make an effort to be reconciled with Edmund Jones before the end of the year. See Diary 67: 27 December 1740: 'I was much concerned for the great uneasiness that has happened . . . I went to see Mr. Edmund Jones . . .'
[113] Diary 65: 14 November 1740.
[114] This society had been arranged during December 1740 and met on 13 February 1741. Diary 66: 22 December 1740.
[115] Diary 67: 29 December 1740.
[116] Ibid., 30 December 1740.
[117] Diary 69: 13 February 1741; JHS, XXVI, 94; MTU, pp. 34–5.
[118] Trevecka Letter 312; JHS, XXXV, No. 2 (June 1950), 24. The letter comprises of twenty-six closely written pages. Extracts are published in the *Proceedings of the Wesley Historical Society*, XVII, Part 3. See also R. T. Jenkins, *Y Cofiadur* (1935), 22.
[119] Harris does not say which letter was read. It was possibly the one dated 9 November 1740, in which Whitefield opposed Wesley's doctrine of perfection. Whitefield, *Works*, I, p. 219. Where Harris obtained a copy of the letter is not known.
[120] Harris does not inform us of the nature of the six rules but it is possible that they were the ones mentioned earlier.
[121] Diary 68b: 29 January 1741.
[122] Diary 69: 14 February 1741.
[123] MTU, p. 35.
[124] JHS, XXVI, 94; HMGC, p. 170.
[125] Diary 71: 22 March 1741.
[126] Note Harris's words on 14 June 1741: '. . . thought it right to abide in Communion in one Church till they would turn us out . . .'
[127] There are three versions still extant: NLW MS 5984b; Diary 69: 13 February 1741; and Diary 71: 22 March 1741.
[128] The correct date is 14 June and not 15 June as in HMGC, p. 170.

NOTES

[129] This is not sufficiently emphasized in HMGC, pp. 170-1. The appointment of overseers for the societies was significant. It was the creation of a middle tier of workers between the ministers and the exhorters. Harris was making arrangements for his departure 'perhaps for ever'.

[130] Heitzenrater, *Wesley and the People Called Methodists*, pp. 120f.

[131] For Whitefield's reply, see Whitefield, *Journals*, p. 571.

[132] For a further account of the 'Free Grace' controversy, and the events leading up to the separation, see Tyerman, *Life of Whitefield*, I, pp. 462-76.

[133] *Weekly History*, Nos. 13, 14, where Harris described Wesley's doctrine as 'Hellish, Popish and Heretical'.

[134] HHLE, pp. 40-2; A. H. Williams, *John Wesley in Wales* (Cardiff, 1971), pp. xxvii, xxix-xxx.

[135] Diary 71: 23, 29 March; Diary 74: 14 June 1741.

[136] It was during this visit that Whitefield married Elizabeth James of Abergavenny, Tyerman, *Life of Whitefield*, I, pp. 530-5.

[137] Williams, *John Wesley in Wales*, pp. xxvi-xxvii, 10-13. G. T. Roberts in *Bathafarn* (The Journal of the Historical Society of the Methodist Church in Wales), XIII (1958), 47-9.

[138] JWJ, II, p. 509.

[139] Diary 81: 9 November 1741.

[140] Ibid.

[141] His response to Whitefield's words was, 'God forbid!'

[142] *Weekly History*, Nos. 79, 80, where Whitefield suggested: 'It may be worth while to enquire (now Matters are brought to a Crisis) whether or not it may be proper to form our selves into a more close Body and yet not separate from the Church of England.'

[143] As suggested in HMGC, p. 171; cf. JHS, XXVI, 75.

[144] Diary 82: 21 November 1741.

[145] G. H. Jenkins, *The Foundations of Modern Wales*, pp. 375-7.

[146] HHVP, p. 64.

[147] Diary 83: 20 December 1741.

[148] Diary 84: 7 January 1742; JHS, XXVI, 93f., 102-3; HMGC, pp. 171-2; D. E. Jenkins, *Calvinistic Methodist Holy Orders*, pp. 55-6.

[149] While it is known that Rowland, William Williams and David Jenkins were three of the clergymen, the identity of the fourth remains a mystery. Harris had heard on his way to Dugoedydd that Howell Davies did not intend to be present. For David Jenkins of Cellan (d. 1742), see HMGC, pp. 207-8.

[150] There were no Dissenting ministers present. G. T. Roberts, *Howell Harris* (London, 1951), p. 46, suggests that the reason for this was

that other previous meetings which they had attended had resulted in disputes.

151 Trevecka Letter 450. For Whitefield's letter, see G. Whitefield, *Letters* (Edinburgh, 1976), p. 511; Tyerman, *Life of Whitefield*, I, pp. 541–2; Jenkins, *Calvinistic Methodist Holy Orders*, pp. 52–4. For the significance of the letter, see JHS, XXVI, 95 and HMGC, p. 171.

152 Speck, *Stability and Strife*, p. 119; W. S. Gunter, *The Limits of 'Divine Love'*, pp. 124, 141.

153 J. S. Simon, 'The Repeal of the Conventicle Act', *Proceedings of the Wesley Historical Society*, XI, 86–93, 103–37.

154 Tyerman, *Life of Whitefield*, I, p. 486, where it is stated that by 1741, Whitefield was 'to all intents and purposes ... a Dissenting minister. In America, his ministerial associates and friends were almost, without exception, Nonconformists.' It is, therefore, hardly surprising that he was prepared to allow those who wished to communicate with them to do so.

155 Diary 84: 7 January 1742; JHS, XXVI, 103.

156 JWJ, II, pp. 335–6.

157 For the term 'association', see HMGC, pp. 168–9; TL, p. 280.

158 *Weekly History*, No. 61, where Harris states, 'The Devil rages most horribly in the North: My flesh trembles for fear of going there sometimes.'

159 'The Foundation, Aims and Rules of the Societies or Private Meetings that have begun to meet recently in Wales. To which is added some hymns to be sung in the Private Meetings. By men of the Church of England.'

160 For Wesley's Rules, see J. S. Simon, *John Wesley and the Methodist Societies* (London, 1923), pp. 100f.

161 For a precis of the contents, see TL, pp. 251f.

162 17 March and not 18 March as in Harris's Itinerary. Cf. JHS, XXVI, 99

163 *Weekly History*, No. 61, p. 1, 'We had some disputes the last time we met, but we never parted with such broken Hearts and wet Cheeks.'

164 JHS, XXVII, 56.

165 Ibid., p. 58. We are not told the nature of the complaints.

166 Diary 91: 4 July 1742.

167 See Tom Beynon, *Cwmsel a Chefn Sidan* (Caernarfon, 1946), p. 23.

168 Diary 92: 19 July 1742.

169 It was at this meeting that minutes of the Associations were first kept. The minute books are deposited at the NLW; Trevecka MSS 2945, 2946, 2976 and 9977.

170 For John Powell (1708–95), see DWB.

[171] For the term 'Moderator', see TL, p. 280; HMGC, p. 180.
[172] For Herbert Jenkins (1721–72), see DWB.
[173] A discussion on this was held at Trevecka on 29 June 1743. John Richard, one of the exhorters, had claimed that such divisions were 'Popish'. JHS, XLVIII, 47.
[174] JHS, XLVIII, 69.
[175] Diary 108: 28 March 1744.
[176] HHVL, p. 85.
[177] Diary 117: 17 July 1745; also, Diary 109: 25 April 1744.
[178] Simon, *John Wesley and the Methodist Societies*, pp. 98–100.
[179] Though it could be argued that this conclusion cannot be reached in the absence of source material giving an account of Rowland's role, and that Harris gives a distorted view of the development of Methodist organization, the nature, quality and quantity of evidence contained in Harris's Diaries demonstrates clearly the scale of his contribution to the work. There is a consensus that Harris was the architect of Methodist organization in Wales while Rowland was its greatest preacher. POD, p. 34; TM, I, p. 431; LHH, p. 255; G. T. Roberts, *Howell Harris*, p. 50; Emlyn Evans (ed.), R. T. Jenkins, *Cwpanaid o De a Diferion Eraill* (Dinbych, 1997), p. 129; Jenkins, *The Foundations of Modern Wales*, pp. 348–9. The words of William Williams of Pantycelyn are suggestive in this context; Harris claimed that he said in 1763 that 'Mr Rowland did shine in the pulpit, but was not fit for any other place or work', HHRS, p. 188.
[180] *Account of the Progress of the Gospel*, II, No. 2, p. 67; Harris's report to Whitefield, dated 25 January 1743, of his labours following the Watford Association earlier in the month.
[181] Ibid., III, No. 1, p. 46.

The Church of England

[1] Diary 1: 22 May 1735.
[2] Spurr, 'Anglican apologetic', 191.
[3] HHVP, p. 39.
[4] Diary 23a: 9 April 1737; HHDR, pp. 108–9; cf. Tyerman, *Life of Whitefield*, I, p. 201.
[5] Diary 54: 22 March 1740; HHVP, p. 31.
[6] Diary 23a: 2 April 1737.
[7] G. V. Bennett, *The Tory Crisis in Church and State, 1688–1730* (Oxford, 1975), pp. 8–15. Also, Speck, *Stability and Strife*, pp. 91–2, 103–4; Dorothy Marshall, *Eighteenth Century England* (Harlow, 1962), p. 105.

NOTES

8 BA, p. 19.
9 HHDR, p. 108.
10 BA, pp. 19–20.
11 Diary 23a: 8 April 1737.
12 Diary 25: 24 September 1737.
13 Diary 23a: 7 April 1737.
14 Diary 113: 20 September 1744.
15 Diary 25: 21 September 1737. Also, 6 and 8 September 1737.
16 Speck, *Stability and Strife*, pp. 105–6; R. Geraint Gruffydd in Dyfnallt Morgan (ed.), *Y Ferch o Ddolwar Fach*, p. 17.
17 Diary 68b: 25 January 1741.
18 HMGC, pp. 64–8.
19 Griffith Jones, *Welch Piety* (1740–1), p. 13.
20 Mary Clement, *The SPCK and Wales*, p. 53.
21 Diary 54: 21 March 1740.
22 R. Tudur Jones, *Congregationalism in England*, pp. 58–62.
23 Trevecka Letter 2799; STL, I, p. 65. Also, HHLE, p. 44.
24 HHVL, p. 68: 19 May 1745. Cf. Erasmus Saunders, *A View of the State of Religion in the Diocese of St. Davids* (London, 1721; republished Cardiff, 1949).
25 Trevecka Letter 2799.
26 Diary 23a: 1 April 1737.
27 Diary 25: 9 October 1737.
28 Diary 63a: 2 November 1740.
29 Diary 22: 3 February 1737.
30 E.g., Diary 25: 8 September 1737; Diary 113: 20 September 1744.
31 Diary 22: 20 February 1737.
32 Diary 23: 18 March 1737; HHDR, pp. 105–6.
33 Diary 22: 2 February 1737. Harris says that he was 'advised not to go from my own Church by my Minister'.
34 Diary 52: 10 February 1740.
35 HHDR, pp. 108–9.
36 HHVL, p. 249; HHLE, p. 43. Harris did not say which expressions were unacceptable.
37 Frank Baker, *John Wesley and the Church of England* (Nashville, 1970), p. 182.
38 Diary 23a: 2 April 1737.
39 Diary 91: 6 July 1742, '... willing to go from our Church, and tired of the carnal ministers sorely, but must wait [for] God to lead us'; HHVP, pp. 65, 125; HHVL, p. 237.
40 Diary 103: 5 October 1743.
41 HHDR, p. 103.
42 BA, pp. 57–8.

NOTES

43 Diary 23a: 30 March 1737; Diary 54: 22 March 1740; also Trevecka Letter 343.
44 R. Buick Knox, 'Howell Harris and his doctrine of the Church', JHS, L, 36.
45 Diary 131a: 18 May 1748.
46 Ibid.
47 HHVL, p. 115; HHLE, p. 44.
48 D. E. Jenkins, *Calvinistic Methodist Holy Orders*, p. 45; R. T. Jenkins, *Yng Nghysgod Trefeca*, p. 25.
49 R. Tudur Jones, *Hanes Annibynwyr Cymru*, p. 146.
50 'For the unbelieving husband is sanctified by the wife, and the unbelieving wife is sanctified by the husband: else were your children unclean; but now they are holy.' Diary 54: 17 March 1740; HHVP, p. 51.
51 Diary 89: 18 April 1742.
52 HHRS, p. 27: 5 October 1742.
53 HHVP, p. 51: 4 March 1741.
54 HHDR, p. 110.
55 JHS, XXV, 435. Also, XLIX, 78, 24 January 1741.
56 Diary 22: 3 February 1737.
57 Ibid., 20 February 1737.
58 Ibid., 9 February 1737.
59 Ibid., 3 February 1737.
60 Ibid., 20 February 1737.
61 Diary 23a: 25 March, 7 April 1737.
62 Ibid., 26, 27 March 1737.
63 Ibid., 1 April 1737.
64 Ibid., 6 April 1737.
65 Ibid., 8 April 1737.
66 Diary 23: 13 March 1737.
67 Diary 23a: 8 April 1737.
68 Diary 21: 10 April 1737.
69 Ibid., 11 April 1737.
70 Diary 25: 21, 22, 24 September 1737.
71 Diary 21: 10 April 1737.
72 Diary 25: 21 September 1737.
73 Diary 20: 11 February 1737.
74 Diary 52: 9 February 1740.
75 R. Tudur Jones, *Hanes Annibynwyr Cymru*, pp. 143–4.
76 Trevecka Letter 119.
77 Trevecka Letter 303: 25(?) December 1740.
78 JHS, XXIV, 57, 19 December 1740; R. Tudur Jones, *Hanes Annibynwyr Cymru*, p. 145.

NOTES

79 Ibid.
80 Diary 68b: 8 February 1741.
81 Diary 92: 2 August 1742.
82 Diary 54: 18 March 1740.
83 R. Tudur Jones, *Hanes Annibynwyr Cymru*, p. 146.
84 HHVP, p. 48: 26 February 1741.
85 Ibid., p. 48: 27 February 1741. It must be understood, however, that like William Grimshaw of Haworth, Harris 'never grudged the Dissenters the conversion of the unregenerate; only the alienation of his own converts'. See J. D. Walsh, 'The Yorkshire Evangelicals in the eighteenth century', Ph.D. thesis, University of Cambridge, 1956.
86 Diary 54: 7 March 1740.
87 Diary 84: 1 February 1742.
88 HHVP, p. 40: 4 December 1740. Also, M. H. Jones, 'Howell Harris, citizen and patriot', p. 197.
89 Evans, 'The eighteenth century Welsh awakening', p. 187.
90 HHLE, p. 10.
91 Trevecka Letter 362. Cf. R. T. Jenkins, *Yng Nghysgod Trefeca*, p. 21.
92 Trevecka Letter 288: 26 November 1740.
93 D. E. Jenkins, *Calvinistic Methodist Holy Orders*, p. 23.
94 Trevecka Letter 303: 25 December 1740.
95 HMGC, pp. 13–14.
96 Jenkins, *Yng Nghysgod Trefeca*, p. 36n. Also, D. D. Morgan (ed.), R. Tudur Jones, '"Y Dwymyn Ias" a'r "Sentars Sychion"', in *Grym y Gair a Fflam y Ffydd* (Bangor, 1998), pp. 157f.
97 Trevecka Letter 338: 15 May 1741.
98 Diary 123: 5 [4] July 1746. This Diary has been wrongly dated by a later editor. The correct date is in the parentheses.
99 LHH, pp. 208–9.
100 Edmund Jones was known by this title following some prophecies that he made. See DWB.
101 Trevecka Letter 598: 14 August 1742. Also Trevecka Letter 638 (Harris to Whitefield); STL, I, pp. 43f.
102 Watson, *The Early Methodist Class Meeting*, p. 5; *Minutes of the Methodist Conferences* (London, 1862), p. 31; Frank Baker, *John Wesley and the Church of England*, p. 112.
103 POD, p. 73; HHRS, pp. 11–25.
104 HHRS, p. 25; POD, p. 74; HHVP, p. 74.
105 HHRS, p. 20: 20 September 1742.
106 George Whitefield, *Letters* (Edinburgh, 1976), p. 485.
107 HHRS, pp. 49, 51.
108 George Whitefield, *Letters*, p. 511.
109 Diary 25: 7 September 1737.

NOTES

[110] Diary 71: 23 March 1741.
[111] This was also Wesley's view. Baker, *John Wesley and the Church of England*, p. 116.
[112] Diary 62: 14 September 1740.
[113] Trevecka Letter 54: 16 August 1735.
[114] HHRS, p. 211; TM, I, p. 415, but note that it was William Davies who allowed monthly communion. Pryce Davies died on 24 October 1761. JHS, XXXIX, 27.
[115] Diary 96: 25 December 1742.
[116] HHDR, p. 122.
[117] Diary 97: 23 [22] January 1743. Also Jenkins, *Yng Nghysgod Trefeca*, p. 129.
[118] LHH, p. 210. Trevecka Letter 598; see also, Diary 53: 22 February 1740.
[119] A. M. Lyles, *Methodism Mocked* (London, 1960), p. 154; E. J. Bicknell, *The Thirty-Nine Articles of the Church of England* (3rd edn: London, 1955), pp. 351f.
[120] Wesley, *Works*, V, p. 420.
[121] Trevecka Letter 598: 14 August 1742; LHH, p. 209.
[122] HHLE, p. 45.
[123] Diary 110: 6 June 1744.
[124] Diary 90: 23 May 1742.
[125] Ibid.
[126] For Thomas Morgan (1720–99), an Independent minister, see DWB.
[127] R. T. Jenkins, *Yng Nghysgod Trefeca*, pp. 44–5.
[128] Trevecka Letter 592: 9 August 1742.
[129] Trevecka Letter 610: 26 August 1742; Whitefield, *Letters*, p. 426.
[130] Trevecka Letter 621: 3 September 1742; Whitefield, *Letters*, p. 515.
[131] Trevecka MS 2945; JHS, XLVIII, 31.
[132] HHRS, p. 49: 20 August 1743.
[133] This is the title given to the Association meeting by Harris in his Diary. HHRS, p. 51.
[134] HHRS, p. 51, 31 August 1743.
[135] Trevecka MS 2945; JHS, XLVIII, 76.
[136] Ibid., 79.
[137] Diary 110: 1 June 1744.
[138] Ibid., 2, 3 June 1744.
[139] Ibid., 4 June 1744.
[140] Diary 112: 27 June 1744.
[141] The date was 21 September 1744, and not 27 September as in HMGC, p. 442 and JHS, XLIX, 27.
[142] Diary 113: 26 September 1744; LHH, pp. 209–10.
[143] Diary 113: 28 September 1744.

[144] Ibid., 4 November 1744.
[145] HHVL, p. 64: 18 December 1744.
[146] Ibid.
[147] Trevecka Letter 1308: 30 March 1745. The letter is signed by Thomas Price, William Edward, Thomas William, John Belcher and Evan Thomas.
[148] Diary 116: 3, 4 April 1745.
[149] Ibid., 24 April 1745.
[150] Ibid.
[151] For William Jones (1718–73?), see DWB; Also, William Griffith, *Methodistiaeth Fore Môn* (Caernarfon, 1955), pp. 90ff.
[152] Association Records, JHS, L, 52.
[153] Ibid., 86: 14 October 1747.
[154] Diary 127a: 27 October 1747.
[155] Diary 132a: 9 October 1748.
[156] HMGC, p. 196; Hughes-Edwards, 'Development and organisation', 109.
[157] HMGC, p. 199; JHS, XXXVIII, 40.
[158] HHVL, p. 7.
[159] HMGC, p. 197. Also JHS, XLIX, 26.
[160] HHRS, p. 78: 28 August 1760.
[161] *Minutes of the Methodist Conferences*, I, p. 533.
[162] Diary 91: 6 July 1742.

The Opposition to Methodism

[1] HHDR, pp. 41–4.
[2] Trevecka Letter 65: 27 February 1736; LHH, pp. 29–30.
[3] William Williams of Pantycelyn states in his elegy to Harris that he first saw him when he was exhorting the people by the church porch. Thomas Levi, *Casgliad o Hen Farwnadau Cymreig*, p. 30.
[4] BA, pp. 22–3.
[5] Diary 12: 30 March 1736.
[6] Trevecka Letter 70: 29 March 1736 (Howell to Joseph Harris).
[7] Diary 44: 11 May 1739.
[8] BA, p. 25; HHDR, p. 96.
[9] For John Owen (1698–1755), see DWB. He became chancellor of Bangor Cathedral in 1743 and was throughout his life opposed to Methodism. He attempted on more than one occasion to secure a conviction against Methodists for breach of the 1664 Conventicle Act and supported the clergy in the area surrounding his native town of Llanidloes in their actions against them. He was described by one

NOTES

of his fellow clergymen as 'famous for a troublesome litigious temper . . .' (Henllys MS 630, University of Wales, Bangor).

10 BA, p. 53.
11 HHDR, p. 102.
12 Ibid., p. 54.
13 Diary 41: 24 March 1739.
14 Trevecka Letter 162: 21 May 1739.
15 See below.
16 Trevecka Letter 178: 2 August 1739.
17 Trevecka Letter 151: 17 March 1739, from David Perrot, incumbent of Bedwellte and Mynyddislwyn, Monmouthshire; Trevecka Letter 219a: 10 February 1740, from David Davies of Llanbrynmair, Montgomeryshire.
18 Trevecka Letter 330: 18 April 1741; LHH, pp. 157–8.
19 Trevecka Letter 331: 19 April 1741; LHH, p. 159.
20 Trevecka Letter 339: 18 May 1741.
21 Ibid.; LHH, p. 159.
22 The reply was not delivered until eighteen months after its composition. The reason for the delay is not known.
23 Trevecka Letter 343: 14 June 1741. LHH, p. 161.
24 Wesley, *Works*, VII, pp. 273–7; Outler, *John Wesley*, p. 19.
25 Wesley, *Letters*, II, pp. 148–9; V, p. 249.
26 Trevecka Letter 343: 14 June 1741.
27 See chapters 2 and 5.
28 See A. S. Pringle-Pattison, *John Locke: An Essay concerning Human Understanding* (Oxford, 1924), pp. 359–63.
29 Wesley's fourth Annual Conference, during June 1747, also defined 'schism' as 'a causeless breach, rupture, or division, made amongst the members of Christ, among those who are the living body of Christ, and members in particular'. See Conference minutes in Outler, *John Wesley*, p. 172.
30 This was also Wesley's view. In his sermon, 'On Schism' (*Works*, VI, pp. 401–10), he emphasized that in Scripture the word denoted a separation within a church rather than from it. He allowed that 'schism' could be defined as 'a causeless separation from a body of living Christians', provided that it was understood that 'it be not strictly Scriptural' (p. 406).
31 For the terms of the Toleration Act, see Michael R. Watts, *Dissenters*, pp. 259–60; R. Tudur Jones, *Congregationalism in England*, pp. 107–8.
32 Diary 52: 11 February 1740.
33 One of the Justices was Gabriel Wynne of Dolarddyn. The name of the second is not known. For the identity of the clergyman, see MTU, pp.

21–2, where it is suggested that it was Lewis Jones, the recently installed incumbent of nearby Llanymawddwy. Jones was an ardent opposer of Methodism. The name of the incumbent at Cemais was Vaughan Jones. Harris's only clue to his identity is that his surname was 'Jones'.

[34] For the Conventicle Act (1670), see Watts, *Dissenters*, p. 226; R. Tudur Jones, *Congregationalism in England*, pp. 69–70. For the repeal of the Act, see J. S. Simon, 'The Repeal of the Conventicle Act', *Proceedings of the Wesley Historical Society*, XI, 85–93, 103–8, 130-7.

[35] This was a reference to the case brought against Harris at Monmouth in August 1739.

[36] For Marmaduke Gwynne, see DWB; DEB; A. H. Williams, 'The Gwynnes of Garth, c. 1712–1809', *Brycheiniog*, XIV, 79–96, and XVII, 92–7.

[37] Though Harris does not give a name in his Diary, this was undoubtedly William Wynn (1709–60), the incumbent at Llanbrynmair since 1739. R. Gwilym Hughes, 'William Wynn o Langynhafal', *Llên Cymru*, I, 22f.

[38] Diary 63a: 5 November 1740.

[39] For Jenkin Morgan (d. 1762), see DWB.

[40] 'Cof-lyfr cynulleidfa'r Methodistiaid yn Nhref y Bala', MS 8822, T. C. Edwards Collection, NLW. Translated 'The record book of the Methodist congregation at Bala', it gives an account of the beginnings of Methodism in the town. G. P. Owen, *Atgofion John Evans y Bala* (Caernarfon, 1997), pp. 83f.

[41] Diary 68b: 29 January 1741.

[42] Abbey and Overton, *The English Church*, pp. 530–1.

[43] A. M. Lyles, *Methodism Mocked*, p. 39.

[44] Trevecka Letter 178: 2 August 1739.

[45] BA, p. 53.

[46] Baker, *John Wesley*, p. 182.

[47] Trevecka Letter 339: 18 May 1741.

[48] John Stevenson, *Popular Disturbances in England* (Longman, 1979), p. 32; JWJ, III, pp. 129, 132–3, 191, 224; Jackson (ed.), *Early Methodist Preachers*, I, p. 146.

[49] MTU, p. 19.

[50] Diary 52: 13 February 1740. See LHH, p. 74; TM, I, p. 100.

[51] Diary 72: 13 May 1741.

[52] Ibid., 17 May 1741.

[53] Diary 109: 3 April 1744.

[54] Diary 118: 1 October 1745.

[55] Ibid., 3 October 1745.

[56] Diary 62: 11 September 1740.

NOTES

57 For Robert Jones (1706?–42), see DWB; A. H. Williams, *John Wesley in Wales*, pp. xxii–xxiii.
58 TM, I, p. 84; LHH, p. 126; Edward Morgan, *The Life and Times of Howel Harris, Esq.* (Holywell, 1852), p. 56.
59 Trevecka Letter 174: 14 July 1739.
60 Williams, *Howell Harris*, p. xxii, states that Robert Jones was converted 'in the Methodist sense' by Charles Wesley in 1741, but cf. HMGC, p. 302, where Harris is quoted as saying in November 1741 that he was going '... to Full Moon [Fonmon] Castle to Esquire Jones (that had divided from us on account of doctrine ...)'. It was to Arminianism that Charles Wesley converted Robert Jones, which is hardly a conversion 'in the Methodist sense'. He had been converted prior to 1741, as Henry Davies's letter, dated 1739, proves.
61 Not 16 June as stated in the 'Itinerary'.
62 According to Whitefield's *Journals*, p. 244, in April 1739 Capel Hanbury requested a judge at Monmouth Assizes to prevent both Whitefield and Harris from itinerating and teaching the people. His application must have been refused as it was under the Riot Act that Harris was arrested during June.
63 An account of the trial, and the events leading up to it, is given in chapter 3.
64 Tom Beynon, 'Howell Harris accused of riotous assault at Presteigne and Knighton Quarter Sessions 1740–41', *Radnorshire Society Transactions* (1950), 67f. Also, *The Christian's Amusement* (1740), Issues 5 and 7.
65 Diary 64: 8 October 1740.
66 Diary 68: 14 January 1741.
67 Ibid., 15 January 1741.
68 Trevecka Letter 169.
69 *Gentleman's Magazine* (1744), 504, quoted in LHH, pp. 289–90.
70 For example, Robert Lloyd or Llwyd (1716–92) of Cilcain, Flintshire. See DWB.
71 For Sir Watkin Williams Wynne (d. 1749) of Wynnstay, see DWB. Harris described him as 'one of the greatest enemies of Christ'. HHVL, pp. 51–2.
72 HHVP, p. 214. He fell from his horse and died from his injuries on 26 September 1749.
73 For example, J. D. Walsh, 'Methodism and the Mob in the Eighteenth Century', in E. J. Cunning and Derek Brown (eds.), *Studies in Church History* (Cambridge, 1972), VIII, pp. 213f.; Speck, *Stability and Strife*, pp. 79–81; B. Bushaway, *By Rite* (London, 1982), pp. 190f.; P. Langford, *A Polite and Commercial People:*

NOTES

England 1727–1783 (London, 1989), pp. 264–6; J. F. C. Harrison, *The Common People* (London, 1984), pp. 243f.

[74] J. Wesley, *Works* (Pine), XVIII, p. 5. Also, Arthur P. Witney, 'The basis of opposition to Methodism in England in the eighteenth century', Ph.D. thesis, New York, 1949, 59.

[75] Diary 52: 13 February 1740.

[76] Ibid., 14 February 1740.

[77] Diary 62: 9 September 1740.

[78] Diary 74: 25 June 1741.

[79] Diary 62: 9 September 1740.

[80] Diary 74: 25 June 1741. Also *Weekly History* (1741), Issue 14.

[81] This was on 9 September 1740. For Seward's account, see *The Christian's Amusement* (1740), Issue 2. It appears that he lost the sight of his right eye for some time, and it is possible that an infection may have set in which affected his left eye and later contributed to his death on 22 October. Cf. G. L. Fairs, 'Notes concerning the death of William Seward at Hay', JHS, LVIII, 12–17.

[82] E. P. Thompson, 'The moral economy of the English crowd in the eighteenth century', *Past and Present,* 50 (1971), 76–136.

[83] Ibid.

[84] Walsh, 'Methodism and the mob', pp. 223f.

[85] Diary 74: 25 June 1741.

[86] For John Evans (1723–1817), see DWB; G. P. Owen, *Atgofion John Evans y Bala,* pp. 17f.

[87] John Hughes, *Methodistiaeth Cymru* (3 volumes: Gwrecsam, 1851–6), I, p. 99.

[88] Diary 52: 3 February 1740.

[89] Diary 89: 17 April 1742; Diary 142: 18 March 1750.

[90] Diary 54: 26 March 1740; Diary 62: 11 September 1740; HHVP, pp. 47–8, 50.

[91] R. Malcolmson, *Popular Recreations in English Society, 1700–1850* (Cambridge, 1973), passim.

[92] J. H. Davies, *A Bibliography of Welsh Ballads Printed in the 18th Century* (Part IV: London, 1911), pp. xv–xvi.

[93] For Harry Parry (1709?–1800), see DWB. Also, NLW MS 6729b.

[94]
>Sweet Harry Parry does not go
>To hear the Roundheads or Quakers,
>The men who, in the open-air,
>Have ceased to say their prayers.

My own translation. The original emphasizes that the Methodists were hypocrites.

[95] An *anterliwt*, or interlude, was a dramatic presentation in metre which was popular in Wales in the eighteenth century. Thomas Parry,

NOTES

Hanes Llenyddiaeth Gymraeg hyd 1900 (Caerdydd, 1944), pp. 208–12.
96 For William Roberts (fl. 1745), see DWB.
97 University of Wales, Bangor MS 3212, 483.
98 HMGC, p. 212.
99 For James Erskine (*c.*1678–1754), the son of Charles, fifth Earl of Mar, MP for Clackmannshire (1734–41), and Stirling Burghs (1741–7), a staunch Presbyterian, see DNB.
100 HMGC, pp. 227–8.
101 Ibid., p. 221; Trevecka Letter 1353.
102 MTU, p. 80.
103 HMGC, p. 218.
104 Early Association Records, JHS, L.
105 JHS, XXV, 17–18.
106 Diary 47a: 24 June 1739.
107 Diary 112: 19 June 1744. Trevecka Letter 1191.
108 Diary 47a: 27 January 1739.
109 Diary 113: 18 September 1744. The report which Harris had heard proved false.
110 Diary 41: 20 March 1739.
111 HHVP, p. 73: 10 May 1742.
112 Ibid., p. 102: 18 April 1744.
113 Diary 52: 14 February 1740.
114 Diary 62: 9 September 1740. Quoted by Howell Harris as part of a sermon preached by William Seward.
115 Diary 113: 27, 28, 29 [*sic*] August 1744.
116 Diary 97: 19 January 1743.
117 Diary 62: 9 September 1740.
118 Diary 98: 15 March 1743.
119 Diary 52: 4 February 1740.
120 Diary 130: 17 April 1748.
121 Diary 41: 20 March 1739.
122 Diary 52: 14 February 1740.
123 Diary 62: 9 September 1740.
124 Diary 68b: 29 January 1741.
125 Diary 54: 25 March 1740.
126 *The Christian's Amusement*, No. 2 (September [?] 1740).
127 Diary 62: 9 September 1740.
128 BA, p. 45.
129 Diary 110: 31 May 1744.
130 Diary 145: 11 June 1750.
131 Ibid., 12 June 1750.
132 MTU, pp. 16–17.

[133] Diary 47: 25 July 1739.
[134] Diary 68b: 29 January 1741.
[135] BA, pp. 51–2. For another example, see *Weekly History* (1741), Issue 34, p. 3.
[136] Diary 68b: 4–5, 7 February 1741; Diary 97: 2 January 1743; Diary 101: 27 July 1743; Diary 126: 9 May 1747; Diary 127a: 14 October 1747.
[137] Diary 71: 11 April 1741.
[138] Trevecka Letter 219: 9 February 1740.
[139] Diary 84: 3 February 1742.
[140] Diary 97: 2 January 1743.
[141] Diary 101: 27 July 1743.
[142] Diary 124: 1 November 1746.
[143] Diary 127a: 21 October 1747.
[144] Ibid., 14 October 1747.
[145] Diary 283: 21 October 1751.
[146] Diary 135a: 14 July 1749.
[147] Diary 83: 31 December 1741.
[148] *Y Llenor* (1927), 39.

Controversy and Division

[1] Trevecka MS 3186; LHH, pp. 46–7; HMGC, p. 106. The Diary which would have recorded their first meeting is missing.
[2] Glyn M. Ashton (ed.), Robert Jones, *Drych yr Amseroedd* (first published, 1820; republished, Caerdydd, 1958), p. 80.
[3] HMGC, p. 379; Geraint H. Jenkins, *The Foundations of Modern Wales*, p. 365, '. . . the Methodist movement found itself in turmoil and disarray. Between 1750 and 1762 Methodism lost its impetus and sense of direction.' Also, R. T. Jenkins, *Hanes Cymru yn y Ddeunawfed Ganrif*, p. 90, 'The movement went on . . . in a lame and wounded fashion . . .' (my translation); Ashton (ed.), Jones, *Drych yr Amseroedd*, pp. 78–80, 'The persecution, contempt and slander which the Methodists endured did not do as much harm as the division that occurred' (my translation).
[4] DR, p. 283; HMGC, pp. 388ff.
[5] HMGC, pp. 391–3.
[6] For John Sparks (1726–69), see DWB; HMGC, pp. 268–9.
[7] MTU, p. 187.
[8] For James Relly (1722–78), a cow farrier who was converted under the ministry of George Whitefield and was later to be the founder of the Rellyite sect, see DNB; DWB; DEB.

NOTES

9 For the 'Trevecka Family', as the community became known, see TL, pp. 185–206; LHH, pp. 378–93; Alun Wynne Owen, 'A study of Howell Harris and the Trevecka Family'.
10 Trevecka Letter 2472, in which Harris was invited to return.
11 HMGC, p. 315–16.
12 It is claimed that Rowland was short-tempered. See Owen Thomas, *Cofiant y Parchedig John Jones Talsarn* (Wrexham, [1874]), p. 801.
13 POD, pp. 35f; HMGC, p. 320.
14 Diary 18: 11 January 1737.
15 Diary 93: 4 September 1742; HHVL, p. 8.
16 Diary 113: 4 October 1744; G. T. Roberts, *Howell Harris*, p. 55. Also, Diary 126: 6 May 1747 and Diary 131b: 5 August 1748.
17 Diary 66: 4 December 1740. See HHVP, p. 40.
18 Diary 81: 12 November 1741.
19 Whitefield, *Works*, I, pp. 426–7.
20 Diary 127: 3 June 1747; HHVL, p. 143.
21 R. T. Jenkins, *Hanes Cymru yn y Ddeunawfed Ganrif*, p. 90; R. Tudur Jones, *Hanes Annibynwyr Cymru*, p. 147.
22 For Morgan John Lewis, (1711?–71), a Monmouthshire exhorter, converted under Harris's ministry *c*.1738, see DWB. He was prominent among those who wished the Methodists to secede from the Established Church.
23 Diary 125: 20 January 1747.
24 HHVL, p. 187.
25 HHVP, pp. 40, 143.
26 Diary 146a: 7 December 1750.
27 Diary 125: 20 January 1747.
28 JHS, XXIV, 56.
29 See, for example, HHVL, p. 68 (15 May 1745); ibid., p. 86 (9 February 1746); Diary 122: 1 April, 27 April, 1746; HHVL, p. 104 (18 June 1746); Diary 123: 27 June, 15 July 1746; Diary 132a: 30 November 1748; Diary 133: 2 February 1749; Diary 134: 2 March 1749; Diary 143: 10 April 1750.
30 John Wesley also was accused of being too autocratic. F. Baker, *John Wesley and the Church of England*, p. 202.
31 Jenkins, *Hanes Cymru*, p. 90.
32 Hughes-Edwards, 'Development and organisation', 79; DR, p. 50.
33 Diary 47a: 25 June 1739.
34 Ibid., 4 August 1739.
35 Diary 63: 25 September 1740, 'sweetly agreeing in all'.
36 Diary 49: 18 September 1739.
37 Trevecka Letter 338: 15 May 1741; LHH, pp. 172f.
38 Diary 82: 11 December 1741. I think it unfair to suppose, as in

NOTES

HMGC, p. 317, that Harris regarded these sins as ones committed by Rowland. The prayer is that he may be kept *from* these sins.

39 Diary 83: 20 December 1741.

40 I cannot agree with Alun Wyn Owen when he says in HMGC, p. 320, (a) that the manuscript reader can sense the tension in Harris's mind at the beginning of 1742, (b) that it would have been the easiest thing for Harris and Rowland to start an argument and quarrel. The manuscripts give little indication of any real tension between the two of them up to this time.

41 For an account of this first Association, see HMGC, pp. 171–2, 319.

42 Diary 84: 8 January 1742; JHS, XXVI, 104.

43 Diary 84: 10–11 January 1742.

44 Diary 84: 12 January 1742.

45 JHS, XXVI, 104.

46 The discussion of covenant theology reached its climax in the seventeenth century, in the teachings of Johannes Cocceius (1603–69), a celebrated German theologian, who interpreted the history of salvation in the terms of a series of covenants. Following the collapse of the 'Covenant of Works' as a result of Man's disobedience, a new covenant was revealed, made between God the Father and God the Son, who, in the role of Man's representative, secured salvation through his own personal obedience, the benefits of which are communicated to the elect through faith in Christ. Here, while Harris adopted the strict Calvinist position, Rowland represented a more moderate view, which held that, following the Fall, God sent his Son into the world, to do and suffer whatever was required to secure Man's salvation. God then promised this salvation to all who complied with the terms on which it was offered. Both views were acceptable within Calvinistic circles; the argument was purely academic. G. P. Fisher, *History of Christian Doctrine* (Edinburgh, 1896), pp. 348–50; R. Tudur Jones, *Vavasor Powell* (Abertawe, 1971), pp. 92–5; Charles Hodge, *Systematic Theology*, 3 vols. (London, 1960), II, pp. 354–66; Richard L. Greaves, *John Bunyan* (Abingdon, 1969), pp. 97–111; R. C. Monk, *John Wesley: His Puritan Heritage* (London, 1966), pp. 96–106.

47 Harris gives an account of this episode in Diary 86: 17 March 1742.

48 JHS, XXVI, 109, '. . . on Bro. Rowland not being willing to go according to the Rules of the Society we had dryness . . .' The meaning is unclear.

49 Diary 86: 18 March 1742.

50 DR, pp. 111–14.

51 Diary 62: 5–6 September 1740; Diary 70: 12 March 1741; Diary 71: 22 March 1741; HHVP, p. 72.

NOTES

52 It was a view also held by some Moravians. Towlson, *Moravian and Methodist*, pp. 56–62.
53 J. Wesley, *Letters*, II, pp. 57–65.
54 Fisher, *History of Christian Doctrine*, p. 274; James Atkinson, *Martin Luther* (London, 1968), p. 148.
55 Fisher, *History of Christian Doctrine*, p. 274n.; William Cunningham, *The Reformers and the Theology of the Reformation* (first published 1862, republished Edinburgh, 1967), p. 111.
56 G. F. Nuttall, *The Holy Spirit in Puritan Faith and Experience*, p. 57.
57 E. H. Sugden (ed.), *Sermons*, I, p. 208; II, p. 345.
58 Fisher, *History of Christian Doctrine*, p. 274.
59 J. Wesley, *Letters*, V, p. 358. Letter to Dr Thomas Rutherford, Regius Professor of Divinity at Cambridge and archdeacon of Essex.
60 Ibid., p. 359.
61 Whitefield, *Works*, I, p. 260. A letter from Whitefield to Harris.
62 HHVL, p. 59.
63 Diary 86: 19 March 1742.
64 Diary 88: 24 March 1742, 'The rumour of my disagreeing with Rowland already has cankered and done evil.' JHS, XXXIV, 79; DR, pp. 193–4.
65 Diary 92: 2 August 1742.
66 14 April 1742; see D. E. Jenkins, *Calvinistic Methodist Holy Orders*, p. 66; DR, p. 193.
67 Diary 90: 8 June 1742; JHS, XXXV, 20–1.
68 For Thomas Price (1712–83) of Watford near Caerphilly in Glamorgan, a prominent Methodist and Justice of the Peace, see JHS, XXXIX, 55–62.
69 STL, I, p. 10. Whitefield also warned Harris that he was being 'too censorious' and 'too bigotted'. Whitefield, *Works*, I, pp. 426–7; cf. the same *edited* letter in the *Weekly History* (1742), Issues 79–80.
70 For John Cennick (1718–55), a native of Berkshire, who began preaching at Kingswood, Bristol, in 1739, and sided with Whitefield in the Calvinist controversy of 1740–1, see DNB; DEB; Mathew Wilks (ed.), *The Life of Mr John Cennick* (London, 1819); Tyerman, *Life of Whitefield*, I, pp. 467f.; II, pp. 4f.
71 HHRS, p. 99; Tyerman, *Life of Whitefield*, II, pp. 1f.
72 Harris's excursions to England in 1739 lasted for 2 months, in 1740 for 1½ months, in 1741 for nearly 4 months and in 1742 for over 3 months.
73 Trevecka Letter 705; *Account of the Progress of the Gospel* (1742), II, Issue 1. I do not agree that the contents of this letter could be interpreted as malicious, as suggested in HMGC, p. 323.
74 Diary 96: 4–6 December 1742.

NOTES

[75] Trevecka Letter 745; STL, I, pp. 66–7; *Account of the Progress of the Gospel*, II, Issue 2.

[76] G. T. Roberts, *Howell Harris*, pp. 49–50; R. T. Jenkins in JHS, XXXVI, 83, 'He was deliberately brought in ... to fill a vacuum.'

[77] HMGC, pp. 319, 323.

[78] For example, Diary 97: 5 January 1743, where Harris states that 'Pen can describe nothing of him ... such love and wisdom and Power I never saw met in one man as in him.'

[79] This was certainly Harris's later view. Diary 123: 27 [26] June 1746, where Rowland is accused of 'want of fatherly spirit'. Rowland argued that he did not see himself as a national leader. See also, Diary 115b: 22 January 1745, where Harris suggests that Rowland did not undertake a sufficient number of preaching tours.

[80] Harris was chosen Superintendent at Watford on 6–7 April 1743. Association Records in JHS, XLVIII, 39.

[81] HMGC, p. 323.

[82] Diary 97: 2[3]–3[4] February 1743. Also, Diary 99: 18, 19, 25 May 1743; Diary 100: 29 June 1743; Diary 104: 2 November 1743.

[83] Diary 123: July 15 [14] 1746; a fact recognized by the Moravians at Haverfordwest, who admitted that he had appeared 'some years before the Methodists'. R. Buick Knox, 'Howell Harris and his doctrine of the Church', JHS, L, 9; also, JHS, VI, 6; HHVL, p. 68.

[84] HHRS, pp. 17, 53; Diary 113: 24 October 1744; Diary 115b: 2 January 1745; HHVP, p. 68; Diary 122: 1 April 1746; Diary 132a: 30 November 1748. There are many more.

[85] Harris uses the title 'General Visitor to All the Societies' on 25 January 1743.

[86] Diary 97: 13 January 1743.

[87] HHVL, p. 78.

[88] The creation of an awareness among Calvinistic Methodists of the international dimension of the Revival was the particular contribution of John Lewis, the printer of the Methodist newspapers to which references have already been made. These contained letters from home and abroad giving accounts of the progress of the work. They appeared under four titles between 1740 and 1745; *The Christian's Amusement* (1740), *The Weekly History* (1741–2), *An Account of the Progress of the Gospel* (1743) and *The Christian History* (1744–5). For an assessment of their significance, see D. S. Durden, 'Transatlantic communications and literature in the religious revivals 1735–1745', Ph.D. thesis, University of Hull, 1978, 80–8; S. O'Brien, 'Eighteenth century publishing networks in the first years of transatlantic Evangelicalism', in M. A. Noll, D. W. Bebbington and G. A. Rawlyk (eds.), *Evangelicalism* (Oxford, 1994), p. 38f. For John Lewis (fl.

1728–55), see DWB; JHS, II–V; *Proceedings of Wesley Historical Society*, XXI, 128–30; O'Brien, 'Eighteenth century publishing networks', pp. 48f.

89 Diary 74: 29 June 1941.
90 For the history of the Moravian church, see J. E. Hutton, *A History of the Moravian Church* (London, n.d.); Edward Langton, *History of the Moravian Church* (London, 1956); Towlson, *Moravian and Methodist*, pp. 21–34. For the Moravian church in England, see Podmore, *The Moravian Church in England, 1728–1760*, passim.
91 HHLE, pp. 24–5; Alun Wynne Owen, 'A study of Howell Harris and the Trevecka Family', 7; R. T. Jenkins, *The Moravian Brethren in North Wales* (London, 1938), p. 12; R. W. Evans, 'The eighteenth century Welsh awakening', 180.
92 *Bathafarn*, X, 23, 26. Also HHRS, pp. 25, 38, 41.
93 HHRS, p. 26.
94 HHLE, pp. 59–60.
95 Diary 120: 4 December 1745. Cf., Towlson, *Moravian and Methodist*, p. 129.
96 HHVL, p. 90. See also, ibid., pp. 84, 99, 'Shewed of the Moravians, their cunning, errors, bigotry and evil eye on the Tabernacle.' Wesley also accused the Moravians of 'guile and dissumulation'. Wesley, *Letters*, I, p. 258; Towlson, *Moravian and Methodist*, pp. 27–8.
97 Diary 122: 10 April 1746; HHVL, p. 90. Also, HHVP, p. 128.
98 Towlson, *Moravian and Methodist*, pp. 129–30; Hutton, *A History of the Moravian Church*, pp. 212f.; Podmore, *The Moravian Church in England*, pp. 132–6.
99 HHVL, p. 59: 1 and 3 December 1744.
100 Harris had already accused him of antinomianism in August 1743. See HHRS, p. 51.
101 HHVL, pp. 59–60: 1–3 December 1744.
102 'Letter Days', during which letters from correspondents in various parts of the world were read, were held at Fetter Lane, the Foundry and the Tabernacle. Through them, an awareness was created among those present of the international dimension of the Revival; at the same time, converts were brought to a realization that they were part of a larger body than was visible to them at their meetings. Letter-reading also testified to the magnitude of God's grace in that He was constantly involved in drawing people to Himself simultaneously in many parts of the world. For the significance of 'Letter Days', see Durden, 'Transatlantic communications', 96–108. For an example of the procedure on a 'Letter day' at Whitefield's London Tabernacle, see *An Account of the Progress of the Gospel* (1743), III, pp. 73ff.

NOTES

[103] For example, HHVP, p. 181; HHVL, p. 253.
[104] Earlier references by Harris to Christ's Blood can be seen in Diary 47: 26 July 1739; Diary 52: 31 January, 3 February 1740; Diary 54: 3, 5 March 1740; Diary 54: 15 March 1740.
[105] Diary 120: 4 December 1745. Also, HHVP, p. 115: 13 October 1745.
[106] HHVL, p. 60: 4 December 1744.
[107] Diary 115b: 4 January 1745.
[108] For the Trinitarian controversy, see Abbey and Overton, *The English Church in the Eighteenth Century*, I, pp. 480–529.
[109] Harris was accused of denying the Trinity in Daniel Rowland, *Ymddiddan rhwng Methodist Uniawn-gred ac Un Camsyniol* ([Bryste], 1750), a pamphlet published to condemn Harris's views.
[110] G. P. Fisher, *History of Christian Doctrine*, pp. 136f.
[111] L. Berkhof, *Systematic Theology* (London, 1958), pp. 88–9.
[112] See below.
[113] Diary 115b: 17 January 1745.
[114] Diary 115a: 17 December 1744.
[115] For the Monarchian teachings, see Fisher, *History of Christian Doctrine*, pp. 98–9.
[116] Diary 115a: 17 December 1744.
[117] Diary 115b: 16 February 1745.
[118] Ibid., 23 January 1745.
[119] Ibid., 26 February 1745.
[120] References to the 'Blood' do not totally disappear from the Diary during this period, but they are fewer in number.
[121] Trevecka Letter 621: 3 September 1742.
[122] Diary 115b: 30 January and 16 February 1745. Also, Diary 130: 17 April 1748.
[123] Diary 116: 3 April 1745.
[124] Ibid., 23 April 1745.
[125] HHVL, p. 69: 30 May 1745.
[126] Diary 115b: 30 January, 16 February 1745, 'God has left us because the preaching of the Blood is lost.'
[127] Diary 116: 3 April 1745.
[128] Ibid., 5–6 May 1745.
[129] Diary 117: 3 July 1745.
[130] Ibid., 4 July 1745.
[131] Diary 118: 29 July 1745, 'I find the Enemy strives to weaken and blacken me ...'
[132] Ibid., 30 July 1745, 'Bro. Wesley and the Brethren I find set me out as going to Errors ...' There is no reference to this in Wesley's *Journals*, apart from a cryptic entry on 29 May 1745 (vol. III, p. 178), 'I talked

at large with Howell Harris, not yet carried away by the torrent of Antinomianism. But how long will he be able to stand? Only until he consents to stand neuter. When he is brought not to oppose, he will quickly yield.' For Wesley's opposition to the emphasis on the 'blood and wounds', see Towlson, *Moravian and Methodist*, pp. 138–9.

133 Diary 118: 4 August 1745.
134 Diary 120: 28 October 1745.
135 Ibid., 4 December 1745.
136 Diary 123: 27 [26] June 1746. Harris states that Rowland held that 'the Lord did not set him in the place of a father, else He would fit him for it'.
137 Diary 118: 30 July 1745; TM, I, p. 301.
138 For examples, see HHVP, p. 102; Diary 67: 26 December 1740; Diary 130: 22 February 1742; Diary 115b: 2 January 1745; Hughes-Edwards, 'Development and organisation', 231.
139 Dallimore, *George Whitefield*, II, pp. 231–2.
140 *Weekly History*, VII, Issue 4, pp. 14–15.
141 Diary 116: 2 April 1745.
142 For examples, see Diary 116: 4, 19, 23 April 1745; Diary 118: 30 July 1745.
143 Diary 118: 20 August 1745; Diary 118: 12 September 1745. The problem of losing one's 'first love' – the fading away of the ecstasy and spiritual euphoria that often came with the first stage of conversion – was a well-known danger point and a recurring problem in Methodism; some converts lapsed at this stage. Wesley noted how many came to find relief in the doctrine of predestination: when they felt their first confidence falter, they derived comfort from the idea of 'final perseverance'. John Wesley, 'A plain account of Christian perfection', in *Works*, XI, pp. 366ff., with special reference to Section 13. Also, John Newton, *Works*, 6 vols. (London, 1816), I, pp. 588–9.
144 Diary 120: 4 December 1745.
145 Ibid., 4 January 1746.
146 Ibid., 7 January 1746.
147 Ibid., 8 January 1746.
148 Tyerman, *Life of Whitefield*, II, p. 148.
149 Diary 118: 11 September 1745.
150 Diary 120: 24 November 1745.
151 Diary 121: 21 January 1746.
152 Ibid., 2 May 1746.
153 For James Beaumont (d. 1750), see DWB; TM, I, pp. 223–4; HMGC, pp. 223–5; MTU, pp. 103–6, 113, 150, 156.
154 Diary 73: 11 June 1741.
155 Trevecka Letter 592: 9 August 1742; STL, I, pp. 31–3.

156 HHVP, p. 58.
157 HHVL, p. 61.
158 HMGC, p. 331; Diary 126: 19 May 1746, '[Beaumont] opened his mind about the only use of the Law being only [sic] to shew souls their misery, and then to shew them the Saviour, and not to tell them to do anything. I also declared I thought that was somewhat of antinomianism.'
159 Diary 116: 17 March 1745.
160 HHVL, p. 104.
161 Diary 122: 9–10 April 1746.
162 Ibid., 9 April 1746; TM, I, p. 321.
163 Diary 122: 9 April 1746.
164 Ibid., 10 April 1746.
165 Diary 145: 25 June 1750. This confirms Harris's constant assertion in 1750 that the seeds of the separation were sown in 1746. Also, DR, p. 272.
166 See Diary 122: 10 April 1746.
167 JHS, L, 47–8, 14 April, 1746.
168 JHS, XXXI, 86–90; TM, I, p. 323.
169 HHVL, pp. 94–5, 5, 13 and 14 May 1746.
170 Ibid., p. 98, 26 May 1746.
171 Ibid., p. 102.
172 Diary 123: 27 [26] June 1746.
173 This theme gained prominence in Harris's writings from 1745 onwards. After assuming responsibility for the Tabernacle, he envisaged himself as a negotiator between the various factions involved in the Revival. In February 1746 he wrote: 'the Lord has given me to be a peacemaker and reconciler, and also a means of keeping the brethren in the Church' (HHVL, p. 87. Also, ibid., pp. 78, 88, 90, 104, 117; HHVP, pp. 121, 128, 136; R. Buick Knox, JHS, L, 35; Dallimore, *George Whitefield*, II, pp. 235–9). He was suitably qualified for the task; as Dr Nuttall observed, 'He was ... in touch with many of the religious movements of his time' (HHLE, p. 3). Moreover, being a layman who did not have to confine himself to conveying spirituality through the mediation of any particular form of liturgy, and who was able to move around without restriction, expressing himself in whatever terms were acceptable to those with whom he happened to be in conversation at the time, must surely have been an advantage.
174 Diary 123: 27–8 [26–7] June 1746.
175 Ibid., 8 July 1746.
176 Ibid., 30 September 1746; also, 1 October: 'the Brethren are set against me ...' and 'they are combined against me and blacken me everywhere ...'

NOTES

177 Ibid., 1–2 October 1746.
178 The account of the meeting is taken from Diary 124.
179 Diary 124: 19 October 1746.
180 Ibid., 17 October 1746.
181 Ibid., 16 October 1746.
182 Diary 125: 12 January 1747, '... was drawn out, cutting, to the Tale-barers ...'
183 Diary 124: 6 November 1746.
184 Ibid., 5 December 1746; HHVP, p. 128. Anne was Harris's second daughter. The first was born on 30 August 1745 but died the same day. Diary 118: 30 August 1745. For an account of Harris's courtship and marriage to Anne Williams of Skreen, see Gomer M. Roberts, *Portread o Ddiwygiwr*, pp. 88ff; Geraint Tudur, 'The king's daughter: a reassessment of Anne Harris of Trefeca', in *Journal of Welsh Religious History*, vol. 7 (1999), 55–75.
185 Diary 125.
186 Ibid., 8, 10–12, 20 January 1747.
187 Ibid., 7, 20 January 1747.
188 Diary 124: 27 November 1747.
189 Diary 125: 7 January 1747; HHVP, p. 129.
190 Diary 125: 19 January 1747.
191 Thomas Adams, one of the preachers at Whitefield's Tabernacle, also believed Harris to have been 'too bearing sometimes'. Diary 126: 15 April 1747.
192 Diary 125: 20 January 1747; HHVL, p. 118.
193 He was in England for 171 days compared to 194 in Wales. He was at home for less than fifty days during the whole of the year. 'Itinerary', JHS, X, No 3. Also, HMGC, p. 331.
194 Diary 126: 24 April, 14 May 1747.
195 Harris claimed this at Cirencester, 15 April 1747.
196 Diary 126: 14 May 1747.
197 Ibid., 15 May 1747.
198 Ibid., 20 May 1747.
199 Diary 127: 23 July 1747.
200 Diary 127a: 20 September 1747.
201 Ibid., 24 September 1747.
202 Ibid., 19 September 1747.
203 For further examples of Harris's Partripassian statements, see John Gwili Jenkins, *Hanfod Duw a Pherson Crist* (Liverpool, 1931), pp. 148–66.
204 John Calvin, *Institutes of the Christian Religion* (Philadelphia, 1960), I, pp. xiii, 128ff.; B. B. Warfield, *Calvin and Augustine* (Philadelphia, 1971), pp. 231ff.

NOTES

205 For the doctrine of the Trinity, see Berkhof, *Systematic Theology*, pp. 82f.
206 Nicholas Ludvig von Zinzendorf, *Maxims. Theological Ideas and Sentences, extracted by J. Gambold* (London, 1751), pp. 332–3, 'Yet each denomination is generally possessed of some Jewel (a clearness of truth, a valuable temper) peculiar to itself ...' Also, A. J. Lewis, *Zinzendorf*, p. 151; Senn, *Protestant Spiritual Traditions*, pp. 207–8.
207 Diary 127a: 14 October 1747.
208 Diary 130 and 131a: 12–13 May 1748.
209 Diary 131a: 13 May 1748.
210 Ibid., 26 February 1748.
211 Diary 129: 4 February 1748.
212 G. F. Nuttall, *The Holy Spirit*, p. 43.
213 Diary 131a: 5 May 1748; HMGC, p. 332; HHVP, p. 147.
214 Diary 131a: 17 May 1748.
215 Tyerman, *Life of Whitefield*, II, pp. 184f.
216 HHVL, p. 201.
217 Tyerman, *Life of Whitefield*, II, pp. 184f.; HHVL, pp. 201–2.
218 Diary 131b: 3 August 1748.
219 Diary 96: 7 November 1742; Diary 102: 31 August 1743; HHRS, p. 41, 51.
220 Tyerman, *Life of Whitefield*, II, pp. 145, 183. For Whitefield's recantation of his early enthusiastic reliance on 'impressions' of the Spirit, see 'Letter to the bishop of London' in Whitefield, *Works*, IV, pp. 127–8.
221 Tyerman, *Life of Whitefield*, II, pp. 125–40.
222 Diary 131b: 18 August 1748.
223 Diary 132: 22 August 1748; Diary 132a: 1 October 1748. Harris claims to have travelled between 400 and 500 miles during September, preaching twice, sometimes three times, daily.
224 An account of the relationship between Harris and Sidney Griffith is given in chapter 8.
225 The underlying theme of his sermons was still the Person and Work of Christ, as is attested by his texts during this period; e.g., 20 August – John 1:1 ('In the beginning was the Word, and the Word was with God, and the Word was God'); 22 August – Romans 8:3 ('God sending his own Son in the likeness of sinful flesh'); 14 September – 'Our Saviour's Person'; 23 September – Luke 19:10 ('For the Son of man is come to seek and to save that which was lost'); 2 October – Revelation 12:1 ('And there appeared a great wonder in heaven ...'). All dates are during 1748.
226 Diary 133: 28 December 1748.
227 Ibid.

NOTES

[228] Diary 132a: 30 October 1748.
[229] Ibid., 6 November 1748.
[230] Ibid., 27 November 1748.
[231] Diary 133: 1 February 1749.
[232] Ibid., 27 January, 1 February 1749.
[233] Ibid., 5 January 1749, This was Anne, who had been born on 5 December 1746.
[234] Tyerman, *Life of Whitefield*, II, p. 190.
[235] Diary 133: 7 January 1749, 'I had now a letter from London to invite me to take care of the London Society ...' See Trevecka Letter 1832: 29 November 1748, in STL, II, p. 23.
[236] Diary 133: 26 January 1749; Tyerman, *Life of Whitefield*, II, pp. 188f.
[237] Ibid., p. 189.
[238] Ibid.
[239] Diary 134: 19 February 1749.
[240] HHVP, pp. 115, 117, 121. Also, HHLE, p. 40; Knox, 'Howell Harris and his doctrine of the Church', JHS, L, 35.
[241] Diary 133: 26 January 1749; cf. Dallimore, *George Whitefield*, II, p. 249: 'in reference to Whitefield's hope of union, [Harris] stated, "... it will never do, because neither of the sides can submit to either of the other head – Mr Wesley or Mr Whitefield"...' This sentence, taken out of context, should not be misunderstood. Harris was not opposed to union, but resolute that preliminary talks should clearly define the nature of the union. He was aware of the problems, as in HHVL, pp. 195, 202–3, 208, but at the same time determined that an attempt should be made.
[242] Diary 133: 26 January 1749. Also, HHVL, p. 213: 8 and 12 April 1749.
[243] HHVL, p. 213.
[244] Ibid., p. 222: 26 April 1749. The meeting took place at Bristol on 2 August 1749.
[245] Diary 135a: 26 May 1749. Rowland responded to Harris's moves by saying that he was 'too soft and complying'.
[246] Diary 135a: 25 May 1749; see also Harris's scathing attack on Price on 28 May.
[247] Ibid., 29 May, 2 June.
[248] Ibid., 22 June.
[249] Ibid., 27 May.
[250] See chapter 8.
[251] Diary 135a: 26 July 1749; HHVP, p. 166.
[252] HHVL, p. 231.
[253] Ibid., p. 234. Harris had a third daughter, Elizabeth, who was born on 14 December 1748. She died at Brecon on 8 February 1826.

NOTES

254 Ibid., p. 235.
255 Ibid., p. 233.
256 Ibid., p. 241. 'Mr Brown', who had issued the lease for the Tabernacle in London, objected strongly to Harris. This was later to lead to difficulties as he threatened to withdraw the lease if Harris was allowed to preach there.
257 Diary 137: 2 October 1749.
258 Ibid., 11 October 1749.
259 Diary 138: 20–1 October 1749.
260 Ibid., 28 October 1749.
261 Ibid., 22 October 1749.
262 Diary 139: 8 December 1749.
263 HHVL, p. 250.
264 Diary 141: 31 January 1750.
265 Ibid., 1 February 1750.
266 Ibid., 3 February 1750.
267 Diary 142: 1 March 1750.
268 Ibid., 11 March 1750.
269 Ibid., 15 March 1750.
270 Ibid., 17 March 1750.
271 For William Powell, see HMGC, pp. 238–9.
272 For Thomas William (1717–65), of Eglwysilan, see HMGC, pp. 236–7.
273 Diary 143: 31 March 1750.
274 For Thomas Jones, see HMGC, pp. 219–20.
275 For John Richard, see HMGC, pp. 242–3.
276 Diary 144: 22 April 1750.
277 Diary 143: 1 April 1750.
278 Diary 144: 23 April 1750.
279 Ibid., 7 June 1750.
280 Ibid., 8 June 1750.
281 See chapter 8.
282 Diary 145: 22 June 1750.
283 Tom Beynon, 'Extracts from the Diaries of Howell Harris', *Bathafarn*, X, 41.

The Prophetess

[1] J. E. Griffiths, *Pedigrees of Anglesey and Caernarvonshire Families* (1914), p. 169.
[2] Gwynedd Archives: Poole Collection, Schedule, VII, 1228–9. William Griffith sought legal opinion in 1742 as to the possibility of a court

of equity allowing him to take away his wife's 'pin money'. This would suggest that there were difficulties in the marriage at that early date.

[3] For Peter Williams (1723–96), a native of Carmarthenshire who was converted under the ministry of George Whitefield and who became an author and biblical expositor, see DWB; DEB. Also, Gomer M. Roberts, *Bywyd a Gwaith Peter Williams* (Caerdydd, 1943).

[4] The name of the peninsula which constitutes part of Caernarfonshire.

[5] Roberts, *Bywyd a Gwaith Peter Williams*, p. 27. Williams claimed that a 'gentlewoman of property was effectually converted' during his visit to the area, and that she acknowledged him 'as her spiritual father as long as she lived'. This has been claimed to have been a reference to Sidney Griffith (MTU, p. 153), although TM, I, p. 369, held that it was through Harris's ministry that she was converted. It appears from the evidence of the Diaries that she had already been converted prior to meeting Harris in October 1748.

[6] Trevecka Letter 1828, which states that William Griffith accompanied two Methodist exhorters to Marmaduke Gwynne's house at Garth in 1748, and that 'all the exhorters are welcomed to come to Cefnamwlch'.

[7] Diary 128: 31 October 1747. This was how Harris described the north following the persecution that he suffered there.

[8] Diary 132a: 7 October 1748. Harris's estimate of 8,000–10,000 is probably an exaggeration. Beriah Gwynfe Evans, in *Ymneilltuaeth Cymru ac Apocrypha'r Diwygiad*, pp. 113–14, is extremely suspicious of Harris's figures for his congregations. It is doubtful that they were as large as Harris and the other revivalists of the eighteenth century claimed. Estimates of crowd sizes are always difficult; Harris would probably have erred towards greater success rather than underestimated the number of his auditors.

[9] Trevecka Letter 1824, partly transcribed in HMGC, p. 335.

[10] Diary 133: 2 February 1749.

[11] Ibid., 7 February 1749.

[12] Diary 135a: 18 July 1749. It should be emphasized that this conversation took place on 18 July 1749, and that Harris and Sidney Griffith had met on that date, not on 20 July as in HMGC, p. 337.

[13] Wesley, *Journal*, III, pp. 460–61.

[14] Cf. HMGC, p. 337. The author states that it was Harris who invited Sidney Griffith to accompany him on his journey to Llangeitho, but this view is not supported by Harris's entry in his Diary. The fact that there is no mention that she returned home to pick up any luggage suggests that she had already begun her journey south and was possibly aware that Harris would be calling at Pwllheli.

NOTES

15 Diary 135a: 21 July 1749.
16 Ibid., 25 July 1749. Also, HHVP, p. 166.
17 Diary 135a: 26 July 1749.
18 Ibid., 27 July 1749.
19 Although there is a reference to Harris and Sidney Griffith travelling together from Llangeitho to Trevecka in HMGC, pp. 337–8, the author gives the misleading impression that they went directly from Llangeitho, through Trevecka, to Builth, and that Sidney Griffith returned home immediately after the Association. In fact, their journey took them from Llangeitho to Llanddowror, then on to Carmarthen; from there to Trevecka, over to Bristol, back again to Trevecka and then to Builth.
20 Diary 135a: 28 July 1749. Not as in HMGC, p. 337.
21 Ibid., 29 July 1749.
22 Diary 136: 30 July 1749.
23 Ibid.
24 This was not true, unless Harris meant the first of the gentry in north Wales.
25 Diary 136: 31 July 1749.
26 Ibid., 1 August 1749.
27 Diary 137: 23 September 1749.
28 Ibid., 6 August 1749.
29 Diary 136: 7 August 1749.
30 See HHVL, p. 19, where the author claims 'that there was never any domestic tension at Trevecka on account of Madam Griffith'. This is not true.
31 Diary 136: 9 August 1749.
32 Ibid., 9 August 1749.
33 See HMGC, p. 338, where it is said that Sidney Griffith had been turned out of her home by her husband. This statement is most probably taken from MTU, p. 157. Though Sidney Griffith's marriage was certainly in difficulties, she had not yet been thrown out. See below.
34 Diary 137: 23 September 1749.
35 Ibid., 1 October 1749.
36 Ibid., 23 September 1749.
37 For Watkin Wynne (1717–74), see DWB (Wynne (Wynne-Finch) (Family)).
38 Diary 137: 27–8 September 1749.
39 Ibid., 27 September 1749.
40 Ibid., 23 September 1749.
41 Ibid., 1 October 1749.
42 Harris often found it necessary to correct her, e.g. Diary 137: 23, 24

September 1749. Sidney Griffith did later claim to Harris that she was infallible in her communication of divine messages. See below.
43 For example, Diary 136: 9 August 1749; Diary 137: 30 September; Diary 138: 25, 27 October, and 6–7 November.
44 Diary 137: 24 September 1749.
45 Ibid., 28 September 1749.
46 Ibid.
47 Ibid., 30 September 1749.
48 Ibid., 3 October 1749.
49 Ibid., 29 September 1749.
50 Ibid., 30 September 1749.
51 Ibid.
52 Ibid., 1 October 1749.
53 Ibid., 2 October 1749.
54 Ibid., 1 October 1749.
55 Ibid., 13 October 1749.
56 Diary 138: 17 October 1749.
57 Diary 137: 8 October 1749. It is a passing reference in a prayer that 'she has so many Revelations'. Harris does not give any details of their nature.
58 Diary 137: 3 October 1749.
59 Ibid., 6 October 1749.
60 For a biblical reference to the Urim and Thummim, see Exodus 28.30. They were 'Instruments of divination attached to the breastplate of the [Jewish] high priest; their form is uncertain. The process of divination involved the use of two stones or tablets by means of which an answer of "yes" or "no" could be obtained to important questions.' Dan Cohn-Sherbok, *The Blackwell Dictionary of Judaica* (Oxford, 1992), p. 557.
61 Diary 137: 3 October 1749.
62 Ibid., 6 October 1749.
63 Ibid., 11, 12, 17, 20 October 1749.
64 Ibid., 11 October 1749.
65 Ibid., 12 October 1749.
66 Diary 136: 30 July 1749. Harris was called to Bristol by Whitefield to discuss 'terms of Union among us'. The first meeting, attended by Harris, Whitefield and both Wesleys, took place on 2 August. Further attempts were made in London later in the same year. HHVL, pp. 247–65.
67 Harris was accused by John Wesley. HHVL, p. 249: 10 December 1749. He had mentioned to the Countess of Huntingdon his belief that Harris was hindering the union by keeping Wales to himself. This Harris denied.

[68] Diary 137: 9 October 1749.
[69] Diary 138: 12 November 1749.
[70] Ibid., 14 November 1749.
[71] Ibid., 22 October 1749.
[72] It possible that the term came from a verse similar to Psalm 32:8: 'I will instruct thee and teach thee in the way thou shalt go: I will guide thee with mine eye.'
[73] Diary 138: 22 October 1749.
[74] Ibid., 23 October 1749.
[75] Ibid., 25 October 1749.
[76] Harris often omits the reasons for his disagreements with Sidney Griffith while writing his Diary, saying only that 'storms' or 'tryals' had taken place.
[77] This was the first time she had used this term. Its origin is biblical: Deborah, in Judges 5:7, used it to describe herself. It therefore denotes a godly woman displaying unusual spiritual bravery and strength.
[78] Diary 138: 27 October 1749.
[79] For the Ranters, a seventeenth-century antinomian movement, see Christopher Hill, *The World Turned Upside Down* (London, 1972), passim. For contemporary views on their beliefs, see ibid., pp. 163–8.
[80] For the French Prophets, who believed in miraculous powers and claimed to have attained the state of perfection, see Hillel Schwartz, *The French Prophets*.
[81] The gift of discerning of spirits is the ability to know with assurance whether certain behaviour purporting to be of God is in reality divine, human or satanic.
[82] Diary 138: 27 October 1749.
[83] Ibid.
[84] For Thomas Jones, see HMGC, pp. 219–21.
[85] Diary 138: 29 October 1749.
[86] It was here that Sidney Griffith became ill, not at Llanidloes, as stated in HMGC, p. 339.
[87] Diary 138: 30 October 1749.
[88] Ibid., 2 November 1749.
[89] Ibid., 4 November 1749.
[90] Ibid., 3, 4, 5 November 1749.
[91] Ibid., 6 November 1749.
[92] Diary 139: 21 November 1749.
[93] Sidney Griffith's exact date of birth is not known. After consideration of the relevant factors, it is unlikely that she was more than thirty when she first met Harris in 1748.
[94] Diary 139: 12 November 1749.

NOTES

95 Ibid., 10 November. The meeting there was prearranged and did not occur by chance as suggested in HMGC, p. 339, and POD, p. 116.

96 This probably accounts for the earlier reference in HMGC, p. 338, and MTU, p. 157 that she had been ejected from her home prior to her arrival at Trevecka in September. In fact, she was thrown out after she returned home, and then returned to Trevecka, arriving there on 20 October. During her absence, Harris had expressed the hope that William Griffith 'would drive her away, so that all may see 'tis the Lord brings her [to Trevecka]' (Diary 137: 13 October 1749). If that had already happened, he would have no reason to offer such a prayer.

97 Diary 138: 18 November 1749.

98 Ibid., 19 November 1749.

99 Their wedding anniversary. They were married in 1744.

100 Elizabeth Whitefield, who had been a guest at Trevecka during September 1749, was also opposed to Sidney Griffith and wasted no time in making life difficult for Harris. He wrote on 8 December: 'I saw more of the craft and Cunning of Mrs. Whitefield.' Her attitude led to another 'dreadful Combat with Satan'.

101 HHVL, p. 250.

102 MTU, p. 161.

103 HHVL, p. 255: 30 December 1749 and 1 January 1750.

104 Ibid., p. 257.

105 Ibid., p. 262: 17 January 1750.

106 A view also expressed by his own wife. Diary 141: 3 February 1750.

107 Diary 141: 1 February 1750.

108 W. S. Gunter, *The Limits of 'Love Divine'*, pp. 195f. Also, L. Tyerman, *The Oxford Methodists* (London, 1873), pp. 386–411; Wesley, *Letters*, II, pp. 110f.

109 Diary 141: 9 February 1750.

110 Ibid., 20 February 1750. Also, Diary 142: 3 March 1750.

111 Diary 142: 3 March 1750.

112 Ibid.

113 See, for example, Diary 142: 15 March 1750: Richard Tibbott 'asking what to do when the fathers ... disagree.' See also Trevecka Letter 1913; HMGC, p. 341.

114 Diary 142: 3 March 1750.

115 Ibid., 5 March 1750.

116 Ibid., 11 March 1750. Also, Diary 143: 6 April 1750.

117 Diary 141: 1, 2 February 1750.

118 Ibid., 19 February; Diary 142: 28 February 1750; Diary 143: 23 March, 6 April 1750.

119 Diary 142: 2 March 1750.

NOTES

[120] Ibid., 24, 25 February and 15 March 1750.
[121] Ibid., 25 February 1750.
[122] Ibid., 20 February 1750. For John Sparks, see HMGC, pp. 268–9.
[123] Diary 142: 5 March 1750. For Thomas William, see HMGC, pp. 236–7.
[124] Diary 143: 31 March 1750. For William Powell, Llanfabon, see HMGC, pp. 238–9.
[125] Ibid., 31 March 1750. For John Richard, see HMGC, pp. 242–4.
[126] Diary 141: 9 February 1750.
[127] Ibid., 20 February 1750.
[128] Diary 142: 5, 15 March 1750.
[129] Diary 143: 31 March 1750. It was there that she finally went on 24 April.
[130] Diary 142: 15 March 1750.
[131] 'Arise therefore, and get thee down, and go with them, doubting nothing: for I have sent them.'
[132] Diary 143: 12 April 1750.
[133] Diary 142: 1 March 1750.
[134] Ibid., 9 March 1750.
[135] Diary 144: 26 April 1750.
[136] Ibid., 7 March 1750.
[137] Diary 141: 3 February 1750.
[138] Diary 144: 17 May 1750. Lewis was one of Harris's most faithful supporters but this incident led him to switch his allegiance to Rowland and the clergy.
[139] Ibid., 20 May 1750.
[140] Diary 141: 9 February; Diary 143: 12 April; Diary 144: 17, 21, 26, 28 April, and 9, 29 May 1750.
[141] Diary 144: 28 May 1750.
[142] Diary 142: 16 March 1750.
[143] Diary 144: 8 May 1750.
[144] Ibid., 25 April 1750. The travelling arrangements, while unacceptable to Sidney Griffith, show that Harris was more concerned than he cared to admit about public response to their relationship.
[145] It should be noted that Sidney Griffith was with Harris, mostly at Trevecka, from 24 April, throughout May and the first half of June. The letter attributed to Harris (Trevecka Letter 1932) in HMGC, p. 342, and also in POD, p. 117, could not, therefore, have been written by him to Sidney Griffith. On the day that the letter was written, 3 May 1750, they were together at Builth. The letter was written to a woman, for the author addressed the recipient as 'my Sister'. Furthermore, the letter is signed 'George' and has no relevance to the story of Harris and Sidney Griffith.

[146] Diary 144: 8 June 1750.
[147] Ibid., 26 April 1750.
[148] Ibid., 20 May 1750.
[149] Ibid., 3 May 1750.
[150] Eifion Evans, *Howel Harris*, p. 56.
[151] TM, I, p. 371.
[152] HHVP, p. 198: 1 August 1751.
[153] *Pace* G. H. Jenkins, *The Foundations of Modern Wales*, p. 364, where it is stated that 'the evidence in [Harris's] journal leaves no doubt that his relationship with Madam Griffith was adulterous and that by allowing his heart to rule his head he had brought Welsh Methodism into grave disrepute'. Through reading the same journals I have come to the totally opposite conclusion, that they offer no evidence that the relationship deteriorated into a physical and adulterous association. Harris's phraseology while writing of Sidney Griffith certainly suggests a sexual attraction, but, though it can be said that he was tempted towards adultery, there is nothing in his writings to suggest that any physical act occurred between them. Throughout the episode the Diary records the thoughts and feelings of a man torn between physical lust and spiritual duty; there is no indication that he submitted to his lust. Even though his mental capabilities had deteriorated during the time of the association with Sidney Griffith, the deterioration resulted in a heightened spiritual awareness rather than moral degradation. It is more than likely that, had the relationship become adulterous, the resulting guilt would have totally ruined Harris. This was not the case: his retirement to Trevecka was not prompted by feelings of guilt, and the invitation that he received at the end of the decade from Rowland and Williams to return to the Revival work suggests that they did not believe him guilty of any immoral act.
[154] HMGC, p. 351.
[155] Diary 145: 22 June 1750.
[156] Ibid., 29 June 1750.
[157] DR, p. 277.
[158] R. T. Jenkins in DWB, p. 300.
[159] MTU, p. 162.
[160] Derec Llwyd Morgan, *Taith i Langeitho 1762* (Gwasanaeth Llyfrgell Gwynedd, 1976), p. 6.
[161] HMGC, p. 336, and MTU, p. 154, suggest that Sidney Griffith was initially interested in Daniel Rowland.
[162] Cf. HMGC, p. 343. The conclusion drawn by the author is based on a manuscript incorrectly attributed to Sidney Griffith. See note 145 above.

[163] For example, Diary 137: 8 October 1749; Diary 144: 25 April, 6 May 1750.
[164] TM, I, p. 371.
[165] HHVL, p. 260: 13 January 1750.
[166] Diary 139: 22 November 1749.

Postscript

[1] 'Itinerary' in JHS, X, 38–47.
[2] HHVP, pp. 175, 179, 183–4, 190, 195, 198–9, 211.
[3] Diary 145: 11 June 1750.
[4] HHVP, pp. 181–2.
[5] Diary 145: 4 July 1750. See also TM, I, p. 389.
[6] The first 'General Association' was held at St Nicholas in Glamorganshire. Diary 145: 26–7 July 1750.
[7] Diary 146: 27 September 1750.
[8] Diary 145: 26 July 1750; Diary 146: 26–7 September 1750.
[9] Diary 146: 26 September 1750.
[10] Diary 146a: 15 November 1750.
[11] Translated, 'Dialogue between an orthodox and an erroneous Methodist'.
[12] Ubiquitarians believe in the omnipresence of Christ's body, while Eutychians hold that Christ possessed but one nature.
[13] Diary 152a: 4 July 1751; TM, I, pp. 399–400.
[14] TM, I, p. 401; Diary 158: 1 January 1752.
[15] HHVP, p. 202.
[16] Ibid., p. 204.
[17] Ibid., p. 217.
[18] TM, I, p. 401.
[19] For an account of the 'Trevecka Family', see TL, pp. 185–206; Owen, 'A study of Howell Harris and the Trevecka "family"'; HMGC, pp. 356–77.
[20] Diary 158: 14 February 1752; HHVP, p. 209.
[21] Harris often complained about his health during 1751–2. HHVP, pp. 200–1, 204–5, 216.
[22] 'Itinerary' in JHS, XII, 7.
[23] TL, 187; TM, I, p. 403.
[24] Speck, *Stability and Strife*, p. 28.
[25] HHRS, pp. 62–3.
[26] HHRS, p. 64.
[27] Trevecka Letter 2472; HMGC, p. 398. Rowland and Williams had called at Trevecka as early as 1754, and there remained some contact

between the three revivalists thereafter. HMGC, p. 393.
28 HHRS, pp. 175–6.
29 For the 1762 Revival, see Gomer M. Roberts (ed.), *Hanes Methodistiaeth Galfinaidd Cymru*, II (Caernarfon, 1978), pp. 11ff.; R. Geraint Gruffydd, 'Diwygiad 1762 a William Williams o Bantycelyn', JHS, LIV, 68–75; LV, 4–13.
30 TM, I, p. 412ff.
31 Gomer M. Roberts (ed.), *Hanes Methodistiaeth Galfinaidd Cymru*, II, p. 51.
32 For the College, see TM, I, p. 421; Seymour, *Life and Times of the Countess of Huntingdon*, II, pp. 82f.; Tyerman, *Life of Whitefield*, II, pp. 541f., 555f.
33 'Itinerary' in JHS, XII, 47.
34 Letter, dated 29 July 1773, from the Countess of Huntingdon to William Romaine, in Seymour, *Countess of Huntingdon*, II, pp. 291–2.

Select Bibliography

Manuscript Sources

1. National Library of Wales, Aberystwyth
  i. Calvinistic Methodist Archives
      The Diaries of Howell Harris.
      The Trevecka Letters.
  ii. T. C. Edwards Collection
      MS 8822. 'Cof-lyfr cynulleidfa'r Methodistiaid yn Nhref y Bala'.
  iii. Church in Wales Collection
      Bishops' transcripts of various relevant parish records.

2. University of Wales, Bangor
  MS 34: The Journal of William Seward, 20 July–6 September 1740.

3. Gwynedd County Archives
  Poole Collection.

Printed Material

Abbey, C. J., and Overton, J. H., *The English Church in the Eighteenth Century*, 2 vols. (London, 1878).
Allestree [?], Richard, *The Whole Duty of Man* (London, 1658).
Atkinson, James, *Martin Luther* (London, 1968).
Baker, Frank, *William Grimshaw 1708–63* (London, 1963).
Baker, Frank, *John Wesley and the Church of England* (Nashville, 1970).
Bassett, T. M., *Bedyddwyr Cymru* (Abertawe, 1977).
Bayly, Lewis, *The Practice of Piety* (London, 1610).

SELECT BIBLIOGRAPHY

Bebbington, D. W., *Evangelicalism in Modern Britain: A History from the 1730s to the 1980s* (London, 1989).
Benham, Daniel, *Memoirs of James Hutton* (London, 1856).
Bennett, G. V., *The Tory Crisis in Church and State, 1688–1730* (Oxford, 1975).
Bennett, G. V. and Walsh, J. D. (eds.), *Essays in Modern English Church History* (London, 1966).
Bennett, Richard, *Methodistiaeth Trefaldwyn Uchaf* (Bala, 1929).
Bennett, Richard, *Howell Harris and the Dawn of Revival*, translated by Gomer M. Roberts (Bridgend, 1987).
Berkhof, L., *Systematic Theology* (London, 1958).
Beynon, Tom, *Cwmsel a Chefn Sidan* (Caernarfon, 1946).
Beynon, Tom, *Howell Harris, Reformer and Soldier* (Caernarfon, 1958).
Beynon, Tom, *Howell Harris's Visits to London* (Aberystwyth, 1960).
Beynon, Tom, *Howell Harris's Visits to Pembrokeshire* (Aberystwyth, 1966).
Bicknell, E. J., *A Theological Introduction to the Thirty-Nine Articles of the Church of England* (3rd edn.: London, 1955).
Brown, Dale, *Understanding Pietism* (Grand Rapids, 1978).
Brown-Lawson, A., *John Wesley and the Anglican Evangelicals of the Eighteenth Century* (Durham, 1994).
Bunyan, John, *The Doctrine of Law and Grace Unfolded* (1659).
Bunyan, John, *Jerusalem Sinner* (1688).
Bunyan, John, *Grace Abounding to the Chief of Sinners* (1666: republished, Grand Rapids, 1978).
Bushaway, Bob, *By Rite* (London, 1982).
Calvin, John, *Institutes of the Christian Religion* (Library of Christian Classics, ed. J. T. McNeill: Philadelphia, 1960).
Cavenagh, F. A., *The Life and Work of Griffith Jones* (Cardiff, 1930).
Clement, Mary, *Correspondence and Minutes of the SPCK relating to Wales, 1699–1740* (Cardiff, 1952).
Clement, Mary, *The SPCK and Wales, 1699–1740* (London, 1954).
Cook, Faith, *William Grimshaw of Haworth* (Edinburgh, 1997).
Dallimore, Arnold, *George Whitefield*, 2 vols. (London and Edinburgh, 1970, 1980).
Davies, J. H., *A Bibliography of Welsh Ballads Printed in the 18th Century* (published by the Honourable Society of the Cymmrodorion: London, 1911).
Davies, R. and Rupp, G. (eds.), *A History of the Methodist Church in Great Britain*, vol. 1 (London, 1965).
Duppa, Bryan, *Holy Rules and Helps to Devotion* (London, 1675).
Erb, Peter C., *Pietists* (The Classics of Western Spirituality: London, 1983).

SELECT BIBLIOGRAPHY

Evans, Beriah Gwynfe, *Diwygwyr Cymru* (Caernarfon, 1900).
Evans, Beriah Gwynfe, *Ymneilltuaeth Cymru ac Apocrypha'r Diwygiad* (Treffynnon, 1901).
Evans, Eifion, *Howel Harris, Evangelist* (Cardiff, 1974).
Evans, Eifion, *Daniel Rowland* (Edinburgh, 1985).
Evans, Eifion, *Fire in the Thatch* (Bridgend, 1996).
Evans, Eifion, *Pursued by God* (Bridgend, 1996).
Evans, G. Nesta, *Religion and Politics in Mid-Eighteenth Century Anglesey* (Cardiff, 1953).
Evans, Theophilus, *The History of Modern Enthusiasm, from the Reformation to the Present Time* (London, 1752).
Fisher, G. P., *History of Christian Doctrine* (International Theological Library: 2nd edn: Edinburgh, 1896).
George, M. Dorothy, *London Life in the Eighteenth Century* (Harmondsworth, 1966).
Gill, Frederick C., *Charles Wesley: The First Methodist* (London, 1964).
Greaves, Richard L., *John Bunyan* (Abingdon, 1969).
Griffith, William, *Methodistiaeth Fore Môn* (Caernarfon, 1956).
Gunter, W. Stephen, *The Limits of 'Love Divine'* (Nashville, 1989).
Halévy, É., *La Naissance du Méthodisme en Angleterre* (translated by Bernard Semmel: London, 1971).
Harris, Howell, *The Last Message and Dying Testimony of Howell Harris, Esq.* (Trefeca, 1774).
Harris, Howell, *A Brief Account of the Life of Howell Harris, Esq.* (Trevecka, 1791).
Harrison, J. F. C., *The Common People* (London, 1984).
Heitzenrater, Richard P., *Mirror and Memory: Reflections on Early Methodism* (Nashville, 1989).
Heitzenrater, Richard P., *Wesley and the People Called Methodists* (Nashville, 1995).
Hill, Christopher, *The World Turned Upside Down* (London, 1972).
Hughes, Hugh J., *Life of Howell Harris* (Newport, 1892).
Hughes, John, *Methodistiaeth Cymru*, 3 vols. (Gwrecsam, 1851–6).
Hutton, J. E., *A History of the Moravian Church* (London, 1909).
Jackson, Thomas (ed.), *The Lives of Early Methodist Preachers*, 6 vols. (London, 1865–6).
Jenkins, D. E., *Calvinistic Methodist Holy Orders* (Caernarfon, 1911).
Jenkins, D. E. (ed.), *Religious Societies* (Liverpool, 1935).
Jenkins, Geraint H., *The Foundations of Modern Wales: Wales 1642–1780* (History of Wales, vol. IV: Oxford and Cardiff, 1987).
Jenkins, John Gwili, *Hanfod Duw a Pherson Crist* (Liverpool, 1931).
Jenkins, R. T., *Hanes Cymru yn y Ddeunawfed Ganrif* (Caerdydd, 1931).

SELECT BIBLIOGRAPHY

Jenkins, R. T., *Yr Apêl at Hanes* (Wrecsam, 1930).
Jenkins, R. T., *The Moravian Brethren in North Wales* (London, 1938).
Jenkins, R. T., *Yng Nghysgod Trefeca* (Caernarfon, 1968).
Jones, David, *Life and Times of Griffith Jones* (London, 1902).
Jones, D. J. Odwyn, *Daniel Rowland* (Llandysul, 1938).
Jones, Edmund, *A Geographical, Historical, and Religious Account of the Parish of Aberystruth* (Trevecka, 1779).
Jones, Edmund, *A Relation of Apparitions of Spirits, in the County of Monmouth, and the Principality of Wales* (published posthumously: Newport, 1813).
Jones, J. M. and Morgan, W., *Y Tadau Methodistaidd*, 2 vols. (Abertawe, 1895-7).
Jones, M. H., *Howell Harris* (Aberafan, 1912).
Jones, M. H., *The Trevecka Letters* (Caernarfon, 1932).
Jones, R. Tudur, *Congregationalism in England, 1662-1962* (London, 1962).
Jones, R. Tudur, *Hanes Annibynwyr Cymru* (Abertawe, 1966).
Jones, R. Tudur, *Vavasor Powell* (Abertawe, 1971).
Jones, R. Tudur (D. D. Morgan, ed.), *Grym y Gair a Fflam y Ffydd* (Bangor, 1998).
Jones, Robert, *Drych yr Amseroedd* (first published, 1820; republished (ed. Glyn M. Ashton) Caerdydd, 1958).
Jones, Theophilus, *A History of the County of Brecknock*, 4 vols. (Glanusk, 1911).
Kelly, Thomas, *Griffith Jones, Llanddowror: Pioneer in Adult Education* (Cardiff, 1950).
Knappen, M. M., *Tudor Puritanism* (London, 1939).
Knox, R. A., *Enthusiasm* (first published Oxford, 1950: republished London, 1987).
Langton, Edward, *History of the Moravian Church* (London, 1956).
Lee, Umphrey, *The Historical Backgrounds of Early Methodist Enthusiasm* (New York, 1967).
Levi, Thomas, *Casgliad o Hen Farwnadau Cymreig* (Wrexham, [1872]).
Lewis, A. J., *Zinzendorf, the Ecumenical Pioneer: A Study in the Moravian Contribution to Christian Mission and Unity* (London, 1962).
Lewis, H. Elvet, *Howell Harris* (London, [1911]).
Locke, A. A., *The Hanbury Family* (London, 1916).
Lyles, A. M., *Methodism Mocked* (London, 1960).
Malcolmson, Robert W., *Popular Recreations in English Society, 1700-1850* (Cambridge, 1973).
Marshall, Dorothy, *Eighteenth Century England* (Harlow, 1962).
McLynn, Frank, *The Jacobites* (London, 1985).

SELECT BIBLIOGRAPHY

McNeill, J. T., *The History and Character of Calvinism* (Oxford, 1967).
Monk, R. C., *John Wesley: His Puritan Heritage* (London, 1966).
Morgan, Derec Llwyd, *Y Diwygiad Mawr* (Llandysul, 1981).
Morgan, Dyfnallt (ed.), *Y Ferch o Ddolwar Fach* (Caernarfon, 1977).
Morgan, Edward, *The Life and Times of Howel Harris, Esq.* (Holywell, 1852).
Noll, M. A., Bebbington, D. W. and Rawlyk, G. A. (eds.), *Evangelicalism* (Oxford, 1994).
Nuttall, G. F., *The Holy Spirit in Puritan Faith and Experience* (Oxford, 1946).
Nuttall, G. F., *Visible Saints* (Oxford, 1957).
Nuttall, G. F., *Howel Harris – The Last Enthusiast* (Cardiff, 1965).
Outler, Albert C. (ed.), *John Wesley* (Oxford, 1964).
Owen, G. Dyfnallt, *Ysgolion a Cholegau'r Annibynwyr* (Abertawe, 1939).
Owen, Goronwy P., *Atgofion John Evans y Bala* (Caernarfon, 1997).
Parry, Thomas, *Hanes Llenyddiaeth Gymraeg hyd 1900* (Caerdydd, 1944).
Phillips, Edgar, *Edmund Jones: The Old Prophet* (London, 1959).
Podmore, Colin, *The Moravian Church in England, 1728–1760* (Oxford, 1998).
Porter, Roy, *English Society in the Eighteenth Century* (Harmondsworth, 1982).
Portus, G. V., *Caritas Anglicana: An Historical Inquiry into those Religious and Philanthropical Societies that Flourished in England between the Years 1678 and 1740* (Oxford, 1912).
Pringle-Pattison, A. S., *John Locke: An Essay concerning Human Understanding* (Oxford, 1924).
Rack, Henry D., *Reasonable Enthusiast: John Wesley and the Rise of Methodism* (London, 1989).
Rees, D. Ben, *Haneswyr yr Hen Gorff* (Lerpwl, 1981).
Rees, Thomas, *History of Protestant Nonconformity in Wales* (London, 1861).
Richards, Thomas (ed.), *Er Clod* (Wrecsam, 1934).
Roberts, E. ap Nefydd (ed.), *Corff ac Ysbryd* (Caernarfon, 1988).
Roberts, Gomer M., *Portread o Ddiwygiwr* (Caernarfon, 1969).
Roberts, Gomer M., *Bywyd a Gwaith Peter Williams* (Caerdydd, 1943).
Roberts, Gomer M., *Y Per Ganiedydd*, 2 vols. (Aberystwyth, 1949 and 1958).
Roberts, Gomer M. (ed.), *Selected Trevecka Letters*, 2 vols. (Caernarfon, 1956, 1962).
Roberts, Gomer M. (ed.), *Hanes Methodistiaeth Galfinaidd Cymru*, 2 vols. (Caernarfon, 1973 and 1978).

SELECT BIBLIOGRAPHY

Roberts, Griffith T., *Howell Harris* (London, 1951).
Roberts, Griffith T., *Dadleuon Methodistiaeth Gynnar* (Abertawe, 1970).
Rowland, Daniel, *Ymddiddan rhwng Methodist Uniawn-gred ac Un Camsyniol* ([Bryste], 1750).
Saunders, Erasmus, *A View of the State of Religion in the Diocese of St. Davids* (London, 1721; republished Cardiff, 1949).
Schlenther, Boyd Stanley, *Queen of the Methodists* (Durham, 1997).
Schwartz, Hillel, *The French Prophets* (London, 1980).
Senn, Frank C. (ed.), *Protestant Spiritual Traditions* (New York, 1986).
Seymour, A. C. H., *Life and Times of Selina, Countess of Huntingdon*, 2 vols. (London, 1840).
Simon, J. S., *The Oxford Methodists* (London, 1873).
Simon, J. S., *John Wesley and the Religious Societies* (London, 1921).
Simon, J. S., *John Wesley and the Methodist Societies* (London, 1923).
Speck, W. A., *Stability and Strife* (The New History of England, vol. 6: London, 1977).
Stebbing, Henry, *A Sermon on the New Birth: Occasioned by the Pretentions of the Methodists* (London, 1739).
Stevenson, John, *Popular Disturbances in England, 1700–1870* (London, 1979).
Sugden, E. H. (ed.), *Wesley's Standard Sermons*, 2 vols. (London, 1921).
Sykes, Norman, *Church and State in England in the Eighteenth Century* (The Birkbeck Lectures, 1931–3: Cambridge, 1934).
Thickens, John, *Howel Harris yn Llundain* (Caernarfon, 1938).
Thomas, Edward, *Y Cynghorwyr Methodistaidd* (Conwy, [1904]).
Thomas, Ioan, *Rhad Ras: Ioan Thomas* (Abertawe, 1810; republished, ed. J. Dyfnallt Owen: Caerdydd, 1949).
Thomas, Keith, *Religion and the Decline of Magic* (London, 1973).
Thomas, Owen, *Cofiant y Parchedig John Jones, Talsarn* (Wrexham, [1874]).
Toon, P., *The Emergence of Hyper-Calvinism in English Nonconformity 1689–1765* (London, n.d. [1967]).
Towlson, C. W., *Moravian and Methodist* (London, 1957).
Tucker, R. A., and Liefeld, W., *Daughters of the Church* (Grand Rapids, 1987).
Tyerman, Luke, *The Life and Times of the Rev. John Wesley, M.A.*, 3 vols. (London, 1870).
Tyerman, Luke, *The Oxford Methodists* (London, 1873).
Tyerman, Luke, *The Life and Times of the Rev. George Whitefield*, 2 vols. (London, 1890).
Underdown, David, *Revel, Riot and Rebellion* (Oxford, 1987).
Walker, David (ed.), *A History of the Church in Wales* (Penarth, 1976).
Warfield, B. B., *Calvin and Augustine* (Philadelphia, 1960).

SELECT BIBLIOGRAPHY

Watkins, Owen C., *The Puritan Experience* (London, 1972).
Watson, David Lowes, *The Early Methodist Class Meeting* (Nashville, 1985).
Watts, Michael R., *The Dissenters* (Oxford, 1978).
Welch, Edwin, *Two Calvinistic Methodist Chapels 1743-1811* (London, 1975).
Welch, Edwin, *Spiritual Pilgrim: A Reassessment of the Life of the Countess of Huntingdon* (Cardiff, 1995).
Wendel, François, *Calvin* (London, 1963).
Wesley, Charles, *The Journal of Charles Wesley, M.A.* (ed. John Telford: London, 1909).
Wesley, John, *The Works of the Rev. John Wesley, M.A.*, 32 vols. (printed by William Pine, Bristol, 1771-4).
Wesley, John, *The Works of the Rev. John Wesley, A. M.*, 14 vols. (ed. Thomas Jackson: London, 3rd edition, 1829-31).
Wesley, John, *The Journal of the Rev. John Wesley, A. M.*, 8 vols. (ed. Nehemiah Curnock: London, 1909).
Wesley, John, *The Letters of John Wesley, A. M.*, 8 vols. (ed. John Telford: London, 1931).
White, Eryn M., *Praidd Bach y Bugail Mawr* (Llandysul, 1995).
Whitefield, George, *The Works of George Whitefield*, 6 vols. (London and Edinburgh, 1771).
Whitefield, George, *Journals* (Edinburgh, 1960).
Whitefield, George, *Letters* (Edinburgh, 1976. Facsimile of Whitefield, *Works*, vol. 1, but with additional letters).
Whitehead, John, *The Life of the Rev. John Wesley, M.A.*, 2 vols. (London, 1793-6).
Wilks, M. (ed.), *The Life of Mr John Cennick* (London, 1819).
Williams, A. H., *John Wesley in Wales, 1739-1790* (Cardiff, 1971).
Williams, William, *Drws y Society Profiad* (Aberhonddu, 1777).
Wood, A. Skevington, *The Inextinguishable Blaze* (Exeter, 1960).
Wood, A. Skevington, *The Burning Heart* (Exeter, 1967).
Woodward, Josiah, *An Account of the Rise and Progress of the Religious Societies in the City of London &c, and of their Endeavours for the Reformation of Manners* (4th edn, enlarged: London, 1712).
Worthington, D., *Cofiant y Parch Daniel Rowland* (Caerfyrddin, 1923).
Zinzendorf, N. L. von, *Maxims, Theological Ideas and Sentences* (extracted by J. Gambold: London, 1751).

SELECT BIBLIOGRAPHY

Periodicals

An Account of the Most Remarkable Particulars Relating to the Present Progress of the Gospel, vols. II–IV, National Library of Wales, Aberystwyth.
Bathafarn, The Journal of the Historical Society of the Methodist Church in Wales, 1945–.
The Christian History, vols. V–VII, National Library of Wales, Aberystwyth.
The Christian's Amusement, 1–27 (1740), Bodleian Library: Hope 4o 13.
Y Cofiadur, The Journal of the Historical Society of the Welsh Independents, 1923–.
The Journal of the Historical Society of the Presbyterian Church of Wales, 1916–.
Proceedings of the Wesley Historical Society, 1898–.
The Weekly History, 1–84 (1741–2), Bodleian Library: Hope 4o 13(2).

Articles

Beynon, Tom, 'Howell Harris accused of riotous assault at Presteign and Knighton Quarter Sessions, 1740–41', *Radnorshire Society Transactions* (1950).
Jenkins, G. H., 'An old and much honoured soldier: Griffith Jones, Llanddowror', *Welsh History Review*, 2 (1983).
Jenkins, R. T., 'Hywel Harris y ffermwr', in Emlyn Evans (ed.), *Cwpanaid o De a Diferion Eraill* (Dinbych, 1997).
Jones, M. H., 'Howell Harris, citizen and patriot', *Transactions of the Honourable Society of the Cymmrodorion* (1908–9).
Nuttall, G. F., 'Continental Pietism and the Evangelical movement in Britain', in J. van den Berg and J. P. van Dooren (eds.), *Pietismus und Réveil* (Leiden, 1978).
O'Brien, Susan, 'Eighteenth-century publishing networks in the first years of transatlantic Evangelicalism', in M. A. Noll, D. W. Bebbington and G. A. Rawlyk (eds.), *Evangelicalism* (Oxford, 1994).
Roberts, H. P., 'Nonconformist academies in Wales (1662–1862)', *Transactions of the Honourable Society of the Cymmrodorion* (1928–9).
Thompson, E. P., 'The moral economy of the English crowd in the eighteenth century', *Past and Present*, 50 (1971).
Tudur, Geraint, 'The King's Daughter: a reassessment of Anne Harris of Trefeca', *Journal of Welsh Religious History*, 7 (1999).
Walsh, J. D., 'Origins of the Evangelical revival', in G. V. Bennett and

J. D. Walsh (eds.), *Essays in Modern English Church History: In Memory of Norman Sykes* (London, 1966).

Walsh, J. D., 'Methodism and the mob in the eighteenth century', in G. J. Cumming and Derek Baker (eds.), *Studies in Church History*, vol. VIII (Cambridge, 1971).

Walsh, J. D., 'The Cambridge Methodists', in Peter Brooks (ed.), *Christian Spirituality: Essays in Honour of Gordon Rupp* (London, 1975).

Walsh, J. D., 'Religious societies: Methodist and Evangelical 1738–1800', in W. J. Sheils and Diana Wood (eds.), *Voluntary Religion* (London, 1986).

Walsh, J. D., '"Methodism" and the origins of English-speaking Evangelicalism', in M. A. Noll, D. W. Bebbington and G. A. Rawlyk (eds.), *Evangelicalism* (Oxford, 1994).

Theses

Brunner, D. L., 'The role of Halle Pietists in England (c. 1700–c. 1740) with special reference to the SPCK', D.Phil. thesis, University of Oxford, 1988.

Durden, Diane Susan, 'Transatlantic communications and literature in the religious revivals, 1735–1745', Ph.D. thesis, University of Hull, 1978.

Evans, R. W., 'The eighteenth century Welsh awakening with its relationships to the contemporary English Evangelical Revival', Ph.D. thesis, University of Edinburgh, 1956.

Hughes-Edwards, W. G., 'The development and organisation of the Methodist Society in Wales, 1735–1750', MA thesis, University of Wales, 1966.

Morgan, D. D., 'The development of the Baptist movement in Wales between 1714 and 1815 with special reference to the Evangelical Revival', D.Phil. thesis, University of Oxford, 1986.

Owen, Alun Wynne, 'A study of Howell Harris and the Trevecka "Family" (1752–1760) based upon the Trevecka letters and Diaries and other Methodist archives at the NLW', MA thesis, University of Wales, 1957.

Spurr, John, 'Anglican apologetic and the Restoration Church', D.Phil. thesis, University of Oxford, 1985.

Walsh, J. D., 'The Yorkshire Evangelicals in the eighteenth century with special reference to Methodism', Ph.D. thesis, University of Cambridge, 1956.

Index

Aberdaron 143
Abergavenny 81, 90
Abergorlech 143
Aberthaw 190
Aberthin 116
Account of the Religious Societies in the City of London, An (1697) 32, 65–7, 69
Adams, Thomas 88, 177, 186
Allestree, Richard 92
America 25, 49, 75, 80, 84, 167, 182, 183, 217
Anglesey 116, 143, 148
anterliwt 142
antinomianism 168, 169, 171, 172, 180, 230
Apollos 115, 162
'Apostle of Pembrokeshire' 40
Arminianism 38, 81, 95, 132
Ashburnham estate 13
Association 73, 77, 84–5, 89–91, 182
   Anglo-Welsh 88–9, 159
   authority 79, 85
   Records 74, 113
assurance 17, 40, 45–59, 73, 75, 76, 101, 148, 155–7, 162

Bala 78, 126, 136–40, 142, 145, 146, 148, 149, 199
bands 71, 75
Bangor 92
baptism 34, 76, 98–9, 102
   of the Spirit 98
Baptists 23, 34–5, 68, 76–7, 98, 102, 151
Bath 51
Bayly, Lewis 17, 92
Beaufort, Duke of 132
Beaumont, James 168, 173, 177, 180, 184–5, 187–90, 193–4, 203, 214
Bedwellte 43
Bennett, Richard 31, 41

Betws Diserth 214
Bevan, Arthur 29
Bevan, Bridget 29
Beynon, Tom 1, 9
Bible 25, 42, 181, 193, 213–14, 226
'Bible and Sun' 51, 71
Bideford 66
Billingsgate 198
'Blood of God' 163–4, 177
Boehm, A. W. 29
Böhler, Peter 55, 69
Bolgoed 34, 35, 211
Book of Common Prayer, The 22, 93, 96
Bowen, Edward 143
Bowen, Thomas (Builth) 151
Bowen, Thomas (Llanafan) 143
Brecknockshire Agricultural Society 13
Brecon 143, 231
Breconshire 13, 33, 70, 75, 77, 78, 90, 104, 125, 135, 151, 158, 185, 206, 227, 232
Brief Account of a Trial at Gloucester, A (1744) 136
Bristol 3, 50–1, 58, 69, 72, 85, 110, 112, 117, 147, 153, 202, 220
Bronllys 135, 197, 198
Bryn-melys 214
Builth 203, 204, 212
Bunyan, John 45
Burton, Mr 133

Caeo 113, 170
Caerleon 146
Caernarfonshire 120, 143, 149, 183, 196, 200, 202, 225
Caerphilly 59, 117
Calvin, John 156
Calvinism 28, 39, 63, 78, 80, 86, 101, 193
Calvinists 70, 81, 92, 156, 166, 186, 202, 214, 217

INDEX

Cardiff 50, 66, 69, 105, 144, 191
Cardigan 134
Cardiganshire 73, 78, 82, 136, 154, 220
Carmarthen 28, 181, 188, 202, 209
Carmarthenshire 70, 78, 79, 82, 85, 87, 113, 146, 154, 170, 173, 200, 220
Carno 222
Cathedin 27
Cefn-y-fedwast 117
Cefnamwlch 183, 196, 198, 203, 209, 226, 231
Cemais 125, 129, 133, 137
Cennick, John 88, 157–8, 161–2, 167–8, 169, 206, 208, 214, 215
Charles I 95
Christian's Amusement, The 75, 76, 146
church 124, 129
church government 105, 175
   Episcopacy 97, 124
   Independency 97–8
Church of England 6, 33, 63–4, 78–9, 85, 92–118, 180
   bishops 96
   clergy 94–5, 106, 111, 119–20, 122–3, 130
      opposition to Methodism 120–7
      unawakened 73, 79, 84, 87, 106–7
   disestablishment 130
   doctrine 97, 129
   general loyalty to 92
   Homilies 86, 122
   preaching within 94–5
   'relics of Popery' 95
   renewal of 95–6, 100
   secession from 79, 81–2, 83–4, 87, 88, 93, 97, 101–2, 104–18
   Thirty-nine Articles 86, 93, 107, 122, 124, 125, 127, 129
   weaknesses of 96
Cil-y-cwm 82, 116, 154, 178
circulating schools 28, 41–2, 82
Claggett, Nicholas 30
Clarke, Samuel 163
Clyro 117
communion 15, 16, 52, 79, 83–4, 102, 106–7, 109–10, 182
   in private houses 111
Constantinople, Council of 163
Conventicle Act 83, 125

Cotton, John 53
covenants 40–1, 87, 98, 155
Cwm-iou 28

Dafydd, Philip (Penmaen) 103
Dalton, Edward 30–1, 40, 56, 58
Davies, E. O. 2
Davies, Evan (Haverfordwest) 102
Davies, Henry (Blaen-gwrach) 43, 60, 70, 132
Davies, Howell 40–1, 50, 81–2, 86, 87, 108, 110, 170, 188, 189, 191, 209, 218
Davies, J. H. 1
Davies, James (Merthyr) 43
Davies, Pryce 15, 21, 22, 34, 36, 48, 58–9, 64, 69, 96, 107, 119, 121, 128–9
Davies, Rees (Abergavenny) 43
Defynnog 42, 74, 104, 107, 151, 220
Denbighshire 135, 196, 199
Deneio 120
Dissent 92, 93, 94, 97, 109–10, 120
Dissenters 23–4, 27, 33–7, 39, 43–4, 60–1, 68, 70, 77, 79, 84, 96, 100–4, 106, 112–13, 124, 130, 151, 182
divine retribution 135, 147–8
Doctrine of Law and Grace Unfolded, The (1659) 45
Dolgellau 134
Dugoedydd (Cil-y-cwm) 82, 84, 88, 107, 154, 209
Dummer 49
Duppa, Bryan 16

ecclesiolae in ecclesia 67
Eglwysilan 74, 108
election 39, 45–6, 73
Ellys, Sir Richard 59–60
enthusiasm 19, 22, 25, 94, 103–4, 106, 124, 128, 130, 183, 192–4, 226, 233–4
Erskine, James 143, 144
Erwood 131, 163, 184, 185, 197, 212, 214, 225
Eutychianism 230
Evan, Lewis 134
exhorters 114, 128
   accuse Harris of unorthodoxy 169
   desert Harris 173–4
   loyalty to the Crown 131
   spiritual stiffness 164

INDEX

wishing to be ordained 113–15, 143
Exposition of the Creed (1659) 21
'eye' 181, 189, 211, 212, 213, 214, 222

Farley, Felix 85
Fetter Lane society 51, 53, 69, 71–2
Foelas, Plas y 196, 199
Fonmon Castle 132
Foundry (London) 90
France 4
  fear of French invasion 125
Francis, Enoch 43
Franke, A. H. 29, 67
free grace 39, 45–6, 73, 92
'Free Grace' controversy 80, 86–7
French Prophets 26, 213

Games, John 32, 42, 153
Garth 125, 132
Gellidorchlaethe 174, 177
Gelligaer 78
Georgia 45, 49
Germany 67
Gifford, Andrew 59, 134
Glamorgan 44, 59, 70, 74, 75, 77, 78, 79, 104, 108, 111, 113, 116, 121, 132, 188, 190, 191, 209, 211
Glanyrafon-ddu Ganol (Talyllychau) 87, 145, 155, 157
Gloucester 136, 143, 168, 185, 216, 217
Gloucestershire 182
Glyn (Defynnog) 74, 75, 143, 154, 220
Gonson, Sir John 60
Gore (Radnorshire) 168
'Great Association of all the English Brethren' (1743) 109
Great Ejection (1662) 95
Great Yarmouth 66, 232
Griffith, Sidney 183, 187–9, 192, 194, 195–228, 230, 231
  death 231
  enthusiast 226, 227
  marriage 202–3, 204–5, 216
  opposition to 205–6, 208, 218
  prophetic powers 189, 196, 213–14, 214–15, 216, 226
  role 202, 205, 211–12, 222, 226
Griffith, William 196, 198, 202–3, 215, 222, 231
Griffiths, Hugh (Aberdaron) 143

Griffiths, Mr 136
Groes-wen 87, 116
guns 136, 139, 146
Gwenddwr 43, 45
Gwynne, Marmaduke 125, 132–4, 143, 144

Halévy, Élie 49
Hall, Westley 218
Hanbury, Capel 59–60, 133
Hanbury, Sir Charles Williams 61
Hardwick, Lord Chancellor 59
Harris, Anne (daughter) 176, 185
Harris, Anne (wife) 188, 189, 198, 203–4, 206–8, 209, 211, 214, 215, 216–17, 221, 225, 231
  death 232
Harris, Howell
  accused of becoming a Moravian 162, 169, 170–2
  attitude to popular pastimes 93, 141–2
  autobiography 65–6, 93
  autocratic spirit 184
  barred from communion 107
  and Church of England 20, 33–7, 93–4, 96–7, 104–6, 117–18, 233
  confusion concerning the Trinity 163, 179
  conversion 5, 14ff, 46, 56, 92–3, 106–7
  death 233
  Diaries 1ff, 14, 19, 152, 155
  divine guidance 4, 7, 23–6, 61–2, 90, 97, 108, 183, 190, 193–4, 202, 207, 220–1, 233
  dreams 24–5
  early missions 20, 119
  emphasis on the 'Blood' 162–5, 167, 172–3, 178–9, 184, 188–9
  enthusiasm 5, 20, 23, 25, 173, 181, 192–3, 194, 196, 233–4
  handwriting 2
  Holy Orders 27–30, 48–9, 66, 120, 123–4
  joins militia 232
  lack of humour 153
  letters 11, 219
  loyalty to the Crown 125, 131, 149, 232
  making a will 149

309

INDEX

megalomania 216
organizing skills 91, 152
personality 9, 102–3, 109, 153, 158, 182, 196, 233
position within movement 160f, 172–3, 175
preaching 6–7, 40, 134
precedence 7, 153–4
response to opposition 144–50
retirement 151–2, 231
social standing 13
Superintendent over Wales 89, 159, 210
temptation to atheism 17, 21
theology 19, 38–9, 45–6
views on the Person and Work of Christ 160–1, 165, 167, 171–2, 208
youth 14, 92
Harris, John (St Kenox) 151
Harris, Joseph 2, 11, 13, 22, 28, 29
Harris, Susannah 13, 189, 215
Harris, Thomas 11, 13
'Harris's People' 151
Harry, Miles 43, 59, 76–7
Henllan (Amgoed) 108
Herbert, William 23, 33–4, 39, 98, 100
Hereford 41
Historical Society of the Presbyterian Church of Wales 2
holiness 124, 125
  Rowland's carelessness 218
Holyhead 198
'Holy Living' literature 16–17, 19
Holy Spirit 4–5, 25, 90, 104, 107, 163
Holy Rules and Helps to Devotion (1675) 16
Horneck, Anthony 65
Howell Harris, Reformer and Soldier (1958) 1
Howell Harris's Visits to London (1960) 1
Howell Harris's Visits to Pembrokeshire (1966) 1
Hughes, Lewis 136
Hughes, Morgan 134
Humphreys, Joseph 81, 88, 109–10
Huntingdon, Selina, Countess of 60, 143, 144, 232
Hutton, James 51, 69
hymns 73, 75

Independents 23, 27, 68, 112, 168
infallibility
  Harris accused of claiming 82
  Sidney Griffith 205, 212–13, 226
Ingram, James 143
Interregnum 19
Ireland 198

Jacobites 3, 125, 130
James, Thomas (Crucadarn) 70
Jeffreys, Sister 153
Jenkins, Herbert 89, 97, 177
Jenkins, R. T. 46
Jerusalem Sinner (1688) 45
John the Baptist 124
John, William 133
Jones, David 116
Jones, David (Pembrokeshire) 151
Jones, Edmund (Pontypool) 24, 43, 60–1, 70, 74–7, 101, 103, 104, 121, 177
Jones, Griffith (Llanddowror) 8, 24, 26, 28–32, 34, 36, 38, 40–1, 44, 48, 58–9, 64, 66, 70, 81–2, 94, 101, 103, 126, 154
Jones, M. H. 10, 73
Jones, Robert (Fonmon Castle) 132
Jones, Robert (Llanycil) 126, 129, 136
Jones, Thomas (Cwm-iou) 28, 101
Jones, Thomas (Llanfeugan) 190, 214, 220
Jones, Thomas 133–4
Jones, William (Trefollwyn) 116
Journal of the Historical Society of the Presbyterian Church of Wales 1, 11

Kingswood (Bristol) 49
Knighton 133, 135

Lambeth 71
Lampeter 181
Last Message and Dying Testimony of Howell Harris, The (1774) 97
Laugharne 200
Leipzig 67
Leominster 74
Lewis, David 74
Lewis, Morgan John 153, 174, 177, 221
Lewis, Thomas (Llanfihangel Cwmteuddwr) 39, 101

INDEX

Lewis, Thomas (Blaenau Gwent) 108
Lewis, Thomas (Llan-ddew) 108
Life and Death of Vavasor Powell (1671) 48
Little Newcastle 176
Llanbrynmair 76, 101, 126, 190, 222
Llanddewibrefi 82, 154
Llandeglau 117, 133
Llandeilo 218
Llandeilo Abercywyn 40
Llandinam 121, 145, 178, 214
Llandingad 85
Llandovery 77, 78, 85
Llandyfaelog 146
Llandyfalle 33, 34, 122
Llanddowror 28–30, 41, 42, 44, 48, 64, 67, 68, 82, 94, 200
Llanfaches 103
Llanfair (Caereinion?) 178
Llanfihangel Cwmteuddwr 101, 141
Llanfihangel Tal-y-llyn 14, 64
Llangadog 13
Llangamarch 132
Llangeitho 41–2, 73, 74, 154, 158, 185, 187, 197, 198, 199, 200, 208, 225–6, 232
Llangasty (Tal-y-llyn) 16, 17, 18, 20, 21, 64, 119, 120
Llan-gors 16, 20, 21, 119
Llanidloes 191, 199, 214
Llanlluan 82
Llanmartin 177
Llannor 120, 142
Llansanffraid-yn-Elfael 214
Llanuwchllyn 142
Llanycil 126, 129
Llanymawddwy 131
Lloyd, David (Llandyfalle) 34, 122–3, 129–30
Lloyd, Ned 142
Lloyd, William (Dugoedydd) 82
Lloyd-Jones, D. Martyn 2
Llwyn-llwyd 14, 75
Llwyn-y-berllan 85, 155, 157, 166, 224
Llŷn 196
Llys-y-frân 40
Llywel 206
Locke, John 124
Lodge (Llandinam) 145
London 3, 13, 24, 29, 50, 51, 55, 56–8, 59, 69, 70–2, 80, 90, 98, 105, 109, 111, 112–13, 117, 121, 125, 153, 158, 161, 163, 168, 173, 182, 186, 188, 189, 203, 204, 216, 219, 227
Luther, Martin 156

Machynlleth 136–40, 145, 146, 148
Merioneth 78, 126, 136, 148
Merthyr Cynog 39, 178
Methodism (English) 70, 78, 90–1, 185, 210
Methodism (general) 50, 52, 55, 58–9, 63, 130
  opposition to 85, 99, 119–50
    from Dissenters 100
  socially divisive 141
  union 80–1, 186–7, 210
Methodism (Welsh) 71–2, 79, 81, 84, 86, 88, 90, 110, 162, 190, 192, 195
  and Nonconformity 103
Methodist organization 63–91, 106
Methodists
  charged with disloyalty to Church and state 135
  suspected of being Jesuits 130
'Methodist way' 60, 71, 102
militia 232
miracles 124, 146
mobs 78, 103, 136–42
Mochdre 214
'Moderator' 88, 91, 109, 172
Molther, Philip Henry 53
Monmouth 59, 61–2, 132, 133, 134, 136, 137, 144
Monmouthshire 70, 78, 80, 106, 110, 116, 121, 136, 144, 175, 191, 218, 221
Montgomeryshire 121, 125, 126, 131, 136, 142, 145, 146, 147, 178, 190, 191
Moravians 53, 69–71, 151, 161, 167–9, 183, 187, 205, 208, 210, 215, 227
  Harris's criticism of 161, 170–3
  Harris's defence of 169, 170
  'Letter Days' 162
  Rowland's opposition to 170
  'Sifting Time' 161
Morgan, Jenkin 126, 142, 143, 146, 147
Morgan, Phillip 23, 76, 98
Morgan, Thomas (Henllan) 108
Mynydd Meio 74

INDEX

Nantcwnlle 41
Nature, Design and General Rules of the United Societies (1743) 85, 90
Nature and Necessity of Societies (1737) 69
Neath 104, 111
Newbridge on Wye 222
New Inn (Monmouthshire) 24, 110, 116, 175, 177, 189, 218
Newport (Monmouthshire) 136, 137, 145, 146, 147
Nicaea, Council of 163
Norfolk 232
north Wales 78, 85, 116, 120, 126, 131, 148, 149, 150, 187, 196, 198, 209, 214, 230
Nuttall, G. F. 1, 9, 10, 24

'Old Prophet' *see* Jones, Edmund (Pontypool)
Onslow, Sir Arthur 59
Oulton, John 74–5, 76
Owen, John (Llannor) 120, 128–9
Owens, Thomas 136
Oxford 2, 21, 29, 49, 126, 127

Parry, Harry 142
Parry, Mary 64
Patripassianism 163, 171–2, 181, 230
Pearson, John 21
Pembrokeshire 47, 78, 95, 101, 145, 151, 169, 170, 176, 220, 230
Penboyr 28
Penegoes 136
Penllech 196
Pen-y-bont (Llandeglau) 117
perfection 75
perseverance 73
Pettingall, James 136, 137, 139
Philipps, Sir John 28–9
Phillips, Mary 64
Pietism 67–8
Pontypool 59, 61, 70, 74, 76, 101, 121, 133, 177
Powell, John (Abergwesyn) 69, 76
Powell, John (Aberystruth, later Llanmartin) 75, 88, 177
Powell, Howell (*alias* Harris) 13–14
Powell, Susannah *see* Harris, Susannah
Powell, Thomas 13
Powell, Vavasor 48, 50

Powell, William 190, 191, 219
Practice of Piety, The (1610) 17, 19, 38, 64, 92
preaching 102
 authority 121–2
 field 42, 43, 49–50, 61–2, 83, 125
 lay 82, 89, 123–4
 Methodist 103
 rounds 85
predestination 80
press gang 142–4
Presteigne 133
Pretender 131, 149
Price, Thomas 59, 81, 87, 158, 183, 187, 189, 191, 210
Pugh, Phillip (Cardiganshire) 41, 43, 101
Puritans and Puritanism 3–4, 15, 20, 40, 92, 95, 103, 156, 181
 Civil War 22, 128
Pwllheli 198, 208

Quarter Sessions 133
quietism 5

Radnorshire 42, 117, 133, 168, 197, 214
Ranters 213
rationalism 5
 in theology 94
Rees, Lewis 76, 101
Reformation 3, 156
reformation of manners 7
Relation of Apparitions of Spirits (1813) 24
Religious Societies 32–3, 64–5, 68
Relly, James 151, 177, 186
Relly, John 151
Rhayader 222
Rhosddu 196, 198
Richard, John 143, 190, 219
Riot Act 59–60, 133
Roberts, Gomer M. 2, 11
Roberts, James (Ross) 43, 70, 75
Roberts, William 142
Roman Catholicism 92, 125, 180
Rome 130, 180
Rowland, Daniel 9, 41–2, 43, 45, 74, 81, 82, 86–7, 88–9, 91, 101, 105, 108, 142, 148, 151–2, 153–94, 195, 197, 198, 208, 210, 215, 218–19, 220, 223–4, 229, 230, 232

312

INDEX

character 152
Rowland, John 41
'Rowland's People' 151
Royal Mint 13
Rump (Parliament) 131, 137

Sabellianism 230
Sail, Dibenion a Rheolau'r Societies ... (1742) 85
St Anne's Lane 71
St Mary Hall, Oxford 126
St Nicholas 188, 209
Salisbury 218
salvation 5, 38–9, 49, 52–3, 184
Saul 221
Saunders, Joseph 69
Saunders, Thomas (Llanfaches) 103
Savannah 49
schism 124
  Harris accused of 125, 129
Scotland 75, 158
Scripture Doctrine of the Trinity (1712) 163
Selected Trevecka Letters (1956, 1962) 11
separation (1750) 9, 41, 151–94, 195, 219, 223–4, 229
Seven Years War 232
Seward, William 59, 132, 137, 139, 146, 147
Shaw, John 51–2
societies 32–3, 64–71, 102, 190
  aims 85–6
  buildings 116–17
  disciplined by Harris 165–7, 173, 175, 176, 181, 193, 219, 220
  monthly 74–8
  bi-monthly 76–7
  leaving the Church 104, 107, 111–12, 116
  nature of 110, 114
  registers 69–70, 89
  rules 71–6, 78, 80, 85–6
Society of Ministers 74, 76, 104, 154
Spain 125, 141
  fear of Spanish invasion 131
Sparks, John 151, 219, 220
SPCK 29, 66, 82
Stennet, Joseph 60
Stephen (Book of Acts) 115
steward 71
stillness 53
Swindon 137, 138–41

Tabernacle (London) 97, 105, 157, 158, 160, 161, 166, 167–8, 170, 173, 177, 182, 185–6, 188, 189, 217
Talach-ddu 27
Talgarth 13, 14, 15, 16, 20, 21, 27, 29, 32, 42, 64, 69, 107, 119, 135, 233
Talyllychau 87, 173
Test Acts 92
Thompson, E. P. 139
Tibbott, Richard 143
Tilsley, John 121, 128–9
Toleration Act (1689) 93, 103, 125, 143
Treatise of the Covenant of Grace (1659) 54
Trebinsiwn 16
Tredwstan 20, 23, 27, 112
Trefeca Fach 13
Trefollwyn (Anglesey) 116
Tre-garnedd 198
Trevecka 9, 20, 29, 42, 64, 75, 80, 81, 85, 87, 116, 119, 120, 135, 149, 152, 158, 170, 180, 191, 196, 197, 202, 205, 206, 208, 211, 214, 215, 220, 222, 226, 227, 231, 232
Trevecka College 232
Trevecka Family 13, 152
Trevecka Letters, The (1932) 10
Trinity, doctrine of the 163, 179, 181, 184, 218, 230
  Monarchianism 163
Trosgoed 23, 76
Tyddyn, Llandinam 178
Tŷ-mawr 198

Ubiquitarianism 230
Urim and Thummim 209

Walker, Fowler 60
Walpole, Sir Robert 60
Wapping 71
Watford (Glamorgan) 26, 59, 79–80, 85, 87, 89, 91, 109, 110, 111, 114, 158, 168, 169, 171, 174, 176, 182, 187, 191, 210
Watkins, John 135
Weekly History, The 166
Welsh Calvinistic Methodism 12, 169
Wernos, Y 33, 69
Wesley, Charles 52, 71, 78, 105, 109, 113, 117, 132

INDEX

Wesley, John 12, 26, 29, 36, 45, 46–7, 55, 62, 63, 69, 70–1, 78, 81, 84, 85, 90, 96–7, 105, 106, 107, 109, 117, 123, 132, 136, 155–7, 165, 186, 193, 198, 202, 210, 214, 215, 218
Wesleyan Conferences 90, 117
Westminster 71
Westminster Assembly (1643) 156
Whitefield, Elizabeth 217
Whitefield, George 5, 25, 26, 29, 48–53, 55–7, 59, 63, 69–71, 78, 80, 81, 82–4, 88, 91, 97, 103, 105–6, 107, 108–9, 111, 142, 153, 156–7, 158, 164, 167, 168, 177, 182, 184, 185–6, 188, 189, 197, 202, 210, 217, 219
Journal 12, 25, 49–50, 59
on divine guidance 182–3
to be a bishop 105–6, 183
Whole Duty of Man, The (1658) 16, 19, 22, 38, 64, 92
William, Thomas (Eglwysilan) 108, 111, 190, 192, 219

Williams, David (Pwll-y-pant) 43–4, 46–7, 70, 74–5, 101, 103, 182, 183
Williams, John 42
Williams, Peter 116, 196
Williams, Roger 143
Williams, William (Pantycelyn) 75, 86, 88, 89, 115, 170, 178, 181, 182, 191, 224, 232
Williams, William (Tredwstan) 29
Woodward, Josiah 32, 65–7, 69
Wynne, Cadwaladr 196
Wynne, Watkin 204
Wynne, Sir Watkin Williams 135

Ymddiddan rhwng Methodist Uniawn-gred ac un Camsyniol (1750) 230
Ysbyty Ifan 196, 216
Ystrad-ffin 79

Zinzendorf, Count von 71, 180